From God To Verse

From God To Verse:

Genesis, Exodus, Leviticus, Numbers, and Deuteronomy...
...in rhyme

Seth Brown

RisingPun Productions

To my parents, Jeff and Barbara Brown:

The debt that I owe both of you is substantial
For endless support, both moral and financial.
You believed I could do it. I did it. It's done.
So this page is for you, with love, from your son.

Introduction

So, I guess the obvious question is, "Why?"

Why in God's name would someone translate the entire Torah, line by line, into rhyme? Well, to be perfectly honest, the idea just came to me one day back in 2001, and I knew I had to do it. I didn't know at the time that it would take me nearly a decade to complete, but I didn't really have a choice. Sometimes I just get a sense of purpose and know what needs to be done. Which I guess leads to the next obvious question: "Did God tell you to write this?"

I regret to say that I did not have a dream where God spoke to me and told me to write this. It would make for a better introduction, perhaps, if I had heard a thunderous voice from the sky, or had a vision of angels, or serendipitously discovered a Torah open to a page that talked about verse and knew that I had received a direct message from God. But alas, such was not the case. I just had the idea randomly one day.

However.

There's an old story about a religious man caught in a flood. The flood waters were slowly rising, and the man stood on the porch of his house. A man in a row boat paddled by and told the religious man, "Get in, the waters are rising!" But the religious man said, "No thank you, God will save me." The flood waters kept rising and the man had to go to the second floor of his house. A man in a motor boat drove by and told the religious man, "Get in, the flood is getting worse!" But the religious man said, "No thank you, I have faith that God will save me."

The waters rose and soon the religious man was forced to stand on the peak of his own roof to avoid drowning. A helicopter flew by, and the pilot yelled down, "We're here to rescue you! Hurry!" But the man told the pilot, "No thank you, God will rescue me." The pilot flew away, the waters rose, and the man drowned. The man was sent to heaven, and upon arriving, got to meet God. He asked God, "Why did you let me drown? I had perfect faith that you would rescue me." And God said, "What more did you want? I sent you two boats and a helicopter!"

So, who knows? The answer is: Not me. I don't know how the idea got into my head, I only know that it took up residence and refused to leave until it was a book. You can chalk it up to a lifelong interest in verse, or a divine hand, or pure chance, but if you want to know why I wrote this book, that's the best answer I can give: The idea just came to me. Not necessarily the most satisfying answer, but then again, the truth seldom is.

By way of recompense, let me talk a little bit about what I have tried to do here. So there's this sacred text. This very large, very old, very sacred text. And I had the dual goals of making it as appealing as possible (for maximum enjoyment) while changing it as little as possible (for maximum sacredness).

Now, either one of these things alone seems simple enough. To change it as little as possible, you just leave it as is, and read one of the fine standard translations already on the market. (I can even recommend a few, in my acknowledgements.) Or to make it as appealing as possible, you might cut out all the genealogies and legal codes, keep only the most action-packed stories, and make a movie out of it.

To do both, though, is a little trickier. If the Torah were a friend of mine (and at this point, we've spent enough time together that it's not too much of a stretch), I'd say, "Hey Torah, put your best foot forward, but be yourself." Because when you have a sacred text, it's not really kosher to go cutting out large parts of it just because you don't enjoy ark-building instructions as much as giant floods.

So every single line is there from the original, but the language has been modernized a bit for greater accessibility, and presented in iambic heptameter. There's also a summary of each chapter in 4-8 lines of iambic tetrameter, for children who aren't up to reading the main text. The book is, essentially, a Torah/Bible that has been made friendlier without losing a single line of content.

I hope you enjoy it.

Acknowledgements

First and foremost, I must acknowledge my parents. And not merely because the Ten Commandments tells me to. Back in 2001, I had just graduated from a college with a fairly expensive price tag. And rather than rushing out to get a job, I said to my parents, "I've got this idea for a book, and I was hoping I could try writing full-time for a while. Do you suppose you could help me cover costs for a few months so I can do that?"

At the time, I had not published any books, I did not have a track record as a freelancer, and there was absolutely no reason to believe that I could make a living as a writer. In spite of this, my parents encouraged me to follow my dream, and to write this book in particular. For many reasons, it would have been impossible without them. The rest of my family was also very supportive of both me and my project, so they have my sincere thanks as well.

And then there are my friends, who are, collectively, the finest people in the world. My gratitude to them is outweighed only by the sheer impossibility of thanking them all by name, but if a man's wealth is the quality of friends he has, then I am the wealthiest man that has ever lived. The constant support and encouragement from my friends has been appreciated throughout this project, from those who were working on their own big projects alongside me as I began (Ben and Tom), to those who nearly a decade later are still encouraging me to get my book out into the world (Debbie, who makes every day a delight).

Finally, I must thank the other scholars who have paved the way for me. In creating this text, I used four translations:

1) The Five Books of Moses, by Everett Fox (Schocken Books)
2) The JPS (Jewish Publication Society) Tanakh
3) New Oxford Annotated Bible (revised standard edition)
4) King James Version Bible

Since I have lost what ability to read Hebrew I once had, these translations were essential for my work. Mr. Fox was also kind enough to reply to my letter explaining my project and offer personal encouragement. I thank the Velveteen Rabbi, Rachel Barenblat, whose knowledge of both Torah and poetry was invaluable while I was editing the opening chapters of Genesis for what must have been the 18th time. And last but certainly not least, credit for the cover is due to the talented Daniel Beck.

Contents

GENESIS

Genesis 1

Now, in the beginning when God made the earth
There was nothing at all, no, not even a light.
God said, "Let there be light," and to light He gave birth,
And He liked it, so then He made day, and made night.
He made water, sky, land, plants, and animals too,
And created man, who could make use of it all.
And God saw it was good, all He'd managed to do,
By the time that the end of the sixth day did fall.

[Bereishit]

In the beginning when God was creating the heavens and all of the earth,
When the world was all wild and waste, and of light on the deep oceans there was a dearth,
And the wind of God hovering over the waters, God spoke and said, "Let there be light!"
And indeed, there was light. And God saw it, that light, and He saw that it was good and right.
After seeing his shining creation, God then separated the light from the dark.
So He called the light "Day" and the darkness as "Night" (and the difference between them
     was stark).
And then there was a setting and there was a dawning as earth's creation had begun,
There was evening and then there was morning, and that was the first day, so ending day one.

God said, "Right in the midst of the waters, let there be a firmament, a solid dome
That will separate waters from waters." (since waters above would need less salt and foam)
So God made that expanse of a dome that would separate waters which waved down below
From the waters that still stayed above the expanse He created. And thus it was so.
God had named the expansive dome "Heaven" or "Sky" (and the region it covered was vast).
There was evening and then there was morning, which meant that a second day now had
     gone past.

God said, "Let waters under the sky all be gathered together and into one place.
Let the waters go here, and then there, let the dry land appear so it may shows its face."

It was so. The dry land, God called "Earth", and the gathering of waters, God called it "Seas."
And God saw this was good. (With the gathering waters, these seas He sees, He's pleased
He sees.)
God said, "Let the earth sprout forth with green sprouting growths, with grass and all sorts of
vegetation,
Plants that seed forth their seeds, and fruit trees that bear fruit, both according to their variation."
It was so. The earth brought forth the fruit trees, it brought forth the plants, and the herbs, and
the grass,
And God saw it was good. There was evening and morning, and so a third day came to pass.

God said, "Let there be lights in the sky up above that will separate day from the night,
So they may serve as signs for the set times, the seasons, the days, and the years with their light.
They shall serve as the sky's lights to shine on the earth." It was so, and two great lights God made,
The light greater for daytime, the lesser for night (and some other stars to be displayed).
God placed all of them into the sky, to rule both day and night, and to shine evermore.
And God saw this was good. There was evening and then there was morning, completing day four.

God said, "Let all the waters bring forth swarms of living things, creatures and beasts from
the seas,
And let birds fly above the earth to fill the heavens and sky with formations of Vs.
He created sea monsters and swarms from the waters, and all winged birds from the sky.
And God saw it was good. And God blessed them all, saying "Be fruitful and go multiply.
Fill the waters in all of the seas, and the birds shall increase on the earth as they thrive."
And then there was an evening, and there was a morning, and that was the day numbered five.

God said, "Let the earth bring forth living beings, those of all kinds, from the greatest to least,
Herds of cattle, the ground's creepy-crawlies, and various types of earth's wildlife beasts."
It was so. God created the cattle, and also created wild beasts of all kinds.
And God saw it was good. (And once God had seen this, then another idea sprang to mind:)
God said, "I shall make man in Our image, according to Our likeness this man shall be,
And I give him dominion and rule over cattle, the birds, and the beasts of the sea."
God created man in His own image, both male and female did He create them.
Then God blessed them and said, "Be fertile and increase," and God gave them the whole earth to
sate them.

God said, "Fill up the earth and you shall master it, ruling all creatures that may live there,
From the fish of the sea, to the land's creepy-crawlies, to birds that just fly through the air."
God said, "Here, I give to you all seed-bearing plants, and all trees that have seed-bearing fruit.
They shall be yours for food. And all earth's wildlife will use green plants in that same pursuit.
To all creatures on earth, birds or beasts, that possess life's breath, I give the green plants for food."
It was so. God saw all of the things He had made, and saw that it was good, very good.

There was evening and then there was morning, and that meant the sixth day was finally through.
So the heavens and earth were now finished, and God's work that He had done was finished too.

Genesis 2

On the seventh day, God rested, as was His plan.
So the day become blessed and was a holy day.
From the dust and His own breath, God created man,
And put him in a garden called Eden to play.
God said, "Eat anything that you like but the tree.
Oh, you might want a helper, to not be alone."
So then God made the man fall asleep, so that He
Could take one of his ribs, make a woman from bone.

God completed the work He was doing on the seventh day and said, "I'll take a rest.
And because I have rested on this seventh day, from now on it is holy and blessed."

Now these are the beginnings of heaven and earth, when their creation first came to pass:
At the time of the LORD God's making of the heavens and earth, when not one blade of grass
Had yet sprouted, no bush of the field was yet on the earth, no plants were yet on the plain,
For there was no man yet that could till all the soil, and the LORD God had not made it rain.
But a flow would well up from the ground and then water all soil on the face of the earth.
And the LORD God formed human from humus and dust of the soil, thus to man giving birth.
He blew into his nostrils the breath of life, and that's how man became a living being.

The LORD God planted a garden out in the east, in the land full of pleasure called Eden,
And He placed there the man He had formed. Then the Lord God from there caused to grow
    from the ground
Every species of tree that was pleasant to see, and from which the good food could be found,
With the Tree of Life right in the midst of the garden, and also the Tree of the Knowing
About Good and Evil. (Immortality and knowledge thus both in Eden were growing).
There's a river that flows out from Eden to water the garden, and then it divides
Into four branches. First of the branches is Pishon, that spreads through lands where gold resides,
Through the whole land of Havilah where gold is good, and there's onyx and lapis lazuli.
Now the second river is the Gihon (or Gusher), and through Cush it circles quite truly.
Then the third river's name is Hiddekel (or Tigris), the one which flows east of Assyria.
And the fourth river is the Euphrates. That's all of the four rivers from Eden's area.

The LORD God took the man and set him in the garden of Eden to till it and tend it.
"Of every other tree you may eat quite freely," to the man the LORD God had commanded,
"But eat not from the tree of the Knowing of Good and Evil, that fruit you must not try.
For on that very day that you eat from that tree, as soon as you eat it, you will die."

The LORD God said, "Since it is not good for the man I have made to be living alone,
I will make him a helper that's fitting for him." So the LORD God then formed from the loam
Every beast of the field, every bird of the skies, and brought them to the man by the score
To see what man would name it; and whatever man named a beast was its name ever more.
And the man called out names to the cattle, the birds, and the beasts; all the animals had 'em,
But although every last one of them had been named, there was no fitting helper for Adam.

So the LORD God caused deep sleep to fall upon Adam, took one of his ribs for a plan.
God closed up the flesh, fashioned the rib into woman, and then brought her unto the man.
Man said, "This one is good! She's the bone of my bones, and the flesh of my flesh here displayed.
This one shall be called Woman, since 'twas from the rib of Man that she was fashioned
    and made!"
So a man therefore shall leave his father and mother to go cling instead to his wife,
So the two can become all one flesh. (That's the way things began, and the way of all life).

Genesis 3

Now the snake was the trickiest creature God made,
And he said to the woman, "Can't you eat the tree?"
She said, "God said I can't. I can sit in the shade."
But the snake said, "It's good fruit, so eat it. Trust me."
And so she ate the fruit, and the man ate it too,
Then God said, "I said no! You have made a mistake.
I will punish and place a curse on all of you,
And you must leave the garden, man, woman, and snake."

So the two of them here, both the man and his wife, were naked, but no shame did they feel.
Now the snake was more clever than all other beasts which the LORD God had made in the field.
The snake said to the woman, "Did God really say: You shan't eat any tree in the garden?"
And the woman replied, "We can eat fruit from most, but to one he has not given pardon.

Of the tree in the middle, God said: You shall not eat or touch it at all, lest you die."

The snake said, "You won't die, but God knows that if you eat that tree it will open your eyes.

You'll become just like gods, knowing of good and evil." The woman then saw that the tree

Was both good for eating, and delight to the eyes, and desired for perspicacity.

So she took from its fruit, and ate some of it, then she gave some to her husband as food,

And he ate some as well. Then both opened their eyes and they suddenly knew they were nude.

They sewed fig leaves and made themselves loincloths to wear. Of the LORD God they then
　　　heard the sound,

Moving through the cool garden. The man and his wife hid in trees to avoid being found.

The LORD God then called out to the man and He said "Where are you?" And the man
　　　then replied,

"I heard sounds of You. Since I am naked, I was afraid and I decided to hide."

God asked, "Who was it that told you that you are naked (and caused you to want to be hidden)?

Did you eat from the tree of which I had commanded that eating was strictly forbidden?"

Man said, "It was the woman you gave to be with me, she gave me that fruit, so I ate."

And God said to the woman, "What's this you have done?" And the woman responded,
　　　"The snake

Enticed and convinced me, so I ate." And the LORD God then said to the serpent, "Because

You have done this thing, you will now be more cursed than any animal that ever was.

You will crawl on your belly, eat dust for the rest of your life. Enmity I will spread

Between you and the woman, your offspring and hers; you will wound their heel, they'll wound
　　　your head."

To the woman he said, "I will multiply pregnancy's pain, and the pains of childbirth.

Your desire will be towards your husband, and yet he will rule over you on this earth."

Then to Adam he said, "Because you have done as your wife said, from that tree did you eat

Of which I had commanded: You must not eat it! Cursed shall be the ground under your feet

All because of you. Only with painstaking work shall you eat from the ground ever more.

Let it sprout thorns and thistles for you, yet your food shall be grass that grows from the
　　　earth's floor.

By the sweat of your brow shall you get bread to eat, 'til at last you return to the ground—

For from it you were taken. You are dust, and back to dust you shall return (homeward bound).

The man named his wife Eve, for she was to become the great mother of all of the living.

The LORD God made Adam and his wife coats of skins and clothed them (being somewhat
　　　forgiving).

The Lord God said, "Man has become like one of us, knowing good, knowing evil, and so

Lest he send forth his hand for the Tree of Life's fruit and gain eternal life, he must go."

So the LORD God sent Adam away from the garden of Eden so that he could toil

(And here toil means tilling the ground from which Adam was taken, the very same soil).

Yes, He drove the man out, and placed east of the garden the Cherubim, (fierce winged beasts)

This along with a sword, flaming and ever-turning, to guard the Tree of Life from east.

Genesis 4

Adam had two sons with his wife, Cain and then Abel.
And Abel took care of sheep, Cain worked the farm.
One day out in the field, Cain killed his brother Abel.
God asked him, "Where's Abel? Have you done him harm?"
Cain replied, "I don't know." And God said "You have lied!
I know everything; I know that you brought him death.
From now on, the land will not keep you well supplied."
And then Adam and Eve had another son, Seth.

Now the man knew Eve, knew as his wife, and so she became pregnant and gave birth to Cain,
Saying, "See, I have gotten a son with the help of the Lord." Then she gave birth again.
Now this second son Abel, the brother of Cain, was to become a keeper of sheep.
While Cain (who was the first) would grow into a tiller of soil, from the ground would he reap.
Over the course of time, from the fruit of the soil, Cain gave an offering to the Lord.
As for Abel, he brought the best parts of his flock, a great gift that could not be ignored.
The Lord gave His respect to what Abel had offered, but not to the offering of Cain,
And so Cain was upset and despondent, and his visage fell in a state of disdain.
The Lord said to Cain, "Tell me, why are you upset? And why has your face fallen so low?
Is it not true, that if you intend only good that you will be uplifted from woe?
But if you do not mean to do good, then sin becomes a demon that lies at the door.
Its desire is towards you, although it is something that is possible to rule o'er."

One day Cain said to Abel, his brother, that going out into the field would be good,
But when they arrived there, Cain rose up against Abel, his brother, killed him where he stood.
God asked Cain, "Where is Abel, your brother?" And Cain replied to the Lord God,
    "I don't know.
Am I my brother's keeper, who knows where he is?" God said, "What is this you have
    done? Lo!—
Hear the blood of your brother, it cries out to me from the soil. Thus you now shall be damned
By the soil which opened its mouth to receive the blood of your brother from your hand.
When you till the soil, the soil will no longer yield to you or to your hand yield its strength,
And you shall become a wavering wayfarer, one who will wander the earth at length."
And Cain said to the Lord, "God, this punishment for my crime I cannot bear. For today,
You have driven me out from the face of the soil, and from Your face I must hide away.
Yes, to waywardly wander the earth is my fate, and soon any who meet me will kill me."
But God said to him, "No, for whoever kills Cain shall have sevenfold vengeance on he."

So God put a mark on Cain, to make all who might find him loath to kill him, and face God.
And Cain left the Lord's face to go dwell in the wandering land east of Eden, called Nod.

So Cain knew his wife, she conceived and bore Enoch. Cain founded a city after that,
Which he named for his son Enoch, who fathered Irad, who eventually begat
Mehujael, who begat Methusael, who begat Lamech, who took himself two wives.
One named Adah, the other named Zillah. (Dawn and Dusk, many children did they provide).
Adah bore Jabal, the father of those who live in tents and those who sit amidst cattle.
While his brother Jubal was the father of those who played lyres and made pipe organs rattle.
And Zillah for her part bore Tubal-cain, who forged all blades of both iron and bronze.
Tubal-cain's sister was called Naamah (and there you have listing of some family bonds).
Lamech said to his wives, "Adah and Zillah, hear my voice; wives of Lamech, give your ear
To my speech: I have killed a man for wounding me, and a lad for a few bruises mere.
If Cain is avenged sevenfold, Lamech then seventy-sevenfold, dealing out death!"
Adam knew his wife once again, she bore a son, and decided that she'd name him Seth,
Meaning, "God has provided me another seed in place of Abel," whom Cain had slain.
And to Seth, a son was born, whom he named Enosh. Then men started to praise the Lord's name.

Genesis 5

> Adam had a few children, his children had kids,
> And then their kids had more kids, and more after that.
> And their kids then had more kids, and likewise their kids did,
> And all of their children begat and begat.

This is the record of Adam's generations. When God created man in his way,
In his likeness he created them, male and female, and so on their creation's day
He blessed them and called them Man. Now when Adam had drawn one hundred and thirty
    years breath,
Then he fathered a son in his own likeness, after his image, and he named him Seth.
After Seth was born, Adam lived eight hundred years, during which sons and daughters he sired.
All the days Adam lived totaled nine hundred and thirty years, then he finally expired.

When Seth had lived for one hundred and five years, he fathered Enosh, and so it transpired.
After Enosh's birth, Seth lived eight hundred seven years, some sons and daughters he sired.
All the days that Seth lived totaled nine hundred and twelve years. And then he finally expired.

When Enosh had lived for a full ninety years, he fathered Kenan, and so it transpired.
After Kenan's birth, Enosh lived eight hundred and fifteen years, sons and daughters he sired.
All the days Enosh lived totaled nine hundred and five years. And then he finally expired.

When Kenan had lived seventy years, he then fathered Mahalalel, so it transpired.
Past Mahalalel's birth, Kenan lived eight hundred forty years, sons and daughters he sired.
All the days Kenan lived totaled nine hundred and ten years. And then he finally expired.

When Mahalalel had lived for sixty-five years, he fathered Jared, so it transpired.
After Jared's birth, Mahalalel lived eight hundred thirty years, sons and daughters sired.
The days Mahalalel lived were eight hundred and ninety-five years. And then he expired.

When Jared had lived one hundred and sixty-two years, he fathered Enoch, it transpired.
After Enoch's birth, Jared lived eight hundred years, and then more sons and daughters he sired.
All the days Jared lived totaled nine hundred and sixty-two years. And then he expired.

When Enoch had lived for sixty-five years, he fathered Methuselah, and after that,
Enoch walked in God's ways for three hundred full years, and many sons and daughters begat.
And the days of Enoch totaled three hundred sixty-five years. (Years have that many days)
Then he was no more, for God had taken him (Taken Enoch who had walked in God's ways).

When Methuselah reached one hundred eighty-seven, he fathered Lamech, it transpired.
After Lamech's birth, Methuselah lived seven hundred eighty-two years, kids he sired.
Days Methuselah lived totaled nine hundred and sixty-nine years. And then he expired.

When Lamech had lived for a full hundred and eighty-seven years, he fathered a son.
He named him Noah, saying, "We will have our sorrow relieved, comforted by this one.
All the sorrow of pain when we work with our hands, all the aches that result from our toil,
All the pain we are caused just by working the ground, because of when the Lord cursed the soil."
After Noah's birth, Lamech lived five hundred ninety-five years, sons and daughters he sired.
The days Lamech lived totaled seven hundred seventy-seven years. Then he expired.

Now when Noah was five hundred years old, Shem, Ham, and Japheth he begot at that time.
(And these three sons of Noah's close out the tale of the generations of Adam's line.)

Genesis 6

God saw man had grown evil, was no longer good,
And decided to blot them all out from the land.
But this one man named Noah did just what he should,
And thus God would not hurt him as part of his plan.
God told Noah, "A big flood I'm going to make,
So do just what I say if you want to be fine:
Make an ark out of wood, and be sure that you take
Your whole family, and animals, two of each kind.

When the humans first started to increase on earth, women being born to them in droves,
Sons of God saw how pretty the women were, and they took wives of whomever they chose.
The Lord God said, "My spirit won't remain in man forever, because he is flesh too.
Let the days allowed to him be six score of years, yes, one hundred and twenty will do."
Now, the giants were on the earth back in those days, later too, when the sons of God came
Into the human women, who bore them children, all the heroes of old, men of name.

Now the Lord saw how great was man's evil and wickedness on earth, that man's every thought
From both heart and mind was naught but evil, all day. God was sorry that man he had wrought.
God was saddened He made man on earth, and it pained His heart. God then said, "I will
     blot out
Man, whom I have created, from the very surface of the earth, without any doubt.
All the men, and the beasts, creepy-crawlies, and birds which high up in the air once had soared.
For I am sorry that I have made them." But Noah found favor in eyes of the Lord.

[Noach]

These are the generations and line of Noah. Noah was a just and righteous man.
Blameless in his age, he walked in God's ways, and he sired three sons: Shem, Japheth, and Ham.
Now the earth was corrupted before God, the earth was filled with violence and evildoing.
God looked down at the earth, and saw it was corrupt, for flesh had brought its own way to ruin.

The Lord told Noah, "I have decided to end all flesh. (It seems to have lost its worth.)
The earth fills with wrongdoing because of them. Hark, I bring ruin to both flesh and earth.
Make yourself an ark of gopher wood, make compartments within the ark, and cover it
With pitch on both the inside and out. This is how you shall make it: Three hundred cubits

Is to be the full length of the ark, and the breadth fifty, and thirty cubits as height.
Also, ending within one cubit of the top, be sure that you construct a skylight.
The ark's entrance should be set into its side; make it with lower, second, and third decks."
(A cubit measures nearly a foot and a half, in case these dimensions seem complex)

"As for me, I am going to bring the Flood—waters on earth, bringing ruin to all flesh,
All the flesh with the breath of life in it, from under the sky, all on earth shall perish.
But with you I establish my covenant: You shall come into the ark, and with you
Your sons and your wife and your sons' wives, and from all living things, all flesh, you shall
    take two.
You shall take two of each sort into the ark to keep alive, male and female of each.
From birds after their kind, to every kind of cattle, and all things that crawl on the beach.
Two of each of them shall come to you, so they stay alive. As for you, take for yourself
From all food that is eaten and gather it, so you can store it away on your shelf.

It shall serve as food for you and them." And those were the instructions of God, which He bid.
Noah did so, according to everything that God commanded of him, so he did.

Genesis 7

God told Noah, "Go into the ark that you made;
Because you have been righteous, you will stay alive."
Two by two, all the animals in a parade
Entered into the ark so that they could survive.
And then seven days later, the flood waters came,
And the rain fell for forty days and forty nights.
All the waters rose higher because of the rain,
And all things but the ark were engulfed by its height.

The Lord told Noah, "Come, you and all of your household, into the ark; for I have seen
You are righteous before me in this generation. Take seven pairs of each beast clean,
Both the males and their mates, and of each unclean beast, only two, just one male and his mate.
And from birds of the sky, seven pairs, male and female, so seeds on earth can propagate.
For in seven days I will cause rain on the earth, lasting forty days and forty nights,
And I will blot out all of the living things that I have made from the earth and my sight."
Noah did so, according to everything exactly as the Lord God had commanded.
And so Noah was six hundred years when the Flood came, and waters on the earth expanded.

Noah came, with his sons, wife, and son's wives, into the ark before the Flood's waters rose.
From the animals clean and unclean, birds, and crawling things, two of each came, in two rows.
They came two by two into the ark, male and female, as God had commanded to Noah.
After seven days came the Flood's waters upon the earth, drenching like never before.
In the six hundredth year of the life of Noah, on the second month, seventeenth day,
All the fountains beneath the great deep burst forth, and heaven's floodgates and sluices gave way.

The rain fell on the earth forty days, forty nights. That same day, Noah came with his sons
Shem, Ham, and Japheth, and Noah's wife, and his three sons' wives into the ark all at once.
Them and all wildlife after their kind, all cattle, all things that creep, all things that crawl,
All birds after their kind, and all chirping things, and all things that take to wing in a squall.
They came into the ark to Noah, two and two each of all flesh containing life's breath.
(Every wildlife beast, from the greatest to least, into the ark to be saved from death.)
And those beasts that came, male and female from all flesh they came, as God had
    commanded him.
Then God closed the door, shutting in Noah (because the Flood's waters were too great to swim).

The flood was on the earth for a full forty days. Waters increased and lifted the ark,
It was raised high above the earth; the waters grew and swelled greatly. (None could disembark.)
The ark floated on waters, and when waters had swelled exceedingly over the earth,
Every mountain so high that was under the sky was now covered by the water's girth.
Fifteen cubits higher swelled the waters, the mountains were covered by waters so rife.
Then all flesh that moves on the earth perished—the birds, cattle, beasts, and all the wildlife,
All the swarming things that like to swarm on the earth, and then even the whole of mankind.
All things that had life's breath in their nostrils, all that once was on the dry, firm ground
    had died.
So He blotted out all living things upon earth, man and beast, things that creep in the dark,
Even birds. All were wiped out from earth. Only Noah remained, and his crew on the ark.

<u>Genesis 8</u>

> The flood stayed for a hundred and fifty long days,
> And then God recalled Noah was still in the ark.
> God sent wind so the waters would go on their ways,
> Noah sent birds to scout where he could disembark.
> Noah's raven found nothing, so he sent a dove,
> Which found an olive leaf that it brought back on board.
> Noah knew this meant dry land, sent thanks to above,
> And then he built an altar to worship the Lord.

When the waters had swelled upon earth for a hundred and fifty days, God then paid mind
And remembered both Noah and all living things with Noah on the ark at that time.
God then caused a great wind to blow over the earth, and the waters began to subside.
Fountains of the deep and the sky's floodgates were closed, and no more rain did the sky provide.
So the waters receded continually, and when one hundred fifty days passed,
All the waters abated. The ark came to rest atop Ararat's mountains at last.
On the seventh month, seventeenth day, this occurred. Waters kept sinking from where
    they'd been,
'til the tenth month. Upon the first day of which, tops of the mountains could finally be seen.

After forty days, Noah threw open the window of the ark he'd made, and sent out
A black raven, which went to and fro, until waters dried up from the earth's whereabouts.
Then he sent out a dove, to see whether the waters had dried from the face of the soil.
But the dove could find no resting place for her foot, and so returned to him, being loyal.
She returned to the ark, because water still covered the earth's face, not fully abated.
Noah put out his hand, taking her back into the ark with him. And then Noah waited
Seven days more, and sent out the dove once again from the ark, so dry land it could seek.
The dove then returned late in the evening, and there was a plucked olive leaf in her beak!
By this, Noah knew that all the waters had decreased on earth. Then he waited once more
Seven days, and sent out the dove, but she did not return to him like times gone before.

So it was, in the six hundred and first year, in the first month, and on that month's first day,
All the waters began to dry up from the earth. Noah took the ark's covering away
And he saw that the face of the soil was firm here, much drying ground did he espy.
In the second month, on the twenty-seventh day, the earth was once again finally dry.

God spoke to Noah, saying, "Go out of the ark, with your wife, your sons, and your sons' wives.
All things living with you, all flesh—birds, animals, things that creep, and things that swarm
    in hives,
Have them go out with you, so they can swarm on earth, and on earth be fertile and increase."
And so Noah went out, with his sons, wife, and sons' wives, and all living things were released.
All the birds, creepy-crawlies, all things that move on the earth, went out of the ark by family.
Noah built an altar to the Lord, and took from all clean beasts and birds to offer humbly.
Noah offered them up on the altar. God smelled the sweet odor, and said in his heart,
"I will never again curse the soil for man, though his heart form evil from the start.
I will never again destroy all living things, as I've done; So long as earth persists,
Sowing and harvest, cold and heat, summer and winter, day and night no more shall desist."

Genesis 9

God blessed Noah, and his sons, and said to them all,
"Go be fruitful and multiply, fill up the land.
I give you the whole earth which will serve at your call,
And we're making a covenant. So understand:
I now promise that never again shall there be
A great flood to kill everyone. It won't be so.
And as proof of this covenant you have with Me
You will see in the clouds of the sky a rainbow.

God blessed Noah and all of his sons, and God said to them, "Be fruitful and multiply.
Fill the earth. All the beasts of the earth shall fear you, as will all of the birds in the sky,
All that crawls on the soil, all the fish of the sea, into your hand all of it now passes.
All the living things that move on earth shall be for you, as food, just like all the green grasses,
I now give you all things, although flesh with the blood of its life you are never to eat.
I require a reckoning from the blood of your own lives, just as with wild beasts.
I demand it from mankind, from every man's brother, a reckoning for human life.
Now whoever sheds man's blood, by man shall his blood be shed, (Live by the knife, die by knife.)
For God made mankind in His own image. And as for you, be fruitful and multiply.
Go abound and increase on the earth." Then the Lord said to Noah, and his sons nearby,
"As for me, I establish my covenant now, with both you and your offspring to follow,
And with all living things that are with you: birds, cattle, beasts that come out from the
    ark's hollow,

All the beasts of the earth. I establish my covenant with you: That never again
Shall all flesh be cut off by the waters of a rising Flood, and that never again
Shall there be a Flood to bring the whole earth to ruination." God said: "This is the sign
Of the covenant I make between me and you, and all creatures with you, for all time:
My rainbow I have set in the clouds, to serve as a sign of the covenant between
Me and the earth. And when I bring clouds over the earth, and the bow can clearly be seen,
I will call to mind My covenant between Me and you, and all beings of flesh living,
That the waters shall never again become Flood, to bring ruin to all flesh, unforgiving.
When the rainbow is in the clouds, I will look at it, to call to mind something of worth,
Namely the covenant everlasting between God and all living beings on earth."
God said to Noah, "This is the sign of the covenant I've established between Me
And all living flesh that is on earth." Noah's sons who went out of the ark were just three:
There was Shem, Ham, and Japheth. And Ham was the father of Canaan. These three were
    the sons
Of Noah, and from them the whole earth was peopled, from them all of the earth-folk were spun.
Noah was the first tiller of soil, he planted a vineyard, and like this it went:
When he drank from the wine, he got drunk, and uncovered himself in the midst of his tent.
Ham, the father of Canaan, saw his father's nakedness, told his two brothers outside.
Then Shem and Japheth placed a cloak on both shoulders, walking backwards towards father
    to hide
Noah's nakedness; their faces were turned backwards, so his nakedness they didn't see.
And when Noah awoke from his wine, he learned what his littlest son had done to He.
He said, "Cursed be Canaan. The lowest of slaves may he be to his brothers." And then
He said, "Blessed be the Lord, the God of Shem, let him possess as a servant Canaan.
And may God enlarge Japheth, let him dwell in Shem's tents, may Canaan be servant to them."

Noah lived past the Flood three hundred fifty years, after all the waters did subside.
All his days totaled up to nine hundred and fifty years of living. And then he died.

Genesis 10

> Noah lived to nine hundred and fifty years old,
> And had children, who had more children after that.
> And their children had children, and as you've been told,
> All their children begat, and begat, and begat.

Now these are the generations of the three sons of Noah: Japheth, Ham, and Shem
Sons were born to all Noah's sons after the Flood, and so here we have tried to list them.

The sons of Japheth were Gomer, Magog, Javan, Madai, Tubal, Meshech, and then Tiras.
Gomer's sons were Ashkenaz, Riphath, and Togarmah. (While Gomer was their daddy dearest.)
The sons of Javan were Elishah and Tarshish, the Kittim, and Dodanim as well.
From these sons spread the maritime nations, coast peoples divided by lands where they dwell.
These are all the descendants of Japheth, each one with their own tongue, by clan and by nation.
Ham's descendants were Cush, Mitzrayim, Put, and Canaan (cursed following Noah's libation).
Cush's sons were Seba, Habilah, Sabta, Raamah, Sabteca. Then Raamah had two
He had Sheba and Dedan. Then Cush begot Nimrod, the first mighty man that earth knew.
By God's grace he was a mighty hunter—so mighty an old saying uses his name:
"So like Nimrod, a mighty hunter by God's grace," (as one might praise a hero of fame.)
Now his kingdom began with Babel, Erech, and Accad, all in the land of Shinar.
From this land Ashur set out and built Nineveh, along with city squares and Calah,
And between Nineveh and Calah, the great city of Resen. And then Mitzrayim
Fathered Ludim, Anamim, Lehabim, Naphtuhim, Pathrusim, and the Calushim,
And also the Caphtorim, from where all the Philistines came. Canaan too begot sons:
There was Sidon, his firstborn, and Heth, along with Jebusite and the Amorite ones,
And the Girgashites, Hivites, Arkites, Sinites, Arvadites, Zemarites, and Hamathites.
Afterward, all the Canaanite clans spread abroad. Territory of the Canaanites
Had extended from Sidon, and then as you come toward Gerar, as far out as the Gaza.
And if you were to walk towards Sodom and Gomorrah, and towards Zeboiim and Admah,
There their borders extended as far as Lasha. Now these peoples are the sons of Ham
After their families, after their languages, in a list by their nations and lands.
Children were also born to Shem, ancestor of each one of the descendants of Eber,
And also Japheth's older brother. The sons of Shem began with Elam and with Asshur,
Then came Arpachshad, Lud, and Aram. And Aram had four sons: Uz, Hul, Gether, and Mash.
Arpachshad fathered Shelah, and Shelah had Eber (from whom the name "Hebrews"
    was snatched).
Eber had two sons, the first named Peleg (or "Splitting"), because in his day earth was split.
And the name of his brother was Joktan, and as for children, Joktan had quite a bit:
Almodad, Sheleph, Hazarmaveth, Jerah, Hadoram, Uzal, Diklah, and Obal,
Abimael, Sheba, Ophir, Havilah, and Jobab—Joktan had fathered them all.
All these, Joktan's sons, had settlements from Mesha to the hills near Sephar in the east.
These are the sons of Shem, by their clan and by tongue, by their land, and by nation not least.

All of these are the groupings of Noah's descendants, by origin, by nation, by blood,
And from these descendants the nations were divided upon the earth after the Flood.

Genesis 11

There was only one language in all of the land,
It was spoken by all, from the chiefs to the rabble.
But men had a tower they built as their plan
To reach high up like God, in the city called Babel.
Now God saw they were building and said, "My oh My,
There'll be nothing they can't do if these heights they reach!"
So he went down to stop them from building so high
By confusing their language with all different speech.

All of earth shared the very same language, with one set of words. And as men were migrating
From the east, they found a valley in Shinar's lands, and they settled there, set for creating.
They said to one another, "Come, let us bake bricks, and then burn them in turn through
    and through."
So for them the brick-stone served as building stone, and the bitumen as mortar and glue.
Then they said, "Come, let's build a great city for ourselves, a tower whose top is so high
That it reaches the heavens. Let's make names for ourselves so we and our work will not die,
Otherwise we'll be scattered all over the world!" The Lord came down so that He could see
Both the city and tower man built, seeking power. And then the Lord said, "Here they be,
One people with one language they share among all, and this tower is just the beginning—
In time, there will be nothing to stop them from anything they want to do, even sinning!
Come now, let us go down there and baffle their speech, no two neighbors will then speak
    the same."
So God scattered them over the earth, and they had to stop building, hence Babel was named.
Yes, the city received the name Babel, (like babble), since there God had baffled all speech,
And it was from there that God had scattered all people across the earth's entire reach.

This is Shem's line: Shem lived for one hundred years, fathered Arpachshad, two years past
    the Flood,
After Arpachshad's birth, Shem lived five hundred years, and sired sons and daughters of
    his blood.
When Arpachshad had lived thirty-five years, he fathered Shelah, and after Shelah's birth,
Arpachshad lived four hundred and three years, and then fathered sons and daughters on
    the earth.
When Shelah had lived for thirty years, then he fathered Eber, and after Eber's birth,
Shelah lived for four hundred and three years, and fathered both sons and daughters on the earth.
When Eber had lived thirty-five years, then he fathered Peleg, and after Peleg's birth,

Eber lived for four hundred and thirty years, and fathered sons and daughters on the earth.
When Peleg had lived for thirty years, then he fathered Reu, and after Reu's birth,
Peleg lived for two hundred and nine years, and then fathered sons and daughters on the earth.
When Reu had lived thirty-two years, then he fathered Serug, and after Serug's birth,
Reu lived for two hundred and seven years, and fathered sons and daughters on the earth.
When Serug had lived for thirty years, then he fathered Nahor, and after Nahor's birth,
Serug lived for two hundred more years, and then fathered both sons and daughters on the earth.
When Nahor had lived twenty-nine years, then he fathered Terah, and after Terah's birth,
Nahor lived for one hundred and nineteen years, and fathered sons and daughters on the earth.

When Terah had lived seventy years, then he fathered Abram, and Nahor, and Haran.
Now what follows are the generations of Terah, the line that with Terah began.
Terah fathered Abram, and Nahor, and Haran; and Haran fathered Lot. Then Haran
Died in his father Terah's lifetime, in Ur of the Chaldeans, in his native land.
Both Abram and Nahor took a wife for themselves, the name of Abram's wife was Sarai,
Nahor's wife was named Milcah, daughter of Haran, whom she and Iscah were sired by.
Now Sarai was barren, she had no child. Terah took Abram, his son, and Haran's son
Lot, his son's son, and Sarai his daughter-in-law, the wife of Abram, who was his son;
And all four of them went forth together, Terah with Abram, Lot, and Sarai set out
From Ur of the Chaldeans to go to the land of Canaan, but it then came about
That when they reached the city of Harran, they settled there, feeling no need to move on.
The days of Terah came to two hundred and five years, and then Terah died in Harran.

Genesis 12

The Lord told Abram, "Go to the country I'll show you,
I'll give Canaan to your descendants, one day.
Now to Egypt, in famine, where no one will know you.
Name your wife as your sister, it's safer that way."
So when Abram was in Egypt, he said Sarai
Was his sister, whom Pharaoh was glad to receive.
But plagues fell upon Pharaoh. Then he found out why,
So he said, "Abram, you and your wife now must leave."

[Lech-Lecha]

So the Lord said to Abram, "Go forth from your land, where your kindred and father's house lie,
To the land I will show you. I'll make a great nation of you, and will bless you, and I
Will then make your name great. And you shall be a blessing, I will bless those who bless you too,
And will curse those that curse you, and all of earth's clans shall find blessing for themselves
     through you."

Abram went, as God told him, and Lot went with him. Abram was seventy-five years old
When he left Harran. He took his wife Sarai, his brother's son Lot, and all of their gold,
All the wealth they'd acquired, all people they'd gotten in Harran, and set out to go
To the land of Canaan. When they came to the land of Canaan, Abram did not move slow,
But he passed through the land to the Place of Shechem, as far in as the Sage-Oak of Moreh
(That's a sacred tree known as the "oracle giver", a remarkable piece of flora).
At that time, the Canaanites were still in the land. The Lord appeared to Abram to say,
"I will give this land to your offspring." Abram built an altar to the Lord on that day.
An altar to the Lord who had appeared to him. From there, Abram moved on to the hills
And the mountains east of Bethel, pitching his tent with Ai on the east, Bethel west still.
There he built one more altar to God, and he called out the name of the Lord with his mouth.
Abram then journeyed on, ever journeying towards the Negev, deep in the dry south.

Now there was in the land a great famine, so it was to Egypt that Abram went down,
To sojourn, for the famine was severe. When Abram was about to enter town
He said to his wife Sarai, "Look here, I know that you are a woman fair to behold.
When Egyptians see you, if they think you're my wife, my reception from them will be cold.
They would kill me, although they'd allow you to live. Please say you are my sister, instead.
That way it will go well with me on your account, and because of you I won't be dead."

So when Abram came to Egypt, all the Egyptians saw the woman was very fair;
Pharaoh's courtiers saw her, they praised her to Pharaoh, she was taken into his lair.
It went well with Abram thanks to her, he acquired sheep and oxen, and donkeys and maids,
Servants, she-asses, and even camels. But God plagued Pharaoh and his house with great plagues,
All because of Sarai, Abram's wife. Pharaoh had Abram sent for, and then Pharaoh said,
"What is this that you've done to me! Why did you not say she was your wife, but say instead
That she was just your sister, so that I took her as a wife for myself? Now then, here—
Here's your wife, take her back, and be gone with you both!" Pharaoh called some of his
     men to ear,
And put them in charge of Abram, charged with escorting Abram far away from this mess.
He commanded his men to send Abram away, with his wife and all that he possessed.

Genesis 13

Abram went up from Egypt with Sarai his wife,
Both with Lot and their things, to his altar of old.
But between Abram's herdsmen and Lot's, there was strife,
Even though there was plenty of cattle and gold.
Abram told Lot, "There's no need to argue. We're kin!
Pick some land, right or left, I won't go where you went."
So Lot chose to go east, to Sodom (where men sin),
And it was in Hebron that Abram pitched his tent.

Abram went up from Egypt, into the Negev, with his wife and all that he possessed,
Along with Lot. Now Abram was rich in livestock (cattle and goats with which he'd
    been blessed),
And in silver and gold. So he journeyed on from the Negev to Bethel, to the place
Where his tent had been previously, between Bethel and Ai, at the site of God's grace,

The same site of the altar that he had first built. And there Abram called out the Lord's name.
As for Lot, who had also gone with Abram, he had sheep, oxen, and tents when he came,
The land couldn't support them both staying together, with property of such extent
That they could not remain and both settle together. So there was a great argument
Between all of the herdsmen of Abram's livestock and all Lot's herdsman and cattle-hands.
(And it was at that time that the Canaanites and Perizzites were settled in the land.)

Abram said to Lot, "Please, let there not be a quarrel with you and me, your men and mine,
For we are kinsmen. And is not all of the land before you? Part from me at this time.
If you go to the right, I will go to the left, and if you go left, I will go right."
So Lot lifted his eyes up and saw all the plain of the Jordan, a beautiful sight,
He saw how well-watered it all was, (before God brought ruin to Sodom and Gomorrah,)
Like the garden of God, like the land of Egypt, just as you would be coming towards Zoar.
So Lot chose for himself all the plain of the Jordan. Then Lot journeyed east, and they parted,
Each man left from the other; Abram settled in the land of Canaan, while Lot soon started
To be settled in the cities of the plain, it was near Sodom that he pitched his tent.
Now the men of Sodom were all sinners against God, and sinners of a wicked bent.

So God said to Abram, once Lot parted from him, "Lift your eyes up and see all around
To the north, to the south and Negev, to the east, to the Sea in the west. All the ground

That you see, I give to you and to your offspring, for the ages. I will make your seed
Like the dust of the earth, so if a man could count all the dust of the earth, then indeed
So too could all your offspring be counted. Get up, and now go walk about through the land
Walk throughout its length and walk throughout its breadth, for I am giving it into your hand."
Abram moved his tent, and the place he came to settle and dwell was upon Hebron's sod,
Beside the oaks (or the terebinths) of Mamre. There Abram built an altar to God.

Genesis 14

> In the days of Amraphel the king of Shinar,
> Arioch, Tidal, and Chedorlaomer too,
> They made war with four kings of the east from afar
> In the valley of Siddim (the Salt Sea, to you.)
> Sodom's king fled, his army was beaten, undone,
> And then Lot and his goods became taken in war.
> Abram heard this had happened, took up arms, and won.
> He freed Lot, and Sodom's men could live as before.

Now it was in the days of Amraphel king of Shinar, Arioch king of Ellasar,
Chedorlaomer king of Elam, and Tidal king of Goyim, that they all made war
Against Bera king of Sodom, Birsha king of Gomorrah, Shinab king of Admah,
Shemeber king of Zeboiim, and the king of Zoar (which was then known as Bela).
All the latter joined forces in the limestone valley of Siddim (that's now the Dead Sea).
For twelve years they had served Chedorlaomer, but in the thirteenth year this would not be.
They rebelled, but then in the fourteenth year Chedorlaomer and kings with him in fights
Struck at the Rephaim at Ashteroth-Karnaim, and at Ham, attacked the Zuzites,
Beat the Emim at Shaveh-Kiriathain, the Horites in their hill-country of Seir
As far as El-Paran, which is out by the wilderness. On their way back, they came near
To En-Mishpat, the Judgment Spring now called Kadesh, and conquered from the Amalekites
All their land, and then also all those settled in Hazazon-Tamar, the Amorites.
Then the king of Sodom, the king of Gomorrah, king of Admah, king of Zeboiim,
And the king of Bela (now Zoar), went out to fight them in the valley of Siddim;
To fight Chedorlaomer the king of Elam, Tidal king of Goyim, Amraphel
The king of Shinar, and Arioch king of Ellasar—Four kings against five. The vale
Of Siddim was filled with pits of bitumen. So when Sodom and Gomorrah's kings fled,
They flung themselves into them. Those that remained fled up into the hill-country instead.

And they took all the wealth of Sodom and Gomorrah, and all of their provisions too,
And they also took Lot, the son of Abram's brother, and his possessions, and withdrew;
For he'd settled in Sodom. But one who escaped brought the news to Abram the Hebrew,
Who dwelt near the oaks of Mamre the Amorite, brother of Eshcol and of Aner,
They were Abram's allies. And when Abram heard his kinsman had been taken prisoner,
He took his retainers and his house-born slaves, three hundred eighteen went as far as Dan
In pursuit. And at night, Abram split up his forces against them as his battle plan.
Abram's servants divided and conquered them, and they drove them to Hobah in pursuit,
To the north of Damascus. And Abram returned with his kinsman Lot, and all his loot.
All the property, and all the women, and all other people, Abram had brought back.
So the king of Sodom had gone out to meet Abram when he returned from his attack
Against Chedorlaomer and the kings with him, to the valley of Shaveh (King's Valley).
Melchizedek, the king of Salem brought out bread and wine to celebrate Abram's sally.
And since he was a priest of the highest God, El Elyon, he had blessed Abram by saying,
"Blessed be Abram by El Elyon, founder of heaven and earth, He to whom we are praying.
And blessed be God Most-High, who has kindly delivered your enemies into your hand."
And then Abram gave him a tenth of everything (which is how tithes came into the land).

Now the king of Sodom said to Abram, "Give me the people, take the goods for your own."
Abram said to the king of Sodom, "I raise my hand and swear to the Lord, El Elyon,
The creator of heaven and earth, I shall take from you no thread, not one sandal-strap,
Nothing of yours; lest you say, 'I made Abram rich!', or some other similar claptrap.

I want nothing for me, only what my servants have used up; and then as for the shares
That belong to the men who went with me- Aner, Eshcol, and Mamre- let them take theirs."

Genesis 15

Then the Lord came to Abram inside of a vision,
And said, "Do not fear, Abram. I am your shield."
Abram said, "I have no offspring. What's your provision?"
God said, "Worry not, you shall produce great yield.
Sacrifice me some animals, cut them in two."
Abram did, the sun set, the light started to fade,
And God said, "Your descendants will wander, it's true,
But they'll come out well." Then was a covenant made.

After these things the Lord's word came to Abram in a vision, saying, "Abram, fear not.
I am a shield to you, your reward shall be very great." But Abram said, "My Lord God,
What would you give me? For I shall die cursed and childless, and my home's domestic caretaker
Is Eliezer the Damascan." And then Abram spoke further to his Lord and maker,
"Look, You gave me no child of my own, now my chief servant must serve as my heir."
But God's word came to him, replying, "He will not. For your heir, your own seed you will bear."
He brought Abram outside and said, "Look at the heavens and count the stars. Can you
    count them?"
God continued, "So shall be your offspring." And trust was placed in the Lord God by Abram.
God had deemed this as righteousness on Abram's part, and He said to him, "I am the Lord
The one who brought you out of Ur of the Chaldeans to give you this land as hoard."
Abram asked, "My Lord God, how will I know that I am the one to inherit the land?"
God replied, "Fetch me a calf of three years, a she-goat of three years, a three-year-old ram,
And a turtledove, and a young fledgling." Abram fetched him all of these, cut them in two,
And placed half of each facing the other, except for the birds which he did not cut through.
And though vultures descended to feast on the carcasses, Abram drove them all away.
As the sun set, a deep slumber fell upon Abram, a great darkness and some dismay.
The Lord said to Abram, "Know this, that your offspring will be strangers in a land not theirs,
And the nation shall put them in servitude, and then oppress them for four hundred years.
But then I shall bring judgment upon that same nation, and they will go free with great wealth.
As for you, you will go to your fathers in peace, buried after a long life of health,
At a ripe old age. But in the fourth generation, they will return here once again,
For the iniquity of the Amorites will not be fully complete until then."
It was when the sun set, and the dark of night came, that a smoking oven could be seen,
And a fiery torch appeared near the pieces of the oven, and passed straight between.

And on that day, the Lord made a covenant with Abram, saying, "I give your offspring
All this land, from the River of Egypt to the great river, the Euphrates flowing,
The land of the Kenites, the Kenizzites, the Kadmonites, Hittites, Perizzites as well,
The Rephaim, the Amorites, Canaanites, Girgashites, and where the Jebusites dwell."

Genesis 16

> Though Sarai did not bear any children for Abram,
> She gave her maid Hagar for Abram to try.
> And Hagar managed to have a child with Abram,
> Which made Hagar think she was better than Sarai.
> Then Sarai was mad. Hagar fled, an angel found her
> Who said "Tell Sarai 'sorry,' go back and submit,
> You are pregnant, and that's why your belly is rounder,
> It's a boy, Ishmael will be the name of it."

Now Sarai, Abram's wife, had not borne him a child. She did have, though, an Egyptian maid.
Her name was Hagar. Sarai said to Abram, "Look here, the Lord God has clearly displayed
That he wishes to keep me from bearing children. Please go into my maid where she lies;
Perhaps through her, I shall have a son to rise up." Abram heeded the words of Sarai.
So Sarai, Abram's wife, took Hagar the Egyptian, her maid—after Abram had lived
For ten years in the land of Canaan—and gave her to her husband Abram as wife/gift.
He went in to Hagar and Hagar became pregnant. But when she saw she had conceived,
Her mistress became lowered in her esteem. And so Sarai said to Abram, aggrieved,
"The wrong done to me is your fault! Yes, I myself brought my maid to your bosom; but now
Since she sees she's conceived, she sees me with contempt. May the Lord judge between
    us somehow."

Abram said to Sarai, "Your maid is in your hands. You may deal with her as you see fitting."
Sarai treated her harshly, so she ran away. But God's messenger found Hagar sitting
By a spring of water in the wilderness, by the spring on the road going to Shur.
He said, "Hagar, Sarai's maid, from where have you come, and to where are you going,
    what's more?"
She said, "I am fleeing from my mistress Sarai." And then God's messenger said to her,
"Go return to your mistress and let yourself be treated harshly, and do not demur."
And God's messenger said, "I shall make your seed many, too many to count when I'm done."
And the Lord's messenger said to her, "Behold, now you are pregnant! You will bear a son;
Name him Ishmael, ("God heeds"), for God heeds your suffering. He shall be a wild man,
With his hand against all and all theirs against him, he shall settle among his brethren."

So she called out the name of the Lord who spoke to her, "You are God of Seeing," she said,
"Have I still gone on seeing once the Lord has seen me?" (She was surprised not to be dead.)

And so therefore the well was called Beerlahairoi, ("Well of the Living One Who Sees Me")
And it lies between Kadesh and Bered. (The site where she saw she was seen, all can see.)

Hagar bore a son to Abram, Ishmael was the name Abram had called him at birth.
Abram was eighty-six years old when Hagar bore Ishmael to Abram on this earth.

Genesis 17

> God told Abram, "Let us make a covenant now,
> You'll no longer be Abram, but Abraham, you.
> Your descendants will be many. To keep this vow,
> Have all males circumcised as a sign this is true.
> And Sarai is now Sarah, and she will give birth."
> Abraham laughed and said, "We're too old for this game."
> God said, "I speak the truth, there is no need for mirth,
> Sarah will bear a son to you, Isaac his name."

Now when Abram was ninety-nine years old, the Lord appeared to Abram and said to him,
"I am God the Almighty. Walk in my ways and be wholehearted and blameless of sin.
I set my covenant between Me and you, and I will make of you very many."
Abram threw himself down on his face and then God spoke with him saying, "Look, as for Me,
Here, My covenant is with you, so you shall become the father of a crowd of nations.
And no longer shall your name be Abram, but Abraham shall be your new appellation,
For I make you the father of a crowd of nations. And I make you very fertile,
I will make nations of you; and kings will come out of you, not right now, but in a while.
I establish my covenant 'tween Me and you, and all your seed that comes after you,
As an eternal covenant to be God to you, and to be God to your seed too.
I give both to you and to your offspring the land you have sojourned in, all of Canaan,
To be an everlasting possession. I will be their God." God said to Abraham,
"As for you, you and your offspring are to keep My covenant through all ages to be
This is My covenant which you must keep, between Me and you, and too your progeny:
Every male among you shall be circumcised. You must circumcise flesh of your foreskin,
So it serves as a sign of the covenant 'tween Me and you. Through each generation,
At the age of eight days, every male among you must be circumcised. This is a need
For all of your servants, be they house-born or bought from a foreigner not of your seed.

Yes, they all must be circumcised, house-born and purchased, your offspring and not
    your offspring,
And that way shall My covenant be in your flesh marked as covenant everlasting.
And if any uncircumcised male fails to circumcise from the flesh of his foreskin,
Then that person has broken my covenant, and also shall be cut off from his kin."

God said to Abraham, "As for Sarai your wife, you shall nevermore call her Sarai,
For Sarah is her name. I will bless her, and even give you a son from her, will I.
I will bless her so that she will give rise to nations, kings of people will come from her."
But then Abraham fell on his face and just laughed, and he said to himself, "Yeah, oh sure.
To a hundred-year-old man, will there be kids born? Or shall Sarah at ninety give birth?"
Abraham said to God, "Oh, if only Ishmael might live in your presence on earth."
God said, "Nevertheless, Sarah your wife shall bear you a son, and this shall be his name:
'Isaac', meaning 'he laughs'. I'll establish my covenant with him as one to maintain
For the ages, and for his offspring after him. As for Ishmael, your words I'm heeding:
Behold, I will make him blessed, and make him bear fruit, and I will make him many, exceeding.
He will father twelve chieftains, and I'll make a great nation of him, so shall it commence.
But my covenant I will establish with Issac, whom Sarah will bear one year hence."

When He had finished speaking with Abraham, God then went up, from beside Abraham.
Abraham took Ishmael his son and all slaves that were born in his house, on his land,
And all of those he bought with his money, all males in Abraham's house, born and bought,
And on that same day he circumcised the flesh of their foreskins, as God told him he ought.
And so Abraham was ninety-nine years old when he had his foreskin's flesh circumcised,
And Ishmael his son was thirteen when he had the flesh of his foreskin circumcised.
On that very same day two were circumcised, Abraham, and too his son Ishmael,
And all of his household, both house-born and purchased, were then circumcised with him
    as well.

Genesis 18

Sarah laughed when God told her that she'd have a kid,
But God said, "I can do all things, you will give birth."
Sarah said, "I did not laugh." God said, "Yes you did."
Then the Lord saw that people did sin on the earth,
In Sodom and Gomorrah. He said, "I'll destroy them."
But Abraham said, "You'd kill innocent men.
What if fifty good men lived there? Would you destroy them?"
God: "I would spare them." Abraham: "How about ten?"

[Vayeira]

Now the Lord appeared to him by the oaks of Mamre, as he sat at his tent's front door
In the heat of the day. He looked up, and saw three men near him that were not there before.
When he saw them, he ran from the door of his tent to greet them, and he bowed to the ground.
He said, "My lords, pray, if I've found favor with you, do not pass by this servant you've found.
Pray let water be fetched, just a little, then wash your feet and recline under the tree;
Let me fetch you a morsel of bread to refresh your hearts, then go on with your journey—
After all, you have passed by your servant's way." And the three spoke, "Do just as you have said."
Abraham quickly ran into the tent with Sarah and said, "Quick, we'll need three small breads.
Take three measures of good flour, knead it, make cakes!" Abraham ran to the herd outside,
He took one fine young calf, and gave it to a slave, who prepared it quickly to provide.
Then he fetched cream and milk, and the calf he'd prepared, and placed all of it before the three.
He was standing nearby them right under the tree while they ate. And then they said to he,
"Where is Sarah your wife?" He said, "Here, in the tent." One then said, "I will return to you
In the spring, at the time when life blossoms; and your wife Sarah will blossom a son too!"
Sarah was listening at the door of the tent, behind Abraham, hid from his gaze.
And both Sarah and Abraham were old in years; Sarah no longer had women's ways.
Sarah laughed to herself, saying, "Now that I'm withered and worn, am I now to have pleasure?
With my husband so old?" God said to Abraham, "Now why does Sarah laugh in such measure?
Why does she ask herself, 'shall I really give birth to a child, now that I am so old?'
Is there anything beyond the Lord? I will return to you at the time I've foretold,
In the spring, when life blossoms, and Sarah will have a son." Sarah spoke a fabrication,
Saying, "I did not laugh." For she was afraid. But God said, "You did laugh, on that occasion."

The men rose up from there and looked down toward Sodom, Abraham went with them as escort.
God said to Himself, "Shall I hide from Abraham what I'm about to do, or report?

For this Abraham is to become a great nation, a populous nation as well,
And then all of the nations on earth are to find blessing through Abraham for themselves.
For I have chosen him and known him, he will instruct his sons and his household in trust,
After him to keep walking the ways of the Lord, by doing that which is right and just,
So that God may bring for Abraham what He has promised is to be Abraham's fate."
So God said, "The outcry in Sodom and Gomorrah is great, and their sin has great weight.
I will go down and see if they've done altogether according to the cry I heard.
Great destruction if so. And if not, I will know." And that was the Lord Almighty's word.

So the men turned from there and went toward Sodom, but still Abraham stood before God.
Abraham came close and said, "Will you really kill innocent men along with the flawed?
Perhaps in this big city of guilty men live fifty innocents, are they to die?
Will you not spare the place for the sake of fifty innocents, who might in that place lie?
Heaven forbid that You do a thing like this, that You would bring death to the innocent
Along with the guilty, so both types of men end up rewarded to the same extent.
Indeed, far be it from You to do this! Shall not the judge of all earth do what is just?"
God replied, "If I find in Sodom fifty innocents, then spare the city I must.
I will bear the sin of the whole city for their sake." Then Abraham spoke and said, "Pray,
I have ventured to speak to my Lord God Almighty, and I am but mere dust and clay.
Now, perhaps of the innocent fifty, five will lack—For that, shall none be left alive?
Will the city fall for them?" God said, "I will not bring ruin, if I find there forty-five."
But then Abraham spoke up again and said, "Maybe only forty there are not bad."
God said, "I will not do it, for those forty's sake." Abraham said, "Lord, please don't be mad
If I speak a bit further: Perhaps only thirty such innocent men will be found."
God said, "I will not do it, if I find there thirty such innocent men on the ground."
But then Abraham said, "Pray, I venture to speak to my Lord, if my words he will take.
Maybe only twenty will be found." God said, "I won't bring ruin, for those twenty's sake."
But then Abraham said, "Lord, please don't be mad that I speak up this one last time again:
What if only ten can be found?" God said, "I will not bring ruin, for the sake of the ten."
And the Lord went his way, when He had finished speaking to Abraham, then He departed.
And so Abraham too then returned to his place, where he was 'ere this dialogue started.

Genesis 19

So two angels came to Sodom, and Lot played host.
They told him, "Take your family and get out of town.
This whole city is wicked, and so it will roast,
So get out before fire and brimstone rain down.
Only, don't look behind you when fleeing the slaughter."
Lot's wife looked, and turned into a pillar of salt.
Then Lot lived in the hills, was brought wine by his daughters,
Who lay down with him in a drunken assault.

The two messengers came to Sodom at sunset, as Lot was sitting at Sodom's gate.
When Lot saw them, he rose up to greet them and bowed his head low to the ground,
    saying, "Wait!
Now I pray you, my lords, turn aside to the house of your servant, and there spend the night,
Wash your feet, and then you can wake early to go on your way." They said, "No, that's alright.
We will spend the night out in the streets of the square." But Lot urged them strongly, so instead
They turned his way and came into his house where he made for them a feast and baked flatbread,
And they ate. They had not yet lain down, when the townsfolk, the men of Sodom, young
    and old,
All the people from even the outskirts of town, they encircled the house, feeling bold.
They called out to Lot and said to him, "Where are the two men that came to you on this night?
Bring them out to us, we want to know them more intimately!" Lot was stuck in this plight.
He went out to them, to the entrance, shut the door behind him and he said to the band,
"Pray you, brothers, do not be so wicked. I have two daughters who have not known a man,
Pray let me bring them out to you, and you may deal with them however you think is best,
But to these men do nothing because they've come under the shelter of my roof as guests."
But they said, "Step aside!" And said, "This fellow came to sojourn here, and now wants to judge?
Now we'll do worse things to you than them!" And they pressed hard against Lot
    (a serious nudge.)
They stepped closer to break down the door, but the messengers reached out a hand and
    grabbed Lot,
They pulled him into the house with them and then shut the door. And the men outside
    were caught
By a dazzling light from the messengers, blinding all men at the door, great and small,
So that all of the men at the entrance were unable to locate the door at all.

Then the messengers said to Lot, "Whom else do you have here? A son-in-law, sons, or daughters?
Anyone whom you have in the city, bring them out of this place, for we shall bring slaughter!
We're about to bring ruin upon the whole city, how great is their cry before God!
God has sent us to bring it to ruin." And so Lot went out and spoke to his inlaws.
To his sons-in-law, those who had taken his daughters in marriage, he said, "Up! Get out!
Quick, get out of this place, for God will bring ruin on the city!" But they heard with doubt.
They thought that Lot was joking, it seemed to his son-in-laws that he was like one who jests.
When the dawn came, the messengers urged Lot on, saying, "Up! Take your wife and
     daughters, lest
You end up swept away in the city's iniquity." When he lagged, they grabbed his hand,
And his wife's hand, and also the hands of his two daughters- for the Lord's pity was grand,
And they brought him out and left him outside the city. Then one said, "Escape, for your life!
Do not look behind you, don't stand still on the Plain, but just flee to the hills with your wife.
Otherwise you will be swept away." But Lot said to one of them, "No, pray, my good lord,
Your servant has found favor in your eyes, and you have been gracious to have me aboard,
You have saved my life, but I can't flee to the hills, lest the wickedness cling to me, killing me.
Now pray, that town is near enough for one to flee to—such a small place—I'd live there willingly,
So my life could be saved." He replied, "Very well, I will grant you this favor also,
By not overturning this town which you have mentioned. Now move quickly, escape there, go!
For I am unable to do anything until you have arrived in the town, safe."
Therefore the name of the town was called Zoar (which can be translated as "a small place").

As the sun rose up over the earth and Lot entered Zoar, the Lord rained from the sky
On Sodom and Gomorrah with fire and brimstone, causing all in those cities to die.
And He overturned all of the plain. In those cities all life, man and plant, met a halt.
Now Lot's wife while escaping looked back behind him, and turned into a pillar of salt.
Abraham left early in the morning to where he had stood in the presence of God,
He looked down on the face of Sodom and Gomorrah, and all of the Plain, and was awed.
For he saw the dense smoke of the land rising up like the dense smoke that comes from a furnace.
So it was, when God brought ruin to the plain's cities, he kept Abraham in mind, earnest,
And for his sake, God sent Lot from the overturning, away from the midst of destruction
When He overturned all of the cities where Lot had lived before the two men's instructions.

Lot went up from Zoar and settled in the hills, his two daughters with him to be saved,
For he was afraid to live down in Zoar, therefore all three of them lived in a cave.
The firstborn daughter said to the younger one, "Our father is old, and there is no man
To come in to us, or to know us and consort with us in the way of all the land.
Come, let us make our father drink wine, and lie down with him, so that we may bear offspring."
So that night they made their father drink wine, then the firstborn went in and lay down
     with him.
Now the father knew nothing of her laying down, or her rising up. So the next day,
The firstborn daughter said to the younger daughter, "Look, last night with our father I lay.

Let us have him drink wine tonight too, then you go in and lie with him, he'll never know.
That way our seed will be kept alive." So that night, they made their father drink wine also.
Then the younger one went and lay down with him, but once again Lot was well ignorant
Of her lying down and rising. So by their father, Lot's two daughters became pregnant.
The firstborn had a son Moab (meaning "by father"), who fathered today's Moabites,
And the younger one's son Ben-Ammi ("son of my kinspeople") fathered the Ammonites.

Genesis 20

> Abraham went to Gerar, said, "Sarah's my sister,"
> So king Abimelech had her sent to his tent.
> God told him, "She's Abe's wife, and you'll pay if you kissed her!"
> The king told God, "Don't hurt me, I'm innocent."
> Then he asked Abraham, "Why did you lie to me?"
> Abraham said, "She's my sister, and is my wife."
> Abimelech then gave him sheep and oxen free,
> So that Abraham prayed to God for the king's life.

Abraham journeyed on from there to the Negev, settled down between Kadesh and Shur.
Sojourning in Gerar, Abraham said of Sarah his wife, "That one is my sister."
So Abimelech, King of Gerar, had sent out to have Sarah taken to his side.
But God came to the dreams of Abimelech in the night and said to him, "You must die,
Due to the woman whom you have taken, for that one is another man's wedded wife."
Abimelech had not come near her, and said, "My lord, would you drain a nation of life
Even though it is innocent? Did he not say to me, 'she is my sister?' And plus,
She said, 'He is my brother!' And so with a blameless heart and clean hands I have done thus."
And God said to him in the dream, "I know it was with whole heart you did this, consequently
I have kept you from sinning against Me, which is why I did not let you touch her gently.
But now, give the man's wife back to him, for he is a prophet and he can intercede
On your behalf, so you may live. But if you fail to return the man's wife, then take heed:
Know that you shall die, not only you, but all that are yours will become equally harmed."
In the morning, Abimelech called his servants and told them. They were greatly alarmed.
Abimelech had Abraham summoned and said to him, "What's this to us you have done?
What wrong have I done you that you should bring such great guilt on me and upon
    my kingdom?
Deeds that should not be done, you have done to me." Abimelech said to Abraham more,
"What were you thinking that made you do this thing?" Abraham said, "I told myself before,

'surely there is no fear of God in this place, and they will kill me because of my wife.'
And besides, she is really my sister, my dad's daughter, though my mom didn't give her life.
So she became my wife. And when God's power caused me to wander from my father's house,
I said to her, 'Please do this small kindness for me, of the truth, be quiet like a mouse.
And wherever we travel, say, "He is my brother."' And that's how we got in this jam."
Abimelech took sheep and oxen, slaves and maids, and gave all of them to Abraham,
And returned his wife Sarah to him. Abimelech said, "Here, all my land is before you.
Settle wherever looks good to you." And to Sarah, Abimelech said, "Now, as for you,
I hereby give your brother one thousand pieces of silver, to serve as vindication,
So that those who are with you, and everyone, may overlook your recent situation."
And then Abraham prayed to God and interceded, and God healed Abimelech,
Along with his wife and his slave women, so that they could all bear children at his beck.
For God previously had closed fast and obstructed every womb in his household area
All because of the incident with the wife of Abraham, all on account of Sarah.

Genesis 21

The Lord visited Sarah and gave her a son,
And thus Isaac was born. But Isaac liked to play
With the boy Ishmael, Sarah's maid Hagar's son,
And then Sarah was mad, so she sent them away.
Hagar left with her son, worried for Ishmael,
But God said "Do not fear, for his safety I'll keep."
Abraham and Abimelech's men at a well
Argued, but then they made an agreement with sheep.

The Lord took note of Sarah as He had said, and the Lord dealt with her as He had spoken.
Sarah conceived and bore a son to Abraham in his old age, when life had awoken
In the season of which God had spoken to him, in the spring. Abraham named his son,
Whom Sarah had born to him, "Isaac" (which translates as "He laughs" in old Hebrew tongue).
And then Abraham circumcised Isaac his son at eight days, as the Lord had commanded.
Abraham was one hundred years old when his son Isaac was born, and on the earth landed.
So then Sarah said, "God has made laughter for me, all who hear of it will laugh with me."
And she added, "Who would have said to Abraham that Sarah would nurse sons? But indeed,
I have borne him a son in his old age." The child then grew up and the child was soon weaned,
And so Abraham held a great feast on the day Isaac's weaning had been seen and gleaned.

Sarah saw the son of Hagar the Egyptian, whom she had borne to Abraham, mocking.
She said to Abraham, "Cast this slave-woman out, along with her son. Send them both walking,
For the son of this slave shall not share in the inheritance with my own son, Isaac."
This distressed Abraham since the matter dealt with his son, and looked not to be solved quick.
But God told Abraham, "Do not be distressed about the boy and the slave Sarah blame,
Heed all Sarah tells you, for through Isaac your line will be continued and bear your name.
And now as for the son of the slave-woman, I will also make a nation of him,
For he too is your seed." Early next morning, Abraham took bread and a waterskin,
And gave them to Hagar, he put them on her shoulder, with the child and sent them away.
She went off and she wandered in the wilderness of Beersheva. Until on one day,
When the water was gone from the waterskin, she left the child beneath a bush nearby,
Then she went to sit, far as a bowshot away, thinking, "Let me not see the child die."
So she sat far away, lifted her voice and wept. But God heard the boy's voice from afar.
And God's messenger called to Hagar from heaven and said to her, "What ails you, Hagar?
Do not be afraid, for the Lord has heard the voice of the boy at his present location.
Arise, lift the boy up, and hold him with your hand, for of him I will make a great nation."
So God opened her eyes and Hagar saw before her a well of water, so she went,
Filled the skin up with water, and let the boy drink from it, hoping his thirst would relent.
God was with the boy as he grew up, he lived in the wilderness, became a bowman.
He lived in Paran's wilderness, and his mother got a wife for him from Egypt's land.

At about that time, Abimelech and Phicol, chief of his troops, said to Abraham,
"God is with you in all that you do. So now, swear to me by God, right here where I am,
That you will not deal falsely with me, with my progeny, or their progeny in turn,
But in good faith, as I've dealt with you, deal with me, and with the land in which
    you've sojourned."
Abraham said, "I so swear." But Abraham rebuked Abimelech where he did stand
All because of a well of water that Abimelech's servants had seized beforehand.
Abimelech said, "I don't know who did this thing, and until now you hadn't told me,
I've heard nothing about it until today." So Abraham took some oxen and sheep
And gave them to Abimelech, and the two of them then cut a covenant between them.
And then Abraham set seven ewes of his flock aside. When Abimelech had seen them,
He asked Abraham, "What do these seven ewes that you have set aside mean?" He replied,
"These are seven ewes you should accept from my hand, proof that I've dug this well we've espied."

Therefore that place was known as Beersheva, (which means "Well of seven" or "Well of
    the oath")
For there the two of them swore at Beersheva, and there cut a covenant between them both.
Then Abimelech and Phicol, chief of his troops, arose and returned to the country
And the land of the Philistines. Meanwhile, Abraham planted a tamarisk tree
In Beersheva, and there he did call out the name of the Lord, the Everlasting God.
And so Abraham sojourned in the land of the Philistines for many days abroad.

Genesis 22

Then God tested poor Abraham, and said to him,
"Take your son Isaac, whom you love, your firstborn heir,
Take him up to the mountain and sacrifice him."
Abraham took his son up, and when they got there,
Isaac said, "Where's the sacrifice?" Dad raised his hand,
But the Lord said, "Stop, Abraham! It was a test."
And an angel told him, "You will thrive in the land,
Since you did not withhold your son, you will be blessed."

After these events, God tested Abraham, saying to him, "Abraham!" Without shock,
Abraham replied, "Here I am." God said, "Take your son, the favored one you love, Isaac,
And go to the land of Seeing, Moriah. Offer him there as a burnt offering,
Upon one of the mountains which I will tell you of." So Abraham, the next morning,
Saddled his ass and took with him two servants and his son Isaac, since he was devout.
He split wood for the offering, rose up, and went to the place God had told him about.
On the third day did Abraham lift up his eyes, and he then saw the place from afar.
Abraham told his men, "You stay here with the ass, while the boy and I both go up there,
We will worship and then we'll return to you." Abraham took all the offering wood,
And placed it upon Isaac his son. In his hand, he took firestone and knife where he stood.
So the two of them went off together. Isaac said to his father Abraham, "Father!"
Abraham replied, "Here I am, Isaac, my son." Isaac said, "Please don't think me a bother,
Here are firestone and wood, but now where is the lamb for the offering? I don't perceive it."
Abraham replied, "God will see to the lamb for His own offering, my son. Believe it."
So the two of them went off together, arriving at the place that God had mentioned.
Abraham built the altar there, arranged the wood, and then finally bound Isaac his son,
Placing him on the altar on top of the wood. And then Abraham reached out his hand,
He took up the knife to slay his son. But God's messenger called from heaven, "Abraham!"
The Lord's messenger called to him, "Abraham! Abraham!" Abraham said, "Here I am."
And the messenger said, "Don't raise your hand against the boy, do not do one thing to him.
For I now know that you fear the Lord, since you did not withhold your son, favored, from me."
Abraham lifted up his eyes and saw a ram with its horns caught in the shrubbery.
Abraham took the ram, and then offered it up on the same spot where his son had been.
"Adonai-yireh" ("God Sees") he named the site, so we say, "On God's mountain it is seen."

Now God's messenger called to him from heaven a second time, said, "By myself I swear,
The Lord has said, because you have done this thing and not withheld your son, your favored heir,

I will bless you indeed, I will make your seed many, like heaven's stars up in the sky,
Like the sand on the seashore. The gate of your foes all your seed shall possess by and by,
All the nations of earth shall bless themselves by your seed, because you did heed my command."
Abraham then returned to his servants, and they went together to Beersheva's lands.

So then Abraham stayed in Beersheva. And following all this, Abraham was told,
"Milcah has also borne, sons to Nahor your brother: The firstborn, Utz, is the most old,
And Buz (Utz's brother), Kemuel who fathered Aram, and Chesed, and Hazo,
And Pildash, Jidlaph and Bethuel." Now Bethuel fathered Rebekah, as we know.
These eight Milcah bore to Nahor, Abraham's brother. And his concubine named Reumah,
She had also borne children: She bore Tebah, Gaham, Tahash, and then she bore Maacah.

Genesis 23

> Sarah lived one hundred twenty seven full years.
> Abraham mourned her death, and said to the Hittites,
> "Give me land where I can bury her," through his tears.
> They responded, "Okay, from us, you'll get no fights."
> Abraham said, "Tell Ephron the cave of Machpelah
> Is what I want. I'll pay full price for that cave."
> Ephron said, "I can give it for free to you, fella,"
> But still, Abraham paid, and so bought his wife's grave.

[Chayei Sarah]

Sarah's lifetime in years was one hundred and twenty seven, all the years of her life.
Sarah died in Arba-town (Hebron) in the land of Canaan. Abraham mourned his wife,
So he came to mourn Sarah and weep for her, then he rose up from before his own dead
And he told the Hittites, "I am a sojourner who has settled among you," and said,
"Give me title to a burial site among you, so that I may bury from view
My own dead." And the Hittites responded to him, saying, "Hear us, my lord. Now since you
Are exalted by God in our midst, bury your dead in our choicest burial site.
None among us denies you his plot for your dead." Abraham then bowed to the Hittites.
He bowed low to the Hittites, the folk of the land, and said, "If this is your true request
That I bury my dead out of sight, then hear me, and for me intercede at your best
With Ephron son of Zohar, so that he may give me title to the cave of Machpelah,
Which he owns. It is at the far edge of his land, and I'll pay the full price to that fella.

Let him sell it to me in your presence as burial site." Ephron was sitting there,
With the Hittites. Then Ephron the Hittite arose, giving answer so that all could hear,
"No, my lord, hear me. The field I give you, and give you the cave on that land," Ephron said,
"Here, I give it to you in the presence of my people's sons. Go and bury your dead."
Abraham bowed before the people of the land, speaking to Ephron so all could hear,
"But wait, hear me out, let me pay you the land's price, take it, so I may bury dead there."
Ephron answered to Abraham, "My lord, hear me. This small land has a value, we've said,
Of four hundred silver shekels, what's that between me and you? Go and bury your dead."
Abraham heeded Ephron's terms, weighed out to him the silver, in its full promised weight
Which the Hittites had heard, four hundred silver shekels priced at the going merchants' rate.

So the field of Ephron in Machpelah, near Mamre, the field and the cave therein,
And all trees in the area passed from Ephron to Abraham as his possession,
In the presence of the Hittites, and of all who entered through the town's gates. After that,
Abraham buried Sarah his wife in the cave which in the field of Machpelah sat,
East of Mamre (Hebron) in the land of Canaan. And so it had passed from the Hittites,
The field with the cave in it, into Abraham's possession as a burial site.

Genesis 24

> Abraham was old, and asked his servant to swear,
> "Do not let my son marry one of Canaan's daughters,
> But go to my country and get him one there."
> So the servant left, and found a maiden with water.
> She gave water to him and his mounts from her jar,
> And the servant was pleased with the kindness she carried.
> He asked her to travel back with him afar,
> So Rebekah became Isaac's wife; they were married.

Abraham was now old, well advanced in years, and by the Lord in all things he'd been blessed.
Abraham said to the senior slave of his household, who had charge of all he possessed,
"Put your hand under my thigh and swear by the Lord, God of heaven and God of the earth,
That you won't take a wife for my son from the Canaanites, but from the land of my birth.
Do not take from these women where I've settled, but go to seek wives in my native land,
For Isaac." And the slave said to him, "But what if she does not want to heed my command?
If she won't consent to follow me here, shall I take your son back to your former home?"
Abraham said to him, "Beware. My son must never be brought back to that land to roam.

For the Lord God of heaven, who took me from my father's house and my kin, spoke to me.
And He swore to me saying, 'I give this land to your offspring'—So I have faith that He
Will send a messenger before you, and from there you will then take a wife for my son.
And if that woman won't consent to follow you, your oath-bound duty to me is done.
But you must never take my son back there." The servant then put his hand under the thigh
Of his lord Abraham, and swore to him an oath about this matter, vowed to comply.

So the servant took ten camels from his lord's camels and went out, his lord's goods in hand.
He rose up and went to Aram-of-two-rivers, to Nahor's town just as had been planned.
He had his camels kneel outside town at the water well as the sun set, at the time
When the women go out to draw water. And he said, "Lord, God of that master of mine,
Let today be the day that it goes well for me, deal kindly with my lord Abraham.
Here, I stand beside the spring of water as the townswomen draw from it. Here I am.
Let the maiden to whom I say, 'Please lower your pitcher so that I may have a drink.'
And who says, 'drink, and I will also give your camels some water.' (She'd be it, I think.),
Let her be the one you have decided on for your servant, for Isaac, so I'll know
That you've dealt graciously and in good faith with my master. And this sign will serve to show."

And then just as he had finished speaking, Rebekah came out—she'd been born to Bethuel,
Son of Milcah, wife of Nahor, Abraham's brother—she was as pretty as a jewel.
Now her pitcher was up on her shoulder, and she was fair to look upon, a virgin.
No man had known her. Going down to the spring, she filled her pitcher and came up again.
Then the servant ran towards her and said, "Pray, from your pitcher let me sip a little water."
She replied, "Drink, my lord," as she lowered her pitcher in haste as her good grace had taught her.
She let him drink, and when he had finished she said, "I will water your camels as well."
So she emptied her pitcher and quickly ran to the well to draw for all his camels.

He stood staring at her, silently wondering if the Lord had granted him success.
When the camels had finished, the man took a gold nose ring, half-shekel weight, and bracelets,
Two nice bracelets of gold for her wrists, ten gold shekels in weight. "Pray tell me," the man said,
"Whose daughter are you? And in your father's house is there space where we might rest
    our heads?"
She replied, "I am the daughter of Bethuel, son of Milcah, whom she bore to Nahor."
And she said, "Yes, there's straw. Yes, there's plenty of food. Yes, you may find shelter through
    our door."
The man bowed low in homage to the Lord and said, "Blessed be the Lord, the God of my master
Abraham, who has not withheld his faithfulness from my lord, nor led him to disaster.
As for me, the Lord has guided me on my journey to the house of my master's kin."
And the maiden then ran to her mother's household and relayed all this to those within.

Rebekah had a brother whose name was Laban. Laban ran to the man at the spring,
And as soon as he saw the bracelets on the wrists of his sister, and the gold nose ring,

And as soon as Laban heard Rebekah his sister say, "That's what the man said to me."
He went up to the man who still stood at the wellspring with his camels, and said to he,
"Come in, oh you blessed of the Lord, why are you standing outside when I have prepared
Both the house for you and a place camels can stay?" So the man came in and food was shared.
The man first had unbridled the camels, and they gave the camels some straw and some fodder,
And then gave to the man and those who were with him for the washing of their feet some water.
Food was set before him to eat, but he said, "I will not eat before speaking my word."
Laban said, "Speak on." So the man said, "I'm Abraham's servant, as you may have heard.
The Lord has blessed my master exceedingly, and he's become rich, with oxen and sheep,
He has given him silver and gold, servants and maids, both camels and asses he keeps.
As for Sarah, my master's wife, she bore my master a son after she had grown old,
And he's given him all that he owns. Now my lord made me swear, and here's what I was told:
'You shall not take a wife for my son from the women of the Canaanites, where I dwell.
No, instead you shall go to my father's house, there you will find a wife that will work well.
Take a wife for my son.' I said to my lord, 'What if the woman will not follow me?'
He replied, 'the Lord, Whose ways I've followed will send His messenger to aid your journey.
He will grant you success on your journey, to take from my clan a good wife for my son,
From my father's house. When you have finished this task, only then will your duty be done.
When you come to my clan, if they don't give her to you, your duty is finished that way.'
Now today I came to the well and said, 'Oh Lord, God of my master Abraham, pray,
If you would grant success to my journey, then here, I have stationed myself by the well.
Let the maiden to whom I say, "Please lower your pitcher so that my thirst I may quell."
And who answers, "Drink, and I will also give your camels water." Let her be the one
Whom the Lord has decided should serve as the wife of my good master Abraham's son.'
And before I was even done praying in my heart, Rebekah came out. On her shoulder
Was a pitcher, and she went down to the wellspring and drew water. At that point I told her,
'Oh, please give me a drink.' So she hastily lowered her pitcher and said, 'Here you go.
Drink, and I'll water your camels too.' So I drank, and she watered the camels also.
Then I asked her 'Whose daughter are you?' She said, 'the daughter of Bethuel, son of Nahor,
Whom Milcah bore to him.' So I put the ring and bracelets on her, which you saw before,
And in homage I bowed to the Lord, and blessed Him, God of my master Abraham, One
Who led me on this journey to take the daughter of my master's brother for his son.
So, now, if you will deal truly and faithfully with my lord, then tell me so I'll know,
And if not, tell me, so I'll know whether to turn right or if to the left I should go."

Bethuel and Laban both responded, saying, "By the Lord this matter has been decreed;
We cannot speak to you anything bad or good. Here's Rebekah before you, indeed,
Now take her and go, so that she may be a wife for your master's son, as God has said."
When the servant of Abraham heard their words, he bowed low to the Lord God with his head.
And the servant brought out things of silver and gold, and garments, and gave them to Rebekah,
And he gave presents to her brother and her mother as well, to show he did respect her.

Both he and the men that were with him ate and drank, spent the night. When they woke the
    next day,
He said, "Send me off to my lord." But then her brother and mother said, "Let the girl stay.
Let her stay with us for a few days, maybe ten, after that she can go." He replied,
"Don't delay me, for God has made my journey filled with success. Send me off on my ride,
So that I can return to my master." They said, "Call the maiden and ask her reply."
They called Rebekah and said to her, "Will you go with this man?" She said, "I will go, aye."
So they sent off Rebekah their sister with her nurse, and Abraham's servant and men,
And they blessed Rebekah and said to her, "Our sister, may you become thousands of tens
Of thousands; And may your offspring seize the gates of their foes." She rose, and her maids
    rose too.
And they mounted the camels and followed the man. Then the servant took her and withdrew.

Now Isaac had just come back from Beerlahairoi, for in the Negev he was still dwelling.
And Isaac went out to ponder in the field at night, because he found evening compelling.
Isaac lifted his eyes and saw, look, camels coming. Rebekah lifted her eyes too,
And saw Isaac, got down from the camel, and said to the servant beside her, "Now who
Is the man over there walking in the field to meet us?" The servant said, "That's my lord."
So she took a veil and covered herself. The servant told Isaac all that had occurred.
Isaac brought her into the tent of Sarah, his mother, took Rebekah as his wife,
And he loved her, and so was able to find comfort once his mother left from this life.

Genesis 25

> Abraham took another wife, who bore more kids.
> He was buried in Machpelah's cave, with his wife.
> Ishmael then had children, so many he did,
> While Rebekah and Isaac had two, both in strife.
> Their two children fought. The first, named Esau, was hairy.
> The second, named Jacob, had grabbed at his heel.
> One day Esau was hungry, and Jacob wouldn't share, he
> Demanded Esau's birthright, and struck a deal.

Abraham had now taken another wife, named Keturah, who bore to him Zimran,
Jokshan, Medan, Ishbak, Midian, and Shuah. Jokshan fathered Sheba and Dedan.
Dedan's sons were the Ashurites, Letushites, and Leummites. The sons of Midian
Were Ephah, Epher, Enoch, Abida, and Eldaah. And all of those sons, to a man,

Were the children of Keturah, but Abraham had willed all that he had to Isaac.
And to sons of the concubines Abraham had, he gave gifts, and then told them to walk.
He sent them far away from his son Isaac, while he was still alive, far to the East.

And so these are the days and years of the life of Abraham, which he lived 'ere it ceased:
A full hundred and seventy-five years, then he expired, but to good ripe age he'd lived.
Abraham died both old and contented in days, and was gathered to his relatives.
His sons Isaac and Ishmael buried him in the cave of Machpelah, in the field
Of Ephron son of Zohar the Hittite, facing Mamre, which Abraham in a deal
Had acquired from the Hittites. There Abraham was buried, and his wife Sarah as well.
After Abraham's death, God blessed his son Isaac, and near Beerlahairoi did he dwell.

These are the generations of Ishmael, Abraham's son, that Hagar the Egyptian,
Sarah's maid, bore to Abraham. Here are the names of his sons, ordered by generation:
Nebaioth, who was Ishmael's firstborn, then Kedar, Adbeel and Mibsam, and Mishma,
Then Dumah and Massa, Hadad, Tema, Jetur, and Naphish, and finally Kedmah.

These are the sons of Ishmael, these their names listed by village and tribal corrals,
With twelve leaders for their dozen tribes. And these are the years of the life of Ishmael:
One hundred thirty-seven full years, then Ishmael expired, and did breathe his last.
So he died and was gathered to his relatives. They settled in an area vast,
From Havilah to Shur, which is found before Egypt, if one were to walk toward Assyria;
And they camped alongside all their kinsmen, and he fell among all of them, in that area.

[Toledot]

These are the generations of Isaac, son of Abraham. Abraham fathered Isaac.
Isaac was forty years old when he took Rebekah to wife (after that water well trick),
Yes, Rebekah, daughter of Bethuel the Aramean, from the country Aram,
Sister of Laban the Aramean. Isaac prayed to God that she could be a mom.
He prayed to the Lord on behalf of his wife, for she was barren and she could not bear,
And Rebekah his wife became pregnant, because the Lord God had granted Isaac's prayer.
But the children then struggled together inside her womb, so she said, "If this is so,
Why do I exist?" And she went to inquire of the Lord. God said to her, "You must know
That two nations are in your womb, two peoples born from your body will soon be divided.
One shall be stronger than the other, elder shall serve the younger, as I have decided."
When her days to give birth were at hand, sure enough, twins were in her womb, twins she
    would bear.
The first one came out red, hair all over his body, so they named him "Esau" (or "Hair").
After that, then his brother came out, and his hand to the heel of Esau grabbed hold,
So they named him "Jacob" ("Heel-Holder"). She bore them when Isaac was sixty years old.

The boys grew up: Esau became a skillful hunter, a man of the field outdoors,
But Jacob was a plain man, who stayed among tents. Isaac started to love Esau more,
Because he had a taste for the game he brought, whereas Rebekah, she loved Isaac dearly.
One time Jacob was boiling some stew when Esau came in from the field, and he was weary.
Esau said to Jacob, "Please give me a few bites of that red stuff; I'm weary and tired."
(That's why they called him "Edom" or "Red One", but Jacob was feeding a different desire.)
Jacob said, "Sell me your birthright, now." Esau said, "Okay, here I am dying of hunger,
What good now is a birthright to me?" Jacob said, "Then at once, swear it to me, the younger."
He swore to Jacob and sold his birthright to him. Jacob gave him bread and lentil stew.
Esau ate and drank and rose and went off, and that's how he spurned the birthright he once knew.

Genesis 26

There was famine, so God spoke to Isaac and said,
"Don't go to Egypt," So Isaac stayed in Gerar.
And when asked of his wife, he didn't say they were wed,
But said, "This is my sister, we come from afar."
Abimelech saw them and said, "Hey, she's your wife,
Why'd you lie?" Isaac said, "To be safe, as you know."
The king told everyone to free Isaac from strife,
But he got rich and envied, so he had to go.

Now there was a famine in the land, aside from the first famine in Abraham's days,
So Isaac went to Abimelech, king of the Philistines, to Gerar where he stayed.
The Lord appeared to Isaac and said, "Do not go down to Egypt; continue to dwell
In the land that I tell you of, sojourn in this land, and all things for you will go well.
I will be with you and bless you, to you and your offspring I will give all of these lands,
And I will fulfill the sworn-oath that I swore long ago to your father Abraham.
I will make your seed many, like the stars of heaven, all these lands I give to your seed.
All the nations of earth shall be blessed through them—all because Abraham paid my voice heed.
He kept My charge: My commandments, My laws, My teachings." And so Isaac stayed in Gerar.
When the men of the place asked him about his wife, he said of her, "She is my sister,"
Because he was afraid to say "she's my wife", since he had thought to himself, "Otherwise,
The men of this place will kill me due to Rebekah, so fair to behold in one's eyes."
When some time had passed, the Philistines' king Abimelech looked out a window and saw
Isaac laughing and loving with his wife Rebekah. Abimelech called him, said, "Ah!

So she is your wife! Why then did you say before, 'she is my sister?'" Isaac replied,
"I thought to myself, otherwise on account of her and her beauty, I might have died."
Abimelech said, "What have you done to us! One of the men might have lain with your wife,
And then you would have brought guilt upon us." Abimelech then charged his people, "The life
Of any person who touches this man or his wife shall end in a manner quite grim."

Isaac sowed in that land, and reaped one hundredfold in that same year. The Lord had
    blessed him.
The man grew rich, and kept on increasing his wealth, until Isaac possessed a ton of it:
He had flocks of sheep and herds of oxen, and a large house every Philistine did covet.
So the Philistines, angry with envy, stopped up the wells which had been dug in the days
Of his father Abraham by his father's servants, and filled them up with earth and clay.
Abimelech said to Isaac, "Go far from us, you've become too many to abide."
So Isaac went from there, and encamped in the wadi of Gerar, and there did reside.
Isaac dug anew all of the wells which had been dug in his father Abraham's time,
And which the Philistines had stopped up after Abraham's death in their envious crime.
Isaac gave the wells all of the same names that his father had given to them before.
But when Isaac's servants, digging in the wadi, found a well with a fresh water store,
Then the herdsmen of Gerar did quarrel with Isaac's herdsmen, saying, "This water's ours."
So he named the well "Esek" ("contention"), because they had quarreled with him and been sour.
They dug another well, and they quarreled again, so he named it "Sitnah" ("Animosity").
He moved on from there and dug one more well, but this time of quarreling there was a paucity,
So he named it "Rehoboth" (or "space"), and said, "Now, the Lord has made space for us believers,
So that we may bear fruit and increase in the land." Isaac went up from there to Beersheva.

That night, the Lord appeared to him and said, "I am the God of your father Abraham.
Do not fear, for I am with you. I will bless you and make your seed many in the land,
For the sake of Abraham My servant." He built there an altar, and called the Lord's name.
Isaac pitched his tent there, and his servants began digging a well, all in that place same.
Abimelech went to him from Gerar, with Ahuzzath his aide, and Phicol, troop chief.
Isaac said to them, "Why have you come to me, since you hate me and have caused me
    much grief?
You have sent me away from you." They said, "But now we see that the Lord has been with you,
So we say, let there be an oath treaty between us, and also a covenant too:
That you'll do us no harm, just as we have not harmed you, and have dealt with you at our best,
Always kindly and fairly, and sent you away in peace. Now by the Lord are you blessed."
Then he made them a feast, and they ate and drank. Next morning, they swore oaths to
    one another.
Isaac bade them farewell, and they left him in peace. That same day, Isaac's servants discovered
The well that they'd been digging had water. They said to Isaac, "We have found water! Yay!"
So he named it "Sheva" (or "Oath"), therefore the city is named Beersheva to this day.

Now when Esau was forty years old, he took as a wife Judith, daughter of Be'eri
The Hittite and of Basemath daughter of Elon the Hittite, and made life less merry
For Rebekah and Isaac.

Genesis 27

> Now when Isaac was old and was losing his sight,
> He told Esau, "Go hunt, I'll bless you 'ere I die."
> Now Rebekah heard him, and told Jacob, "Take flight,
> Get some meat and we'll get you that blessing, or try."
> Jacob said, "Esau's hairy!" But mom had a plan,
> Gave him Esau's clothes, put haired goatskins on his skin.
> Isaac asked, "Who are you?" Jacob said, "Esau, man."
> Isaac blessed him before Esau could come back in.

Now when Isaac grew old and his eyes were too dim to see,
Isaac called Esau, his older son, and said to him, "My son!"—"Here I am," replied he.
Isaac said, "I am old now, and don't know the day of my death. So please take up your bow
And your quiver, go out to the field and hunt me down some game, which I love, as you know.
Then prepare me a delicacy such as I like it, bring it to me, I will eat it,
So that I may give to you my blessing before I die and my own life is completed."
But Rebekah was listening as Isaac spoke to his son, so when Esau did run
To the field to hunt down some game to bring home, Rebekah said to Jacob her son,
"Look, I was listening as your father was speaking to your brother Esau, and said,
'Bring me game and then make me a dish, I'll eat it and bless you before God 'ere I'm dead.'
So now, my son, please listen to what I command you: Go to the flock, fetch me two kids,
Some choice ones, and I will make them into a delicacy, the type which he has bid.
You bring it to your father, and he will eat, so that he may bless you before he dies."
Jacob said to Rebekah his mother, "But my brother Esau has hair on all sides,
While I have smooth skin. If my father should feel my skin, I'll seem like a trickster, or worse.
I'll bring a curse, and not a blessing, upon myself." His mother said to him, "Your curse,
My dear son, shall be on me; just listen to what I say, go now, and fetch them for me."
He went and took the kids and brought them to his mother, and she made a delicacy,
Such as his father loved. Rebekah then took the garments of Esau her older son,
The best ones in the house, and dressed her younger son Jacob in them. And when she was done,
He was covered in skins of the goat kids, with fur on his hands, and the smooth of his neck,
Then she placed in the hand of her son Jacob the dish she'd made, to complete the effect.

He came to his father and said, "Father!" Isaac replied, "Here I am. Which son are you?"
Jacob said to his father, "I'm Esau, your firstborn. I have done as you told me to.
Pray, arise and eat from the game I have hunted, so you may give your blessing to me."
Isaac said to his son, "How did you find it so quickly, my son?" Jacob said, "You see,
The Lord your God made it go well for me." Isaac said to Jacob, "My son, please come closer
So that I may feel you and know if you are my son Esau, or if you are a poser."
Jacob moved close to Isaac his father, who felt him and said, "The voice is Jacob's voice,
But the hands are Esau's hands." He didn't recognize him (which may have made Jacob rejoice),
For his hands were like the hands of Esau his brother: Hairy. He was just to be blessed,
When Isaac asked once more, "Are you truly my son Esau?" Jacob replied, "I am. Yes."
So then Isaac said, "Bring it to me, and I will eat my son's game, so that I may bless you."
Jacob served him and he ate, brought him wine and he drank, then Isaac his father said, "Yes, you,
Come closer and then kiss me, my son." He came close and kissed him. Now Isaac smelled
    his clothes,
And blessed him saying, "The smell of my son smells like the blessed fields of God in my nose.
May God give you from the dew of heaven, the fat of the earth, plenty of wine and grain.
May peoples serve you, and tribes bow down to you, and as lord over your brothers you'll reign.
Let your mother's sons bow to you. Cursed be those who curse you, those who bless you will
    be blessed."
And as soon as Isaac finished blessing Jacob, and from Isaac's presence Jacob left,
Esau his brother came back from his hunting, bringing his father a sweet dish of game.
He then said to his father, "Rise and eat this delicacy, and bless me in your name."
Isaac his father said to him, "Which son are you?" He said, "I am your firstborn, Esau."
Isaac trembled greatly and said, "Who was it then, that just brought me some game for my maw?
I ate of it before you came, and gave my blessing to him, now he must remain blessed."
When Esau heard his father's words, he cried out greatly and bitterly, very distressed.
He said to his father, "Bless me, me too, father!" Isaac said, "Your brother came with guile
And he took away your blessing." Esau said, "Is that why he was named in such a style?
He is named Jacob, Heel-Sneak, for he has now sneaked against me and cheated me twice,
He took my firstborn birthright, and now he has taken my blessing; that's really not nice."
Esau said, "Haven't you reserved a blessing for me?" Isaac answered, to Esau spoke,
"Look, I've made him your master, and gave him all of his brothers for servants, that's no joke.
I've sustained him with grain and wine. What then, my son, am I still able to do for you?"
Esau said to his father, "Have you but one blessing, father? Bless me, father, me too!"
And Esau raised his voice and wept. Then his father Isaac answered, said to him with love,
"Look, away from the fat of the earth must you dwell, from the dew of the heavens above,
You shall live by the sword, and you shall serve your brother, but one day you'll brandish
    your sword,
And will break his yoke from your neck." Esau hated Jacob due to his unjust reward,
And the blessing which Isaac had given him. So Esau said to himself, "Any day,
The days of mourning for my father will come, and then my brother Jacob I will slay."

But Rebekah was told of the words of her elder son Esau, so she called and sent
For her younger son Jacob and said to him, "Your brother Esau has a vengeful bent.
He's consoling himself by planning to kill you. So now, my son, listen to my voice
Flee at once to Haran, to my brother Laban. You don't really have much of a choice.
Stay with him for a while, until your brother's anger subsides, and from you turns away,
Until he forgets what you did to him. Then I'll send and have you brought back on that day—

For why should I lose both of you in the same day?" So Rebekah then said to Isaac,
"I loathe my life because of these Hittite women. If Jacob took a wife from their stock,
A wife from the daughters of Heth, such as these women which are the daughters of the land,
From the native women, then why should I live? Why on earth should I continue to stand?"

Genesis 28

> Isaac told Jacob, "Don't take a Canaanite wife,"
> Esau heard this, and married a non-Canaanite.
> Jacob left for Haran, had the dream of his life,
> Where God spoke to him, blessed him, and made all things right.
> He awoke and said, "This place is great! God is here!"
> And he named the place Bethel (It was Luz before).
> Jacob vowed, "If the Lord will protect me from fear,
> He is my God, and I'll tithe him from all my store."

So Isaac called for Jacob, he blessed him and then he commanded him, saying to him,
"You shall not take a wife from the Canaanites. Rise, and go to the country of Aram,
To the house of Bethuel, your mother's father, and from there take for yourself a wife,
From the daughters of Laban, your mother's brother. May God Almighty bless you in life,
May he make you be fruitful and multiply, so that a host of people you become,
And may he give the blessing of Abraham to you and to your offspring yet to come,
So that you may inherit the land of your sojourning, which God gave to Abraham."
So then Isaac sent Jacob off; he went to the country of Aram, to meet Laban,
Son of Bethuel the Aramean, brother of Rebekah, the mother of two:
Namely Jacob and Esau. Now Esau, when he saw that Isaac bid Jacob adieu,
And had blessed him and sent him to the country of Aram to take a wife from that sector,
Charging him, "You shall not take a wife from the Canaanites, so go elsewhere to select her,"

And that Jacob had heeded his father and mother and gone to the land of Aram,
Well then, Esau, he saw that women from Canaan did not make his father Isaac calm.
So Esau went to Ishmael and took to wife, in addition to those he'd betrothed,
One Mahalath, the daughter of Abraham's son Ishmael, sister of Nebaioth.

[Vayetze]

Jacob left from Beersheva and set out for Haran, and came upon a certain place.
Since the sun had set, he spent the night there, and took a stone as a pillow for his face.
He lay his head upon it, and lay down there. He dreamt a ladder was set on the ground,
With its top in the heavens, and God's messengers upon it were going up and down.
And here God was standing over him. He said, "I am the Lord, the God of Abraham
Your father and the God of Isaac. The land where you lie, to you and your seed I grant.
All your offspring will be like the dust of the earth, you shall burst forth north, south, east,
      and west.
All the clans of the earth shall bless themselves through you and also through your seed will
      be blessed.
I am with you, will watch over you wheresoever you go, bring you back to this soil
Indeed, I will not leave you until I have done what I've spoken to you (being loyal)."
Jacob woke from his sleep and said, "Surely, God is in this place, and I, I knew it not!"
He was awestruck and said, "How awesome is this place! It's none other than a house of God,
And that's heaven's gate!" He started early, and took the stone on which he'd let his head drop,
And set it up as a standing pillar, a marker of stone, and poured oil on top.
And he named the place "Beth El" ("House of God"), although the city was named Luz formerly.
Jacob then made a vow, saying, "If God will be with me, and will keep watch over me
On this journey I'm making, and will give me food to eat, and also clothing to wear,
And if I return safely to my father's house—then the Lord shall be my God, I swear.
And this stone I've set up as a pillar shall become a house of God for all to view,
And of everything that You give me, I shall set aside one tenth as a tithe for You."

Genesis 29

        Jacob came to a well with a stone on the top,
        Which he moved to give Laban (his uncle)'s sheep water.
        Jacob kissed Rachel. Laban met him and said, "Stop,
        What would you want to work for me?" He said, "Your daughter!"
        Laban said, "Seven years, then I'll give her to you."
        Jacob said, "It's a deal." And then seven years passed.
        Laban gave Leah. Jacob said, "Leah won't do,
        I want Rachel!" Years later, he got her at last.

Jacob picked up his feet and went on his journey to the land where the Easterners dwell,
Looked around and saw there a well in the field, and three sheep lying down by the well,
For it was from that well that they gave the sheep water, but on the well's mouth was a stone
Which was so large, they'd roll it off to let the sheep drink, and put it back when they were done.
Jacob said to them, "Brothers, where are you from?" They said, "We are from Haran." He
    asked them,
"Do you know Laban son of Nahor?" They said, "Yes, we do." He said, "Is all well with him?"
They said, "It is well; And here comes Rachel his daughter, girl of shear beauty, with the flock."
Jacob said, "But it is still broad daylight, too early to gather up all the livestock,
So go give the sheep water and take them to pasture." But they said, "This we cannot do
Until all the flocks have been gathered, only then is the stone moved to let water through."
While he still spoke to them, Rachel came with her father's flock, for she was a shepherdess.
Now when Jacob saw Rachel, daughter of Laban, there grew in him a great happiness.
When he saw the sheep of Laban his mother's brother, he neared, rolled the stone from the well,
And gave water to the sheep of Laban his mother's brother—Then Jacob kissed Rachel.
He kissed her, then he lifted his voice and wept, telling her that he was her father's kin,
That he was Rebekah's son. So Rachel did run to give her father information.
Now as soon as Laban heard of Jacob, the son of his sister, he ran out to meet him,
He embraced Jacob and then he kissed Jacob, and then brought him into his house to greet him.
Jacob told Laban all that had happened. Laban told him, "Truly, you're my flesh and bone."
And he stayed with Laban for a month. Laban said to Jacob, "Though you're kin of my own,
It seems silly to serve me for nothing, so tell me, what do you desire as a wage?"
Now Laban had two daughters, the older named Leah, Rachel the one of younger age.
Leah had tender eyes, but Rachel was quite shapely, so Jacob fell in love with her.
He told Laban, "I will serve you for seven years all for Rachel, your younger daughter."
Laban said, "Better that I should give her to you than to some outsider. Stay with me."
And so Jacob served seven years for Rachel, but to Jacob, mere days it seemed to be,

Due to his great love for Rachel. When he was done, Jacob said to Laban, "Come now, sir,
Give me my wife, for my term of work is completed, so that I may come into her."
Laban gathered all people of that place together for a feast. And that very night,
He took his daughter Leah and brought her to Jacob, who went into her (without sight).
Laban also gave Zilpah his maid to Leah his daughter. When morning came to be,
Surprise! Here—she was Leah! He said to Laban, "What is this that you have done to me?
Was I not in your service for Rachel? Why have you deceived me?" Laban calmly said,
"It is not our practice to give the younger one away before the firstborn is wed.
Just wait until this one's bridal week is completed, and we'll give you that one also,
Provided that you serve me for seven more years in return for this." Jacob did so.
He completed the bridal week for this one, then Laban gave him his daughter Rachel
As a wife. Laban gave Rachel his daughter Bilhah his maid to be her maid as well.
So Jacob came into Rachel also, and gave her more love than Leah had collected.
Then he served Laban for seven more years. Now when the Lord saw that Leah was rejected,
The Lord opened her womb, but Rachel remained barren. Leah conceived and bore a son,
Who she named "Reuben" ("See, a son!"), for she said, "Surely, the Lord has seen my affliction.
Surely now my husband will love me." She conceived again and bore one more son and said,
"Surely, the Lord has heard that I'm unloved, so to me a second son he has granted."
And she named him "Shimon" ("Hearing"). She conceived again and then she bore another son,
And she said, "Now this time my husband will be joined to me, for I have borne him three sons."
Therefore, he was named "Levi" (or "Joining"). She conceived again, and bore a son once more,
And she said, "This time I will give thanks to the Lord, because after all, this one makes four."
And that's why she called his name "Judah" (which means "Giving Thanks") Then Leah stopped
    giving birth
After she had borne her husband Jacob four children, all of which were boys, on the earth.

Genesis 30

Rachel envied her sister who bore Jacob sons,
So she said, "Take my maid." Leah gave her maid too,
And with both of their maids, Jacob bore little ones,
And then Leah, and Rachel. He had quite a few.
Laban said once again, "What do you want for pay?"
Jacob said, "The striped sheep from your flock that is ripe."
Laban said okay, then moved his striped sheep away.
But then Jacob made sure the strong sheep bore a stripe.

When Rachel saw she'd born no children to Jacob, she envied her sister and said
To her husband Jacob, "Come now, give me children, or otherwise I will be dead."
Jacob's anger flared up against Rachel and he said, "Am I to take the place of God,
Who has withheld from you the fruit of the womb?" She said, "Here is my maidservant Bilhah;
Come in to her, so she may bear on my knees, so through her I may bear children also."
So she gave him her maid Bilhah as concubine, and then into her Jacob did go.
Bilhah conceived and bore a son to Jacob, which Rachel adopted, saying gladly,
"God has done me justice, yes, he has heard my voice, and he has given a son to me!"
Therefore, she named him "Dan" ("He Has Done Justice"). And Bilhah, Rachel's maid,
    conceived again,
And she bore Jacob a second son. Rachel said, "Now with Leah, I no more contend.
I have struggled a struggle of God with my sister, and finally I have prevailed!"
So she named him "Naftali" ("My Struggle"). Now when Leah saw that her own womb had failed,
She took Zilpah her maid and gave her to Jacob as a concubine for him to know.
Zilpah, Leah's maid, bore a son to Jacob. Then Leah said, "What good fortune!" And so,
She named him "Gad" (or "Fortune") Then Zilpah, maid of Leah, bore Jacob a second son.
Leah said, "Happiness! They'll call me happy." So "Asher" ("Happiness") she named that one.

In the days of wheat harvest, once Reuben went and found "love-apples" (mandrakes) in the field.
He then brought them to Leah, his mother. Rachel said to Leah, "Pray, share your son's yield."
Leah said to Rachel, "Was the fact that you took my husband so paltry in your sight
That you now want to take my son's mandrakes too?" Rachel said, "Fine, he'll lie with
    you tonight,
In exchange for your son's mandrakes." So that night, when Jacob came home from the field, tired,
Leah went out to meet him and said, "You must come in to me, for tonight you've been hired.
I have hired you for my son's mandrakes." So he lay with her that night, and God paid heed.
God paid heed to Leah, so that she conceived and bore Jacob a fifth son from that deed.
Leah said, "God has given me my hired wages, since I gave my maid to my husband."
So she called his name "Issachar" (or "There is Hire"). And once again, Leah was pregnant.
She conceived again and bore a sixth son to Jacob. Leah said, "God gave me a gift
This time my husband will surely prize me, for I have borne him six sons, here is the sixth."
So she named him "Zebulun" (or "Prince"). Afterwards she bore a daughter, Dinah by name.
But God kept Rachel in mind, God heeded her, and opened her womb so that she became
Pregnant. Rachel conceived and bore a son. She said, "My reproach, God has taken away."
So she named him "Joseph" ("He Adds"), saying, "May God add another son for me one day."
Now once Rachel had borne Joseph, Jacob said to Laban, "Give me leave to go back home.
Give me my wives and children, for whom I served you. I'll return to the land of my own.
Indeed, you know what services that I have rendered for you." Laban said to him, "Pray,
Indulge me. I have now become wealthy, and the Lord has blessed me because you did stay."
He said on, "Specify the wages that I owe you, and I will pay you, being fair."
Jacob said to Laban, "You know how I have served you, and how your flocks fared in my care.

For you had just a few before I came, and now to a multitude it has increased,
Since the Lord has blessed you at my every step. Yet, my own house has not gotten the least."
Laban said, "What shall I give you?" Jacob said, "Don't give me anything, only do this,
And if you do this one thing for me, I will return to tend and watch your flock in bliss:
Let me go over your whole flock today, removing all heads that are speckled and spotted,
Every dark-colored sheep, spotted or speckled goat, and so shall my wages be allotted.
In this way may my honesty clearly be seen in the future when you come to check;
If you see in my flock any lamb that's not dark, or a goat with neither spot nor speck,
Then it will be from theft." Laban said, "Very well, let it be done as you have just stated."
But on that very day, Laban went to his flock to have the animals separated.
He took all the he-goats that were spotted or streaked, and all she-goats with speckles or spots,
Every one with white on it, and every dark lamb, and to his sons, he handed the lot.
Then he put three-days journey between Jacob and himself, while Jacob tended the rest.
Jacob took fresh rods of poplar, almond, and plane trees, and peeled them as he saw best.
He peeled white peelings in them, exposing the white on the rods in a pattern of stripes.
(Folks believed animals who saw patterns while they mated would bear offspring of that type.)
Then he set them in front of the goats at the water troughs, where they would come drink, in heat.
Therefore goats were in heat by the rods, and the flock bore striped and speckled and
　　　spotted meat.
But the sheep, Jacob set apart, and had them face all the streaked and dark ones Laban owned;
So he made special herds for himself, but Laban's flocks were left out to randomly roam.
Now whenever robust animals were in heat, Jacob would place the rods in their sight,
So they'd mate by the rods. But he'd not put the rods near the weak animals lacking might.
The result was that feeble ones became Laban's, while to Jacob, the strong ones accrued.
Jacob soon grew exceedingly wealthy with flocks, maids and slaves, camels, and donkeys too.

Genesis 31

Laban's sons all said, "Jacob took our father's wealth."
God told Jacob, "Go back to the place you were born."
Jacob put his whole family on camels, in stealth,
And then left in the dark. Laban woke the next morn,
And learned Jacob had fled. He chased him for a week,
Finally catching him saying, "Why do this bad act,
Rob my things?" Jacob said, "I don't have what you seek,
Even search." Laban said, "Okay, let's make a pact."

Now he heard the words of Laban's sons, who were saying, "That Jacob has taken away
All that was our father's, and from what was our father's, he's built his great wealth of today."
Jacob saw that Laban's manner toward him was also no longer as kind as before.
Then the Lord said to Jacob, "Return to the land of your fathers, your birthplace of yore.
I will be with you." So Jacob sent and had Rachel and Leah called out to the field,
To his animals. And he said to them, "By your father's face has his heart been revealed.
Now his manner toward me is not as in the past. But my father's God has been with me.
You both know I've served your father with all my might, yet he cheats me and won't pay my fee.
He has cheated me, constantly changing my wages, yet God won't let him do me ill.
If he said, 'speckled ones shall be your wages,' with speckled animals the flock would fill.
And if he said, 'the striped ones shall be your wages,' then the striped ones would make up
    the flock.
So you see, God has taken away from your father and given to me his livestock.

Once, when the animals were in heat, I had a dream. I lifted my eyes and I saw
That the he-goats which mated with the flock had stripes, spots, and speckles, from foot up to jaw.
And God's messenger said to me in the dream, 'Jacob!' I said, 'Here I am.' Then he said,
'lift up your eyes and see, all the he-goats which mate with the flock—speckled, striped,
    and spotted.
For I have seen all that Laban is doing to you. I am the God of Bethel, where
You anointed the pillar, where you vowed a vow to Me. Now rise, and get out of here.
Leave this land, and return to your native land.'" Rachel and Leah both answered him, saying,
"Do we still have inheritance-share in our father's house that would be reason for staying?
He regards us as outsiders, for he has sold us, and gobbled up our purchase price.
Indeed, all the wealth God took away from him and gave to you belongs to us, by right.
It's for us and our children, so now, whatever God has told to you, Jacob, do so."
So then Jacob rose, lifted his children and wives on the camels, and prepared to go.

Jacob led away all of his livestock, all of his wealth, and all the flocks he'd acquired
In the Aram-country, to come home to his father Isaac who in Canaan was mired.
Now Laban had gone to shear his sheep, while Rachel stole the household idols of her dad.
And Jacob kept Laban in the dark by not telling him that he was running like mad.
So he fled, with all that he had, he rose and crossed the Euphrates, heading to the hills.
He went toward the hill country of Gilead. On the third day, Laban learned of his ills.
He took his kinsmen with him and set after Jacob, pursuing him for seven days.
He caught up with him in the hill country of Gilead, but on that night, in sleep's haze,
God came to Laban the Aramean in a dream, and said to him, "You must beware.
Do not speak to Jacob, good or ill." When Laban finally caught up to Jacob, then there
Jacob had pitched his tent in the mountains; Laban was camped with his kin in Gilead.
Laban said to Jacob, "What did you mean by running away secretly from my pad?
You kept me in the dark, led my daughters away like captives; Why'd you flee secretly?
You didn't tell me. For I would have sent you off with lyres and musical festivity,
And what's more, you didn't even allow me to give my grandchildren a nice goodbye kiss.
You have done foolishly! And it's now in my power to injure you greatly for this.
But then yesterday night, the God of your father spoke to me, saying, 'You must beware.
Do not speak to Jacob, good or ill.' Okay, say you fled since you missed your father's lair.
Tell me, why did you steal my gods?" Jacob answered and said to Laban, "Well, you see,
I was very afraid, for I thought that by force you would take back your daughters from me.
As for whomever you find with your gods, they shall not live. In your kin's presence I swear it.
If you recognize anything of yours in my possession, take it, for I won't bear it."
Jacob did not know that Rachel had stolen them. Laban then went into Jacob's tent,
And into Leah's tent, and the maidservants' tents, but of his gods he found no fragment.
Then he went out of Leah's tent and into Rachel's, but Rachel was one step ahead,
She had taken the gods and put them underneath a camel's cushion, where she rested.
Laban felt all around the tent, but did not find a thing, as they were 'neath Rachel's seat.
She said to her father, "Don't let my lord be angry that I do not rise up to greet,
For the ways of women are upon me." So he searched, but no household gods did he find.
Jacob then became upset and took up his grievance with Laban. Jacob spoke his mind.
He said to Laban, "What's my offense? What's my sin that made you pursue me with such speed,
That you've rummaged through all my things, feeling my wares. What of yours have you found
    with this deed?
Take whatever you've found and display it here so that your kinsmen and mine may consider it.
It has been twenty years now that I have served you, and my loyalty has been inveterate.
Your ewes and she-goats have not had miscarriages, the rams from your flock I have not eaten,
I have brought you none torn by beasts—I have made good the loss, from my own hand it
    was beaten.
Stolen by day or night, regardless. Oft, by day the heat would consume me, frost by night,
And sleep fled from my eyes. Twenty years in your house I have now lived like this, is that right?
I've served you fourteen years for your two daughters, and six more years for the flock, we agree,
Yet you've changed my wages ten times over. Had not the God of my father been with me,

The God of Abraham and the Terror of Isaac, else you would have sent me off, broke.
But God saw my affliction, the toil of my hands, and last night He passed judgment and spoke."

Laban answered Jacob, "The daughters are my daughters, the children are my children too.
All the animals are my own animals—All that you see, it is mine. This is true,
But to my daughters, what can I do to them now, or to children they've given birth to?
So now come, let us cut covenant, you and I, so there's witness between me and you."
Jacob took a stone and set it up as a pillar, and said to his kin, "Gather stones."
They fetched stones and they made a mound. Then they ate by the mound, making the
　　　covenant known.
Laban named it "Yegar-sahaduta" ("Mound-Witness"), while Jacob had named it "Gal-ed".
(Which also means "Mound-Witness", but in Hebrew tongue, not in Aramaic.) Laban said,
"This mound is a witness between me and you this day." That is why Gal-ed was so named,
And also "Mitzpah" ("Guardpost"), because he said, "May the Lord guard us from each
　　　other's games.
If you should ever ill-treat my daughters, or take other wives—though no human is near,
God Himself is a witness between me and you." And Laban then said to Jacob, "Here.
Here is this mound. Here is the pillar that I have sunk between me and you, as witness.
This mound is a witness, and the pillar is also one, that toward you I won't transgress.
I will not cross past this mound to you, nor you cross this mound and pillar towards me, for ill.
May God of Abraham and the God of Nahor (their fathers' God) judge between us still."
Jacob swore by the Terror of his father Isaac, then sacrificed food on the height
Of the mountain, and called his kinsmen to eat bread, which they did, and up there spent
　　　the night.

Genesis 32

> Jacob went home, sent Esau word he was arriving.
> He heard Esau'd meet him with 400 men.
> Jacob picked many gifts from his wealth which was thriving,
> Told servants to take them to Esau, and when
> They were asked, "Whom do you serve? And where are
> you going?"
> They'd say, "I serve Jacob, these gifts are for you,
> And he's right behind us." (Though they'd no way of knowing
> That Jacob was wrestling a man the night through.)

Early in the morn, Laban kissed his sons and daughters and blessed them, before heading home.
Now as Jacob went on his way, he met God's messengers on the same path he did roam.
When he saw them, Jacob said, "This is a camp of God!" And he named that place "Mahanaim".
(And that means "Double-Camp", because Jacob had camped there, and God's messengers had
     camped by him.)

[Vayishlach]

Jacob sent messengers to his brother Esau, in the land of Seir, Edom's country.
He had sent them ahead and commanded them saying, "To my lord Esau, say thusly:
'Here is what Jacob, your servant, says: I have sojourned with Laban and rested 'til now,
I've acquired both male and female slaves, flocks of sheep, oxen, donkeys, and cows.
I have sent this message for you to hear, my lord, in the hope that I will gain your favor.'"
Then the messengers came back to Jacob and said, "We have ill tidings you will not savor.
We came to your brother, to Esau, but he's already coming to meet you, with men.
Now four hundred men are coming with him." Jacob was exceedingly scared and frightened.
He divided the people with him, and the flocks, oxen, and camels into two camps,
Saying to himself, "If Esau strikes at one, the other may yet escape from those scamps."
Jacob then said, "God of my father Abraham, God of my father Isaac, O Lord,
Who said to me, 'return to your native land, and then I shall give to you a reward.'
I am unworthy of all the good faith and kindness you've steadfastly shown to Your servant.
With my staff alone I crossed this Jordan, and now have become two camps. My faith is fervent.
Pray save me from the hand of my brother, the hand of Esau, for of him I'm afraid.
I fear that Esau may come and strike me down, mothers and children alike to be slayed.
But you've said, 'I will deal well with you, I will make your offspring like the sand of the sea,
An abundant amount that's too many to count.' That's the promise that you made to me."

After spending the night there, he took gifts for his brother Esau from what was at hand:

A full two hundred she-goats, and twenty young kids, and two hundred ewes, and twenty rams,

Thirty milch camels and their young, forty cows, ten bulls, and twenty she-asses, ten males.

Jacob handed them over to his servants, herd by herd, and gave his servants details.

He said, "Cross on ahead of me, leave room between herds." To the servants in front he said,

"When my brother Esau meets you and asks of you, 'Whose man are you? To where do you head?

And whose animals are those ahead of you?' Then say, 'By your servant Jacob they're owned;

They are gifts for my lord Esau, and Jacob is behind us, his arrival postponed.'"

Jacob gave the same charge to the second and third groups, and all groups that walked with
     the herds,

Saying, "When you should come upon Esau, my brother, then speak to him using these words:

You shall say, 'And your servant Jacob is behind us.'" For Jacob had thought in this case,

"I will wipe the rage from the face of Esau by sending presents ahead of my face,

And when we're face to face, maybe my face will please him, and he will be gracious and kind."

So the gift went ahead, while he stayed in the camp for the night, but no sleep did he find.

He arose in the night and he took his two wives, his two maids, and his eleven kids,

To the Jabbok crossing, where he sent them across, and then also sent all that was his.

Jacob was left alone. And a man wrestled with him until dawn came up in the sky.

When he saw that he could not prevail against Jacob, he touched the socket of his thigh.

And the socket of Jacob's thigh was dislocated as he wrestled with him. He said,

"Let me go, for the dawn has come up!" But he said, "I will not let you go, but instead,

I will hold on until you have blessed me." He asked, "What is your name?" "Jacob," he replied.

Then the man said, "'Jacob' ('Heel-Sneak') shall no more be your name, but a name with
     more pride.

You shall be named 'Israel' ('God-Fighter'), for you have fought with God and man,
     and prevailed."

And then Jacob asked, "Tell me your name!" But he said, "Don't ask for such things to
     be revealed."

(For names of the divine give power over them.) So he blessed Jacob, and took his leave.

Jacob named the place "Peniel" ("Face of God"), for "I've seen God face to face, I believe,

Yet my life has been saved." The sun rose on him as he crossed Peniel, limping along

On his thigh; which is why the Children of Israel to this day believe it is wrong

To eat of the thigh muscle and sinew that lies on the inner socket of the thigh,

For that sciatic nerve is the socket of muscle where Jacob was touched by that guy.

Genesis 33

Jacob, he saw that Esau and his men drew near.
They hugged each other. Esau said, "Why the big show?"
Jacob said, "To gain your favor. Isn't it clear?"
Esau said, "I have plenty, there's nothing you owe."
Jacob said, "No, please take it, I'm so glad you're kind.
God has given me plenty, I've plenty to share."
Esau said, "Let's go. I will not leave you behind."
Jacob said, "No, don't slow down for me, it's not fair."

Jacob lifted his eyes and saw Esau approaching, and with him were four hundred men.
He divided the children among Leah, Rachel, and also the two handmaidens.
He put the handmaidens and their children first, with Leah and her children right behind,
And Rachel and Joseph behind them, while Jacob himself went to the head of the line.
He bowed low to the ground seven times, until he neared his brother. Esau came to meet him,
And then Esau embraced Jacob, flinging himself around his neck, and kissed him to greet him.
They both wept. Esau lifted his eyes and saw all of the women and children and said,
"Who are these with you?" He said, "Children with whom your servant has by God
    been favored."
Then the maids came close, they and their children bowed low. Leah and her children did
    the same.
Then Joseph and Rachel came close and bowed low. Esau said, "What do you mean by
    this game?"
Jacob said, "To find favor in my lord's eyes." Esau said, "My brother, I have enough.
Let what is yours remain yours." But Jacob said, "Please, if I've found favor, accept this stuff.
Take these gifts from my hand, for I have, after all, seen your face as one sees that of God,
You've been gracious to me. Take this gift I bring you, for God's favor shown me leaves me awed.
I have more than enough." And he pressed him, so he took it. Then Esau said, "Let us go.
Let us travel onwards, I shall go at your side." But Jacob said to him, "My lord knows
That the children are frail, and the flocks and herds in my care are still nursing, and weak.
If we were to push them hard for one single day, they would die. So now heed what I speak:
Pray let my lord cross on ahead of his servant, while I travel slowly, in the rear,
At the pace of the cattle before me, and the children, 'til I reach my lord in Seir."
Esau said, "Let me leave with you some of my men." Jacob said, "That is unnecessary.
I wish only to find favor with you." So Esau left that same day, and did not tarry.

He started back to Seir, while Jacob went to Succot, and built himself a house and home.
And he built sheds for his livestock, therefore since then as "Succot" ("Sheds") that place has
    been known.

Jacob came home in peace to the city of Shechem, which is in the land of Canaan,
He encamped facing the city after his homecoming from the country of Aram.
Then he purchased the parcel of land where he pitched his tent, from the children of Hamor.
Hamor (or "Donkey") was the father of Shechem, who shared the name that the city bore.
And the price of purchase was one hundred kesitahs, worth one hundred lambs, as the deal.
There he set up an altar and called it "El Elohe Yisrael" ("God, God of Israel")

Genesis 34

> Leah's daughter, named Dinah, went out in the land.
> Shechem forced himself on her, and wanted to wed.
> Shechem then told his dad Hamor what he had planned,
> Who went looking for Jacob, found his sons instead.
> Hamor said, "My son wants Dinah. What is the price?"
> They said, "You must be circumcised, all your domain."
> When they did so, two of Jacob's sons that enticed
> Them before killed the men while they were still in pain.

Now Dinah, Leah's daughter, whom she'd borne to Jacob, went to see the girls of the land.
Shechem son of Hamor the Hivvite, prince of the land, saw her, and forced her with his hand.
He took her and lay with her by force. And his spirit drew him to Dinah, Jacob's daughter;
He loved Dinah and spoke to her tenderly. So Shechem stated to Hamor, his father,
"Get me this girl as a wife!" Now Jacob heard he'd defiled his daughter Dinah with violence,
But his sons were out in the fields with the livestock, so Jacob waited for them in silence.
Then Hamor, Shechem's father, went out to Jacob to speak with him, but Jacob's sons came;
They came back from the fields when they heard what happened, exceedingly upset and pained.
For Shechem had done a disgrace in Israel by lying with Jacob's daughter forcefully.
Such a thing is not to be done. Hamor spoke with them and tried to convince them resourcefully.
He said, "My son Shechem, he longs for your daughter, so please give her to him as a wife.
Intermarry with us, give us your daughters, and take ours for yourselves. Join us in life!
Dwell among us, the land will be open to you, dwell and trade in it, gain property."
And Shechem said to her father and to her brothers, "Please do this one favor for me:

I will pay you whatever you ask, and a dowry and gifts as much as you can name,
I will give you whatever you want, just give me the girl Dinah as my wife to claim."

Jacob's sons answered Shechem and Hamor his father deceitfully due to his deed,
For Shechem had defiled their sister Dinah. They said to them, "Our words you must heed.
We cannot do this thing, giving our sister to men with foreskins—Disgrace in our eyes.
Only on one condition will we comply: All males among you must be circumcised.
Then we'll give you our daughters, and we'll take your daughters for ourselves, and settle with you,
To become one people. But if you don't heed us and circumcise yourselves, then we're through,
We will take our daughter and go." Their words seemed good in the eyes of Hamor and his son,
And the young man Shechem wanted Jacob's daughter, so he quickly set to see it done.
Now Shechem was respected in his father's house, so he and Hamor went to the gate.
At the gate of the city they spoke to the townsmen and said, "These men bring peace, not hate.
Let them settle in the land and travel in it, for the land is large enough for them.
Let us take their daughters as wives for ourselves and let us give our own daughters to them.
But there is one condition to these men's compliance, to settle with us as one kin,
That every male of ours will be circumcised, just as they have removed their own foreskin.
All their livestock, beasts, and property shall be ours! Let's comply so they settle with us."
So they heeded Hamor and Shechem his son, all at the city's gate, with little fuss.
All the males who went out of the city's gate were circumcised. When three days had gone by,
While they were still in pain, two of Jacob's sons, brothers of Dinah, Simeon and Levi,
Each took their sword and came upon the city, feeling secure, and killed all of the males.
And Hamor and his son Shechem they also killed by the sword, which slashes and impales.
They took Dinah from Shechem's house and went off. Then Jacob's other sons found all the slain,
(Whom had all been defeated quite easily since they were still off their guard from the pain),
And they plundered the town, because their sister had been defiled. They seized their livestock,
All their sheep, oxen, donkeys, all in the city and the field, all their wealth in stock.
All their children and wives, all that was in the houses, they captured and plundered the lot.
But Jacob said to Simeon and Levi, "Far too much trouble for me you have brought.
You've made me odious to the men of the land, the Canaanites and the Perizzites.
My men are few in number, so if the two of them should launch an attack and unite,
They could band against me, and I will be destroyed, me and my household lost in this war."
But Simeon and Levi answered him, "Should our sister Dinah be treated like a whore?"

Genesis 35

God told Jacob, "Arise, go to Bethel, and then
Build an altar to God." So he set out that way.
Jacob built the altar, named El-Bethel. Again,
God appeared once more to Jacob, this time to say:
"You, named Jacob, your name's now Israel instead."
And He blessed him. To Benjamin, Rachel gave birth,
And then once she bore Jacob's twelfth son, she was dead.
And then Isaac died after nine score years on earth.

Now the Lord said to Jacob, "Arise, go to Bethel and stay there, and there build an altar
To the God who appeared to you when you fled your brother Esau." And he did not falter.
Jacob said to his household and all with him, "Rid yourself of all foreign deities.
Remove them from your midst, purify yourselves, change your clothes, rise, come to Bethel
    with me.
There I will build an altar to the God who answered me on the day of my distress,
Who has been with me all places that I have gone." And the people agreed and said, "Yes."
So they gave Jacob all of the foreign gods they had, and all sacred rings in their ears,
And Jacob buried them under the oak near Shechem, to stay there for thousands of years.
As they moved on, upon all the towns that were near where they journeyed, a fear of God fell,
So that they did not chase the sons of Jacob. And Jacob came back to Luz (now Bethel),
In the land of Canaan, he and all that were with him. And Jacob built an altar there,
And he called the place "El-Bethel" ("Godhead") for that was where God unto him had appeared,
When he fled from his brother. Now Deborah, the nurse of Rebekah, died in their keeping.
She was buried below Bethel, under an oak named "Allon Bacuth" (or "Oak of Weeping").

God appeared again to Jacob, when he came back from the country of Aram, and blessed him.
God said to him, "You who are named Jacob, you shall be named Jacob no more." God
    addressed him,
"For your name shall be Israel!" God called his name "Israel", and God said to him too,
"I am God Almighty, be fertile and increase, nation and nations shall come from you,
Kings shall spring from your loins. The land I gave to Abraham and Isaac, to you I give it,
And to your offspring after you I give the land." Then God left before Jacob could pivot.
God went up from beside him, where He'd spoken with him. And Jacob set up at that site
A stone pillar where God spoke to him, he poured oil and drink offerings on the granite.
Jacob named the place where God had spoke to him "Bethel" ("House of God"). They left Bethel.
But when they were still some distance short of Ephrath, a hard childbirth came to Rachel.

She had difficult labor, but at its hardest, the midwife told her, "Don't be afraid,
For this one is another son for you." But as Rachel died and her life slipped away,
She named him "Ben-Oni" ("Son of My Suffering"), but his father named him "Benjamin",
(Or "Son of the Right Hand"). Rachel died. It was the road to Ephrath she was buried in.
(That's now Bethlehem.) Jacob set a pillar which remains on Rachel's grave to this day.
Israel journeyed on, pitching his tent beyond Migdal-Eder ("Herd-Tower"), to stay.
While Israel stayed in that land, Reuben went and lay with Bilhah, his dad's concubine.
And Israel found out. Now the sons of Jacob numbered twelve, twelve strong boys from his line.
The sons of Leah: Jacob's firstborn Reuben, Simeon, Levi, and Judah, Issachar,
And Zebulun. The sons of Rachel: Joseph and Benjamin. Then the sons of Bilhah,
Rachel's maid: Dan and Naphtali. And the sons of Zilpah, Leah's maid: Asher and Gad
These are Jacob's sons who were born to him in the country of Aram. Twelve sons he had.

Jacob came home to Isaac his father at Mamre, in Arba (which is now Hebron),
Where both Abraham and Isaac had sojourned once. And in years, Isaac was getting on.
The days of Isaac's life were one hundred and eighty years, when he breathed his last and died.
Isaac died and was gathered to his kinspeople, at ripe old age, in years satisfied.
He was buried by his sons Esau and Jacob (now Israel), both there to preside.

Genesis 36

> Now Esau (or Edom) had taken some wives
> From the Canaanite women, and after he did,
> Each one of the three women created some lives,
> Bearing Esau's children, who then had their own kids.

These are the generations of Esau (Edom). He took wives from the women of Canaan:
Adah daughter of Elon the Hittite, and Oholibamah daughter of Anah and
Granddaughter of Zibeon the Hittite, and Basemath the daughter of Ishmael
Sister of Nebaioth. Adah bore Eliphaz to Esau, Basemath bore Reuel,
And Oholibamah bore Jeush, Jalam, and Korah. Those were the sons of Esau,
Who were born to him in the land of Canaan. Esau decided to journey abroad.
He took his wives, his sons and his daughters, all members of his household, cattle and beasts,
All his animals, and everything he had gained while in Canaan, from greatest to least.
He went off into another land, away from Jacob his brother, on his account,
For together, they had too much livestock to feed, and the land couldn't support that amount.
So Esau settled in the hill-country of Seir (Esau is Edom, please be aware).
This is the line of Esau, father of the Edomites, in the hill-country of Seir:

Now these are the names of the sons of Esau: Eliphaz son of Esau's wife Adah,
And Reuel son of Basemath, the wife of Esau. And then the sons of Eliphaz:
There were Teman, Omar, Zepho, Gatam, and Kenaz. Now Timna was a concubine
To Eliphaz son of Esau, and she bore Amalek to Eliphaz, in his line.
Those were the sons of Esau's wife Adah. And these are the sons of Reuel: Nahath,
And Zerah, and Shammah and Mizzah. And those were the sons of Esau's wife Basemath.
These are the sons of Oholibamah, Anah's daughter, granddaughter of Zibeon
(Whose name can mean "hyena"), and Esau's wife. Oholibamah bore Esau three sons:
Jeush, Jalam, and Korah. These are the clans of Esau's sons: The sons of Eliphaz,
His firstborn: The clans Teman, Omar, Zepho, Korah, Gatam, Amalek, and Kenaz.
Those are the clans of Eliphaz in the land of Edom. Those are the sons of Adah.
These are the sons of Esau's son Reuel: the clans Nahath, Zerah, Shammah, and Mizzah;
Those are the clans of Reuel in the land of Edom, sons of Basemath, Esau's wife.
And these are the sons of Esau's wife Oholibamah, the ones to whom she gave life:
Clans Jeush, Jalam, and Korah; these are the clans of Esau's wife Oholibamah,
Daughter of Anah, Esau's wife. Those are the sons and clans of Edom, who was Esau.

These are the sons of Seir the Horite, who were settled in the land: Shobal and Lotan,
Zibeon, and Anah, and Dishon, and Ezer, and Dishan. Those were the Horite clans,
The children of Seir in the land of Edom. The sons of Lotan were Hemam and Hori,
And Lotan's sister was Timna (the concubine who was mentioned before in the story).
These are the sons of Shobal: Alvan, and Manahath, and Ebal, Onam and Shepho.
These are the sons of Zibeon: Aiah and Anah—the Anah who found long ago
The hot springs in the wilderness, while pasturing the asses of Zibeon his father.
And these are the children of Anah: his son Dishon, and Oholibamah his daughter.
And these are the children of Dishon: There were Hemdan, Eshban, and Ithran and Cheran.
These are the sons of Ezer: Bilhan, Zaavan, and Akan. These are the sons of Dishan:
Uz and Aran. These are the clans of the Horites: the clans Zibeon, Shobal, Lotan,
Anah, Dishon, Ezer, and Dishan. Those are the Horite families, by clan, in Seir's land.

These are the kings who reigned in Edom, before any king o'er the Israelites reigned.
Bela son of Beor reigned in Edom as king, and "Dinhabah" was his city's name.
When Bela died, Jobab son of Zerah, from Bozrah, became king and reigned in his stead.
When Jobab died, Husham from the land of the Temanites then became king in his stead.
When Husham died, Hadad son of Bedad succeeded him as king, and reigned in his stead,
(The Hadad who defeated Midian in Moab) "Avith" was the city he led.
When Hadad died, Samlah of Masrekah succeeded him as king, and reigned in his stead.
When Samlah died, Saul of Rehoboth-on-the-River became king and reigned in his stead.
When Saul died, Baal-hanan son of Achbor succeeded him and became king in his stead.
When Baal-hanan son of Achbor died, Hadar became the next king, and reigned in his stead.
"Pau" was his city's name, and his wife's name was Mehetabel, the daughter of Matred,

Daughter of Me-zahab. These are the names of the clans of Esau, by name, place, and clan:
The clans Timna, Alvah, Jetheth, Oholibamah, Elah, Pinon, Kenaz, Teman,
Mibzar, Magdeil, and Iram. Those are the clans of Edom, listed by their habitations
In the land of their holdings. And that is Esau, the father of the Edomite nation.

Genesis 37

Israel loved Joseph best of all of his sons,
And gave him a coat of many colors to wear.
Joseph's brothers were mad they weren't the most loved ones.
Then Joseph had a dream he decided to share.
He told his brothers, "Listen to this dream I had:
Your sheaves all bowed to mine, and stars bowed to me too."
They threw him in a pit, took his coat, and were mad,
Sold him as a slave, through Reuben asked them not to.

[Vayeshev]

Jacob settled in the land where his father Isaac had sojourned, the land of Canaan.
These are the generations of Jacob. Joseph, at just seventeen years old, was a man.
Joseph tended the flocks along with all his brothers, helped the sons of his father's wives
Bilhah and Zilpah. And Joseph brought their father ill reports about all of their lives.
Now Israel loved Joseph above all his sons, for he was the son of his old age,
So he made him a coat ornamented in many colors, the cause of much outrage.
For when his brothers saw that their father loved Joseph much more than any of his brothers,
They despised him, and could not speak peacefully to him, for being loved more than all others.
Now Joseph had a dream which he told to his brothers—from then on, they hated him more—
He said to them, "Pray, hear this dream that I have dreamt: We were out binding sheaves by
    the score
In the field, when suddenly my sheaf arose, it was standing upright, and behold,
Your sheaves circled around it and bowed down to my sheaf!" They hated what they had
    been told.
His brothers said to him, "Would you reign over us? Would you rule over us like a king?"
From then on, Joseph was hated even more for the talk of his dreams that he would bring.
He dreamt another dream, and shared it with his brothers, saying, "I dreamt another dream:
Now the sun and the moon and eleven stars were bowing down to me; what could it mean?"

When he told the dream to his father and his brothers, his father rebuked him and said,
"What is this dream that you have dreamt? Are we to come, I, your brothers, and mother,
    who's dead,
And all bow down before you?" His brothers were envious, his father kept it in mind.

Now his brothers went to tend their father's flock of sheep in Shechem, and at that same time,
Israel said to Joseph, "Aren't your brothers pasturing the flock of sheep in Shechem?
Come here, and I will send you to them." Joseph said to Israel, "Okay, here I am."
Israel said to him, "Come, go see how your brothers are faring, and how fare the sheep,
And bring word back to me." So he sent Joseph out from Hebron, where the valley was steep.
Joseph came to Shechem, and a man came upon him while he was roaming in the field.
The man asked him, "What do you seek?" He answered, "I seek my brothers." And then
    he appealed,
"Tell me, where do they pasture their sheep?" The man said, "They've moved on from here. I
    heard them say,
'let us go to Dothan.'" So Joseph followed them to Dothan, and found them in that way.
They saw him from afar, and before he got near, they conspired against him to slay him.
They said to one another, "Here comes the dream master, and now is the time to repay him.
Let us kill him and throw him in one of these pits, we can then say 'A savage beast ate him.'
Then let's see what becomes of his dreams!" Upon hearing their plans, Reuben tried to
    abate them.
He tried to rescue Joseph and said, "Let us not take his life. Don't let his blood be shed!
Don't lay one hand upon him, but throw him into this pit in the wilderness instead."
He intended to save Joseph from them and then return him to his father intact.
When Joseph came to his brothers, they took his coat, with the many colors from his back.
Then they took Joseph and cast him into the pit. The pit was empty, no water in it.
And they sat down to eat their food, but when they lifted their eyes and looked up in a minute,
They saw a caravan of Ishmaelites coming from Gilead, all in a band,
And their camels bore balm, balsam, and laudanum to be taken down to Egypt land.
Judah said to his brothers, "What do we gain by killing our brother, hiding his blood?
Come, let us sell him to the Ishmaelites, but let not our own hand shed Joseph's blood.
For he is, after all, our brother and our flesh." And his brothers all agreed to it.
When the Midianite men, the merchants, passed by, they all pulled Joseph out of the pit,
And his brothers sold Joseph for twenty pieces of silver to the Ishmaelites.
They took him to Egypt, so when Reuben returned to the pit, he was nowhere in sight.
Now when Reuben saw that Joseph wasn't there, he rent his clothes (having failed his rescue).
He returned to his brothers and said, "The boy isn't there! What am I supposed to do?"
Then they took Joseph's coat, and they slaughtered a kid, dipped the coat in the blood of the goat.
They had it sent to their father and said, "We found this. Look at it; is this your son's coat?"
Jacob recognized it, and said, "My son's coat! He's been devoured by some savage beast!
Joseph has, no doubt, been torn to pieces!" Jacob rent his clothes, and his mourning increased.

He put sackcloth on his loins and mourned his son for many days, thinking Joseph was dead.
All his sons and daughters arose to comfort him, but he refused to be comforted.
He said, "No, I will go down to my son in mourning, to Sheol!" (to Hell, or "the grave")
Thus his father wept for him. Meanwhile, the Midianites had sold him as a slave.
They had sold Joseph into Egypt to Potiphar, who served as Pharaoh's chief steward,
A court-officer of Pharaoh's, and in addition, the Captain of the palace Guard.

Genesis 38

> Judah married Shua, and brought three sons to life.
> There was Er, Onan, and Shelah. God made Er die.
> Onan would not bear children with Tamar, Er's wife,
> So God killed him as well. One day Judah walked by,
> But Tamar wore a veil and so she was disguised.
> Judah wanted to sleep with her, she asked the price
> Of his staff, which he gave. She stayed unrecognized
> 'til returning his staff. Then Tamar gave birth, twice.

At about that time, Judah went down away from his brothers, and turned his camp aside
Towards an Adullamite man whose name was Hirah, and that's where Judah had found a bride.
Judah saw the daughter of a Canaanite man whose name was Shua; she was the one.
He took her as a wife and came into her. She became pregnant and bore him a son,
He named him "Er". Then she became pregnant again, bearing a son whom she named "Onan".
Once again she bore a son, and named him "Shelah"; meanwhile he did lie in Chezib land.
Judah took a wife for Er, his firstborn. The date was palmed off on a girl named Tamar.
But Judah's firstborn Er was evil in the Lord's eyes, and so he did not make it far.
The Lord caused him to die. Then Judah said to Onan, "Come into the wife of your brother,
Do a brother-in-law's duty, preserve his seed, so the widow may still be a mother."
But Onan knew that the seed would not be his, and his vexation at this was profound.
So whenever he came into his brother's wife, he let it fall to waste on the ground,
That way Onan did not provide seed for his brother. In the Lord's eyes, this was evil,
So He caused him to die as well. Then Judah said to Tamar his daughter-in-law, "Still,
Sit as a widow in the house of your father until Shelah my son is grown up."
For he said to himself, "Otherwise he will die like his brothers from Tamar's bad luck."
So Tamar went and stayed in the house of her father. And after that, many days passed.
Then Shua's daughter, Judah's wife, died. And when Judah had finished his mourning at last,

He went up with Hirah the Adullamite to Timnah to see his sheepshearers' keep.

And Tamar was told, "Here, your father-in-law is going to Timnah to shear his sheep."

Tamar took off her widow's clothes, covered her face with a veil, wrapped herself, and sat down

By the entrance to Enayim ("Two Wells") which is on the road that leads to Timnah town,

For she saw that Shelah had grown up, yet she had not been given to him as a wife.

When Judah saw her, he thought that she was a whore, for she was dressed like one of that life,

With her face covered up. He went over to her and said, "Come, let me come in to you."

(For he did not know that it was Tamar his daughter-in-law, with her face hid from view.)

She said, "What will you give me for coming in to me?" He said, "I myself will have sent

A goat kid from my flock." She said, "I will need a pledge, until I receive your payment."

He said, "What pledge shall I give you?" She said, "Your seal, your cord, and the staff in
     your hand."

So he gave them to her and then came in to her, and by Judah she became pregnant.

She rose and went away, then she took off her veil, and put on her widow's clothes once more.

Now when Judah had sent the goat kid by his friend the Adullamite, to set the score,

He was sent to fetch the pledge from the woman, but he couldn't find her to get what was owed.

So he asked the townspeople, "Where is the cult prostitute near Enayim by the road?"

They said, "There's no cult prostitute here!" So he went back to Judah, and said with a frown,

"I couldn't find her, and also, the townspeople said, 'there's no cult-prostitute in this town."

Judah said, "Let her keep my pledge for herself, otherwise we'll become a laughing-stock.

I did send her the kid, but you could not find her, and all over the town you did walk."

Three months later, Judah was told, "Tamar your daughter-in-law has been playing the whore,

In fact, she is with child from harlotry!" Judah said, "These are things she must burn for;

Bring her out and let her be burned!" But as she was being brought out, a message she sent

To her father-in-law saying, "By the man to whom these things belong I am pregnant."

And she said, "Here are seal and cords and staff, now recognize, pray, to whom they belong."

Judah recognized them and said, "She is in the right, while I have been wrong all along!

For I should have given her to Shelah my son." And he did not lie with her again.

The time came for Tamar to give birth, there were twins in her womb. She was in labor, when

One of them put a hand out. The midwife tied a scarlet thread to his hand signifying

That he had come out first. But just then he pulled back his hand, and his brother
     came out crying.

And she said, "What a breach you have breached for yourself!" So "Perez" (or "Breach") was
     the boy's name.

Then his brother came out, the red thread on his hand, so "Zerah" ("Red of Dawn") he became.

Genesis 39

Joseph was in Egypt, servant to Potiphar.
God made Joseph successful in all he would do,
So his master liked him, gave him rights that stretched far.
Now the master's wife asked, "Let me lie down with you."
But he said, "No." Then one day, she grabbed his coat faster,
Said, "Lie down with me!" He said "No!", then he fled.
But he left his coat, so then the girl told the master,
That he tried to force her to join him in bed.

Now when Joseph was brought down to Egypt, Potiphar, who served as Pharaoh's chief steward,
An Egyptian man, a court official of Pharaoh's, and also Captain of the guard,
Had acquired Joseph from the hands of the Ishmaelites, who had brought him down there.
And the Lord was with Joseph and so he was a man blessed with success beyond compare.
Joseph stayed in the house of his lord the Egyptian, who saw that The Lord was with him,
And also that the Lord brought success onto everything that Joseph had his hand in.
Joseph found favor with him and waited on him, so he set him over his household,
And all things that he owned. And as soon as Joseph as the household chief had been enrolled,
The Lord blessed the Egyptian's house because of Joseph. His blessing was on everything,
All things in the house and in the fields owned by the Egyptian received the Lord's blessing.
So he left all that he had in Joseph's hands, and with him there, he had just one concern:
The bread that he ate. Joseph was well-built and nice to look at (like his mother, in turn).
After some time, the wife of the master laid eyes upon Joseph and said, "Lie with me!"
But Joseph refused, saying to his lord's wife, "Look, with me here, my lord is worry-free.
All belonging to him he has placed in my hands; in this house, I rule as much as he,
And he has withheld not one thing from me, except you, for you are his wife. Don't you see?
So how could I do this evil to him? It would be a sin against God, in addition!"
Though she coaxed Joseph day after day to lie with her and be with her, he did not listen.
Now one day, he came to the house to work, and none of the men were inside the homestead.
She grabbed him by his coat and said, "Lie with me!" But he left his coat in her hand and fled.
He escaped outside, but when she saw that he'd fled outside and left the coat in her hand,
She called in her house-servants and said to them, "See! He has brought to us a Hebrew man
To have play with us. He came to me, to lie with me, but I yelled out in a loud voice,
And when he heard my scream, he left his coat and fled outside, since he did not have
     much choice."
Now she kept his coat next to her until his master came home, then she told him the tale,
"The Hebrew servant who you brought to us came to me to have play with me, but did fail.

I yelled out, and he left his coat with me and fled." When his lord heard the words his wife spoke,
Saying, "This is what your servant has done to me," then his anger was fully provoked.
Joseph's lord had him put in the dungeon, the place where the king's prisoners were confined.
But while Joseph was there in the dungeon, the Lord was with him, and was faithful and kind.
The Lord made the chief jailer find favor with Joseph. The chief jailer put in his hands
All the prisoners in the dungeon. All that got done, got done because of Joseph's commands.
The chief jailer did not supervise anything; Joseph worked so well, there was no need,
Because the Lord was with him, and no matter what Joseph did, the Lord made it succeed.

Genesis 40

Joseph wound up in jail, with cupbearer and baker,
Who both told to Joseph the dreams that they had.
The first said, "A three-branched vine became a grape maker,
I put them in Pharaoh's hand." He said, "Be glad,
It means he'll set you free in three days. Mention me!"
Then the baker said, "Let me tell you my dream too:
Birds were eating from three baskets on my head." He
Replied, "You will be dead in three days." Both came true.

Some time later, the cupbearer and baker of Egypt's king had both given offense
To their lord, the king of Egypt. Pharaoh was angry with his two officials, and hence,
He took his chief cupbearer and chief baker, and had them taken into custody
In the house of the captain of the guard, the same dungeon where Joseph happened to be.
The guard captain appointed Joseph to attend them. In custody, they spent much time,
And the two of them—both the cupbearer and baker of Pharaoh who had been confined—
They both had dreams, each man with his own dream that had its own meaning on that
    single night.
When Joseph came to them in the morning and saw them, their depression was in plain sight.
He asked Pharaoh's officials, in custody with him, "Why do you appear sad today?"
They replied, "We have dreamt dreams, and there's no interpreter to tell us what the dreams say."
Joseph said to them, "Are not all interpretations from God? Pray, tell your dreams to me."
The chief cupbearer told his dream to Joseph. He said, "In my dream, a vine I did see.
There was a vine in front of me, and on the vine were three branches each with winding shapes,
And just as it was budding, the blossoms came out, and the clusters ripened into grapes.

Then the Pharaoh's cup was in my hand. I picked the grapes and squeezed them into
    Pharaoh's cup,
And put the cup in Pharaoh's hand." Joseph said to him, "Here's what your dream means,
    listen up:
The three branches are three days, in three days Pharaoh will lift up your head, your post restored,
And you shall again place Pharaoh's cup in his hand, like you did as cupbearer before.
But please keep me in mind when it goes well for you, kindly mention my name to Pharaoh,
So that you will free me from this place. For in truth, I was kidnapped—stolen!—long ago,
From the land of the Hebrews. And here too I've done nothing to merit a dungeon stay."
When the chief baker saw that the interpretation was good, he decided to say,
"I also had a dream of that type. On my head were three wicker baskets of bread,
And in the topmost basket were all kinds of baked goods for Pharaoh. But then the birds fed!
The birds ate the food out of the basket atop my head." Joseph then gave his reply,
"Here's the interpretation: The three baskets are three days, and when three days have gone by,
Pharaoh will lift up your head—from off of your body!—and then hang you up from a tree,
And the birds will all pick at your flesh." On the third day, Pharaoh's birthday, it came to be
That he held a great banquet for all of his servants, and lifted the heads of a pair:
His chief cupbearer and his chief baker were singled out from all of those who were there.
He restored the chief cupbearer to his cupbearership, to put the cup once again
In the hand of Pharaoh. But the chief baker he hanged, all just as Joseph told the men.
It all happened according to what Joseph gave as interpretations from their dreams.
But the cupbearer did not keep Joseph in mind, he forgot his promise to redeem.

Genesis 41

    Pharaoh had two dreams. First, seven cows fat and round
    Walked up out of the Nile, followed by seven lean.
    Then the same thing with grain. So Pharaoh asked around,
    "Who can interpret dreams and tell me what they mean?"
    The cupbearer said, "Joseph does things of this sort,"
    Joseph said, "Seven good years, but then seven bad.
    So your dream means save food." Pharaoh said, "Run my court!
    You are wise." And through famine, saved food Egypt had.

Pharaoh had a dream after two years that he was standing out by the stream of the Nile,
When out of the Nile came seven cows, fat of flesh, fair to look at, sturdy, and virile.
The cows grazed in the reed grass, but then seven other cows came from the Nile close behind,
Ill to look at and lean of flesh, these new cows stood on the Nile's bank near the first kind.
Then the ugly and skinny cows ate up the seven cows sturdy and fair to look at.
Pharaoh woke from this dream, but then he fell asleep to dream a second time after that:
Seven ears of grain, solid and healthy, grew on one stalk. Seven more ears sprung up near,
But the seven new ears of grain had been scorched by the east wind, and so they were lean ears.
Then the lean ears devoured the seven full ears. Pharaoh awoke: It was all a dream!
But in the morning his spirit was agitated, so he sent throughout his regime
To have all the wise-men and magicians of Egypt brought in to give interpretation.
Pharaoh told his dream to them, but none of them could find meaning or present revelation.
Then the chief cupbearer spoke to Pharaoh and said, "Now of my faults I must make admission.
At one point Pharaoh was angry with his servants, placed me in custody in his prison,
In the house of the captain of the guard, myself and the chief baker. And we both dreamt.
That one night we each dreamt dreams with their own meanings, but to understand,
     failed our attempt.
Now a young Hebrew lad was in there with us, a servant of the captain of the guard.
When we told him our dreams, he interpreted them for us, (which we had both found too hard).
He told each of us what our dreams meant. And it was just as he interpreted to us:
I was restored to my position, and the other was hanged and is now a carcass."
Pharaoh sent and had Joseph called. They rushed him out of the dungeon. He shaved,
     changed his clothes,
Then he came before Pharaoh. And Pharaoh said, "I dreamt a dream. What it means,
     no one knows.
But I heard it said of you that when you hear a dream, you can give an interpretation."
Joseph answered, "Not I! God will answer what is good for Pharaoh in this situation."
Pharaoh said to Joseph, "In my dream, I was standing on the Nile's bank, when behold,
Out of the Nile came seven cows, fat of flesh, fair of form," (their good health he extolled,)
"And they grazed in the reed grass. And then seven other cows came from the Nile close behind,
And these new seven were scrawny, ill, and ugly. In all Egypt, I've not seen their kind.
I had never seen any in such ill-condition, and then the ill cows ate the strong,
But when they ate the first cows, you could not tell, because they looked as ill as all along.
Then I woke. I saw also in my dream, on one stalk grew seven healthy ears of grain,
And then seven more stalks, thin and scorched by the east wind, sprung up behind them
     on the plain.
Then the thin, withered ears ate the seven good ears. Now, I've spoken with all my magicians,
But none of them can give me a good explanation. To do so, Joseph, is your mission."
Joseph said to Pharaoh, "Your two dreams are the same. God has revealed His plan to Pharaoh.
Here, the seven good cows stand for seven years, the seven good ears, seven years also.

The dream is one dream. The seven ugly and lean cows that followed them are seven years,
And the seven ears of grain that were hollow, shriveled, and scorched by the east wind, those ears
Will be seven years of famine! Just as I've told Pharaoh, God has revealed his plan:
Here, immediately ahead are seven years of abundance in all Egypt's land.
After them shall arise seven years of harsh famine, when all abundance is forgotten.
And the famine will ravage the land, with abundance no more. All the crops will grow rotten.
As the land becomes ravaged by famine, no trace of the plenty before shall remain,
For the famine that comes after will be exceedingly heavy, destroying all grain.
Now as for Pharaoh having the same dream twice, it means that God has determined the matter,
And that God will soon carry it out. So now let Pharaoh save Egypt from being shattered.
Now let Pharaoh select a discreet and wise man, set him over the land of Egypt.
And let Pharaoh take steps to appoint overseers for the land who are well-equipped,
To take one fifth of all Egypt's produce in the seven years when plenty fills the land.
Let them gather the food of these good years ahead, and pile it up under Pharaoh's hand.
All the food will be stored in the cities, and kept under guard, to act as a reserve
So that during the seven year famine that strikes Egypt, we'll live on food we've preserved."
Joseph's plan was deemed good by Pharaoh and his servants. Pharaoh said to his servants, "Well,
Could we find us another man like him, a man in whom the spirit of God would dwell?"
So Pharaoh said to Joseph, "Since God made this known to you, there are none as wise as you.
You shall be the one over my house, and my servants will do as you tell them to do.
Only by the throne shall I be greater than you." Pharaoh to Joseph said one more thing,
"See, I put you in charge of the land of Egypt!" Then Pharaoh removed his signet-ring;
He took it from his hand, placed it on Joseph's hand, and had him dressed in fine linen clothes,
And then put a gold chain on his neck, had him mount the second chariot of Pharaoh's,
And they called out before him, "Abrek!" (which can mean "Attention!" or sometimes
    "Bow the knee!")
So it was that Pharaoh placed Joseph over all the land of Egypt to oversee.
Pharaoh said to Joseph, "I am Pharaoh, but without your leave, no man in the area
Of Egypt shall raise hand or foot." Pharaoh then gave Joseph the name "Zaphenath Paneah"
(Which means "God speaks and He lives"). Pharaoh gave him Asenath, the daughter
    of Potiphera,
Priest of On, as a wife. So Joseph's influence went out over Egypt in that era.
Joseph was thirty years old when he entered the service of Pharaoh, king of Egypt.
Joseph went out from Pharaoh's presence and went through all the land of Egypt, well-equipped.
During the seven years of abundance, the land produced plenty. He gathered the grain,
And collected all kinds of provisions from those seven years which graced Egypt's domain.
He stored grain in each city, and put in the city the grain from the fields around it.
Joseph piled up grain, like the sand of the sea, until there were too many to count it.
Now Joseph fathered two sons by Asenath, daughter of Potiphera, priest of On,
Before the years of famine came. Joseph gave the name of "Manasseh" to the firstborn,

(Which translates as "He Who Makes Forget") meaning, "God made me forget all of
    my hardships,
And all my father's house." And he named the second "Ephraim" ("Double Fruit") from his lips,
Meaning, "God has made me bear fruit in the land of my affliction." The seven years ended,
And abundance in Egypt gave way to a seven year famine, as Joseph portended.
A great famine struck in all the lands, but in the land of Egypt there was bread throughout.
But when even all Egypt's lands felt famine, for bread the people to Pharaoh cried out.
Pharaoh said to all of the Egyptians, "Go to Joseph, whatever he tells you, do!"
So when famine had spread through the land, Joseph opened the storehouses where
    grain accrued.
He gave rations to all the Egyptians, since famine in Egypt was slow gaining strength.
And all lands came to Egypt for rations, to Joseph, since famine had struck the world's length.

Genesis 42

Food was scarce. Jacob heard Egypt still had supplies,
So he sent his sons there. Joseph knew them on sight,
But did not reveal himself. He said, "Are you spies?"
They said, "We're ten of twelve brothers, one's home this night,
And one's gone." Joseph said, "Are you honest? If so,
Bring your brother from home as proof you do not lie."
So they went back to tell Jacob. Jacob said, "No,
Don't take Benjamin. If he's lost, from grief I'll die."

Now when Jacob saw that there were rations to be had in Egypt, he said to his sons,
"Why do you keep just looking at one another? I've heard in Egypt, there are rations.
Go down to Egypt and buy us food rations from there, so that we may live and not die."
So ten of Joseph's brothers went down to buy some rationed grain from Egypt's large supply.
But Jacob did not send Benjamin, Joseph's brother, for he said, "What if he is harmed?"
The sons of Israel were among those that came to buy rations; they came in a swarm,
For the famine was in the land of Canaan. Joseph was governor over the land,
It was he who dispensed rations to the land's people. Before him, his brothers did stand.
They came and bowed to him, with their heads to the ground. When Joseph saw his brothers,
    he knew
Who they were, but pretended not to recognize them and spoke as a stranger might do.

He spoke harshly to them and said, "Where do you come from?" They said, "From the
    land of Canaan,
To buy food rations." And though Joseph recognized them, for their part, they never caught on.
And Joseph was reminded of dreams he had dreamt of them. He said to them, "You are spies!
It's the land's weakness that you have come to see!" They replied, "No, we came to buy supplies.
My lord, your servants have come to buy food rations. We are all sons of a single man,
We are honest, your servants have never been spies." He said, "No, you now spy on the land!
It's the land's weakness that you have come to see!" They said, "Your servants are twelve,
    we are brothers,
Sons of one man in Canaan, the youngest is with our father, and no more is the other."
Joseph said to them, "It's just as I have told you, 'You are spies!'—Here is how you'll be tested:
As Pharaoh lives, unless your youngest brother comes here, at this place you shall be arrested.
You shall not leave this place. Send one of you to fetch him, the rest shall as prisoners remain.
That way we will test your words and see whether there is truth in you, or if you just feign
And as Pharaoh lives, you are indeed spies!" He moved them into custody for three days.
Joseph said to them on the third day, "Do this and you shall live, for I follow God's ways:
If you are honest, let one of you brothers stay as a prisoner in custody,
And the rest of you go back to your households with famine-rations for your family.
Then bring your youngest brother back to me, to prove your words truthful, and you will not die."
They prepared to do so, but the brothers said to one another, "We cannot deny
We have guilt in regards to our brother—we saw his distress of heart as he implored,
And we listened not. That's why this distress has come upon us: His distress, we ignored."
Reuben spoke up and said, "Didn't I tell you 'don't sin against the child!' But you would not hear.
So now reckoning has come for his blood." They did not know that they had caught Joseph's ear,
For he'd spoken to them through an interpreter (so they did not know he understood).
Joseph turned away from them and wept, but returned and spoke to them as soon as he could.
Joseph had Simeon taken away from them, and bound up and fettered before their eyes.
Then Joseph ordered that their bags be filled with grain, and each man's silver returned likewise,
And that they should be given provisions for their journey. Joseph's men did so for them.
Then they loaded their rations onto their donkeys, and departed from that place. But then,
As one opened his sack to give his donkey fodder at the night camp, there in his pack
Was his silver. He said to his brothers, "My silver has been given back, in my sack!"
Their hearts gave way, and they trembled to one another, saying, "What has God done to us?"
They came home to their father Jacob, in the land of Canaan, bearing Egypt's surplus.
They recounted all that had befallen them, saying, "The man, governor of the land,
Spoke harshly with us, since he mistook us for spies and thought some evil deeds we had planned.
Now we said to him, 'We are honest, we have never been spies. We are twelve, brothers all,
Sons of our father. One is no more, and the youngest is in Canaan, at father's call.'
Then the man, the lord of the land, said to us, 'Here's how I'll tell if you are honest men:
Leave one of you brothers here with me, and bring food to your household to face the famine.
But bring your youngest brother back to me, so that I may know you are honest, not spies.
Then I will give your brother back to you, you may travel as you see best in your eyes.'"

But when all of them emptied their sacks, there was each man's pouch of silver, filled and
    unlightened.
They looked at their pouches full of silver, both they and their father, and then became
    frightened.
Then their father Jacob said to them, "Why is it always me that you boys must bereave?
Joseph is no more, Simeon is no more, and now for Benjamin you would have me grieve!
All this has come upon me." Reuben said to his father, "My two sons you may destroy
If I do not bring him back to you. Put him in my hands, and I'll return you the boy."
But he said, "My son is not to go down with you, for his brother is already dead.
And he is left alone. Should some harm befall him on the path which you now wish to tread,
You will send down to Sheol (down to the grave) in sorrow every gray hair on my head."

Genesis 43

But the famine was bad, so they had to go back,
Taking Benjamin. Jacob told them, "Take some gifts,"
In the hopes it would make the man's anger grow slack.
So they took them and then went back down to Egypt.
Joseph greeted them, asking "How's your dad of years?"
They said, "He's in good health." Joseph saw Benjamin
And asked, "Is this the youngest?", then wept many tears,
Overcome with the feelings he could not hold in.

Now the famine was grave in the land, so when they'd finished eating the rations they'd brought
Up from Egypt, their father told them, "Return there, buy us more rations." But Judah thought.
Judah told him, "The man had warned us, 'You shall not see my face unless your brother's
    with you.'
So if you will let our brother go with us, we'll go down there and buy rations to give you.
But if you will not let him go, we will not go down, because the man said to us all,
'You shall not see my face unless your brother is with you.'" This made Israel's face fall.
He said, "Why did you serve me so ill, telling this man that another brother you've got?"
They replied, "The man asked about us, and about our family, and kept asking a lot.
Saying things like, 'Is your father still alive? Do you have another brother?' And so
We responded accordingly. Could we know he'd say, 'Bring your brother down'? Could
    we know?"
Judah said to his father Israel, "Send the lad in my care, we'll be on our way,
So we may live and not die—we, you, and our children. The boy's safety I pledge this day.

I will act as his pledge, at my hand you may seek him. If I don't bring him back to you,
And set him before you, then I'll forever bear the guilt that my duty I couldn't do.
Indeed, had we not lingered, we could have been there and back twice in this time we just spake."
Then their father Israel said to them all, "If it must be so, then do this thing: Take.
Take some of the choice produce of this land in your baggage, take them as gifts to the man—
Some balsam, honey, balm and laudanum, pistachios and almonds. Take in your hand
Silver doubled, two times over all of the silver that you found returned in your packs,
Return it in your hand, perhaps it was an oversight; if so they might want it back.
Take your brother too. Rise and return to the man, and may God Almighty grant to you
Mercy from the man, so he'll release your other brother to you, and Benjamin too.
As for me, if I must be bereaved, then I must be bereaved." The brothers took the gift,
Silver two times over and Benjamin as well, and went down to Egypt, to Joseph.
There they stood before him, and when Joseph saw Benjamin with them, he told his
    house steward,
"Take those men in the house, and then slaughter an animal, have it prepared and procured,
For it is with me that these man shall dine this noon." The man did just as Joseph instructed,
He brought the men into Joseph's house, but the men were afraid at how they'd been conducted.
They were frightened to be there and said, "It's because of the silver that we've been brought in,
All that silver returned in our packs last time makes us look like we've committed a sin.
They will take offense, roll on us, fall on us, seize us as slaves, and our asses as well."
So they went to the chief steward of Joseph's house at the entrance and said, "We must tell.
Please my lord, hear us out. We came down here before to buy rations, but that very night,
When we camped and then opened our packs, each man's silver was in the packs, stacked
    to full height.
But we've brought it back here in our hand, and more silver as well to buy food rations here.
We do not know who put our silver in our packs." He replied, "All is well, do not fear.
Your God, the God of your father must have put treasure in your bags for you, I've been paid,
Since your silver has already come to me." And Simeon before them he conveyed.
Then the man had them come into Joseph's house, and gave them water for washing their feet,
And gave their asses food. They prepared the gifts, until Joseph came back at noon to eat.
When Joseph came home, they gave him the gifts they'd brought to the house, from their hand,
    and then bowed.
They bowed low to the ground before him. Joseph greeted them, asked of their welfare aloud,
"Is your old father well, the one of whom you spoke? Is he still in good health?" They replied,
"It is well with your servant our father, he is in good health, and gladly has not died."
They bowed in homage. Joseph then lifted his eyes up and saw his brother Benjamin,
The son of his mother, and he said, "Is this your youngest brother, the one you mentioned?"
Then he said to him, "May God be gracious to you, my boy." With that, Joseph hurried out.
For he was overcome with feelings for his brother, and had to weep to let it out.
Joseph entered a chamber and wept there. He then washed his face, and returned, in control.
He said, "Serve bread!" They served him by himself, and them by themselves, with their own
    bread and rolls,

The Egyptians who ate with him by themselves, for with Hebrews they would not break bread.
(Such things are an abomination for Egyptians.) In his presence, they were seated,
The firstborn according to his firstborn-rank, the youngest according to his youth-rank.
And the brothers all stared at each other, astonished. (Was this an elaborate prank?)
Joseph had courses taken to them from his table, especially for Benjamin,
Whose food portions were five times as large as theirs were. Then they drank and were
    merry with him.

Genesis 44

Joseph told his steward, "Fill their bags up with food,
And then put my best goblet in Benjamin's sack."
Then the steward said to them, "Why were you so rude,
Is good kindness repaid with ill robbery back?"
Joseph said, "The thief must stay, you others may go."
Judah said, "Please my lord, that is too much to face.
Our dad will die of grief if that boy's not in tow,
So I beg you, let me stay here and take his place.

He commanded the steward of his house and said, "Fill the men's packs with food, to the brim,
Put each man's silver into his pack. And put my goblet in the pack of Benjamin,
Yes my best silver goblet, put it in the youngest's pack, with the silver for his rations."
So the man did as Joseph had told him. At daybreak, the men were sent off, with their asses.
They had just left the city, and had not gone far, when Joseph said to his steward, "Rise!
Get up, follow those men, and when you have caught up with them, say to them, 'I am surprised!
Why have you repaid good with ill? For is this not what my lord drinks with, this very cup,
And he also divines with it. You have done wrong by this.'" So when the steward caught up,
He spoke those words to them. To the steward they said, "Why does my lord speak words
    such as these?
Heaven forbid your servants should do such a thing. Now remember, my lord, if you please,
That the money we found in our sacks we brought back, all the way from the land of Canaan.
So how could we steal silver or gold from the house of your lord? This charge shall not go on.
Let whichever of your servants found with the goblet die, and then we shall be your slaves."
He replied, "Let it be as you say, a servant shall be made of the cup-stealing knave,
But the rest of you shall go free." So each one hastened to lower his pack to the ground,
Each man opened his pack, then he searched from the eldest to youngest. The goblet was found!

'twas in Benjamin's pack. They rent their clothes, reloaded their asses, returned to the city.
Judah and his brothers came to the house of Joseph, who was still there, seeking his pity.
They flung themselves on the ground before him. Joseph said, "What deed is this that
you have done?
Do you not know that a man like me can divine?" Judah said, "What thing can be spoken?
What can we say to my lord? How can we plead? How can we prove that we are innocent?
God has uncovered the crime of your servants, so here we are, to be my lord's servants,
We, and the one in whose hand the goblet was found." But then Joseph said, "Heaven Forbid!
No, far be it from me to make all of you my servants for what just one of you did.
The man in whose possession the goblet was found, he shall become a servant to me,
But the rest of you, go back in peace to your father."

[Vayigash]

                          Judah neared, and offered a plea:
"Please, my lord, pray let your servant speak a few words in the ears of my lord of our woe,
And please don't let your anger flare up against your servant, for you are like the Pharaoh.
My lord asked of his servants, 'do you have a father or another brother?' We said,
'We do have an old father, and a young child of his old age, one whose brother is dead,
So that he alone is left of his mother, his father loves him.' And then you decreed
To your servants, 'Bring him down to me, for I wish to set my eyes upon him, indeed.'
Then we said to my lord, 'the lad can't leave his father, if he left, his father would die.'
But you said to your servants, 'If your youngest brother does not come down with you hereby,
You shall not see my face again.' Now it was when we went back to my father, your servant,
We told him my lord's words, and our father said, 'Go back and buy us some rations, it's urgent!'
But we said, 'We can't go down. If our youngest brother is with us, then we will go down,
For if he is not with us, then we cannot see the man's face.' This made my father frown.
Now your servant, my father, told us, 'You yourselves know that my wife bore two sons to me.
One is gone from me, and I said, "He has been torn by a beast, torn to pieces, surely."
And I've not seen him since. Now if you take away this one from before my face as well,
Then should harm befall him, you will bring down my white head and grey hairs in grief to Sheol.'
So now, when I come back to your servant, my father, and the young lad is not with us,
The lad with whom his own life is so bound up, when he sees that the lad is not with us,
He will die. And your servants will send the grey hairs of our father to Sheol in grief.
For your servant pledged himself to my father for the boy's safety, a concern in chief.
I said, 'If I do not bring him back to you, I will forever be guilty before you.'
So now, pray let this servant of yours stay instead of the lad, to be a servant for you,
But let this lad go back with his brothers. How can I return to my father without him?
Then I would have to see the ill-fortune that would fall on my father, and all about him.

Genesis 45

Joseph could not control himself and he cried out,
"All but my guests, leave now!" Then he cried and he said,
"I am Joseph, your brother!" His brothers had doubt,
But he told them, "Don't be sad, God sent me ahead
To insure your survival. Now go tell our dad
That I rule here." And Pharaoh gave them the land's best.
So they told Jacob Joseph still lived. He was glad,
And said, "I must see him while there's breath in my chest!"

Then Joseph could no longer restrain himself before all of his attendants, and cried,
"Now, have everyone withdraw from me!" No one else but Joseph's brothers was left inside.
Joseph made himself known to his brothers, his weeping so loud, it could be heard by others;
The Egyptians heard, and even Pharaoh's household heard. And then Joseph said to his brothers,
"I am Joseph. Is my father still alive?" But his brothers were not able to answer,
For they were dumbfounded by his presence. Joseph told them all, "Come close to me.
    Advance, sirs."
They came close. Joseph said, "I am Joseph your brother, he whom you sold into Egypt.
But now, don't be distressed or upset with yourselves that you sold me here. It's in the script,
For it was to save life that God sent me ahead of you. There have been two years of famine,
And five more years of famine are still to come, the land will yield no harvest to examine.
So God sent me ahead of you to make sure that you stay living on earth, and survive.
So you see, it was not you that sent me here, but God. And see how he has made me thrive:
He has made me a father to Pharaoh, and the lord of all Pharaoh's household as well,
And also ruler over the whole land of Egypt, the place where I currently dwell.
Make haste, go back to my father and say to him, 'this is what your son Joseph does say,
"God has made me the lord of all Egypt, so come down to me here, and do not delay.
You shall stay in the region of Goshen, you shall be near me, you, and your sons, and their sons,
Your flocks, your herds, and all that is yours. I'll sustain you through the coming five
    years of famine.
Otherwise, you and your household and all that is yours will be reduced to poverty."'
Here, your eyes see, and my brother Benjamin's eyes see, the one speaking to you is me.
So tell my father of all the weight that I carry in Egypt, and all that you've seen.
And make haste, bring my father down here!" Joseph flung himself on his brother Benjamin,
Then he wept as he hugged the neck of Benjamin, who wept on Joseph's neck in release.
Joseph kissed all his brothers and wept on them. Only then could they speak to him in peace.

The news reached Pharaoh's palace, "Joseph's brothers have come." Pharaoh and his servants
   were pleased.
Pharaoh said to Joseph, "Say to your brothers, 'do as follows, load up all of your beasts,
And go down to the land of Canaan. Fetch your father and your households, and come to me.
I will give you the best that Egypt has to offer; the fat of the land you will eat!'
Command them also, 'do this, take wagons from Egypt for your little ones and your wives,
Carry your father down and come! Do not regard with regret things from your former lives,
For the best that Egypt has to offer shall be yours.'" The sons of Israel did so,
Joseph gave them wagons and food for the journey as he'd been commanded by Pharaoh.
To each of them he gave a change of clothes, but to Benjamin he gave a great extent,
Three hundred silver pieces and five changes of clothes. And then to his father he sent
Ten male asses, all loaded with the best of Egypt, ten she-asses with grain and bread,
And provisions for his father on the journey. Then he sent off his brothers ahead.
As they went off, Joseph said to his brothers, "Don't quarrel with each other on the way."
They went up from Egypt, came to the land of Canaan, where their father Jacob did stay.
And they told him, "Joseph, he is still alive! Now he's the ruler of all Egypt's land!"
His heart failed, for he did not believe them. But then they spoke to him of Joseph's command,
And when they spoke to their father of Joseph's words, the words Joseph had spoken to them,
And when he saw the wagons that Joseph had sent for the purpose of transporting him,
Then their father Jacob's spirit came to life. And Israel (who is Jacob) then said,
"It's enough! Joseph my son is still alive; I must go see him before I am dead!"

Genesis 46

> So Israel set out with all things he held dear,
> To Beersheba, where to God he made sacrifice.
> God appeared and said, "Jacob?" He said, "I am here."
> God said, "Do not fear Egypt, I shall make it nice."
> Joseph came out to meet Israel at Goshen,
> Joseph said, "Your location here I'll help you keep.
> When Pharaoh asks you what you do, all of your men
> Should say 'shepherding', since he hates men who tend sheep.

So then Israel set out with all he had, came to Beersheba, offered sacrifice
To the God of his father Isaac. God called to Israel in visions of the night.
God said, "Jacob! Jacob!" He said, "Here I am." God said, "I am God, God of your father.
Do not be afraid to go down to Egypt, for a great nation I'll make of you there.

I Myself will go down with you to Egypt, and I Myself will bring you up again.
Joseph shall lay his hand on your eyes when you die." Jacob set out from Beersheba then.
The sons of Israel carried Jacob their father, their wives, and their little-ones too
In the wagons which Pharaoh had sent to transport him. And they took what they had accrued,
All their livestock and all of the property that they had gained in the land of Canaan.
They came to Egypt, Jacob and his offspring with him, his sons, and the sons of his sons,
Jacob's daughters and Jacob's sons' daughters; all his offspring he brought with him to Egypt.

Now these are the names of the sons of Israel who came down to Egypt on the trip:
Jacob and his sons: Jacob's firstborn Reuben. His sons: Enoch, Pallu, Carmi, Hezron.
Simeon's sons: Jemuel, Jamin, Ohad, Jachin, Zohar, and Saul (a Canaanite's son).
LevI's sons: Gershon, Kehat, and Merari. Judah's sons: Shelah, Perez, Onan, Er,
And Zerah—but Onan and Er died in the land of Canaan. And Perez's sons were:
Hezron and Hamul. The sons of Issachar were: Puvah, Iob, Shimron, and Tola.
Zebulun's sons were: Sered, Elon, and Jahleel. And those were the sons born by Leah.
Leah bore those sons to Jacob, along with his daughter Dinah, in Aram-country,
Hence the persons among all the daughters and sons of Jacob numbered thirty and three.
Gad's sons: Ziphion, Haggi, Shuni, Ezbon, Eri, Arodi, Areli. All Gad's.
Asher's sons: Imnah, Ishvah, Ishvi, Beriah, and Serah, the sister that they had.
And Beriah's sons Heber and Malchiel. Those were the sons that were born by Zilpah,
Whom Laban gave to Leah his daughter. Zilpah bore Jacob sixteen persons in all.

The sons of Rachel, Jacob's wife: Joseph and Benjamin. Then in the land of Egypt,
Asenath, daughter of Potiphera, priest of On, bore Joseph two sons from her hips:
Their names were Manasseh and Ephraim. The sons of Benjamin were: Ard, and Huppim,
Bela, and Becher, and Ashbel, and Gera, and Naaman, Ehi, and Rosh, and Muppim.
Those were the sons of Rachel that were born to Jacob. In all, there were fourteen of them.
While Dan's only son was: Hushim. NaphtalI's sons were: Jahzeel, Guni, Jezer, Shillem.
Those were the sons of Bilhah, whom Laban had given to Rachel his daughter as maid,
Bilhah bore all of these sons to Jacob. They were seven persons, when fully arrayed.
All the persons who came into Egypt with Jacob, the ones that were his own offspring,
Aside from the wives of Jacob's sons, there were sixty-six persons when finished counting.
And then Joseph's sons, who were born to him in Egypt, they numbered two. So it would be,
That the total number of all Joseph's household that came to Egypt was seventy.

Now Jacob had sent Judah ahead of him to Joseph, to point the way to Goshen.
When they came to the region of Goshen, Joseph had his chariot harnessed, and then
He went up to Goshen to meet his father Israel, presenting himself to him.
Joseph flung himself around his neck, and wept on it until in tears his face did swim.
Israel said to Joseph, "Now I can die, since I have seen your face—you're still alive!"
Joseph said to his brothers and his father's household, "Here is a plan so we can thrive:

I will go up and tell the news to Pharaoh, saying, 'My brothers and father's household,
Who were in the land of Canaan have come to me. They are shepherds, their calling of old.
They have always been breeders of livestock, they brought all they have, all their flocks
      and their herds.'
Now when Pharaoh has you called and says, 'What is your occupation?' Then you must answer,
'Your servants have been breeders of livestock from our youth, both we and also our fathers.'
So that you may all settle in the region of Goshen to practice your occupation.
For to the Egyptians, every shepherd of flocks is no more than an abomination."

Genesis 47

> So Pharaoh asked Joseph's brothers, "What do you do?"
> And they said, "We are shepherds." So Pharaoh said, "Well,
> Stay in Goshen." Meanwhile, Egypt's famine just grew,
> So they all came to Joseph, who had bread to sell.
> He sold it for their money, and then for their sheep,
> And when sheep ran out, they gave their land to have bread.
> Joseph asked one-fifth tribute, the rest they could keep.
> Jacob told him, "Don't bury me here when I'm dead."

So Joseph came and told Pharaoh, "My father and my brothers, with their sheep and oxen
And all that is theirs, came from the land of Canaan and are now in the land of Goshen."
From the circle of his brothers, Joseph picked five men, and presented them to Pharaoh.
Pharaoh said to his brothers, "What is it that you do?" And they responded, "As you know,
We your servants are shepherds of flocks, like our fathers before us. And now we have come
To sojourn in the land, for there's no pasture for the flocks of your servants where we're from.
Famine is severe in Canaan's land. Pray let your servants stay in the land of Goshen."
Pharaoh said to Joseph, "So your fathers and brothers have come to you, these goodly men.
The land of Egypt lies before you, so have them settle in the best parts of the land.
Let them stay in the region of Goshen. And if you know capable men in their band,
You should put them in charge of my livestock." Joseph brought his father Jacob to Pharaoh.
Jacob gave Pharaoh a blessing of greeting. Pharaoh said to Jacob, "I'd like to know
Just how many are the days and years of your life?" Jacob said to Pharaoh in reply,
"The days and years of my sojourn here on earth have been one hundred thirty years gone by.
Few and ill-fated have been the days and years of my life. They have not reached the life-span
Of my fathers' lives during their sojourns." Jacob gave Pharaoh a farewell-blessing, and

Left his presence. So Joseph then settled his father and brothers, gave them property
In the best part of Egypt's land, in the region of Rameses, as Pharaoh had decreed.
Joseph sustained his father, his brothers, and his father's household, as numbers dictated

But there was no bread in all the land, due to the food shortage the famine had created.
Both the land of Egypt and the land of Canaan were completely depleted from famine.
Joseph gathered up all of the silver that was found in the lands of Egypt and Canaan,
As a payment for rations they'd bought. Then Joseph brought the silver into Pharaoh's house.
When the silver in the land of Egypt and in the land of Canaan had all run out,
The Egyptians all came to Joseph and said, "Give us bread! Shall we die in front of you
Just because all our silver is gone?" Joseph said, "Give me your livestock, and that will do.
I will give you bread in exchange for your livestock, since the silver no longer amasses."
So they brought their livestock to Joseph, who gave them bread for horses, sheep, cattle, and asses.
He got them through that year by allowing them to exchange all of their livestock for bread.
But when that year had ended, they came back to him during the following year and said,
"We can't hide from my lord that if the silver has run out, and all our livestock you own,
There is nothing remaining for my lord aside from our soil and our flesh and bones.
Why should we die in front of your eyes, and not only us, but also our land and soil?
Take both us and our land for the bread, and from now on as serfs for Pharaoh we will toil.
Give us seeds so that we may live and not die, and so the soil won't become desolate."
So Joseph acquired all of the farm land in Egypt for Pharaoh at a speedy rate,
For each of the Egyptians sold his field because the famine was just too much to bear,
So the land all went over to Pharaoh. And as for the people who were living there,
Joseph transferred them into the cities from one edge of Egypt to the other edge.
Only the land of the priests he did not acquire, because the priests had Pharaoh's pledge.
They received an allotment from Pharaoh and managed to live off of that allocation.
Therefore they did not sell their land to Joseph, but instead stayed at their former location.
Joseph said to the people, "Since on this day I have bought you and your land for Pharaoh,
You shall have seed. Now here is the seed for you, which in the land of Pharaoh you shall sow.
And at harvest time, you shall give a fifth to Pharaoh. The other four fifths are for you,
As more seed for the field, and as food for you, and for your household, your little ones too."
They said, "You saved our lives! May it please our lord, from now on Pharaoh by us
　　shall be served."
And Joseph made it into a land law in Egypt, which still to this day is observed,
That the fifth part of all land shall go to Pharaoh, the exception being the priests' soil.

And so Israel stayed in the land of Egypt, in the land of Goshen, being loyal.
They obtained holdings in it, bore fruit, multiplied, until they were exceedingly rife.

[Vayechi]

Jacob lived seventeen years in the land of Egypt so that the span of Jacob's life

Came to one hundred and forty-seven years. When the time came for Israel to die,
He called his son Joseph and said, "If I've gained your favor, put your hand under my thigh,
Swear that you'll deal with me in good faith and truth; pray do not bury me in Egypt.
When I lie down with my fathers, carry me from Egypt, and bury me in their crypt."
Joseph told him, "I will do according to what you have spoken." But Israel said,
"Swear to me!" So Joseph swore to him. And then Israel bowed at the head of his bed.

Genesis 48

Later, Joseph was told, "Now your father is ill."
So he went with his two sons to see him in bed.
Jacob said, "Your two sons will be like mine, they will,
But your other sons will remain all yours instead.
Let me bless Ephraim and Manasseh." Joseph
Brought Ephraim to his left hand, Manasseh right.
But Israel crossed hands, blessing Manasseh left,
And giving Ephraim blessings of greater might.

Some time later Joseph was told, "Your father is ill." So he took with him his two sons,
Manasseh and Ephraim. And Jacob was told, "To see you, your son Joseph now comes."
Israel gathered his strength, and said to Joseph as he (Israel) sat up in bed,
"El Shaddai appeared to me at Luz in the land of Canaan, and he blessed me, and said,
'I will make you bear fruit and be many, and make you into a host of peoples too;
And I will grant this land as a holding for the ages to your offspring after you.'
Now your two sons born to you in Egypt, 'ere I came to you in Egypt at that time,
Shall be mine. Ephraim and Manasseh, no less than Reuben and Simeon, shall be mine.
But your progeny born to you after them shall be yours, called by the name of their brothers
In their inheritance. For when I was returning from that country, Rachel your mother
Died on me, in the land of Canaan, on the way, still some distance away from Ephrath.
And I buried her there on the road to Ephrath (which is now Bethlehem), on that path."
Now when Israel saw Joseph's sons, he said, "Who are these?" Joseph said to his father,
"They are my sons, whom God has given to me here." And Israel said, "Bring them closer.
Bring them up to me so I can bless them." For Israel's eyes with old age had turned dim,
And he could not see. Joseph brought them close to him, and he kissed them and then
    embraced them.
Israel said to Joseph, "I never expected that your face again I would see,
And yet here, God has let me see your children too." Joseph then removed them from his knees.

And they all bowed low to the ground. Joseph took both of them, Ephraim with his right hand,
To Israel's left, and Manasseh with his left hand, to the right of Israel's stand,
And brought them close to him. But Israel stretched out his right hand, laying it on the head
Of Ephraim (though he was the younger, and normally firstborn receive that instead),
And his left hand on Manasseh's head. He crossed his arms (Manasseh's firstborn right
    thus docked).
He blessed Joseph and said, "The God in whose ways my fathers Abraham and Isaac walked,
The God who has been my shepherd ever since the day that I was born, until this day,
The messenger who has redeemed me from ill fortune, may he bless the lads. And then pray,
May my name and my line be continued through them, and too my fathers' names, Abraham,
And Isaac. May they teem like fish and become multitudes all through the midst of the land."
When Joseph saw that his father placed his right hand on Ephraim's head, he thought it wrong;
So he took hold of his father's hand to move it to Manasseh's head, where it belonged.
Joseph said to his father, "Not so, father, this one is firstborn, place hand on his head."
But his father refused, saying, "I know, my son, I know. From him too, tribes shall be bred.
He too shall be great, and yet his younger brother will be greater than he, his offspring
Shall become a great multitude of nations." So then he blessed them on that day, saying,
"By you shall Israel give blessings, saying: God made you like Ephraim and Manasseh."
And by speaking their names in that order, Israel put Ephraim before Manasseh.
Then Israel said to Joseph, "Here, I am about to die, but God will be with you.
He will have you return to the land of your fathers. And now, one more thing must I do.
Now I give you one portion, one shoulder, one mountain slope more than your brothers' reward,
Which I once took away from the hand of the Amorite with my bow and with my sword."

Genesis 49

> Jacob told his sons, "Reuben, you are my first born,
> Simeon and Levi are a pair quite angry.
> Judah, you are a lion that praise will adorn
> From all people. Zebulun shall dwell by the sea.
> Issachar is an ass, Dan a snake by the road,
> Gad shall raid the raiders, Asher will have rich bread.
> Naphtali is a hind, Joseph's a wild colt,
> Benjamin is a wolf." Jacob stopped, and was dead.

Jacob then called his sons and said, "Gather round, that I may tell you of what shall befall you
In days yet to come. Gather and hear, sons of Jacob, your father Israel who called you.

Reuben, you are my firstborn. Not only my might, but also the first fruit of my vigor,
Both surpassing in rank and surpassing in honor. In these virtues, there were none bigger.
As unstable as water, you surpass no more—for when you mounted your father's bed,
You defiled it and brought disgrace—he went up to my couch, and the couch he mounted.
Now Simeon and Levi are brothers, weapons of violence are their swords. Such cruelty,
Let my person not come to their council nor ever be counted in their assembly.
For in anger they kill men, wantonly maim bulls. Cursed be their anger, too fierce to quell,
And their fury so harsh. I will split them up in Jacob, scatter them in Israel.
You, O Judah, your brothers shall praise you. Your hand shall be on the nape of your foes' necks.
And your father's sons, they shall bow down to you. A lion's whelp, Judah commands respect.
From prey, my son, you have gone up. He squats and crouches like a lion, the king of beasts.
Who dares rouse him up? The scepter won't depart him, nor the ruler's staff leave from his feet,
Until Shiloh comes and people's homage is his. He ties up his ass-foal to a vine,
His young colt to a choice crimson tendril, and then Judah washes his garment in wine,
His robe in blood of grapes. His eyes darker than wine, his teeth whiter than milk. Zebulun,
He shall dwell on the seashore as haven for boats, and his own flank shall rest on Sidon.
Issachar, a strong-boned ass, crouching in the sheepfolds, saw the good of the resting turf,
And how pleasant the land. So he bent his shoulder to bear, and became a toiling serf.
Dan his people shall judge, as one tribe of Israel's, and be a serpent by the road,
A viper by the path who bites the horse's heel, so it throws off its passenger load.
I wait for your deliverance, Lord! Gad shall be raided by raiders, but raid their heels.
Asher's food shall be rich, for it is royal dainties befitting a king he shall yield.
Naphtali is a hind let loose which yields lovely fawns. Joseph, a young wild ass.
A wild ass by a spring, donkeys along a wall. Archers all assailed him as he passed,
Shot at him bitterly, yet his bow remained firm, and his arms and hands both stayed agile,
By the means of the Mighty One of Jacob up there, the Shepherd, the Stone of Israel.
By your father's God, may he help you, and Shaddai (Almighty), blessings may he bestow
Upon you; blessings both from the heavens above, and of the ocean crouching below,
Blessings of the breast and womb. The blessings of your father surpass the blessings of old,
Of my ancestors, of mountains eternal, to the boundaries of hills with age untold.
May they rest on the head of Joseph, on the brow of the one chosen out of his brothers.
Benjamin is a ravenous wolf. In the morning his foe is the prey he devours.
Then in the evening, he divides up the spoils." All these are the tribes of Israel, twelve,
And this is what their father told them, giving each an appropriate blessing farewell.
Then he charged them and said, "Soon I will be gathered to my kin, so please bury me right.
Bury me with my fathers in the cave which is in the field of Ephron the Hittite,
At the cave in the field of Machpelah, which faces Mamre, in the land of Canaan.
The same field Abraham bought as a burial holding once from the Hittite Ephron.
There they buried Abraham and his wife Sarah, there they buried Isaac and his wife
Rebekah. And there I buried Leah—... The field and cave in it, bought from the Hittites."
And when Jacob had finally finished charging his sons and giving them instructions,
Then he gathered his feet up onto the bed, breathed his last, and was gathered to his kin.

Genesis 50

Joseph wept on his father, then made this demand
To the Pharaoh's court, "Tell Pharaoh that I have sworn
To my father I'd bury him in Canaan's land."
Pharaoh said, "I will grant this request as you mourn."
So all Jacob's sons buried him in the same cave
Of Machpelah, where Abraham buried his wife.
Joseph's brothers apologized, and he forgave,
And saw grandchildren before the end of his life.

Joseph flung himself onto his father's face, wept over him and then kissed him as well.
Joseph ordered the physicians in his service to embalm his father Israel.
They embalmed him. It took forty days for him, the full timespan that embalming requires.
And the Egyptians wept for him seventy days. Now when the days of weeping expired,
Joseph spoke to the household of Pharaoh and said, "Pray, if I've found favor in your eyes,
Speak in Pharaoh's ears, saying, 'My father made me swear an oath to him before he died.
He said, "Look, I am dying. In my burial site I dug for myself long ago
In the land of Canaan, there you must bury me." So pray, now grant me your leave to go,
And to bury my father there, and return.'" Pharaoh said, "Go up and bury your father,
As he had you swear, since you have made an oath." So Joseph went up to bury his father,
And with him went up all Pharaoh's servants, the elders of his household and all Egypt,
All of Joseph's household, all his brothers and father's household, they all went on the trip.
Only their little-ones, their sheep and their oxen did they leave in the land of Goshen.
And along with him also went chariots and horsemen. His troop was heavy with men.
When they came to Goren Ha-Atad ("Bramble Threshing Floor") in the land beyond the Jordan,
They took up a lament, an exceedingly heavy lament (for sorrow is important).
He held seven days mourning for his father. When the Canaanite inhabitants saw
All the mourning at Goren Ha-Atad, the Canaanites stared and were stricken with awe.
They said, "This is such mourning for Egypt." So "Mourning-Meadow of Egypt" it was branded,
(Or "Abel-Mizraim"), beyond the Jordan. Thus his sons did as their father commanded.
They all carried him back to the land of Canaan, buried him in a cave in the field
Of Machpelah, the burial-site which Abraham got Ephron the Hittite to yield,
Facing Mamre. Then Joseph returned to Egypt, he, his brothers, and all of the herd
Who had gone up with Joseph to bury his father, after his father was interred.

When Joseph's brothers saw that their father was dead, they said, "What if Joseph bears a grudge,
And decides to repay us for all of the ill that we caused him, serving as our judge?"

So they sent Joseph a message which said, "Before he died, your father commanded us,
'say this to Joseph, "Pray, forgive your brothers' sin and offense, harm caused by animus."'
Pray forgive the offense of the servants of your father's God!" Joseph wept as they spoke.
Then his brothers came, flung themselves down before him, and said, "Here we are, slaves
    to your yoke."
But Joseph said to them, "Do not be afraid. For am I to be your judge in God's place?
Though you planned harm against me, God planned it for good, to bring this day about
    in his grace—
So that many will be kept alive. So now, don't be afraid. I myself will provide
For both you and your children." And he gave them comfort, and spoke to them kindly besides.

So Joseph stayed in Egypt, with his father's household. He lived to one hundred and ten.
Joseph lived long enough to see Ephraim's grandchildren of the third generation,
And also the sons of Machir, son of Manasseh, were adopted on Joseph's knees.
Joseph said to his brothers, "I am dying, but God will take notice of you, surely,
And bring you up from this land to the land which he promised in an oath to Abraham,
To Isaac, and to Jacob." Joseph had the sons of Israel swear an oath to him,
Saying, "Once God takes notice of you, you must bring my bones up from here." And Joseph died,
At one hundred and ten. They embalmed him, put him in a coffin in Egypt to bide.

EXODUS

Exodus 1

Now Joseph died, but Israel's children increased,
They were many in number and filled up the land.
A new king who had not known Joseph in the least
Rose in Egypt, and said, "This Israelite band
Is too mighty, too many, to be left to thrive.
Let's deal shrewdly with them, kill their sons with our guile."
Yet this order was not obeyed by the midwives,
So Pharaoh said, "Each son born, throw into the Nile."

[Shemot]

These are the names of the children of Israel, coming into Egypt's land,
With Jacob, each man coming with his household: Reuben, Simeon, Levi, Judah, and Dan,
Issachar, Zebulun, Benjamin, and Naftali, Gad, and Asher went on the trip.
All of Jacob's issue totaled seventy persons—Joseph had remained in Egypt.

Now Joseph died, and all of his brothers, and all of that generation before long.
Yet the Children of Israel bore fruit and swarmed, grew (in number) exceedingly strong.
The land filled up with them. Now a new king arose over Egypt, who'd not known Joseph.
And he said to his people, "Look, these people, these Children of Israel in excess,
They are stronger in number than we are—too strong! Come now, let us deal shrewdly with them,
Otherwise they will increase, and if war occurs, join our enemies whom we condemn,
And they'll make war upon us, escaping the land." So they brought in oppressive taskmasters
To afflict the Israelites with forced labor, hoping these burdens would bring disaster.
They built storage-cities for Pharaoh: Pithom and Raamses. But the more they were oppressed,
The more numerous they became, bursting forth, until the Egyptians were all distressed.
They felt dread of the Children of Israel, so they oppressed them into servitude.
They embittered their lives with harsh labor at mortar and bricks. Crushing labor ensued
In the field. All kinds of subservience made their life bitter, harsh labor the worst.

Now the king of Egypt said to the Hebrews' midwives, (Shiphrah was the name of the first,

And the second was named Puah), "When you help Hebrew women give birth, look at the stone.
If the child on that birthstool is a boy, kill him. But if it's a girl, leave her alone."
But the midwives held God in awe, and they did not do as the king of Egypt commanded.
They let male children live. And so the king of Egypt called for the midwives and demanded,
"Why have you done this thing, letting the children live?" And the midwives replied to Pharaoh,
"Because the Hebrew women are not like Egyptian women. They are vigorous, so,
Before the midwife can reach them, they've given birth." God dealt well with the midwives he saw.
And the people grew many and mighty in number. Since the midwives held God in awe,
He made them households. Then Pharaoh charged all of his people, and this command
    he did give:
"Every son that is born, you shall cast to the Nile, but you shall let every daughter live."

Exodus 2

> Now a daughter of Levi gave birth to a son,
> Whom she put in an ark, which Pharaoh's daughter found.
> She required a nurse, got the mother as one,
> And then named the boy Moses, pulled out and not drowned.
> Moses grew up, and saw the burdens of his brothers.
> He saw an Egyptian man strike a Hebrew,
> So then Moses struck back. He feared he'd be discovered.
> The Israelites prayed for help. God heard, and knew.

Now a man from the house of Levi went and took a daughter of Levi as his wife.
The woman became pregnant and bore a son. When she saw him, and how good was his life,
She hid him, for three months. And when she could no longer hide him, she built him a small ark,
A small basket of wicker reeds, caulked with bitumen and pitch, on which he could embark.
So she placed the child in it, and placed the small ark in the bullreeds on the Nile's shore.
And his sister had stationed herself at a distance, to learn what the boy had in store.
Now Pharaoh's daughter went down to bathe at the Nile, and her maidservants walked beside it.
She saw the small ark among the reeds and sent her maid to fetch it as soon as she'd spied it.
When she opened it, she saw that it was a child. A boy crying, whom she pitied so.
She said, "This must be a Hebrew child." And his sister said to the daughter of Pharaoh,
"Shall I go call a nurse from the Hebrew women who can suckle for you this young child?"
Pharaoh's daughter said, "Yes, go." The maiden went and called the mother of that very child.

Pharaoh's daughter said to her, "Have this child go with you. Take him and then nurse him
    for me.
And I myself will pay you your wages." So the woman took him and nursed him fully.
The child grew, she brought him to Pharaoh's daughter, he became her son. She gave him
    the name:
"Moses" ("He Who Pulls Out"), for she said, "I pulled him out of the water from which he came."
Now some years later, Moses grew up. He went out to his people and witnessed their toil.
He saw an Egyptian striking a Hebrew, one of his people, which made his blood boil.
He turned this way and that way, and since he saw nobody there, struck down the Egyptian,
And hid him in the sand. The next day he went out and saw toughs scuffling—Hebrew men.
So he said to the one in the wrong, "Why do you strike your fellow?" To which he replied,
"Who made you prince and judge of us? Will you kill me as you killed the Egyptian who died?"
Moses became afraid and thought, "Surely the matter is known." And indeed, Pharaoh knew.
Pharaoh heard of the matter and sought to kill Moses, but from Pharaoh's face, Moses flew.
Moses settled in Midian, sat by a well. Now, Midian's priest had seven daughters.
And they came out to draw from the well, fill the troughs, and to give their father's flocks
    some water.
Shepherds came up and drove them away. But Moses rose to their defense, watered their flock.
When they came home to their father Reuel, he said, "Why'd you come home so soon from
    your walk?"
They said, "An Egyptian rescued us from the hand of the shepherds, and he also drew,
Yes, he even drew water for us." He said, "So where is he? Why is he not with you?
Why have you left the man behind? Call him, so that he may share in our bread and our life."
Moses was content to stay with the man who gave him his daughter Zipporah as wife.
She gave birth to a son, and he named him "Gershom" (Or "Sojourner There") For Moses said,
"I've been a sojourner in a foreign land." Many years later, Egypt's king was dead.
The Children of Israel groaned from servitude, and cried out. Their cry from servitude
Came up to God. God heeded their cry, God called to mind the covenants that had accrued.
God remembered his covenant with Abraham, and with Isaac, and with Jacob too.
God saw the Children of Israel, and God took notice of their condition. God knew.

Exodus 3

One day, shepherding, Moses saw a bush aflame.
God called out, "Moses!" Moses replied, "Here I am."
God said, "I've seen your suffering. That's why I came.
Go to Pharaoh, for My people, you will bring them
Out of Egypt." But Moses said, "What will I say
When they ask who is bringing them out of Egypt?"
God said, "I am that I am. This you shall convey.
Egypt's king won't let go, so Egypt shall be stripped."

Moses, while he was keeping and shepherding the flock of Jethro his father-in-law,
Priest of Midian, led the flock behind the wilderness, came to the mountain of God,
To Horeb. The Lord's messenger was seen by him in a flame of fire out of a bush.
He saw the bush aflame, yet it was not consumed by the fire (which is odd for a bush).
Moses said, "Let me turn aside, see this great sight—why the bush does not burn up in flame."
When the Lord saw that he turned aside to see, from the midst of the bush God called his name.
He said, "Moses! Moses!" Moses said, "Here I am." God said, "Don't come closer to this sound,
Remove your sandals from your feet, for the place on which you are standing is holy ground."
God said, "I am the God of your father, the God of Abraham, the God of Isaac,
And the God of Jacob." Moses hid his face, for he was afraid to gaze upon God.
Then the Lord said, "I have seen my people's affliction in Egypt, their cry I have heard
In the face of their taskmasters. Yes, all their sufferings I have known as they occurred.
So I've come down to rescue them from harsh oppression felt under the Egyptians' hand,
To bring them out of that land and into a large and broad and goodly and spacious land.
To a land that is flowing with milk and with honey, to the place of the Canaanites,
Of the Hittites, and the Amorites, of the Perizzites, the Hivvites, and Jebusites.
Now behold, the cry of the Children of Israel has come to me, and I have seen
The oppression with which the Egyptians oppress them. The time has come to intervene.
So now, come, for I will send you to Pharaoh. Bring my people, the Children of Israel,
Out of Egypt." Moses said to God, "Who am I, that I should bring Pharaoh this appeal,
And bring the Children of Israel out of Egypt?" God said, "I will be there with you,
And this shall be your sign I've sent you: when the people have been brought from Egypt by you,
By this mountain you all will serve God." Moses said, "I'll come to the Children of Israel
And I'll say, 'the God of your fathers has sent me to you.' Then they'll ask me to reveal

My Lord's name. They will ask me, 'What is His name' What shall I say to them?" God said
 to Moses,
"EHYEH-ASHER-EHYEH" ("I AM THAT I AM") And God said, "When a man this
 question poses,
You will say this to the Children of Israel: 'EHYEH sends me to you.'" God said further,
"This is what you will say to the Children of Israel: 'the LORD, the God of your fathers,
The God of Abraham, the God of Isaac, and the God of Jacob, sends me to you.'
That is my name forever, that is my memorial for all generations through.
Go and gather the elders of Israel. Say to them: 'the LORD, God of your fathers,
The God of Abraham, of Isaac, and of Jacob, has been seen by me and avers,
"I have taken account of you and noticed what things are done to you now in Egypt,
And I have declared: I will bring you up from Egypt's affliction which now has you gripped,
To the land of the Canaanites, the Hittites, the Amorites, and Perizzites as well,
Of the Hivites, and Jebusites, to a land flowing with milk and honey where you'll dwell.'"
They will heed your voice, and you will come, you and Israel's elders, to see Egypt's king
And say to him, 'the Lord, God of the Hebrews, has met with us, now let us be going,
To journey three days into the wilderness and give offerings to the LORD, our God.'
But I know that Egypt's king will not let you go, even under a strong hand or rod.
So I will send forth my hand and strike Egypt with all my wonders I'll do in its midst.
After that he will let you go. And the good favor of the Egyptians I'll enlist
For this people. When you go, you shall not go empty-handed; For each woman shall take
From her neighbor and the sojourner in her house objects of silver and golden make,
And clothing. They will borrow all these things from the people who are living in Egypt,
And you shall put them on your sons and your daughters, and by this means Egypt will
 be stripped."

Exodus 4

Moses said, "They won't trust me." God said, "See your staff?
Now it is a snake. They will take that as a sign."
Moses said, "I'm no speaker, I'd just make a gaffe."
God said, "Whose power makes speakers of men? It's mine!
So now, go!" Moses said, "Please, choose someone instead."
God said, "You speak to Aaron, he'll speak to the crowd."
And so Moses told Aaron just what God had said,
And then Aaron told all of the people, who bowed.

Moses spoke up and said, "They will not believe me, they won't trust me, my voice they
    won't heed.
Rather, they will say, 'the Lord has not been seen by you!'" The Lord then said to him, "Indeed,
What is that in your hand?" Moses said, "A staff." God said, "Throw it to the ground." So he did.
He threw it on the ground, and it became a snake, and from its face Moses fled and hid.
The Lord said to Moses, "Send forth your hand, seize it by the tail,"—Moses sent his hand out,
Took hold of it, and it became a staff in his fist—"so that they may trust without doubt
That the LORD, God of their fathers, God of Abraham, God of Isaac, God of Jacob,
Has been seen by you." The LORD said further to Moses, "Put your hand into your bosom."
He put it in his bosom, and then took it out, and his hand was as leprous as snow.
Then God said to Moses, "Now put your hand back into your bosom."—And Moses did so.
He put his hand back into his bosom, and when he took it from his bosom once more,
It was no longer leprous, but restored to be like the rest of his flesh, like before.—
"Now if they don't believe you and don't trust the first sign, they will trust in this second sign.
And if they do not trust even those two signs, and do not heed your voice, things will be fine:
You shall then from the Nile take some water, and pour it out on the dry ground with your hand.
And the water you take from the Nile will turn into blood when it falls on the dry land."
Moses said to the LORD, "Please my Lord, I am no man of words, and have never been one,
Neither in the past nor now that you have spoken to your servant. I'm heavy of tongue.
I am slow of speech, slow of mouth, and slow of tongue." The LORD said to him, "Who gives
    man speech?
Who makes one mute or deaf, makes one seeing or blind? Is it not I, the LORD, that does each?
So now, go! I myself will be there with your mouth, and instruct you what you are to speak."
But he said, "Please, my Lord, pray send somebody else." And the LORD's anger flared,
    and was piqued.
He became angry with Moses, and said, "Is there not your brother, Aaron, the Levite?
I know he can speak well, and look, he is coming out to meet you. Once you're in his sight,
His heart will be glad. You shall speak to him, you shall put words in his mouth. I will be there,
With both your mouth and his mouth, and I shall instruct you as to what to do. Have no fear.
He shall speak for you to the people. He shall be a mouth for you, you for him, a god.
And take this rod with you in your hand, with which you shall perform the signs, using this rod."
Moses went back to Jethro his father-in-law, and said, "Pray let me go and return
To my brothers in Egypt, to see whether they're still alive, for I have been concerned."
Jethro said to Moses, "Go in peace." Now the Lord spoke to Moses in Midian and said,
"Go, return to Egypt, for all of the men who were once trying to kill you are dead."
So Moses took his wife and sons, mounted them on an ass, and returned to Egypt's land;
And Moses took the rod of God in his hand. The LORD then gave to Moses this command,
"When you return to Egypt, see that all signs I've put in your hand, you show to Pharaoh.
Yet I will harden his heart, and make it strong-willed, so he will not let the people go.
Then you shall say to Pharaoh, 'the Lord says this: "My son, of firstborn-rank, is Israel.
I said to you, 'let My son go, that he may serve Me,' but you have refused to do well.

If you refuse to let him go, then behold, now I will slay your own son, your firstborn.""

On the way, at the night camp, the LORD met him and sought to make him die before the morn.
So Zipporah took flint and cut off her son's foreskin, then touched it to his legs and said,
"Surely you are a bridegroom of blood to me." And when He released him, then she added,
"You're a bridegroom of blood to me because of the circumcision, that is what I meant."

Now the LORD said to Aaron, "Go out to meet Moses in the wilderness." So he went,
He met him at the mountain of God, and kissed him. Moses told Aaron all the LORD's words
With which he had been sent, and all of the signs with which He had charged Moses.
    Aaron heard.
Moses and Aaron went, gathering all the elders of the Children of Israel.
Aaron spoke all the words the Lord had spoken to Moses, and performed the signs as well,
All in front of the people's eyes. The people trusted, saw that the LORD had taken note
Of the Children of Israel, and had seen their affliction. In homage, they bowed low.

Exodus 5

> After that, Moses and Aaron went to Pharaoh,
> And told him, "The Lord God says: Set my people free!"
> Pharaoh said, "This God you speak of, I do not know.
> I will not let this people go, they work for me."
> Pharaoh told his men angrily, "Make every one
> Of those slaves now work harder, oppressed like a curse."
> Moses came to the Lord and asked, "What have you done?
> Since I've spoken to Pharaoh, things only got worse!"

Afterward, Moses and Aaron came and told Pharaoh, "The Lord God of Israel says:
'let My people go, so they may offer a festival to me in the wilderness.'"
But the Pharaoh said, "Who is the LORD that I should heed his voice and let Israel go?
I do not know the LORD, nor care one whit for this LORD, and I won't let Israel go."
They said, "The God of the Hebrews has met with us; pray let us go for three days' journey
Into the wilderness to give offerings to the LORD our God, lest he be angry,
And confront us with pestilence or sword!" The king of Egypt said to them, "For what reason,
Moses and Aaron, do you take the people from their burdens? I do not find this pleasing.

Now go back to your burdens!" And Pharaoh said, "Too many are the people of the land,
And now you would have them cease from their burdens?" So that day, Pharaoh issued
    a command
To the foremen, the taskmasters, and slave-drivers of the people. He said, "Now, no more.
You shall no longer give straw to the people to make their bricks as you have done before.
Let them gather the straw for themselves. But impose on them still the same quota of bricks.
Don't reduce their burden, for they are lazy, which is why they have cried out with their tricks,
Saying, 'let us go give offerings to our God!' So now, let their labor be more hard.
They will do heavy labor, and so to false words, they will no longer give their regard."
The slave-drivers and foremen of the people went out and said to them, "Pharaoh says this:
I will not give you straw, you must get the straw for yourselves wherever you can find it,
And your work shall not be lightened in the least." The people scattered throughout Egypt's land,
Gleaning stubble for straw. But the taskmasters pressed them, repeating the Pharaoh's command,
"Finish your tasks, each day's work, just as when there was straw." And the Israelites' foremen,
Whom the slave-drivers of Pharaoh had set in place over all their people, were beaten.
The taskmasters told them, "For what reason have you not completed your brick-making work?
Both today and yesterday you failed to produce like before. This task you cannot shirk."
The foremen of the Children of Israel came and cried out to Pharaoh, and they said,
"Why do you do this to your servants? No straw is being given to us, and instead,
They just tell us 'Make bricks!' And your servants are beaten, when it is your people at fault."
He replied, "You are lazy! That is why you say, 'let us go serve the God we exalt.'
So now go, serve your work-duty. No straw will be given to you, yet you must produce
The full quota of bricks!" The foremen of the Israelites suffered from this abuse.
They saw that they were in an ill plight, when they said, "You must still reach each day's
    full brick quota."
(Because to make bricks, first one needs straw, and the Pharaoh was not giving them one iota.)
They met Moses and Aaron, who had set themselves to meet them as they came from Pharaoh.
They said to them, "May the LORD see you and judge you for making the Pharaoh hate us so.
You've made us loathsome to Pharaoh and his servants, giving them a sword with which to
    slay us."
Moses went back to the LORD and said, "O my Lord, why have you brought us harm to
    dismay us?
For what reason have you dealt so ill with this people? For what reason have you sent me?
Since I came to Pharaoh to speak in your name, with this people he has dealt terribly.
And you still have not rescued your people, you have not delivered them and set them free."

Exodus 6

> God told Moses, "See what I do with a strong hand,
> For I am the Lord, seen by your fathers of old.
> I will bring you out from burdens in Egypt's land,
> And deliver you to a new land, as I told
> To Isaac, Jacob, and Abraham long ago."
> Moses spoke to the people, but they paid no heed.
> God told Moses, "Tell Pharaoh: Let My people go!"
> Moses said, "My thick lips can't accomplish this deed."

The Lord said to Moses, "Now you'll see what I will do to Pharaoh, for with a strong hand
I shall make him let them go, and with a strong hand I shall make him drive them from his land."

[Va'eira]

God spoke to Moses and said to him, "I am the Lord, who has been seen by Abraham,
By Isaac, and by Jacob, as El Shaddai, but by my name LORD was not known to them.
I did also establish my covenant with them, to give them the land of Canaan,
The land of their sojournings, where they had sojourned. And I've also heard the moans go on
From the Children of Israel, for the Egyptians are holding them in servitude,
And I have called to mind and remembered my covenant. So tell all Israel's brood:
I am the LORD; I will bring you out from beneath the burdens of Egypt and its harm,
I will deliver you from their servitude, I will redeem you with an outstretched arm,
With great acts of judgment. I will take you to be My people, and I will be your God.
And you shall know that I am the Lord your God, who brings you out from beneath Egypt's rod.
I will bring you into the land which I swore to give to Abraham, Isaac, and Jacob.
I will give it to you for a possession, I the LORD." But when these words Moses spake of
To the Children of Israel, they did not heed him, their spirits by labor brought low.
The Lord spoke to Moses and said, "Go in, and tell Pharaoh king of Egypt to let go
The Children of Israel from his land." Moses spoke before the Lord, appealing, "Here,
If the Israelites did not heed me, how will Pharaoh heed me, with my speech unclear?"
The LORD spoke to Moses and to Aaron, and charged them concerning the Israelites
And Pharaoh king of Egypt, to bring the Israelites from Egypt's land, and their plight.

These are the heads of their fathers' houses: The sons of Reuben, firstborn of Israel:
Enoch and Pallu, Hezron and Carmi; those are Reuben's clan-families as they are hailed.

And the sons of Simeon: Jemuel, Jamin, and Ohad, Jachin, and Zohar, and Saul
(The son of a Canaanite woman); those are the clan-families of Simeon, all.
These are the names of the sons of Levi according to their generations: Gershon,
Kehath, and Merari. LevI's life for one hundred and thirty-seven years went on.
The sons of Gershon: Libni and Shimei, by their clans. And the sons of Kehath: Amram,
Izhar, Hebron, and Uzziel; And Kehath had one hundred and thirty-three years lifespan.
The sons of Merari: Mahli and Mushi. These, the Levite clans by generation.
Amram took for himself as wife his aunt Jochebed, who bore him Moses and Aaron.
The years of Amram's life were one hundred and thirty-seven years. These are Izhar's sons:
Korah, Nepheg, and Zichri. And the sons of Uzziel: Mishael, Sithri, and Elzaphan.
Aaron took to wife Elisheba, daughter of Amminadab, sister of Nahshon.
She bore him Nadab and Abihu, and Eleazar and Ithamar. Now Korah's sons:
Assir, Elkanah, and Abiasaph. Those are the families of the Korahites.
Eleazar son of Aaron took for himself one of Putiel's daughters as a wife.
She bore him Phinehas. These are the heads of the fathers' houses of Levites by clan.
That's the same Aaron and Moses to whom the Lord said, "Bring the Israelites from that land,
Bring them forth from the land of Egypt, troop by troop." It was they who had spoke to Pharaoh
Egypt's king, to bring the Israelites out of Egypt, that Moses and Aaron we know.
So it happened that on the day when the Lord spoke to Moses in the land of Egypt,
He said to Moses, "I am the Lord; you shall speak to Pharaoh Egypt's king with your lips
All that I speak to you." But Moses then appealed before the Lord, and said, "Here, see,
If I am of impeded lips and unclear speech (which I am), how will Pharaoh heed me?"

Exodus 7

> The Lord told Moses, "Pharaoh won't listen to you,
> So have Aaron drop his staff; I'll make it a snake."
> But then Egypt's magicians did this same thing too.
> The Lord said, "I will strike every river and lake,
> Turning water to blood." Aaron raised his staff high,
> And God did this. But Pharaoh's strong will would not bend.
> God said, "Tell Pharaoh to free My people, or I
> Will cause swarms of frogs into your land to ascend."

The Lord said to Moses, "See, I will place you in the role of a god to the Pharaoh,
And your brother Aaron will be your prophet. You shall speak all I command you, and so

Aaron your brother shall speak it all to Pharaoh, so that he will let go from his land
All the Children of Israel. But I will harden his heart; he won't heed your command.
I will make My signs and wonders many in the land of Egypt, yet Pharaoh won't heed,
So I will set My hand over Egypt, and bring out My forces, My people, My breed,
The Children of Israel, from Egypt with great acts of judgment; All Egypt shall know
That I am the Lord, when I stretch My hand out over Egypt so My people may go,
And bring out the Children of Israel from their midst." Moses and Aaron did as told,
As the Lord has commanded them, they did. Now at this time, Moses was eighty years old,
Aaron was eighty-three years old, when they spoke to the Pharaoh. The Lord said to Aaron,
And to Moses, "When Pharaoh tells you, 'Produce a miracle.' Then you'll say to Aaron,
'take your staff and throw it down before Pharaoh, so that it shall turn into a serpent.'"
Moses and Aaron came to Pharaoh, they did as the Lord commanded, in all extents.
Aaron threw down his staff before Pharaoh and his servants, and it turned into a snake.
Pharaoh called for his wise-men and sorcerers, so that a similar sign they could make.
So in turn, the Egyptian magicians did the same, with their occult arts and their spells.
Each one of them threw down their staffs and their rods, and then these turned into serpents
    as well.
But the staff of Aaron swallowed up their staffs. Yet strong-willed and hard remained
    Pharaoh's heart.
And Pharaoh did not heed Moses and Aaron, just as the Lord had spoken at the start.

The Lord said to Moses, "Pharaoh's heart is stubborn, he will not let the people go free.
Go to Pharaoh in the morning as he goes out to the Nile, and wait where he will be,
By the shore of the Nile. And take you the staff that has changed into a snake in your hand.
Then say to him, 'the Lord, the God of the Hebrews, has sent me to you with this command:
"Let My people go, so that they may serve Me in the wilderness." But you've paid no heed.
You have not listened so far. The Lord says, "You shall know that I am the Lord by this deed."
See, I will strike the Nile's water with the staff in my hand; And into blood it will change.
And the fish in the Nile will all die. And the Nile will reek with a stink both foul and strange.
The Egyptians will no more be able to drink the water of the Nile without harm.'"
The Lord said to Moses, "Say to Aaron: Take your staff, and stretch out your hand and your arm
Over the waters of Egypt, over their rivers, over their canals, and their ponds,
Over all of their bodies of water, and let them become blood, and waters beyond.
There will be blood throughout all the land of Egypt, even in vessels of stone and wood."
Moses and Aaron did just as the Lord commanded them. He raised the staff where he stood
And struck the water in the Nile, before the eyes of the Pharaoh and all of his servants,
And then all of the water that was in the Nile turned to blood, underneath their observance.
All the fish that were in the Nile died, the Nile reeked, the Egyptians couldn't drink from
    the Nile;
For there was blood throughout the whole land of Egypt, and the waters had turned red and vile.

But then Egypt's magicians produced the same thing with occult-arts and spells they invoked.
And the heart of Pharaoh remained stubborn and strong-willed, not heeding them, as the
    Lord spoke.
So Pharaoh turned and went into his palace, paying no attention to even this.
But all Egypt had to dig around the Nile for water, since its waters were amiss.
They could not drink from the waters of the Nile. Seven days passed once the Lord struck
    the Nile,
Then the Lord said to Moses, "Go tell Pharaoh, 'let My people go, else I'll get hostile.
Send them free to go worship Me. If you refuse, I shall plague your whole country with frogs.
The whole Nile will be swarming with frogs, they will come up into your house, denser than fog,
They shall enter your bedroom, your bed, and climb into the houses of all your servants,
Into your people's houses, your ovens, your kneading bowls, and even into your pants.
Onto you, onto your people, onto all of your servants will this frog plague ascend.'"

Exodus 8

> Pharaoh told Moses and Aaron, "Please ask the Lord
> To remove all these frogs; I'll let your people go!"
> So God caused the removal of all the frog-horde,
> But when Pharaoh saw he could breathe, then he said, "No."
> God had Aaron make gnats from the dust and the sand,
> A feat Egypt's magicians could not replicate.
> Then God sent insect swarms throughout all Egypt's land,
> Except Goshen, where His people had their estate.

The Lord said to Moses, "Say to Aaron, 'stretch out your hand with your staff, let it extend
Over the rivers, the canals, and the ponds, and bring up frogs on the land of Egypt.'"
Aaron stretched out his hand over Egypt's waters (the hand in which Aaron's rod was gripped),
And the frog-horde ascended and covered the land of Egypt. Now all Egypt's magicians
Did the same with their spells, making frogs ascend on Egypt's land in its froggy condition.
Pharaoh had Moses and Aaron summoned, and said, "Plead with the Lord to remove the frogs,
From both me and my people, and I shall let his people go free, no more to be flogged,
So that they may go sacrifice offerings to the Lord." And Moses said to Pharaoh,
"Have this triumph over me: You may choose when I plead with the Lord to make the frogs go.
When shall I plead for you, for your servants, for your people, to have the frogs leave from you,
And your houses, so that they'll remain only in the Nile?" He said, "Tomorrow will do."

Moses said, "As you say, then, so that you will know that there is none like the Lord our God.
The frogs shall be removed from you, from your houses, from your servants, and land where
      they trod,
They shall leave from the people and only remain in the Nile." Moses and Aaron went
From the presence of Pharaoh, and Moses cried out to the Lord of the predicament
Of the frogs which He had afflicted on Pharaoh. The Lord acted by Moses's words:
The frogs died away, from the houses, from the courtyards, and from the fields out near the herds.
So they piled them up in heaps, till the land stank, but when Pharaoh saw the worst was through,
He made his heart both heavy and stubborn, and would not heed them, as God said he would do.

The Lord said to Moses, "Say to Aaron, 'stretch out your staff and strike the dust of the land,
It will become gnats throughout the land of Egypt.'" They did so. Aaron stretched out his hand
With his staff, and he struck the dust of the ground and the gnats came upon man and on beast;
All the dust of the earth became gnats throughout all of Egypt, from the west to the east.
The magicians attempted to do the same, to bring forth gnats with their spells, but could not.
Gnats were on man and beast. The magicians said to Pharaoh, "This is the finger of God!"
But Pharaoh's heart remained strong-willed, and he did not heed them, just as the Lord
      had foretold.
The Lord said to Moses, "Rise early in the morning, and go stand before the Pharaoh,
As he goes out to the water, and say to him, 'thus says the Lord: Let My people go,
So that they may serve Me. If you do not let My people free, I will send swarms of flies,
Upon you, on your servants, and upon your people and your houses, till they cloud your eyes.
The houses of Egypt shall be full of the insects, along with the ground where they stand.
But on that day I will set apart the region of Goshen, which is My people's land,
So that there will be no insects there, so that you may know in this land, I am the Lord.
I will put a distinction between My people and your people which can't be ignored.
On the morrow this sign shall occur.'" The Lord did so, and swarms came into Pharaoh's palace,
Into his servant's houses, and throughout all Egypt, the land suffered from insects' malice.
Pharaoh had Moses and Aaron summoned and said, "Go slaughter to your God in the land."
Moses said, "It would not be right to do this, since the Egyptians would not understand.
Since what we slaughter as offerings is abominable to the Egyptian mind,
If we slaughtered these offerings in their sight that displeased them, then they might be inclined
To stone us. Let us go three days' journey into the wilderness, and we'll slaughter there,
Giving offerings to the Lord our God, as he has commanded us. This would be fair."
Pharaoh said, "I will let you go sacrifice to the Lord your God in the wilderness,
Only don't go too far. Plead for me." Moses said, "Once I leave you, the Lord I'll address.
I will plead with the Lord that the swarms of insects leave Pharaoh and his people tomorrow,
Only let not Pharaoh be deceitful with us again, keeping us here with great sorrow,
And not letting the people go sacrifice to the Lord." Moses left from Pharaoh's presence,
And then pleaded with God. The Lord acted by Moses's words, removed insects unpleasant.
He removed them from Pharaoh, from servants, from his people, not one remained to cause woe.
But Pharaoh's heart was heavy and stubborn once more, and he would not let the people go.

Exodus 9

> God told Moses, "Tell Pharaoh: Let My people go!
> Otherwise, all the Egyptian cattle will die."
> Pharaoh's heart remained stubborn, and still he said no,
> Even when plagued with boils, he just would not comply.
> So the Lord sent down hail, across all Egypt's land,
> Striking all the men, cattle, and crops in the field.
> Pharaoh said, "I was wrong! I will heed your command!"
> But as soon as the hail stopped, Pharaoh would not yield.

The Lord told Moses, "Go to Pharaoh and tell him, 'thus says the Lord, God of the Hebrews:
Let My people go, so that they may worship Me. And if to send them free, you refuse,
And continue to hold them, the Lord's hand will fall upon all your livestock in the fields—
On the horses, donkeys, camels, oxen, and sheep—with a pestilence that will not yield.
And the Lord will distinguish between the livestock of Israel and that of Egypt,
So that nothing belonging to Israel dies while the fields are by pestilence gripped.'"
The Lord set a fixed time, saying, "On the morrow, the Lord will do this thing in the land."
The Lord did so the next day, all Egypt's livestock died, while Israel's continued to stand.
Now when Pharaoh sent inquiries, he learned not one of Israel's livestock was laid low,
But his heart remained heavy with stubbornness, and so he did not let the people go.

The Lord said to Moses and to Aaron, "Take handfuls of soot from a furnace. Let Moses
Toss it into the sky, before Pharaoh's eyes, it shall become fine-dust that it exposes.
It shall be a fine-dust over all Egypt's land, and on man and beast will become boils,
And the boils shall sprout into blisters all throughout Egypt, afflicting them at their toils."
They took soot from a furnace, and stood before Pharaoh, and Moses tossed it to the sky;
It became boils which sprouted on man and on beast. The magicians who were standing by
Were unable to stand before Moses because of the boils on them and all Egypt.
But the Lord hardened Pharaoh's heart, and he did not heed them, just as was in the Lord's script.
The Lord said to Moses, "Early in the morning, place yourself before Pharaoh and say,
'thus says the Lord, the God of the Hebrews: Let My people go, to serve Me in their way.
For this time I will send my plagues against your heart, against your people, and servants too,
So that you may know that there is none like Me in all the earth, that could do what I do.
For by now I could have sent forth My hand and struck you and your people with pestilence,
And you would have vanished from the land; Yet I've spared you just so you could see
   My portents,

And in order that My name might be declared through all the earth. And yet you still cause sorrow
With your thwarting My people, not letting them go. So you shall see, at this time tomorrow,
I will rain down a hail that's exceedingly heavy, like none that has ever been seen
In the land of Egypt from the day it was founded until now. Send word by all means
To give refuge to your livestock and all of yours in the fields; for all beasts and all men
Who are found outside and not bought indoors to shelter shall have the hail rained upon them,
And they will die.'" Whoever feared the Lord among Pharaoh's servants fled quickly inside,
With their own servants and livestock, but those who ignored the Lord left their holdings outside.
The Lord said to Moses, "Stretch your hand to the sky, let hail fall upon all Egypt's land,
Both on man and on beast, and on all of the plants of the field that in Egypt now stand."
Moses held out his staff to the sky, and the Lord sent forth thunder, and hail, and fire.
Fire streamed to the ground as the Lord rained down hail upon Egypt's land, in his great ire.
There was hail, with fire flashing amidst all the hail, as it heavily rained to the earth,
A hailstorm the like of which had never been in all Egypt since the day of its birth.
Throughout all of Egypt, hail struck down all that was in the open fields, from man to beast;
All the plants of the field were struck by hail as well, and the trees were shattered and deceased.
Only in the region of Goshen, where the Children of Israel were, was no hail.
Pharaoh sent for Moses and Aaron and said to them, "This time I have sinned, I have failed.
The Lord is in the right, and both I and my people are in the wrong. Plead with the Lord!
For there has been enough of God's thunder and this hail. I'll let you go, you have my word,
Stay here no longer." Moses said to him, "Once I leave the city, I'll spread out my hands
To the Lord, and the thunder and hail will stop, so you may know that the Lord rules this land.
But I know that both you and your servants still do not stand in fear before the Lord God."
(Now the flax and the barley were ruined, for the barley was in ears, the flax in the bud,
But the wheat and the rye were not stricken, for they ripen late. This fact can't be ignored.)
Moses left Pharaoh, going outside of the city, and spread out his hands to the Lord:

So the thunder and hail stopped, the rain no more poured down on earth, but then when Pharaoh saw
That the rain and the hail and the thunder had ceased, he continued to sin like before.
He made his heart hard and stubborn, his and his servants'. His heart's strong will would not be broken,
And he did not let the Children of Israel go, just as God (through Moses) had spoken.

Exodus 10

The Lord told Moses, "Go forth to Pharaoh again,
Who has hardened his heart so I may show my signs."
Moses and Aaron told Pharaoh, "Send free our men,
Or a great swarm of locusts shall cloud your designs."
When the locusts came, Pharaoh said, "Pardon my sin!
Have the Lord your God blow all these locusts away!"
God did so, but Pharaoh once more thickened his skin.
Then God sent darkness, which was received the same way.

[Bo]

The Lord said to Moses, "Go to Pharaoh, for I have made his heart hard with stubbornness,
And made his servants' hearts heavy and stubborn also, in order that I may impress
These signs of Mine upon them, and in order that you may tell to the ears of your son,
And your son's son how I have made sport of Egypt, and all the wonders which I have done.
You shall tell of the signs that I have placed upon them, so that you know I am the Lord."
Moses and Aaron went to Pharaoh, and then said to him, "These are the words of the Lord,
The God of the Hebrews: How long will you refuse to come humble yourself before Me?
Let My people go, so that they may serve Me. For if you still refuse to send them free,
On the morrow, I shall bring the locust-horde into your land, covering the ground's face
So that no one will be able to see the ground, they'll consume what few plants have escaped,
They'll destroy what survived from the hail, they'll consume all the trees that now grow in
    the field,
They will fill your house, your servants' houses, all houses in Egypt, and they will not yield.
It shall be a plague as your fathers never saw, nor your fathers' fathers in their day,
From their first day on earth until now." With that, Moses left Pharaoh, and went on his way.
Pharaoh's servants said to him, "How long shall this one be a snare to us? Let the men go,
So that they may serve the Lord their God. Can't you see that Egypt is lost? Don't you yet know?"
Moses and Aaron were brought back to Pharaoh, who said to them, "Go serve the Lord
    your God—
Who are the ones to go?" Moses said, "With our young ones, with our elders we go to God,
With our sons, with our daughters, with our sheep and oxen, we will go to worship the Lord,
For we all must observe the Lord's festival." Pharaoh told them, "Oh, you'll be with the Lord,
As soon as I let you all go with your children—which I won't. You have evil intent.
I can see on your faces that you want to leave. Well, you can't, you don't have my consent.

So now go, all you males, and just males, to worship the Lord, for that is what you desire."
And they were expelled from Pharaoh's presence, without the leave that they had come to acquire.

The Lord told Moses, "Stretch out your hand over the land of Egypt for the locust-horde,
And it will ascend over the land of Egypt, eating all plants the hail has ignored."
Moses stretched out his staff over Egypt's land, and the Lord led in a wind from the east
To blow against the land all that day and all night, until morning when it finally ceased,
Having borne in the horde of locusts. They ascended upon all the land of Egypt,
Settling in an exceedingly dense cloud by which all Egypt's territory was gripped.
There had never before been a locust-horde like it, and never would be one again.
They hid the ground from view, so the ground became dark. They consumed all the plants
    of the land;
All the fruit of the trees that the hail had not killed were consumed, 'til no green thing remained,
Neither of tree, or plant, or the grass of the field, in all the land under Egypt's reign.
In haste, Pharaoh had Moses and Aaron summoned, and said to them, "I've sinned by this crime,
Sinned against the Lord your God, and also against you. So pray, bear my sin this one time.
Forgive my offense, and plead with the Lord your God, only to remove this death from me."
He went out from Pharaoh and pleaded with the Lord, who reversed a strong wind from the sea,
Causing the wind to shift to a strong west sea wind which bore all of the locusts away
Into the Sea of Reeds, until not one locust remained in Egypt's land on that day.
But the Lord hardened Pharaoh's heart, and he did not let the Children of Israel go.

The Lord said to Moses, "Stretch your hand towards the sky, and let there be a darkness below
Over all the land of Egypt; this darkness they will feel!" Moses reached out towards the sky,
And there was gloomy darkness throughout all of Egypt for three days, clouding every eye
So a man could not see his brother, nor get up from his spot, yet where Israel dwelled,
There was light. Pharaoh had Moses called and said, "Go serve the Lord, just beasts
    will be withheld.
Only your sheep and oxen shall be left behind, even your children may go with you."
Moses said, "You must also give us sacrifices and offerings. This will not do.
We need them to offer to our Lord; even our livestock must go with us. Not one hoof
May remain behind; for from them we select offerings for our Lord, thus my reproof.
We do not know with what we will worship the Lord until the moment that we arrive."
But the Lord hardened Pharaoh's heart, so he would not let them go, even though hard
    they strived.
Pharaoh said to him, "Be gone from my sight! And take care you do not see my face again,
For on that day, you'll die." Moses said, "As you say, I shall never see your face again."

Exodus 11

The Lord told Moses, "One more plague I bring Pharaoh,
After which, he will set you free, and drive you out.
Tell the people to get gold from neighbors they know."
Moses told them the Lord's words, since he was devout.
He told them, "God has said: In the midst of the night,
All the firstborn of Egypt, from Pharaoh to maid,
They shall die. But your own firstborn shall be alright,
And by this shall my portents and signs be displayed.

The Lord said to Moses, "I shall bring one more plague upon Egypt and upon Pharaoh;
After that he will send you free from here, and it will be finished when he lets you go.
He will drive you out one and all. Now, pray speak in the ears of the people, that they ask,
Each man of his neighbor and each woman of hers, gold and silver objects for our task."
And the Lord gave the people favor in the eyes of Egypt, and Moses also
Was regarded as great in Egypt, in the eyes of the people and slaves of Pharaoh.
Moses said, "The Lord says: At midnight I will go forth throughout the midst of Egypt's lands,
And all firstborn shall die throughout Egypt, from firstborn of Pharaoh who sits in command
On his throne, to the firstborn of the slave girl behind the mill, to all firstborn of beasts.
All firstborn shall die, causing a cry throughout Egypt such as has never been released,
And the like of which shall never be heard again. But against the Children of Israel,
Not dog shall be sharp of tongue, against a man or beast, so that you may see it revealed,
And that you may know that the Lord makes between Israel and Egypt differentiation.
Then all these servants of yours shall come down to me, and bow down to me on that occasion,
Saying, 'Go out, you and all who follow you.' And after that I will indeed go out."
He went out from Pharaoh's presence in flaming anger. The Lord said to Moses, "Have no doubt,
Pharaoh will not heed you, so that my portents may throughout Egypt's land be multiplied."
Now both Moses and Aaron had performed all these wonders where by Pharaoh they were spied,
But the Lord had made Pharaoh's heart heavy with stubbornness, not heeding Moses's demand,
And so Pharaoh still would not let the Children of Israel go free out of his land.

Exodus 12

The Lord said, "On the tenth day of this month, prepare.
Slay a lamb, dab the blood on the posts of your door.
Eat just matzot (unleavened bread), and then beware,
For you're eating a Passover meal to the Lord.
That night, I shall go through Egypt slaying firstborn,
But the blood is a sign; I'll pass over those dwellings."
The Lord did so that night. Egypt cried out, forlorn.
The Israelites ran. (Bread had no time for swelling.)

The Lord said to Moses and to Aaron in the land of Egypt, "Let this month (Nisan)
And its new moon be for you the beginning of months, first of the year as time goes on.
Tell all Israel's community that on the tenth of this month, ten days from new moon,
Each of them shall take one lamb per family, one lamb per household to be used as a boon.
Now if there are too few in the house for a lamb, then you'll share with a neighbor next door
By accounting for the number of persons, each by how much lamb you can eat, no more.
A hale and hearty unblemished lamb shall be yours, a yearling, taken from goats and sheep,
And until the fourteenth day after this new moon, it shall be yours in safety to keep.
Then the whole of Israel's community shall slaughter their lambs in evening's twilight.
They shall take some of the blood and put it on the lintel, and both doorposts, left and right,
Of the houses in which they will eat it. And on that same night, all the flesh they shall eat,
Roasted in fire, with matzot (unleavened bread) and with bitter herbs. But I repeat,
Do not eat any of it raw, or boiled in water, but all roasted over a fire,
From its head to its legs to its innards, all parts of it must be consumed in the pyre.
You are not to leave any over until morning. What's left in the morning you shall burn.
This is how you shall eat it: Your hips girded for travel, sandals on your feet in turn,
And your staves in your hand; and you shall eat it in haste—a Passover meal to the Lord.
I will proceed through the land of Egypt that night and strike down in Egypt all firstborn,
From man to beast, and on all the gods of Egypt I shall render judgment, I the Lord.
Now the blood shall be a sign for you on the houses where you are, and serve as a ward:
When I see the blood, I will pass over you, the plague will not fall upon you to slay,
When I strike down the land of Egypt. This day shall be for you a memorial day:
You shall celebrate it as a festival to the Lord throughout your generations,
As a law for the ages you'll celebrate it. Seven days, you'll eat bread unleavened,
On the very first day you'll remove all leaven from your houses, for whoever eats
Anything leavened, from the first day to the seventh, shall be cut off from Israel's fleet.

And on the first day, a holy convocation, one for you on the seventh day too,
No kind of work shall be done then, only food to be eaten may be prepared by you.
And keep the Festival of Matzot, for on this same day, I have brought your forces out
From the land of Egypt. Keep this day through the ages as a law to follow throughout.
In the first month, on the fourteenth day of the month, at sunset, you are to eat matzot,
Until the twenty-first day of the month at sunset. For seven days, no leavened mote
Is to be found in your houses, for whosoever eats what is leavened, that person
Shall be cut off from Israel's community, whether sojourner or native son.
Anything that is leavened you shall not eat; In all your dwellings you shall eat matzot."
Moses had all the elders of Israel called and said to all of them, "Now, take note:
Pick out lambs for yourselves according to clan, and slaughter the Passover offering.
Then take a bunch of hyssop, dip it in the blood in the basin, and then do this thing:
Touch the lintel and two doorposts with some of the blood in the basin. Not one of you
Is to go out from the entrance of your house until morning. For the Lord will pass through
To smite the Egyptians, and when He sees blood on the lintel and posts, He will pass over
The entrance, and not let the Destroyer enter your house to slay you. He will pass over.
You are to keep this rite as a law for you and your children, for all ages preserve it.
When you enter the land which the Lord will give you, as He promised, then you shall observe it.
And when your children ask you, 'What does this service mean to you?' Then you'll say in reply,
'It is the Passover sacrifice to the Lord, Who passed over the houses, passed by
The houses of the Children of Israel in Egypt, when the Egyptians he slew,
But he saved our houses.'" Then the people bowed low in homage, as they were meant to do.
And the Children of Israel went and did so, according to what the Lord commanded.
As He had commanded Moses and Aaron, so they did, just as the Lord demanded.

Now it was in the middle of the night that the Lord struck down all of Egypt's firstborn,
From the firstborn of Pharaoh who sits on his throne to the low dungeon captive's firstborn,
And each and every firstborn of beast. Pharaoh rose at night, he and all his courtiers,
And all of Egypt. For there was no house in which the death of someone did not occur.
Pharaoh had Moses and Aaron called in the night, and said, "Arise, depart and go out
From the midst of my people, both you and the Children of Israel, go be devout.
Go serve the Lord according to your words. Take your flocks and herds, as you said, just begone!
And even bring a blessing on me!" The Egyptians then strongly urged the people on,
To send them out in haste from the land and make them leave, for they said, "We are all
    dead men!"
So the people took their dough before it was leavened, their kneading-bowls bound up with them
In their clothing, upon their shoulders. Now the Israelites had done Moses's bidding,
They had asked of the Egyptians objects of silver and gold, and clothing that was fitting.
The Lord had given the people favor in the eyes of the Egyptians. And Egypt
Let themselves be asked of, and gave what was requested. And so the Egyptians were stripped.

The Israelites journeyed from Raamses to Succoth, near six hundred thousand on foot,
(That's just menfolk, and not counting children). A riffraff had also gone with them afoot,
And some sheep and some oxen, an exceedingly heavy amount of livestock it was.
Now they baked the dough which they had brought out of Egypt into cakes of matzot because
It had not leavened, since they had been driven out of Egypt, and they could not delay;
Nor had they prepared any provisions for themselves, because haste had carried the day.
The time that the Israelites had lived in Egypt was four hundred and thirty years.
At the end of those four hundred and thirty years, to the day, the Lord's force disappeared.
The Lord's forces all went out from the land of Egypt, a watch-keeping night for the Lord,
To bring them out of Egypt; that same night is still the night of watch-keeping for the Lord
Over all of the Children of Israel, throughout all the generations of Israel.
And the Lord said to Moses and to Aaron, "This is the law of the Passover meal:
Any foreign son is not to eat of it, but any man's servant which he has bought—
Provided he is circumcised, he may eat it. But a settler and hired-hand may not.
In one house it is to be eaten, you are not to bring any of the flesh outside,
And you are not to break a bone of it. By these laws, all of Israel must abide.
Now when a sojourner sojourns with you, and would make the Passover meal to the Lord,
Every male with him must be circumcised, then he may come near to offer in accord,
And will be regarded as a native of the land. But no foreskinned man may eat it.
One Instruction shall serve for the native and for the stranger who sojourns in your midst.
All the Children of Israel did so, as the Lord commanded Moses and Aaron,
So they did. It was on the same day, when the Lord freed the Israelites, every one,
From the land of Egypt by their forces. On that day when the bringing out had been done,

Exodus 13

The Lord told Moses, "Hallow to me each firstborn."
Moses told all the people, "Remember this day.
The Lord brought you from Egypt, and as He has sworn,
Brings you into a land filled with plenty, to stay.
For a week, you shall eat matzot, nothing fermented.
The firstborn beasts, you shall redeem every one.
By a lamb, firstborn donkeys can be represented,
And headbands shall help redeem each firstborn son.

The Lord spoke to Moses and said, "Hallow to me every firstborn, each breacher of womb
Among the Children of Israel, of man or beast, it is mine regardless of whom."

Moses said to the people, "Remember this day, on which you came out from Egypt's land,
From a house of bondage, how the Lord freed you from it by the force of a mighty hand,
And brought you out from here. No leavened bread may be eaten. Today you are going free,
In the new moon of the month of Ripe-Grain ("Abib", or later "Nisan") And it shall be,
When the Lord has brought you into the land of the Canaanites, Hittites, and Amorites,
Of the Hivites and Jebusites, which He swore to your fathers to give you by all rights,
A land flowing with milk and honey, then at the month's new moon you must act in accord:
Seven days you shall eat matzot, and on the seventh day, a festival to the Lord.
Matzot are to be eaten for the seven days; nothing leavened shall be seen with you,
Throughout all of your territory. And you shall tell your son on that day what you do,
Telling him, 'It is because of what the Lord did for me, when I went out of Egypt.'
It shall be a sign on your hand, and a reminder between your eyes of the Lord's script—
In order that the Lord's teachings and law may be in your mouth—that with a mighty hand
The Lord brought you out of Egypt. You are to keep this law at the set-times that are planned
And appointed, from year to year. When the Lord brings you to the land of the Canaanites,
As He swore to you and to your fathers, and gives it to you, then you shall do these rites:
You are to transfer each breacher of a womb to the Lord, all of your owned beasts' firstlings,
The males are for the Lord. Every firstling ass you shall redeem with a lamb that you bring;
If you do not redeem it, then break its neck. And every firstborn of men, of your sons,
You are to redeem. And when in time your child asks of you, "What does this mean?"
 Your response
Shall be this: "With a mighty hand the Lord brought us out of Egypt, the house of bondage.
When Pharaoh would not let us go, stubbornly would not send us free, then the Lord, as judge,
Killed every firstborn throughout the land of Egypt, the firstborn both of beast and of man.
Therefore I myself sacrifice every male firstling to the Lord. And as for my clan,
Every firstborn among my sons I redeem. So it shall be as a mark on your hand
And as headbands or symbols between your eyes on your forehead, that with a mighty hand,
The Lord brought us out of Egypt."

[Beshalach]

      Now it was, when Pharaoh had sent all the people free,
That God did not lead them by the way of the Philistines' land, although nearer it be.
For God said to Himself, "What if the people see war, and then have a quick change of heart,
And return to Egypt!" So God had them progress on a roundabout path from the start,
By way of the wilderness at the Sea of Reeds (which is now known as the Red Sea).
And the Children of Israel went up from Egypt's land , all armed and battle-ready.
Now Moses had taken Joseph's bones with him, for he had made the Israelites swear,
By an oath saying, "God will take account of you, so carry my bones with you from here."
They moved on from Succoth and encamped at Etham at the edge of the vast wilderness.
The Lord went before them by day in a cloud column to lead the way. In night's darkness,

In a pillar of fire, to give them light, so they could travel by both day and night.
And the cloud pillar by day, and the pillar of fire by night didn't leave the people's sight.

Exodus 14

God told Moses, "Tell your people: Go to the sea.
The Egyptians will think you are trapped, and give chase."
The Israelites asked Moses, "Why'd we go free?
Better to be Egypt's slaves than die in this place."
Moses raised his hand, and the Lord parted the seas;
The Israelites fled on the strip of dry land.
The Egyptians gave chase, but were brought to their knees
As the waters returned when Moses raised his hand.

The Lord said to Moses, "Tell the Children of Israel to turn back, not to go on,
And encamp before Pi-ha-hiroth, between Migdol and the sea, before Baal-zephon;
Opposite it you shall encamp, by the sea, facing it. As for Pharaoh, he will say
Of the Children of Israel, 'they are confused in the land, they have now gone astray.
The wilderness has closed them in.' I shall harden Pharaoh's heart so he will pursue them,
And I will gain glory over Pharaoh and all of his army, so the Egyptians
Will know that I am the Lord." And they did so. Now when the king of Egypt was informed
That the people had fled, Pharaoh's heart (and his servants') had changed in regards to
    their swarm.
They said, "What is this that we have done, that we have let Israel go from servitude?"
He had his chariot harnessed, and took his fighting-men with him, and as he pursued,
He took six hundred picked chariots, and all chariots in Egypt that were equipped,
Officers riding all of them. Now the Lord made the heart of Pharaoh, king of Egypt,
Stubborn so that he pursued the Children of Israel, as they departed boldly.
The Egyptians pursued them, and chased them, and then overtook them encamped by the sea.
All the chariot-horses of Pharaoh, his horsemen, his army, by Pi-ha-hiroth,
Before Baal-zephon. As Pharaoh drew near, the Israelites to receive him were loath.
They caught sight of Egypt chasing after them, and were afraid, and cried out to the Lord.
They said to Moses, "Were there no graves in Egypt, so that we must die here from their horde?
Is that why you have taken us into the wilderness? Look what you have done to us
By your bringing us out of Egypt. Did we not while in Egypt explain to you thus,
Saying, 'leave us alone, so that we can serve Egypt! For, better to be Egypt's slaves
Than to die in the wilderness!'" But Moses said to the people, "Do not be afraid.

Stand fast and see the deliverance of the Lord which he will work for you on this day,
For the Egyptians whom you can see now you shall never see again after today.
The Lord will battle for you; you hold your peace." The Lord said to Moses, "Why do you cry
Out to me? Tell the Children of Israel to march forward. And you, hold your staff high,
Stretch your hand over the sea and split it, so that the Israelites may all come through,
Through the midst of the sea, upon dry land. But I will harden Egypt's heart, so they too
Will go in to the sea after them. And I shall gain glory through Pharaoh and his horde,
And his chariots and his riders; then the Egyptians shall know that I am the Lord,
When I gain glory over Pharaoh, and his chariots and riders." God's messenger
That had been going before the camp of Israel moved to follow behind where they were,
And the pillar of cloud moved from in front of them to behind them, between the two camps
Of Egypt and Israel. A cloud of darkness for Egypt, but for Israel, a lamp.
Here it lit up the night, so the two camps did not come near one another through the night.
Moses stretched his hand out over the sea, and the Lord caused it to go back with his might,
With a fierce east wind that blew all night, making the sea into firm ground. The waters split.
The Children of Israel came into the midst of the sea on dry land due to it,
The waters as a wall on their right and their left. But the Egyptians came in pursuit,
Into the sea after them. All of Pharaoh's horses, chariots, and riders to boot.
Now at daybreak's watch, the Lord looked down on Egypt's army from His pillar of cloud fire,
And He panicked the camp of Egypt, loosening all their chariot wheels and tires,
So they drove much slower. The Egyptians said, "Let us flee from the Israelites,
For the Lord makes war for them against us Egyptians, and we cannot conquer His might."
Then the Lord said to Moses, "Stretch your hand over the sea, and the waters shall return
Upon Egypt, on its chariots, and upon its riders." Moses then took his turn,
Stretching his hand over the sea, and at daybreak, the sea returned to its normal state.
And the Egyptians fled at the sea's approach, but the Lord routed them to their wet fate.
The waters returned, covering the chariots and the riders and all Pharaoh's force
That had followed the Israelites to the sea. Not even one remained, in due course.
But the Children of Israel marched through the sea on dry ground, waters for them a wall
On their right and their left. So the Lord on that day from Egypt delivered Israel.
Israel saw Egypt dead by the seashore, and the Lord's might against them which did thus.
The people held the Lord in awe, they trusted in the Lord and in His servant Moses.

Exodus 15

Moses and all the Israelites sang a song:
"I will sing to the Lord, who has brought victory.
I shall honor the Lord, who is mighty and strong,
And has buried the enemy under the sea.
Who is like You, O Lord? You stretched out Your right hand,
And our enemies were swallowed. Long may You reign."
The Israelites came to the wilderness land,
Where the water was bitter and made them complain.

Then Moses and the Children of Israel sang this song to the Lord, and they said this:
I will sing to the Lord, for He has triumphed gloriously over all in his midst;
The horse and its rider he flung into the sea. The Lord is my might, my song, my strength;
He has become deliverance for me. This is my God, and I will praise Him at length,
The God of my father, I exalt Him. The Lord is a man of war, Lord is His name!
Pharaoh's chariots and his army He hurled into the sea, his officers of fame
Sank in the Sea of Reeds. Oceans covered them, and they went down in the depths like a stone.
Your right-hand, O Lord, glorious in power, Your right hand, O Lord, did shatter the foe.
In Your great triumph You smashed your foes, You sent forth Your fury, it consumed them
    like chaff.
By the breath of Your nostrils the waters piled up, the floods stood like a wall cut in half,
The deeps froze in the heart of the sea. The foe said, "I will pursue, I will overtake,
I will divide the spoil, my desire shall have its fill of them, then leave them in my wake.
I shall draw my sword and subdue them with my hand." But with Your breath You made
    the wind blow,
The sea covered them, and they all sank, as if lead, in the majestic waters below.

Who is like You, O Lord, among the gods? Who is like You, majestic in holiness,
Awesome in splendor, feared in praises, doer of wonders, glorious deeds You possess.
You stretched out Your right hand, the earth swallowed them. You have led with mercy and
    steadfast love
The people You redeemed, guided them in Your strength to Your holy pasture spoken of.
The people heard, they shuddered; the settlers of Philistia all writhed in agony,
And the clans of Edom were dismayed, Moav's chieftains were all trembling frightenedly;
All the dwellers in Canaan melted away. There dread and anguish descended on them;
Before the might of Your arm, they fell still as stone. Until Your people crossed, O Hashem,

Until they crossed, the people You fashioned and ransomed. You brought them and planted
 them there,
On the mountain of Your own inheritance, Lord, which You made as Your own dwelling lair,
The sanctuary, O Lord, which Your hands established. Let the Lord reign eternally!
For the horses of Pharaoh came with their riders and their chariots into the sea,
But the Lord turned back the sea's waters against them, while Israelites marched on dry land
Through the midst of the sea. Now Miriam the prophetess, Aaron's sister, in her hand
Took a tambourine, and all the women went out after her with their own tambourines,
And with dancing. Then Miriam chanted to them, "Sing to the Lord, Whose triumph you've seen,
For He has triumphed gloriously; the horse and rider He has hurled into the sea."

Moses had Israel set out from the Sea of Reeds, for Shur at Egypt's boundary,
To the wilderness. They traveled three days in the wilderness, and no water was found.
They came to Marah, but could not drink water there, as 'twas bitter and marred from
 the ground.
Hence they named the place Marah. The people grumbled at Moses, saying, "What shall
 we drink?"
He cried out to the Lord, and the Lord showed him a piece of wood to toss into the drink.
Moses threw it into the water, and the water became sweet. There He imposed law,
And judgment for them, and there He tested them. He said, "If you will heed the Lord your God,
Hearken to His voice and do what's right in His eyes, giving ear to all His commandments,
And keeping all His laws: All the sickness I brought upon Egypt, to you I'll prevent.
I shall not impose it on you, for I am the Lord, your healer." They came to Elim,
There were twelve springs of water and seventy palms, and they encamped by the water's rim.

Exodus 16

All the Children of Israel grumbled, and said,
"I wish we were in Egypt, and not starving here."
The Lord told Moses, "I will rain down lots of bread."
And just as God had spoken, the food did appear.
Moses told all the Israelites, "Here's a warning:
Do not keep your food for the next day, unless
It's the Sabbath, in which case, save it for the morning.
You can't gather food then; it's a day of rest.

They moved on from Elim, the whole community of the Israelites, and they came
To the wilderness of Syn, which lies between Elim and Sinai, a region untamed,
On the fifteenth day after the second New Moon after they departed Egypt's land.
And they grumbled, the whole Israelite community, grumbling to the last man
Against Moses and Aaron. The Israelites said to them, "Better that we had died
By the hand of the Lord in the land of Egypt, where we had food and were satisfied!
Now instead of eating bread and sitting by fleshpots, you've brought us to this wilderness
To bring death by starvation to this congregation. This situation is a mess."
The Lord said to Moses, "Behold, I will cause bread from the sky to rain down upon you,
And the people shall go out each day to gather that day's portion—And so I will view
Whether they follow My instruction or not. So I shall test them. But on the sixth day,
When they prepare what they have brought in, it shall be double-portion of all other days."
(For it had to last them through the Sabbath, when gathering was not permitted.) And so,
Moses and Aaron said to all the Children of Israel, "At sunset you shall know
That it's the Lord who brought you out of Egypt's land. At daybreak, you shall see the
    Lord's glory:
When He heeds your grumblings against the Lord—For who are we that you tell us
    your sad story?
Why grumble against us?" Moses said, "Since the Lord gives you flesh to eat at each sunset,
And at daybreak, bread to eat until you are full, since the Lord hears that you are upset,
He heeds your grumblings against Him; what is our part? You grumble not to us, but the Lord!"
Moses told Aaron, "Tell the whole Israelite community: Come near to the Lord,
For he has heard your grumblings." And as Aaron spoke to the Israelite congregation,
They faced the wilderness, and here: In the clouds, the Lord's glory made a manifestation.
The Lord spoke to Moses and said, "I have heeded the grumblings of the Israelites.
Speak to them and say: At evening you shall eat flesh, and shall have bread by the morning's light,
And you shall know that I am the Lord your God." Now at sunset, there came a horde of quail.
It covered the camp. And at daybreak, a fall of dew covered the camp with a veil.
When the fall of dew lifted, upon the surface of the wilderness was something fine,
Something flaky and fine as frost on the ground. When they saw it, it could not be defined.
Each man said to his brother, "What is it?" ("Man hu?") "This is what's-it-called." (Or "This
    is manna.")
Moses said to them, "This is the bread the Lord has given you to eat. Gather the manna.
This is the word the Lord has commanded: Gather it, each man as much as he will eat,
One omer per person (near two quarts) for as many of you as are in your tent's suite.
Each of you shall fetch for your own tent." And the Children of Israel did so, and gleaned,
Some gleaned more and some less, but measured by the omer, no man had a shortage of means.
Each man gathered according to what he could eat. Moses said, "You shall leave none
    till morning."
But some of them did not heed Moses, and left it out until then, ignoring his warning;
It became wormy, maggot-infested, and reeked. And with these people, Moses was mad.
They gleaned it each morning, each man what he could eat, before the sun melted what they had.

Now on the sixth day, they gathered a double-portion of manna, two omers for each.
All the community's leaders came and told Moses, who said, "It's as in the Lord's speech:
Tomorrow is a Sabbath ("Ceasing"), a day of rest, holy Sabbath for the Lord.
Whatever you would bake, bake, and boil what you'd boil; Let the rest until morning be stored."
They put it aside until morning, as Moses had commanded, and it did not reek,
And it was free of maggots (for this time they followed the orders which the Lord did speak).
Moses said, "Eat it today, for today is the Lord's Sabbath, none shall be in the field.
For six days you shall gather, but on the seventh day is Sabbath, there shall be no yield."
But on the seventh day, some people went out to glean, and found nothing (due to this clause).
The Lord said to Moses, "How long will you men refuse to keep My commandments and laws?
You see the Lord has given you the Sabbath, and on the sixth day, gives you two days' bread.
Now let each man remain in his spot on the seventh day, no man outside his place tread."
So the people remained inactive on the seventh day. "Manna", Israel named the food.
It was like coriander seed, whitish, and tasted like wafers and honey, quite good.
Moses said, "This is what the Lord has commanded: You shall keep safe one omer of it
Throughout your generations, in order that they may see the bread which I had you eat
In the wilderness when I brought you out of the land of Egypt." Moses told Aaron,
"Take a jar, put one omer of manna in it, and place it before the Lord. Once done,
It shall be kept safe throughout your generations." As the Lord had commanded to Moses,
Aaron put it aside before the Testimony, for safekeeping from what time imposes.
And the Israelites ate the manna for forty years, until they reached settled land,
They ate the manna until they came to the bordering edge of the land called Canaan.
(Now an omer is one tenth of an ephah, so these measurements you can understand).

Exodus 17

All the Children of Israel grumbled again,
Telling Moses, "You must give us water to drink!"
The Lord told Moses, "Go to Horeb's rock, and then
Strike the rock. I'll make water appear, in a blink."
Amalek warred with Israel. So the next day,
Moses went to the mountain, staff of God in hand.
While his hands were raised, the war went Israel's way,
So he kept them high, so tired he could not stand.

They moved on, the whole community of the Israelites, on from Syn's wilderness,
By stages, at the Lord's bidding. They encamped at Rephidim, where they were waterless;

There was no water for the people to drink. The people quarreled with Moses and said,
"Give us water to drink!" Moses said, "Why do you quarrel with me where we have been led?
Why do you test the Lord?" The people thirsted for water, still against Moses they grumbled.
They said, "Why did you bring us up from Egypt, to bring us death when from thirst we
    all crumble,
And to kill our children and our livestock with thirst too?" So Moses cried out to the Lord,
"What shall I do with this people? 'Ere long, they'll be stoning me! I must placate this horde."
The Lord said to Moses, "Go before the people, take some of Israel's elders with you,
And take the staff with which you struck the Nile in your hand, and set out. I'll stand there
    before you
On the rock at Horeb. You are to strike the rock, and then water the rock shall emit
And the people shall drink." Moses did so, and the elders of Israel witnessed it.
He named the place "Massah" ("Testing"), and "Meribah" ("Quarreling"), due to the quarreling
Of the Children of Israel, and due to their testing of the Lord, always asking,
"Is the Lord among us, or not?" Then Amalek came, upon Israel he made war,
In Rephidim. Moses said to Joshua, "Choose us some men, and go out to the fore,
Go make war against Amalek. Tomorrow I'll place myself on the top of the hill,
With the staff of God in my hand." Joshua did what he was told, as Moses had willed,
To make war against Amalek. Now Moses, Aaron, and Hur went up to the hill's top.
And whenever Moses raised his hand, Israel prevailed, but when he dropped it, it stopped;
And whenever he set his hand down, Amalek prevailed. Heavy grew Moses's hands;
So they took a stone and placed it under him and he sat down on it, too tired to stand,
While Aaron and Hur supported his hands for him, one on each side, to keep them in check.
So his hands remained steadfast until sunset, and Joshua defeated Amalek,
And his people as well, with the sword. The Lord said to Moses, "Write this as a memorial
In an account, and recite it to Joshua, as a promise from times immemorial:
I will utterly blot out the memory of Amalek from under heaven's sky."
Moses built an altar and named it "Adonai-nissi" ("My banner is Adonai")
With the Lord as his banner, he said, "Yes, it means a hand on the Lord's banner and throne!
The Lord will be at war against Amalek for the ages, through each generation."

Exodus 18

Jethro, Moses's father-in-law, heard the tale
Of what Moses had done. He set out for his tent.
Moses told him how God had made sure they'd prevail,
Jethro said, "Bless the Lord, and the rescue He sent."
The next day, Moses judged all the people, all day.
Jethro saw this, and said, "You can't do this alone!
Select trustworthy judges to help, and that way,
All the small matters, they can decide on their own."

[Yitro]

Now Jethro, priest of Midian, father-in-law of Moses, heard of all God had done
For Moses and His people Israel, how the Lord had saved them from Egypt, and won.
So Jethro took Zipporah, the wife of Moses, after she had been sent away home,
And her two sons, of whom one was named Gershom ("Sojourner There"), for when
    Moses did roam,
He said, "I have become a sojourner in a foreign land." And the other son's name
Was Eliezer ("God's Help"), because, "The God of my father is my help, for he came
And rescued me from Pharaoh's sword." Jethro, Moses's father-in-law, came with his sons
And his wife to Moses, to the wilderness, where Moses was encamped at God's mountain.
He had word sent to Moses, "I, Jethro your father-in-law, shall be coming to you,
And your wife and her two sons with her." Moses went out to meet Jethro, paid him his due.
Moses bowed and kissed him, and they asked after each other's welfare, then entered the tent.
Moses then told his father-in-law all the Lord had done to Pharaoh, every event,
And to Egypt, for Israel's sake, all the hardships that did befall them on their way,
And how the Lord had rescued them. Jethro was jubilant for the Lord's kindness, that they
Had been rescued from the land of Egypt by Him. Jethro then said, "Blessed be the Lord,
Who has rescued you from the Egyptians and from Pharaoh, He who has rescued His horde
From under Egypt's hand. Now I know that the Lord is greater than all gods before hailed—
For when the Egyptians dealt proudly with the people, in that matter the Lord prevailed."
Jethro, Moses's father-in-law, brought burnt offering and sacrifices for God,
And Aaron and the elders of Israel came to eat bread in the presence of God,
With the father-in-law of Moses. On the morrow, Moses sat as a magistrate
To judge the people, who stood before him from sunrise until the sun did dissipate.
When his father-in-law had seen all of the things Moses did for the people, he said,
"Now what kind of thing is this you do for the people, you putting it all on your head?

Why do you sit and act alone, while the whole people will stand before you morn to night?"
Moses said to his father-in-law, "The people come to me to inquire of God's might.
When they ask about God, and when there is a matter of law, that comes to me alone.
I judge between the man and his neighbor, and I make God's instructions and His laws known."
Then the father-in-law of Moses said to him, "This matter is not good as you do it!
You will wear yourself out, and these people as well; it's too much for one man to go through it.
You can't do this alone, it's too heavy for you. So now heed my voice, I will advise
So that God may be there with you: You represent the people before God, acting wise.
You shall bring matters to God, and you should teach the people all of God's laws
      and instructions.
You should let them know where to go, what deeds to do, and on what deeds there are
      some obstructions.
But you, you must have vision and seek out from all the people the most capable men,
Those who hold God in awe, men of truth who spurn ill-gotten gains, and once you have
      found them,
Set them over the people as chiefs of thousands, chiefs of hundreds, and fifties, and tens,
So that they may judge the people at all times. So shall it be, thus achieving your ends.
They shall bring every great matter to you, but every small matter, they'll judge by themselves.
Make it easier for you, let them share your burden, and don't take it all on yourself.
If you do so in this matter, when God commands you, then you will be able to stand,
And also these people will return home in peace." Moses paid heed to Jethro's command,
He did everything as he had said, choosing capable men from all over Israel,
Placed them over the people, as chiefs of thousands, hundreds, fifties, and tens to appeal.
They would judge the people at all times, with the great matters brought up to Moses's hand,
But small matters they'd judge by themselves. Moses sent Jethro off, and went home to his land.

Exodus 19

On the third new moon after they'd left Egypt's land,
They came to SinaI's mountain, and camped at that place.
Moses went up to God, who gave him this command:
"Keep My covenant, and you shall have My good grace."
God came down in a pillar of flame and of cloud,
To the top of the mountain, which Moses ascended.
The sound of the shofar was growing more loud.
God said, "If people climb up, their lives will be ended."

On the third new moon after the Children of Israel had gone forth from Egypt's land,
On that very day, they came to the wilderness of Sinai. Having journeyed, their band,
From Rephidim, they came to the wilderness of Sinai, where they encamped and pitched tents.
There Israel encamped, opposite from the mountain. And then up to God, Moses went.
And the Lord called to him from the mountain, saying, "To the House of Jacob you shall tell,
Yes, to the Children of Israel you shall tell these words, 'You yourselves saw and beheld
What I did to Egypt, how I bore you on eagle's wings and brought you to Me. Now then,
If you will heed My voice and keep My covenant, you shall be My treasure among men.
Indeed, all the earth is Mine, but you shall be to Me a kingdom of priests, holy nation.'
These are the words you are to speak to the Children of Israel, this your obligation."
Moses came and summoned the elders of the people, and set before them all these words,
With which the Lord had commanded him. And the people all answered as one when they heard,
Saying, "All that the Lord has spoken, we will do." And Moses brought their words to the Lord.
The Lord said to Moses, "Here, I am coming to you in a thick cloud. This is in ord-
er that the people may hear when I speak with you, and so they may trust in you forever."
And Moses told the words of the people to the Lord. The Lord said to Moses, however,
"Go to the people, make them holy, both today and tomorrow, let them scrub their clothes.
Let them be ready for the third day, for on the third day the Lord shall come down and close,
In the sight of the people, upon Mount Sinai. You shall set bounds for them round about,
Saying, 'Beware of going up the mountain or touching any of it that sticks out;
For whoever touches the mountain shall be put to death. No hand shall touch him, not one,
But he is to be stoned or shot, whether beast or man, he shall not live for what was done.'
When the ram's-horn trumpet sounds a long blast, only then may they on the mountain ascend."
Moses went down from the mountain to the people, he made them holy and had them tend
To their clothes, washing them. Then he said to the people, "Be ready before the third day,
Do not touch woman." Now on the third day, at daybreak, of lightning there was a display,

Thunder-sounds and a heavy cloud on the mountain, and a strong blasting of the shofar.
(A ram's horn). And all of the people that were in camp trembled, overwhelmed from afar.
Moses brought the people out toward God, from the camp; they all stood at the foot of
    the mountain.
Now Mount Sinai was all in smoke, because the Lord had come down on it in a fire fountain;
The smoke rose like the smoke of a furnace—dense smoke, and the whole mountain trembled
    exceedingly.
Now the shofar sound kept growing stronger and stronger, as Moses kept speaking repeatedly,
And God kept answering him in thunderous voice, and the Lord came down on Mount Sinai,
To the top of the mountain. The Lord called up Moses to the mountaintop in the sky,
And so Moses went up. The Lord said to Moses, "Go down and warn the people below,
Otherwise they will break through to the Lord to see, and many will die from the Lord's glow;
Even the priests who approach the Lord must make themselves holy, and be well purified,
Otherwise the Lord will burst out against them." But Moses said to the Lord, "They're denied.
The people cannot go up to Mount Sinai, for You Yourself gave a warning to us,
Saying, 'Fix boundaries for the mountain and make it holy.'" The Lord said to him, "Do thus:
Go down, and come up with Aaron, but the priests and people must not break through to ascend
To the Lord, lest He burst out against them." Moses went down to the people and told them.

Exodus 20

> God said, "I am the Lord your God. Worship no other.
> Don't take My name in vain. Keep the Sabbath day,
> For God rested then. Honor your father and mother.
> Don't murder. Don't commit adultery and stray.
> Don't steal. Don't bear false witness at your fellow man.
> And don't covet your neighbor's wife, house, or things there."
> The Lord told Moses to build an altar, but plan
> To use dirt and rough stones, no iron tool to prepare.

God spoke all these words, saying, "I am the Lord your God who brought you out from
    Egypt's land,
From the house of bondage. You are not to have other gods besides Me; such shall be banned.
You are not to make yourself a carved-image or likeness of things from heaven above,
Or things on earth below, or in waters beneath the earth; these things, make no image of.
You shall not bow down to them or serve them. For I the Lord your God am a jealous God,
Visiting the iniquity of the fathers on the sons, for actions that were flawed,

To the third and fourth generations of those who hate Me. But showing firm loyalty
To the thousandth generation of those who keep My commandments and those who love Me.
You are not to take the name of the Lord your God in vain, or swear falsely by His name,
For the Lord will not clear one who swears falsely by His name, or one who takes it in vain.
Remember the Sabbath day and keep it holy, for six days you shall do all your work,
But the seventh day is Sabbath for the Lord your God: You are not to do any work,
Not you, nor your son, nor your daughter, not your servant, nor your maid, nor even your beast,
Nor the sojourner that is within your gates is to do any work, even the least.
For in six days the Lord made the heavens, the earth, and the sea, and all that is in it.
And He rested on the seventh day, so the Lord blessed the Sabbath day and hallowed it.
Honor your father and your mother, so that your days may be prolonged and may endure
On the land which the Lord your God gives you. You shall not murder. You shall not adulter.
You shall not bear false witness against your neighbor. You shall not covet your neighbor's house,
You shall not covet your neighbor's wife, or his servant, his maid, his ox, donkey, or mouse,
No, not anything that is your neighbor's." Now all of the people were seeing the lightning,
The thunder, the sound of the shofar, and the mountain smoking. The effect was frightening.
When the people saw it, they fell back and stood at a distance. Then to Moses they said,
"You speak to us, and we will heed your words, but don't let God speak to us, or we'll be dead."
Moses said to the people, "Do not be afraid, for it is to test you God has come,
In order that you will remain in awe of Him, and so to sin you will not succumb."
And the people stood far away, while Moses approached the thick dark cloud where
    God had been.
The Lord said to Moses, "Tell this to the Children of Israel: 'You yourselves have seen
That it was from the heavens that I spoke with you. Therefore, make no silver gods beside Me,
Nor are you to make gods of gold for yourselves. With an altar of earth, you shall provide Me.
Sacrifice on it burnt offerings, sacrifices of peace, and your oxen and sheep.
At each place where I cause My name to be mentioned, I will come bless you, this you shall reap.
But if you make an altar of stone for Me, do not build it of stones that have been hewn,
For by wielding your iron tool on it you will have profaned it, thus draining its boon.
And you shall not ascend My altar by steps, so your nudeness on it won't be laid bare.'"
(For the Egyptians wore short skirts, and if they climbed high, then people would probably stare).

Exodus 21

"When you get a serf, he shall serve you for six years,
But in year seven, you are to let him go free.
Handmaids shall not go out as a male slave appears.
He who kills a man, death shall be his penalty.
If the death was an accident, God shall provide
A place that he can flee, so he won't have to die.
But if it was planned murder, there's nowhere to hide.
That's a tooth for a tooth, and an eye for an eye."

[Mishpatim]

Now these are the rules that you shall set before them: When you acquire a Hebrew slave,
He shall serve for six years, but go free in the seventh year, though no last payment he gave.
If he came by himself, he shall leave by himself; if he had a wife, with him she goes.
If his master gave him a wife, and she bore him sons or daughters, she and all of those
Shall remain as her master's, and the slave shall leave by himself. But if the slave should say,
"I love my master, my wife, and my children; I do not want to go free—I will stay,"
Then his master shall take him before God to judge, and bring him to the doorpost or door.
And his master shall pierce his ear with an awl, and he shall serve that master ever more.
When a man sells his daughter as maidservant, she shall not be freed as male slaves are.
If she is displeasing to her master, who chose her for himself, then he cannot bar
Her redemption-price. He may not sell her to foreigners, since he broke faith; she was cheated.
But if he designated her for his son, then as a free woman she must be treated.
If he takes another for himself, then her food, clothes, and marital oils shall not fade.
If he fails to do these three things for her, then she shall go free, no money to be paid.
He who strikes a man so he dies shall be put to death. But if it was not by design,
But an act of God (accidental), then to him a place of refuge I shall assign.
Yet when one man schemes against another, and treacherously kills with cunning intent,
From My very altar you shall take him, to die. No refuge to this man shall be lent.
He who strikes his father or his mother shall be put to death. He who steals a man,
Whether he sells him or is found holding him, shall be put to death. He who in the land
Curses or insults his father or his mother shall be put to death. When men contend,
And a man strikes his neighbor with a stone or fist, and the struck one does not meet his end,
But instead of dying, merely takes to his bed: If he can arise and walk outside
On his crutch, he that struck him shall go clear unpunished, except that he then must provide

A payment for the loss of his time spent idle, and a cure so he may be well-healed.
When a man strikes his slave or handmaid with a rod, so he dies from the rod he did wield,
It is to be avenged. But if he should survive for a day or two, no vengeance take,
For he is his master's property. When two men fight, and one of them makes the mistake
Of hurting a woman who is pregnant, so that a miscarriage results from the blow,
But no other harm does occur, he shall be fined as the woman's husband chooses so,
The payment to be based on the judges' agreement. But if other damage ensues,
You shall give life for life, eye for eye, tooth for tooth, hand for hand, foot for foot,
     bruise for bruise,
Burn for burn, wound for wound. When a man strikes the eye of his slave, either sex,
     and destroys it,
He shall let the slave go for the sake of the eye. (Thus violence hurts the one who employs it).
If he breaks off the tooth of his serf or handmaid, he shall send him free on tooth's account.
When an ox gores a man or a woman to death, the ox shall be stoned, and no amount
Of its flesh shall be eaten, but the owner of the ox is unpunished, in the clear.
However, if the ox was known to have gored innocent people before in that year,
And the owner, though warned, failed to guard it, and it kills a woman or man sometime hence,
The ox is to be stoned, and its owner as well shall be put to death for this offense.
If a ransom is established for him, then to redeem his life, he must pay it all.
Whether it gores a son or a daughter, this judgment remains and may not be forestalled.
If the ox gores a slave, male or female, then he shall make silver payment to the master,
Thirty shekels he shall give, and the ox shall be stoned as punishment for this disaster.
When a man opens up a pit, or digs a pit, and does not cover it up again,
And an ox or ass falls into it, the one responsible for the pit must pay then
The dead animal's price in silver to the owner, though he keeps the dead animal.
When a man's ox should injure a neighbor's ox, so that it dies, the dead ox they shall sell,
Splitting the price gained from it, and also splitting the dead ox. But if the owner knew
That the ox had a habit of goring, and didn't guard it, then he is to pay his due:
He must pay with an ox in the place of the ox, while the dead ox as his own shall stay.
Now when a man steals an ox or sheep, and kills it or sells it, then in place he shall pay
Five oxen for an ox, and four sheep for a sheep. Now if in the act of tunneling,
The thief is caught and is stuck down so that he dies, there is no blood-guilt on his accounting.

Exodus 22

"If a man gives his neighbor a donkey to guard,
And it dies without anyone seeing the cause,
Then the man has no guilt if by beasts it was scarred,
But must pay if he's stolen it. These are the laws.
You shall not maltreat strangers, not in any way,
Because once you were strangers, back in Egypt's land.
Don't afflict any widows or orphans, for they
Will cry out to me, and you will die by My hand."

Now when a man steals an ox or sheep, and kills it or sells it, then in place he shall pay
Five oxen for an ox, and four sheep for a sheep. Now if in the act of breaking in,
The thief is caught and is struck down so that he dies, there is no blood-guilt dealing with him.
But if the sun has risen on him, there is blood-guilt on his account; he can't be killed,
Instead he is to pay, and if he has nothing, he shall be sold for his stealing guilt.
Now if what he stole is found in his hand, be ox, donkey, or lamb, and is still alive,
Then he is to pay twofold (instead of the rates for what's gone, which is four times or five).
When a man lets his livestock loose to graze in other men's fields or graze vineyards bare,
He shall pay the best-part of his own field or vineyard, to make restitution that's fair.
When a fire breaks out and reaches hedges, thorns, sheaves, or grain, or consumes the whole field,
He who started the fire must make restitution, to compensate for loss of yield.
When a man gives silver or goods to his neighbor for safekeeping, and from that one's grounds
They are stolen, if the thief is caught he shall pay twofold. If the thief cannot be found,
The owner of the house shall come near to God's judgment, to make sure that he did not steal
Property from his neighbor. In all matters of transgression, whether for ox, or wheel,
Or donkeys, or sheep, or clothes, or any kind of loss where one party says, "This is it,"
Then the case of both parties shall come before God's judgment to determine what is fit.
Whomever God's judgment declares guilty shall pay to his neighbor twofold of the charge.
When a man gives his neighbor a donkey, an ox, a lamb, or any beast small or large
For safekeeping, and it dies, or is crippled or captured, and no witness saw or heard,
An oath of the Lord shall be between them to see if one laid hands on the other's herd.
The owner must accept this form of arbitration, no restitution to be made.
But if the animal was stolen from the neighbor, then its owner is to be paid.
If it was torn to pieces by beasts of the wild, he is to bring it as evidence;
For since this could happen to anyone, for what was torn, he need not pay recompense.
When a man borrows an animal from his neighbor, and it is crippled or it dies,
If the owner was not with it, he must pay; if the owner was there, no fine applies.

If it was hired, the hiring-price is received (covering the loss of the owner).
When a man seduces a virgin who has not been paid for and then lies down with her,
He must make her his wife by the payment of a bridal price. If her father refuses
And will not give her to him, he still must pay a virgin's bridal price. (Silver he loses.)
A sorceress you are not to let live. Whoever lies with beasts shall be put to death.
He who sacrifices to other gods shall be destroyed, never again to draw breath,
Only sacrifice to the Lord. Now a sojourner you may not maltreat or oppress,
For you were sojourners in the land of Egypt. You shall not maltreat the defenseless.
Any widow or orphan you shall not afflict, for if you do so in any way,
They will cry out to Me, and I shall heed their cry, and My wrath shall flare up on that day,
And I will kill you with the sword, so that your wives become widows, your children orphans.
If you lend money to My people, to the poor one beside you, the afflicted one,
You shall not act toward him like a creditor, you shall not charge him excessive interest.
If you take a man's cloak as collateral, return it by dusk so he may be dressed,
For it is his only clothing, sole covering for his skin, in what else shall he sleep?
If he cries out to Me, I will pay heed, for I am compassionate. Mercy I keep.
You are not to curse God, nor the ruler among your people. You are not to delay
Offering the first fruit of your grape harvest, and the first flow from your wine press's spray.
The firstborn of your sons you shall give to Me. Do the same with your oxen and your sheep:
For the first seven days let it be with its mother, on the eighth day, give it to Me.
You shall be holy men to Me, men consecrated to Me, and so let it be known.
Flesh that is torn by beasts in the field, you shall not eat. To the dogs it is to be thrown.

Exodus 23

"If you share in false rumors, you share in the guilt.
Do not favor one side in a legal dispute.
Don't take bribes, or the scales of justice will tilt.
And do not oppress strangers, for you've walked their route.
You shall hold a feast for Me three times every year,
One of matzot, one harvest, one gathering in.
All your enemies blocking your path I shall clear,
But do not worship their gods, that would be a sin."

You shall not carry false rumors. Do not throw your hand in with the guilty to become
A malicious witness. You shall not side with a multitude to do evil or wrong.

And you are not to testify in a quarrel as to turn it towards the multitude,

So to turn away from justice. Even a poor man you shall not favor in disputes.

When you come across your enemy's ox or ass gone astray, then return it to him.

When you see the ass of one who hates you crouched under its burden, don't leave it to him;

Though you'd like to abandon him, you must help him. You shall not ignore rights of the poor;

You shall not subvert their rights in legal disputes. From a false charge, be sure you stay far.

Do not kill the clear and innocent, for I don't acquit the guilty and treacherous.

Do not take bribes, for bribes blind the clear-sighted, and twist the words of the
     just and righteous.

You shall not oppress a sojourner, for you yourselves know how it feels to be sojourning,

For you were sojourners in the land of Egypt. For six years, sow your land, keep soil turning,

And gather its produce. But in the seventh year, you shall let it lie fallow and rest,

So the poor of your people may eat it, and what they leave, the field's beasts may digest.

Do so with your vineyard and your olive grove. For six days, you are to do your labor,

But on the seventh day you shall cease from work so your ox and ass may rest in leisure,

And the son of your handmaid and the sojourner may pause for breath and so be refreshed.

In all things that I have told you, be on your guard. Other gods' names shall not ride your breath.

Make no mention of the names of other gods, they shall not be heard in your mouth or throat.

Three times a year you shall hold a festival for Me. You shall keep the Feast of Matzot:

Eating matzot for seven days as I commanded you, in the new moon of ripe grain,

At the set-time in the month of Abib, for it was then that out of Egypt you came,

And no one is to come before Me empty-handed; and then the Feast of Shavuot,

("Weeks" of Harvest-Cutting) of the first fruits of your labor, which in the field you've sowed;

And the Feast of Sukkot ("Huts" of In-gathering), the grape harvest that ends up the year,

When you gather in your work's yield from the field. Three times a year, all your
     males shall appear

Before the true Lord. You shall not offer the blood of My sacrifice with leavened bread,

Or let the fat of My offering lie out overnight until morn has arrived.

The choicest firstling fruits of your soil you shall bring into the house of the Lord, your God.

You shall not boil a kid in its mother's milk. Behold, I send a messenger abroad

Before you, to care for you and guard you on the way to the place which I have prepared.

Beware of him and heed his voice, do not rebel against him, your offense he won't bear,

He shall not pardon your offense, for My Name is with him. Heed his voice, do all I say,

And then I will be an enemy to your enemies, a foe to foes in your way.

When my messenger goes before you and brings you to the Amorites and the Hittites,

To the Perizzites, and to the Canaanites, to the Hivites, and to the Jebusites,

And I cause them to perish, you shall not bow down to their gods, you are not to serve them,

You are not to do as they do, but to smash their pillars, and then to overthrow them.

You are to serve the Lord your God, and He will give blessing to both your food and your water.

I will remove sickness from your midst, there will be no miscarriage of son or of daughter,

And no barren ones in your land. I will let you enjoy the full number of your days.

I will send forth My terror before you, and I will throw into a panicky haze

All the peoples who you come among; I will give you all your enemies by the neck,
So that they turn tail. I will send a hornet-plague of despair before you to affect
And drive out the Hivites, Canaanites, and Hittites. I will not drive them out in one year,
Lest the land become desolate and the wild beasts multiply against you, causing fear.
Little by little, I will drive them out before you, until you've borne fruit and increased,
And possess the land. And I will set your borders from the Sea of Reeds (that is, Red Sea)
To the Sea of the Philistines (Mediterranean Sea), from the Euphrates River
In the north to the Negev desert of the south. And into your hand, I shall deliver
The inhabitants settled in the land, so that you may drive them all out before you.
You shall not cut a covenant with them or with their gods. Make no treaties between you.
They are not to remain in your land, otherwise they might cause you to sin against Me,
Indeed, if you were to serve their gods, then as a snare against you it would prove to be.

Exodus 24

Now the Lord said to Moses, "Go up to the Lord,
Let no others approach." He did as he was guided.
And the people all told him, "We'll act in accord
With the words God has spoken that you have provided."
The Lord told Moses, "Go up the mountain, and stay,
I will give you stone tablets of My Commandments."
So atop the high mountain, on the seventh day,
Moses stayed forty days once he'd made the ascent.

Now to Moses, He said, "Come up to the Lord, you and Aaron, Nadab, and Abihu,
And seventy of Israel's elders, and bow down from afar. Now Moses, just you
Shall come near the Lord. They are not to come near the Lord, and as for the people below,
They shall not even go up with Moses at all." Moses went to let the people know.
He recounted to them all the Lord's words and all the judgments, and the people responded
In one voice, saying, "All the words that the Lord has spoken, we will do. So we are bonded."
Moses then wrote down all the words of the Lord. He woke early in the morning to build
An altar at the foot of the mountain, and twelve pillars for twelve tribes of Israel.
Then he sent young lads of the Children of Israel, who offered up burnt offerings,
And then slaughtered bulls as sacrifices of peace to the Lord. Moses took some basins,
And put half of the blood in them, tossing the other half of blood against the altar.
Then he took the record of the covenant and read it so all the people could hear.

They said, "All that the Lord has spoken, we will do faithfully, we will heed and obey."
Moses took the blood, tossed it on the people, and said, "This blood I toss on you today
Is the blood of the covenant that the Lord has cut with you concerning all these words."
Then Moses and Aaron, Nadab and Abihu, and of Israel's elders a herd
Of seventy, all went up. And they saw the God of Israel. And under His feet
It was as if a sapphire-tiled pavement, as if it were the heavens complete,
Pure and clearer than sky. Yet against the representatives of the Israelites,
He did not send forth His hand. They beheld God-ness, and they ate and drank to
    praise this sight.
The Lord said to Moses, "Come up to Me on the mountain and wait there, so I may give
Tablets of stone to you, the teachings and commandments to instruct them how they should live,
I have written them down so that you may teach them." Moses rose, as did his attendant
Joshua, and Moses went up to the mountain of God. To the elders he had said,
"Wait here for us until we return to you. Here, Aaron and Hur will wait here with you.
Anyone with a legal matter shall approach them." So then Moses went up into
The mountain, and the cloud covered the mountain; The Glory of God settled on Sinai.
The cloud covered it for six days, but on the seventh day, He told Moses to draw nigh.
He called to Moses from the midst of the cloud. And the sight of the Glory of the Lord
Was a consuming flame atop the mountain in the eyes of the Israelite horde.
Moses went into the midst of the cloud, ascending the mountain of heavenly light.
And then Moses remained on the mountain, Mount Sinai, for forty days and forty nights.

Exodus 25

> The Lord told Moses, "Those who would make contributions
> Of their own free will, let them build Me a shrine.
> Make a dwelling, an ark, with precise execution,
> With table and lampstand of the same design."

[Terumah]

Now the Lord spoke to Moses and said, "Speak to the Israelites, so that they may bring
Gifts to Me. From every man whose heart makes him willing, you shall accept my offering.
And these are the gifts you shall accept from them: gold, silver, bronze, blue, purple, and crimson,
Fine linens, goats' hair, rams' skins dyed red, tanned leather skins, (all to be used for construction),
Acacia wood, oil for lighting, spices for anointing oil and for fragrant incense,
Onyx stones, stones for setting on the ephod (priest's garment) and breastpiece for
    those raiments.

Let them make Me a holy-shrine, a sanctuary, so that in their midst I may dwell.
According to all that I show you concerning the pattern of the Tabernacle,
And the pattern for building all its instruments and furnishings, is how you shall make it.
They shall make an ark of acacia wood, two and a half cubits the length you shall make it,
A cubit and a half wide, a cubit and a half high. Overlay it with pure gold,
Overlay it inside and out, and all around its rim, a gold molding you shall mold.
You shall cast for it four rings of gold, putting them on its four feet: Two rings on one side,
And two rings on the other side. You shall make poles of acacia wood, the ark to guide.
Overlay them with gold and insert them into the rings found on both sides of the ark,
So the ark may be carried with them. In the rings of the ark, the poles shall remain. Hark,
They shall not be removed from it. And you are to put in the ark the Testimony
Which I give you. You shall make a penance-cover of pure gold, of which the length shall be
Two and a half cubits, and a cubit and a half wide. You shall make two cherubim
Of gold, of hammered-work, at the two ends of the penance-cover you are to make them.
Make one cherub at one end, and one cherub at the other end. (Now keep it in mind
That these cherubim were winged beasts, not cute babies as we think of in modern times.)
From the cover itself you shall make the two cherubim, keeping the whole thing one piece.
And the cherubim shall have their wings spreading upward, shielding the cover with their wings;
Their faces shall face each other, down towards the cover the cherubim's faces shall face.
Place the cover atop the ark, and in the ark, the Testimony I give you, place.
There I will meet with you and from above the cover, from between the two cherubim
On the ark of the Testimony, I will speak to you of all the things I command,
My command to you concerning the Israelites. You shall make a table comprised
Of acacia wood, two cubits long, one cubit wide, and one and a half cubits high.
You shall overlay it with pure gold. You shall make a rim of gold for it, all around.
You shall make a border for it, one hand's breadth wide, and here too, a gold rim all around.
You shall make for it four rings of gold, to be put at the corners, where its four legs are.
The rings shall be close to the rim, as holders for the poles to carry the table far.
You shall make the poles of acacia wood, and overlay them with gold, so that the table
May be carried by them. You are to make its jars and its jugs and its bowls and its ladles,
From which offerings are poured; Of pure gold you shall make them. On the table you shall set
The shewbread (Bread of the Presence), before My presence, regularly. (Do not forget).

You shall make a lampstand of pure gold, you shall make it of hammered-work, its base,
    its branches,
Its cups, its calyxes, its petals shall be made from it. From its sides issue six branches,
Three branches from one side, three branches from the other side. On one branch shall be
    three cups
Shaped like almond-blossoms, each with calyx and petals, and on the other branch going up,
Three cups like almond-blossoms, with calyx and petals, so for all six branches from the base
Of the lamp. And on the lampstand itself, four almond-cups, calyx and petals in place,

A calyx under two branches, all from the same piece, a calyx under a branch pair,
From the same piece, a calyx beneath two branches, all formed from this one lamp piece,
    with care,
And so on for all six of the lampstand's branches. Their calyxes and stems shall be from it,
All of hammered-work, all of pure gold, and all made of one piece, with all else being from it.
You shall make its lamps, seven lamps, and mount them as to light up the space in front of it.
And its tongs and trays shall be pure gold. From an ingot of pure gold they are to make it,
Along with all these implements and furnishings. Now see that you take into account,
And follow the building-patterns for making them which is shown to you upon the mount.

Exodus 26

"Now the tabernacle shall require ten curtains,
With fifty loops each, curtains five to a side.
Use acacia wood for all the boards, and be certain
The holy shrine is curtained off from outside."

Now as for the tabernacle-dwelling, the inner part, you shall make it from ten curtains
Of fine twisted linen, of blue and purple and crimson, and you shall also be certain
To include cherubim, skillfully worked according to the designer's craftsmanship.
The length of each curtain shall be twenty-eight cubits, and the width shall be four cubits.
Each curtain shall have the same measurements. Five curtains are to be joined to one another,
And the other five curtains shall also be joined to one another (but not the other).
You shall make loops of blue on the edge of the curtain that is outermost of one set,
And do the same with the edge of the curtain that is outermost of the other set.
Fifty loops you shall make on the first curtain, and you are also to make fifty loops
On the edge of the other set's outermost curtain, so each loop is facing a loop.
You shall make fifty clasps of gold, and join the curtains to each other using the clasps,
So that the tabernacle-dwelling may be one piece once all of these steps have elapsed.

You shall make curtains of goats' hair over the Tabernacle as a whole, for a tent.
You shall make eleven of them. The length of each shall be thirty cubits in extent,
And the width of each shall be four cubits. You shall join five of the curtains separately,
And the other six curtains by themselves, but then double over the sixth tapestry
At the front of the tent. You shall make fifty loops at the edge of one set's end-curtain,
And fifty loops at the edge of the joining curtain. You shall make fifty clasps of bronze,
And you shall bring the clasps into the loops, to join the tent together into one piece.

As for the excess tent-curtain that overlaps, let that half-curtain hang in the back
Of the tabernacle. The extra cubits at either end where the curtain goes slack
Shall hang over the sides of the tent on both sides, so the Tabernacle will be covered.
You shall make for the tent a covering of rams' skins dyed red, and you shall make above it
A covering of tanned leather skins. You are to make for the Tabernacle some boards
Of acacia wood, standing upright; Ten cubits shall be the length of each upright board,
And a cubit and a half, the width. Each board shall have two pegs, parallel to each other,
And so shall you make all the boards for the Tabernacle, with pegs opposite each other.
You shall make the boards for the Tabernacle with twenty boards facing the Negev, south,
Making forty silver sockets beneath the twenty boards. Two sockets serving as mouths
To catch the pegs beneath each board, and two sockets beneath each other board for its pegs.
As for the northern wall of the Tabernacle, twenty boards, with sockets to catch pegs,
Forty silver sockets, two sockets beneath each board, and two beneath each other board.
As for the rear of the Tabernacle, seawards, facing west, you are to make six boards.
And make two boards for the back corners of the Tabernacle, which though separate below,
Shall be coupled together above in one ring, and for those two boards, it shall be so,
For they shall form the two corners. Then there will be eight rear boards, with sixteen
    silver sockets,
Two sockets beneath each board, and two sockets beneath each other board, in place to lock it.
You shall make bars of acacia wood, five for boards on one side of the Tabernacle,
Five bars for the boards on the other side, and five bars for the rear, west towards the sea's pull.
And the middle bar halfway up the boards shall run from one end to the other, right through.
You shall overlay the boards with gold, and make their rings of gold, to put the bars into,
And the bars shall be overlaid with gold as well. The Tabernacle you shall fashion
According to the building-patterns for it which you were granted to see on the mountain.

You shall make a curtain of blue, purple, and crimson, and linen that is finely twined;
They shall make it with craftsmanship, with cherubim to be included in the design.
You shall hang it upon four pillars of acacia, overlaid with gold, hooks of gold,
Set in four silver sockets; you shall hang the curtain beneath the clasps designed to hold.
You shall carry into there, inside of the curtain, the ark of the Testimony;
The curtain shall separate for you the Holy place and the Holiest of Holies.
You shall place the penance-cover on the ark of Testimony (of the Covenant),
In the Holiest of Holy places. You shall place the table outside the curtain,
And the lampstand across from the table on the Tabernacle's south side, but note well:
The table you shall put on the north side. You are to make a screen for the tent's portal,
Of blue, purple, and crimson, and fine twisted linen, embroidered with embroidery.
You shall make for the screen five pillars of acacia wood, and those pillars are to be
Overlaid with gold, and their hooks also shall be of gold. Finally, you are to cast
Five sockets of bronze for them, to hold the gold hooks so the tent-screen can be hung at last.

Exodus 27

> "Of acacia wood too shall the altar be made,
> With five cubits a side, and then three cubits tall.
> Build a courtyard where the altar can be displayed,
> And make bronze the material you use for all."

You shall make the altar of acacia wood, five cubits in length, five cubits in width—
The altar shall be square, and three cubits high. You shall make horns on its four corners with
The horns being of one piece with it. You shall overlay it with bronze. You shall make pans
For removing its ashes, its scrapers, basins, flesh-hooks, firepans—all its implements
You are to make of bronze. You shall make a lattice for it, a bronze network as a grating,
And shall make on its four corners four rings of bronze which are to be set on the bronze netting.
You shall set it beneath the altar's ledge, so that to the altar's middle it extends.
You shall make poles for the altar, poles of acacia wood, and overlay them with bronze.
The poles shall be inserted into the rings, so they remain on the altar's two sides
When the altar is carried. You shall make it hollow, with boards. As was shown to your eyes
On the mountain, so shall it be made. You are to make for the Tabernacle a courtyard:
On the Negev side, hangings of fine twined linen, one side one hundred cubits long southward,
With its twenty posts and their twenty sockets of bronze, the hooks of the posts and
　　their bandings
Of silver. And same with the northern border, lengthwise, one hundred cubits of hangings,
With its twenty posts and twenty sockets of bronze, and the posts' hooks and their
　　bandings silver.
And along the courtyard's width on the west side, hangings of fifty cubits, on sea border,
With its ten posts and ten sockets. And along the courtyard's width on the east towards sunrise,
Fifty cubits: fifteen cubits of hangings with their three posts and sockets for one side,
And for the other side, fifteen cubits of hangings with their posts, three, and sockets, three.
And for the courtyard's gate, a screen of twenty cubits, blue, purple, and crimson it shall be,
Of fine twisted linen, embroidered with embroidery, their posts, four, their sockets, four.
All the posts all around the courtyard shall be banded with silver, their hooks of silver,
And their sockets of bronze. The length of the courtyard shall be one hundred cubits, the width
Shall be fifty cubits throughout, and the height shall be five cubits with hangings of twist-
ed fine linen, with their sockets of bronze. All the implements of the Tabernacle
For all its service, all its pegs, and all the pegs of the courtyard, shall be bronze in full.

Now you shall command the Children of Israel to fetch you oil from olives pure beaten,
For the light, so the lamp may be set up to burn regularly. In the Tent of Meeting,
Outside of the curtain that is drawn over the Testimony, Aaron and his sons
Shall arrange it and set it up from sunset until daybreak before the Lord's presence.
It shall burn from evening to morning, as a law for the ages, one perpetual,
Forever to be observed through your generations, by the Children of Israel.

Exodus 28

> "You shall make holy garments: The sacred ephod,
> With the breastplate of judgment, and tunic of blue
> Make a gold plate, engrave it with "Holy to God",
> And the priests shall wear these when their duties they do."

Now bring near to you your brother Aaron and his sons from amidst the Israelites,
To be priests for Me; Aaron, Nadab, Abihu, Eleazar, Ithamar to do rites,
Aaron's sons. You shall make holy garments for Aaron your brother, for glory and beauty.
You shall speak to all who are skilled, whom I have filled with the wisdom of craft, of their duty,
To make Aaron's garments, consecrating him so that he can serve as a priest for Me.
These are the garments they shall make: breastpiece, ephod, robe, checkered tunic (braided to be),
Headdress, and sash. So they shall make holy garments for your brother Aaron and his sons,
To serve as priests to Me. And they are to take gold, blue, purple, crimson, and fine linen.
They shall make the ephod of gold, blue, purple, crimson, and fine linen, worked in designs.
It shall have attached two shoulder-pieces, joined at its two edges, so it shall be joined.
The designed band of the ephod, on it, shall be made like it, from materials same,
Of gold, blue, purple, crimson, fine twisted linen. Take two onyx stones, engrave the names
Of the Children of Israel on them. Six of their names on one stone, the six remaining
On the second stone, in their order of birth. Like stone-cutter's work, with seal engravings,
You shall engrave the two stones with the names of the Children of Israel; and also
You shall make them surrounded and bordered by frames of gold braids. You shall place the two stones
On the shoulders of the ephod, for the Children of Israel as stones of remembrance.
Aaron shall carry their names on his two shoulders, for remembrance before the Lord's presence.

You shall make braids of gold and two chains of pure gold, you are to make them braided
    like cords,
And shall put the rope chains on the braids. You shall make the breastpiece of Judgment
    (of the Lord)
Skillfully worked, you shall make it like you made the ephod; of gold, blue, purple, crimson,
And of fine twisted linen you shall make it. It shall be square, doubled over. A span
Shall be its length and a span its width. Set in it mounted stones, four rows of stone in full.
The first row of stones shall be a carnelian, and a topaz, and a carbuncle.
The second row: emerald, sapphire, and diamond. The third row: jacinth, agate, amethyst.
The fourth row: beryl, onyx, and jasper. Frame them with gold braids where each one's setting is.
The stones shall be with the names of the Children of Israel, twelve as their names prescribe,
They shall be engraved like signet-seal engravings, each one with its name, for the twelve tribes.

You shall make on the breastpiece braided chains of cord, of pure gold. You shall make,
    on breastpiece,
Two gold rings, and you shall attach the two rings to the breastpiece's two ends, one to each.
And you shall attach the two gold chains to the two rings which lie at the breastpiece's ends,
And you shall put them on the ephod's shoulder-piece, facing frontward. Make two more
    gold rings,
And place them on the two ends of the breastpiece, on the inner edge, facing the ephod.
Make two gold rings and put them below the ephod's two shoulder-pieces facing frontward,
Across from its joint, above the designed band of the ephod. The breastpiece they shall tie
From its rings to the rings of the ephod with a blue cord, on the designed band to lie,
Attached so the breastpiece does not come loose from the ephod. Aaron shall bear, for his part,
The names of the Children of Israel on the breastpiece of Judgment over his heart,
Whenever he comes into the Holy place, for remembrance, before the Lord's presence,
Regularly. You shall put the Urim and the Thummim in the breastpiece of Judgment,
So that they will be over Aaron's heart when he comes before the presence of the Lord.
So Aaron shall bear the breastpiece of Judgment for the Children of Israel, thus worn
Over his heart, before the Lord's presence, regularly. You shall make the ephod's robe
All of blue. In the middle of it shall be a head-opening, with seam for its o-
pening, all around, of woven work, like the opening of armor, so it won't split.
You shall make on its skirts all around the hem blue, purple, and crimson pomegranates,
And bells of gold between them, all around: bell of gold and pomegranate, bell of gold
And pomegranate, on the ephod's robe, all around. (For it was thought in days of old
That the sound of a bell would drive demons away. It also warns that humans draw near.)
It shall be put on Aaron while he ministers, so that the sound of it is heard clear
When he comes into the Holy place before the Lord's presence, and heard when he goes out,
So that he does not die. You shall make a plate of pure gold, and on it you shall carve out
Signet engravings, inscribed with "Holiness for the Lord". You shall attach a blue thread
To the headdress, to be on the front of the headdress. It shall be on Aaron's forehead.

So Aaron shall bear iniquity from all the holy things that the Israelites
Offer as sacrifices, all their gifts of holiness—on Aaron's head this alights
Regularly, for winning acceptance for them before the Lord's presence, for their sinning.
You shall make the checkered tunic of fine linen, you shall make the headdress of fine linen,
And you shall make an embroidered sash. As for Aaron's sons, you shall make tunics for them,
You shall make them sashes, and you shall make them turbans, for glory and for adornment.
You are to put them on Aaron your brother, and his sons with him clothed in them shall be.
You shall anoint them, you shall ordain them, you shall consecrate them to be priests for Me.
You shall make them linen breeches to cover nakedness; from hips to thighs they'll extend.
They are to be worn by Aaron and by his sons whenever they come into the Tent
Of Meeting, or when they approach the altar to minister at the sanctuary,
So they do not bear guilt and die. This, a law for all time, for him and his progeny.

Exodus 29

> "Now the priests you must consecrate, and this is how:
> Take two rams, and a bull, a breadbasket as well.
> Offer them up to me as a sign of your vow,
> And amidst all the Israelites I shall dwell."

Now this is the thing that you shall do to them to consecrate them to serve Me as priests:
Take a young bull from the herd, and two rams unblemished, and unleavened bread (use no yeast)
And flat unleavened cakes mixed with oil, and unleavened wafers that with oil are spread;
You shall make them of wheat flour. Put them in one basket, and bring them in the basket,
Along with the bull and the two rams. And Aaron and his sons you shall bring to the door
Of the Tent of Meeting, and wash them with water. Take the holy clothes mentioned before
And clothe Aaron—With the tunic, the robe of the ephod, the ephod, and the breastpiece,
Gird him with the designed band of the ephod, then the headdress on his head you shall place,
And you shall put the holy diadem on the headdress. Take the oil of anointing
And pour it on his head, as so to anoint him. And his sons you shall then forward bring
And clothe them in tunics. You shall gird them with a sash, Aaron and his sons, and shall wind
Turbans for them. And so the right of the priesthood is one that shall be theirs for all time.
So you shall ordain Aaron and his sons. To the Tent of Meeting you shall bring the bull,
And Aaron and his sons shall lay their hands upon the bull's head. You shall slaughter the bull
In the Lord's presence, at the entrance of the Tent of Meeting, and take some of the blood
From the bull and put it on the altar's horns with your finger. Toss the rest of the blood
Against the base of the altar. You shall take all of the fat that covers the entrails,
The appendage above the liver, the two kidneys and the fat on them this entails,

And turn them into smoke upon the altar. As for the bull's flesh, its dung and its skin,
You shall burn it with fire, outside the camp; It is a purification offering.
Then you shall take the first ram, and Aaron and his sons shall place their hands on the ram's head.
You shall slay the ram, take its blood, and toss it on the altar, all around sprinkling red.
You shall cut up the ram into sections, and wash its entrails and its legs, and put them
On its quarters and on its head, and you shall turn to smoke on the altar the whole ram.
It is an offering to the Lord, a sweet odor, a burnt offering to the Lord.
You shall take the second ram, Aaron and his sons shall place hands on its head like before.
You shall slay this ram, take some of its blood, and place it on the ridge of Aaron's right ear
And on the ridge of the right ears of Aaron's sons, and on thumbs of the right hands of theirs,
And the big toes of their right feet. Toss the rest of the blood on the altar all around.
You shall take some anointing oil and some of the blood that now on the altar is found,
And shall toss it on Aaron and his garments, and his sons and his sons' garments also,
So that he and his garments may be hallowed, and his sons and his sons' garments hallowed.
You are to take the fat parts from the ram, the fat tail, the fat covering the entrails,
The appendage above the liver, the two kidneys and the fat on them this entails,
And the right thigh, for this is the ram of ordination. And then add one loaf of bread,
One cake of oil-bread, and one wafer, all from the basket of bread that is unleavened
In the Lord's presence. You shall place them all on Aaron's palms and on the palms of his sons,
And you shall elevate them as an elevation-offering, in the Lord's presence.
You shall take them from their hands and turn them to smoke upon the altar, with the contents
Of the offering, as a sweet odor, it shall be a burnt offering for the Lord.
You shall take the breast from Aaron's ram of ordination and elevate it upward
As an elevation-offering, in the Lord's presence; it is to be your portion.
You shall hallow the breast for the elevation-offering, and thigh contribution
The thigh of the offering that is elevated, raised from the ram of ordination,
From what is Aaron's and from what is his sons'. It shall be for all time an allocation
For Aaron and his sons from the Children of Israel, it is a gift for the priests;
And it shall be a gift from the Children of Israel, from their offerings of peace,
Their raised contributions for the Lord. Now the garments of holiness that are Aaron's
Shall belong to his sons after him, so they may be anointed and ordained in them.
The one of his sons serving as priest in his stead shall wear the garments for seven days,
The one who comes into the Tent of Meeting to officiate in the Holy place.
You shall take the ram of ordination and shall in the Holy place boil its flesh.
Aaron and his sons shall eat the ram's flesh, along with the bread that is in the basket
At the entrance of the Tent of Meeting. These things which purify shall only be eaten
By those who have been ordained and consecrated. They are holy; laymen may not eat them.
Now if any flesh of ordination or bread should remain when morning comes to be,
You shall burn what remains in the fire, it shall not be eaten, because it is holy.
You shall do so for Aaron and his sons, according to all I have commanded you,
You shall ordain them for seven days. And for each day you shall make ready a bull, too,

As a purification offering. You shall cleanse the altar through purification,
And you are to anoint it to hallow it. For seven days you shall do this purgation
To the altar, to consecrate it; And the altar will become an altar most holy.
Whatever touches the altar shall become holy. You shall offer regularly
On the altar: Year-old lambs, two each day. The first lamb you shall sacrifice at daybreak,
And the second lamb you shall sacrifice at twilight. And with the first lamb you shall take
A tenth-measure of choice flour, with one quarter-gallon of oil mixed in, and libation
Of a quarter-gallon of wine. And you shall offer the second lamb at day's cessation,
Making the same grain-gifts and libations you made for morning. It shall be a sweet odor,
A burnt offering for the Lord. It shall be through your generations as a regular
Offering, at the entrance of the Tent of Meeting, before the Lord. For it is there
That I will meet with you, there I will speak to you. I will meet the Israelites there,
And by My Glory it will be consecrated. I will consecrate the Tent of Meeting
And the altar. I will hallow Aaron and his sons to be priests for Me by priesting.
And I will dwell amidst the Children of Israel and I will be a God for them,
So that they may know that I am the Lord, their God, who has brought them out of Egypt's land,
That I might dwell among the Children of Israel, Myself. I am the Lord, their God.

Exodus 30

> "You shall make a wood altar for burning incense.
> Everyone shall contribute one half-shekel in.
> Make a bronze basin, and start constructing the Tent.
> And don't copy the holy incense, that's a sin."

You shall make an altar to burn incense upon, you shall make it of acacia wood,
It shall be one cubit long and one cubit wide, it shall be square, and two cubits high,
With horns from it of one piece with it. Overlay it with pure gold, its top and its sides
All around, and its horns. You shall make a gold rim all around. And make two rings of gold,
To go under its rim on its two sides, make them on its two sides, for holders of poles,
So that it may be carried by them. Make the poles of acacia wood, and overlay
Them with gold. Place it in front of the curtain over the Ark of the Testimony,
In front of the penance-cover over the Testimony, where I will meet with you.
And Aaron shall burn fragrant incense on it; every morning, when the lamps he tends to,
He shall burn incense. And when he lights the lamps at night, he shall also burn incense then,
A regular incense offering before the Lord's presence through your generations.
You shall not offer any outsider's incense on it, offerings burnt or of grain,
Nor shall you pour a libation on it. Once a year Aaron is to purge out sin's stain,

Purifying the horns of the altar, with blood from the offering of purification.
Purification shall be performed on the altar once per year, through your generations;
It is most holy to the Lord."

[Ki Tisa]

                    Now the Lord spoke to Moses, and He said, "When you take
A census of the Israelites, in counting them, each man shall give for his life's sake
A ransom for his life to the Lord upon being counted, so no plague shall befall them
When you count them. This is what they are to give, everyone that goes through the
        counting, all them:
Half a shekel, sanctuary weight (Twenty gerahs or twenty grains makes up a shekel).
Half a shekel, an offering for the Lord. Everyone that is entered in the record,
From the age of twenty years and upward, shall pay the offering of the Lord to live.
The rich shall not pay more, and the poor shall not pay less than half a shekel when they give
The Lord's offering, as ransom for your lives. You shall take the money of atonement
From the Children of Israel and assign it for the service of the Meeting Tent,
So it shall serve for the Israelites as a remembrance before the Lord's presence,
To atone for yourselves." Now the Lord spoke to Moses and said, "Make a basin of bronze,
Its pedestal of bronze, for washing; place it between the altar and Tent of Meeting.
You shall put water in it, so Aaron and his sons may wash their hands and feet therein.
When they come into the Tent of Meeting, they shall wash with water, so they do not die,
Or when they approach the altar to serve, and burn offerings to the Lord up on high,
They shall wash their hands and their feet, so they do not die. It shall be a law for the ages
For them—For both him and his sons, throughout their generations." Now the Lord spoke
        to Moses,
Saying, "As for you, take choice fragrant spices. Flowing-myrrh- five hundred. Cinnamon spice-
Half as much (two hundred and fifty). Fragrant cane- two hundred and fifty will suffice.
Cassia- five hundred. (Now these measures are in shekel-weights from the sanctuary.)
And one hin of olive oil. And you shall make from it an anointing oil that's holy,
A compound of ingredients expertly blended, to be anointing oil holy.
You shall anoint the Tent of Meeting with it, and also the ark of Testimony,
And the table and all its implements, the lampstand and all its implements as well,
The altars for incense and burnt offerings, implements, the basin and pedestal.
You shall hallow them, so they become most holy. All that touches them shall be holy.
And Aaron and his sons you shall anoint, you shall hallow them to serve as priests for Me.
And speak to the Children of Israel and say, 'this shall be holy anointing oil,
It shall be for me throughout your generations. And its holiness you shall not spoil
By pouring it on any human body (aside from the priests). You are not to make
Any other that is like it, from the same composition. For it is to be sac-
red, and shall remain so for you. Any man who mixes compounds like it or does pour
Any of it on an outsider shall be cut off from his kinspeople forevermore.'"

Now the Lord said to Moses, "Take fragrant spices, stacte, onycha, and galbanum,
These spices with clear incense, in equal parts. You shall make with it incense, a perfume,
Blended expertly, salted, pure and holy. Powderize some of it with a firm beating,
And you are to put some of it in front of the Testimony in the Tent of Meeting,
Where I will meet with you; It shall be most holy for you. As for the incense you make,
You are not to make any like it in the same proportions; such would be a mistake.
It shall be sacred holiness to you, to be sacred for the Lord. So any man
That makes any incense like it to savor it shall be cut off from his kin and clan."

Exodus 31

Then the Lord said to Moses, "I've called Bezalel,
Whom I filled up with wisdom to make what I've shown.
From the ark to the basin, he'll make it all well."
And then God gave to Moses two tablets of stone.

Now the Lord spoke to Moses, and said, "See, I have called by name the one called Bezalel,
Son of Uri, son of Hur, of the tribe of Judah. In him, the breath of God does dwell.
I have filled him with the spirit of God, in knowledge, discernment, and ability
In all kinds of workmanship, to make designs, working in gold, silver, bronze, filigree,
In stonecutting for setting stones, and carving of wood—work in all kinds of craft he can.
And here, I give with him Oholiab son of Ahisamach, of the tribe of Dan.
I have given all skillful men skill, so they may make all that I have commanded you:
The Tent of Meeting, the ark of Testimony, and penance-cover over it too,
All the Tent's implements, table and implements, pure lampstand and implements as well,
The altars for incense and burnt offerings, implements, basin and its pedestal,
Garments of office, holy garments for Aaron the priest and the garments of his sons
For priesting, and anointing oil, and incense for sanctuary offerings (holy ones).
According to all that I have commanded you, they shall make it, as I have designed."
Now the Lord said to Moses: Speak to the Children of Israel and say, "Keep in mind
That you must keep My Sabbaths, for it is a sign between Me and you, throughout all time,
To know that I, the Lord, hallow you. You shall keep the Sabbath holy and sanctified,
For it is holy to you. Whoever profanes it shall be put to death for his sin,
For whoever does work on it, that person shall be cut off from among all his kin.
Six days shall work be done, but on the seventh day is Sabbath, of ceasing and of rest,
Holy to the Lord; whoever does work on the Sabbath day is to be put to death.

The Children of Israel shall keep the Sabbath, to observe it through their generations
As a covenant for all time. It is a sign to last for the ages in duration,
Between Me and the Israelites. For in six days, the Lord made the heavens and earth,
But on the seventh day, He ceased and paused for breath (This rest how the Sabbath
    got its birth)."
Now when He finished speaking with Moses on Mount Sinai, He gave to Moses, unflawed,
The two tablets of Testimony, tablets of stone, written with the finger of God.

Exodus 32

> Now when Moses was late, all the people cried out,
> "Aaron, make us a god!" So he gathered their gold,
> Made a calf, which they worshipped and reveled about.
> God said, "Moses, your people don't do what they're told."
> Moses came down the mountain with tablets in hand,
> And of singing and choral prayer, he heard the sound.
> When he saw the calf, how they ignored God's command,
> Moses angrily smashed the tablets to the ground.

When the people saw that Moses was late in coming down from the mountain in the skies,
The people gathered themselves together against Aaron and said to him, "Now, arise,
Make us a god who will go before us, for this Moses who brought us from Egypt's land,
As for this man, we do not know what has become of him, so now we need a new plan."
Aaron said to them, "Take off the gold rings which are in the ears of your wives, daughters, sons,
And bring them to me." All the people took gold rings from their ears, bringing them to Aaron.
He took them from their hand, cast them into a mold, and made it into a molten calf.
Then they said, "This is your God, O Israel, who brought you from Egypt on his behalf!"
When Aaron saw this, he built an altar before it, and Aaron then called out to say,
"Tomorrow is a festival to the Lord." The people started early the next day,
Offered burnt offerings and brought peace offerings. The people sat down to eat and drink,
And arose to frolic. And the Lord said to Moses, "Go down, they've gone over the brink!
For your people whom you brought up from Egypt's land have corrupted themselves,
    causing ruin.
They have been quick to turn aside from the way that I commanded them, and in so doing,
They have made themselves a molten calf, they have bowed to it, even sacrificed to it,
And they have said, 'this is your God, O Israel, who brought you from the land of Egypt!'"

And the Lord said to Moses, "I see these people, they are a people stiff and hard-necked.
So now leave me alone, so my anger may flare against them, causing them to be wrecked,
Though you, Moses, I will make into a great nation." Moses implored the Lord, his God,
Saying, "Why, O Lord, should your anger flare against your people whom you spared from
    the rod,
Whom you brought out of the land of Egypt with great power and with a mighty hand, why?
Why should the Egyptians be able to say, 'He brought them out only to let them die,
He delivered them with ill intent, to kill them in the mountains, burn them from the soil.'?
Turn from your flaming anger, O Lord, and repent of this ill against your people loyal.
Recall Your servants Abraham, Isaac, and Israel, to whom You Yourself have sworn:
I will make your seed many like stars in the heavens, and give to the offspring you've borne
All this land which I've promised, so that they may have it as a possession everlasting."
And the Lord repented of the ill He had planned for His people, for their gold calf-casting.
Now Moses turned to come down the mountain, the two tablets of Testimony in hand,
Tablets inscribed on both sides, with writing on one, and on the other one just as grand.
And the tablets were God's work, the writing was God's writing, all written on the tablets.
Now when Joshua heard the sound of the people as they shouted, he said to Moses,
"The sound of war is in the camp." But Moses said, "That is not the sound of victory,
Not the tune of prevailing, nor the tune of failing defeat, something else it must be—
It's the sound of singing that I hear!" And it was, when Moses neared the camp and he saw
The calf and the dancing, Moses's anger flared up, and he threw the tablets of law
From his hands, smashing them at the foot of the mountain. He took the calf that they had made,
Burned it with fire, ground it to powder, and scattered it so on the water it laid,
And he made the Children of Israel drink it. Then Moses turned and said to Aaron,
"What did this people do to you, that you have brought upon them such a terrible sin?"
Aaron said, "Let my lord's anger not flare up, for you yourself know how this people is,
They are set on evil. They told me, 'Make us a god to lead us, for that man Moses,
The one who brought us up from the land of Egypt, we do not know what happened to him.'
So I said to them, 'Whoever has gold, remove it.' They took it off and turned it in,
They gave it all to me, and then I threw it into the fire, and out came this calf."
Now when Moses saw that the people had gotten out of control due to Aaron's gaffe,
And that Aaron had let it get so bad that they were derided by the enemy,
Moses stood at the gate of the camp and said, "Whoever is for the Lord, come to me!"
All the sons of Levi rallied to Moses there, and he said to the sons of Levi,
"Thus says the Lord, the God of Israel: Each man among you, put your sword on your thigh,
Proceed back and forth from gate to gate throughout the camp, every man his brother to slay,
Every man his neighbor, every man his kinsman." And the sons of Levi did obey.
They did as Moses bid them. And on that day, three thousand men of the people did fall.
Moses said, "Be ordained to the Lord today, even though it has had high cost for all,
Every man at the cost of his son, at the cost of his brother, has suffered much sorrow,
So that the Lord may bestow a blessing upon you today." Now it was on the morrow,

Moses said to the people, "You have been guilty of a terrible sin, and so now
I will go up to the Lord, perhaps I can make atonement for your sin (the gold cow)."
Moses went back to the Lord and said, "Alas, this people has done a terrible sin,
They have made themselves a god of gold. Now if you would only forgive and bear their sin...
But if you will not, then pray, blot me out of the record that you have written, in haste."
The Lord said to Moses, "He who sins against Me, him from My record shall be erased.
Only him. So now go, lead the people to the place of which I have spoken to you, and behold;
My messenger shall go before you, but on the day of My accounting, have them told,
On that day I will call them to account for their sin." And then the Lord sent down a plague,
Plaguing the people for making the calf, for what they did with the calf that Aaron made.

Exodus 33

The Lord told Moses, "Go to the land that I swore
I would give you. I will send a messenger first,
But I will not go with you as I have before,
For your people are hard-necked, my anger might burst."
Moses went to the Tent where he met with the Lord,
Saying, "If You don't go with us, don't make us go.
For Your presence is what makes us great," he implored.
And the Lord favored Moses, said, "Let it be so."

The Lord said to Moses, "Go up from here, you and the people you brought from Egypt's land,
To the land of which I swore to Abraham, Isaac, and Jacob, saying, 'In the hand
Of your offspring shall I give it.' I will send a messenger before you to drive out
Canaanites, Amorites, Hittites, Perizzites, Hivites, Jebusites from lands thereabouts.
You shall go to a land flowing with milk and honey. But—I will not go in your midst,
For you are a hard-necked people, otherwise I'd destroy you." When the people heard this,
When they heard these harsh words and ill tidings, they mourned, no man put on
    himself ornaments.
The Lord said to Moses, "Tell the Children of Israel: You are all stubborn-necked men.
If for one moment I were to go up in your midst, I would destroy you. So for now,
Take off your ornaments so I may consider what I am to do with you, and how."
So the Children of Israel stripped themselves of ornaments at the foot of the Mount,
And remained stripped of their ornaments from then on. Now Moses would take
    himself the Tent,

And go far outside the camp to pitch it. Moses called it the Tent of Meeting because
Those who sought God would go out to the Tent of Meeting outside of the camp. And it was,
That whenever Moses would go out to the Tent, all the people would stand and arise,
Each man at the entrance of his own tent, and they would gaze after Moses with their eyes
Until Moses had entered the Tent. And whenever Moses would come into the Tent,
Then the column of cloud would come down, and stand at the Tent's entrance after its descent.
And He would speak with Moses, and all the people would see a standing column of cloud
At the Tent's entrance, and all the people would rise, and each man at his tent's entrance bowed.
And the Lord would speak to Moses, face to face, as a man speaks to his neighbor or friend.
Now when he would return to the camp, the youth Joshua, son of Nun, his attendant,
Would not stray from within the Tent. Moses said to the Lord, "See, now You have said to me,
'Bring this people up,' but You have not let me know whom You'll send with me on this journey.
And You said, 'I have known you by name, and you have gained My favor,' so if this is true,
If I've gained favor in Your eyes, pray let me know Your ways, so I may truly know You,
And continue to find favor in Your eyes. See, this nation is Your people, so please."
The Lord said, "If My presence were to go with you, would it cause you rest more at ease?"
Moses said, "If Your presence does not go with us, then please do not bring us up from here.
For how else shall the fact that both I and Your people have found Your favor be made clear?
Is it not precisely in that You go with us that we are distinct, having Your grace,
Your people and I, thus separated from every other people on the earth's face?"
The Lord said to Moses, "I shall do as you ask, for you have found favor in My eyes,
And I have known you by name." And he said, "Let me see Your Glory, to be realized."
The Lord said, "I Myself shall cause all of My Goodliness to pass in front of your face
I will call out the name of the Lord before you, and I show grace to whom I show grace,
And I show mercy to those I show mercy to." But he said, "You cannot see My face,
For no human can see Me and live." The Lord said, "See, now here is a place next to Me.
Station yourself on the rock, and when My Glory and My Presence pass by, it shall be,
I will place you in the cleft of the rock, and screen you with My hand, until I've passed through.
Then I will remove My hand, you shall see My back, but My face shall not be seen by you."

Exodus 34

The Lord told Moses, "Carve two more tablets of stone,
And I'll write the same words as the ones that you broke."
Moses carved two more tablets, like those he had thrown,
And he climbed up the mountain. And then the Lord spoke:
"Don't make molten gods for yourselves! Firstborn are mine.
Keep my feasts, keep the Sabbath, and keep all my ways.
Write these words down, a covenant that is divine."
Moses scribed the ten commandments, stayed forty days.

Then the Lord said to Moses, "Carve yourself two tablets of stone similar to the first,
And I will write on these tablets the words that were on the first tablets, the ones you burst.
And be ready by morning; go up in the morning to Mount Sinai, wait there for Me,
On the top of the mountain. No man shall go up with you, and no one else is to be
On the mountain at all. Nor shall sheep or oxen graze down at the foot of this mountain."
So Moses carved two tablets of stone like the first ones, and early with the rising sun
In the morning he went up to Mount Sinai, as God had commanded him. In his hand,
He took the two stone tablets. The Lord came down in the cloud, there beside Moses to stand,
And called out the name of the Lord. The Lord passed before his face, and then called out,
    "The Lord,
The Lord God, showing mercy and grace, slow to anger, abounding in faith to his horde,
Being loyal to the thousandth generation, bearing iniquity, sin, transgression,
Yet He does not clear the guilty, visiting iniquities of fathers on the sons,
And upon sons' sons, to the third and fourth generations." Moses hastened to bow low,
In homage, saying, "Pray if I've found favor with You, O my Lord, pray let my Lord go
Among us. Yes, we are a hard-necked people, so forgive our iniquity and sin,
And make us Your inheritance, make us Your own." He said, "Here, I cut a covenant.
Before all your people I will work wonders which in the whole world have never been viewed.
Then the people with you shall see how awesome is the Lord's work which I will do with you.
Mark well what I command you today. For I shall drive out before you the Amorites,
And the Canaanites, and the Hittites, and the Perizzites, the Hivites, and Jebusites.
Beware that you cut no covenant with the inhabitants of the lands where you go
Otherwise they will become a snare among you. Instead, their altars you shall bring low,
You shall pull them down, their pillars you shall smash, their tree-poles you are to cut
    down and maim.
For you are not to bow down before other gods, for the Lord, Jealous One is his name,

He is a jealous God. If you cut covenant with the inhabitants of the land,

When they go whoring after their gods and sacrifice to them, they will call you on hand

To eat their offerings. And should you take from among their daughters as wives for your sons,

Their women will go whoring after their gods, and cause your sons to be whoring ones.

You shall not make molten gods for yourselves! You shall observe the Feast of Unleavened Bread.

For seven days you shall eat matzot, as I commanded you, at the time appointed

In the month of Abib, for in the month of Abib's ripe grain, you went out of Egypt.

Every breacher of a womb is mine, every male ox and sheep that from a womb is ripped,

But the firstling donkey you shall redeem with a sheep, and if you should fail to redeem,

You shall break its neck. Each firstborn among your sons you must redeem. No one shall be seen

Before my presence empty-handed. For six days you shall work, but on the seventh day,

You shall cease, at plowing, at grain-cutting, you shall cease. Harvest or not, you must obey.

The Feast of Weeks you shall make for yourselves, the first fruits of the wheat cutting, and also,

The Festival of Ingathering as year turns. Three times a year it shall be so:

All your males shall be seen before the presence of the Lord God, the God of Israel.

For I shall drive out nations before your path, widen your territory where you dwell,

So no man covets your land when you go to appear before the Lord your God's presence

Three times a year. You shall not offer blood for My sacrifice with a thing that ferments.

You shall not leave the Passover sacrifice until morning. The first fruits of your soil,

The choicest of them, you shall bring into the house of the Lord your God. You shall not boil

A kid in the milk of its mother." And the Lord said to Moses, "You, write down these words,

For in accordance with these words, I cut a covenant with you, and Israel's herds."

Now he was there beside the Lord for forty days and forty nights; he did not eat bread,

Did not drink water, but wrote down on the tablets the terms of the covenant instead,

The Ten Commandments. Now when Moses came down from Mount Sinai with the tablets in hand,

The two tablets of Testimony with Moses, when Moses came down from the mountain,

He did not know that the skin of his face was radiant because he'd spoken with Him.

Aaron and all the Children of Israel saw that his face's skin was radiant,

So they were afraid to approach him. Moses called to them, and then did Aaron approach,

Along with the leaders of the community, returning to Moses, and he spoke.

He spoke to them, and afterward all of the Children of Israel chose to draw nigh,

And he commanded them everything that the Lord had spoken to him on Mount Sinai.

Now when Moses had finished speaking with them, Moses put a veil over his face.

Whenever Moses would come before the Lord's presence, to speak with Him, he would displace

The veil, until he had gone out. And when he came out to tell all the Israelites

What he had been commanded, the Children of Israel saw Moses's face was bright.

They would see his face, see the skin of the face of Moses—And it was radiating!

But then Moses would replace the veil on his face, until he went in to speak with Him.

Exodus 35

> Moses told all the Israelites, "God commanded
> That all may contribute to build for the Lord."
> And when these contributions to Moses were handed,
> He said, "Bezalel shall design every board."

[Vayakhel]

Now Moses gathered the whole community of the Israelites and said to them,
"These are the words that the Lord has commanded, that you should do them and
    adhere to them:
For six days work shall be made, but on the seventh day, there shall be holiness for you,
Sabbath of rest for the Lord. Whoever works on it shall be put to death if they do.
You shall not let fire burn anywhere throughout all your settlements on the Sabbath day."
Now Moses spoke to the whole community of the Children of Israel to say,
"This is the thing the Lord has commanded, saying: Take from yourselves a raised-offering
For the Lord. A gift for the Lord from whoever's mind and heart makes them willing to bring
The Lord's contribution: gold, and silver, and bronze, blue-violet, and purple, and crimson,
Fine linens, goats' hair, rams' skins dyed red, tanned leather skins, (all to be used for construction),
Acacia wood, oil for lighting, spices for anointing oil and for fragrant incense,
Onyx stones, stones for setting on the ephod (priest's garment) and breastpiece for
    those raiments.
And everyone who is skilled among you shall come and shall make all that the Lord
    does command:
The Tabernacle, its tent and cover, its clasps and boards, its bars and pillars to stand,
And its sockets. The ark and its poles, the penance-cover and the curtain for the screen,
The table and its poles and all its implements, and the Bread of Presence to be seen,
And the lampstand for lighting and its implements and its lamps, and the oil for lighting,
And the altar for incense and its poles, fragrant incense, and the oil for anointing,
And the entrance curtain for the entrance of the Tabernacle, the Dwelling's entrance,
The altar for burnt-offerings, its bronze-mesh lattice, its poles and all its implements,
The basin and its pedestal, the hangings of the courtyard, its pillars and its sockets,
And the screen for the gate of the courtyard, the pegs of the Tabernacle (made to lock it),
And the pegs of the courtyard, and their cords, garments for Holy Shrine officiating,
Holy garments for Aaron the priest, and the garments of Aaron's sons for their priesting."
So the whole Israelite community went out from Moses's presence, and then
Everyone whose heart moved him, and everyone whose spirit made him willing, all those men

Brought the Lord's contribution for work on the Tent of Meeting, for all its construction,
For that service and for the holy garments. Then women and men alike, everyone
Whose hearts moved them brought brooches, earrings, signet rings, necklaces, gold objects
    of all kinds,
Every man moved to give elevation offerings of gold to the Lord by his mind,
And everyone who had in their possession blue, purple, crimson, fine linen, goats' hair,
Rams' skins dyed red, and tanned leather skins, brought them. Everyone that elevated a share,
A raised contribution of silver and bronze, they brought the contribution of the Lord.
And everyone that had acacia wood for the work of constructing the planks and boards,
They brought that. And all skilled women spun with their own hands, and they brought their
    spinning—the blue,
The purple, the crimson, and the fine-linen, and every one of the women who knew
How to do so with skill spun the goats' hair. And the chieftains brought onyx stones,
    stones for setting,
For the ephod and for the breastpiece, and the fragrant spices and the oil for the lighting,
For the anointing oil, and the fragrant incense. Each Israelite woman and man
Whose heart moved them to bring anything for the work that the Lord had given His command
For them to make through Moses, they brought it. An offering to the Lord, one of free will.
Moses said to the Children of Israel, "See, the Lord has called by name Bezalel
Son of Uri, son of Hur, of the tribe of Judah, He has filled him with Godly breath,
With the Spirit of God, in skill, ability, and knowledge of all crafts in full breadth,
To design designs, make them in gold, silver, bronze, the carving of stones for setting each,
And the carving of wood, to make all kinds of crafts of designed workmanship, and to teach,
The Lord put all this skill in his mind, he and Oholiab son of Ahisamach,
Of the tribe of Dan. He has filled them with the skill to design workmanship of all stocks,
Of the jewel-cutter, designer, embroiderer, in blue, purple, crimson, linen fine,
And of the weaver, makers of all kinds of workmanship, and designers of designs.

Exodus 36

Then the people brought so much that Moses said, "Stop!
We have all that we need for constructing the shrine."
Then the curtains were measured, fifty loops on top,
And they all were assembled, as had been designed.

So shall Bezalel and Oholiab make work, and every man whom the Lord has filled
With knowledge and ability to construct the Holy place, these men able and skilled

Shall do all the work that the Lord has commanded. So then Moses called for Bezalel,
For Oholiab, and for all skilled, able men the Lord had filled with wisdom as well,
All whose hearts made them willing to come do the work, to do it. And from Moses they got
All the gifts for constructing the Holy place that the Children of Israel had brought.
They continued to bring him freewill offerings every morning; and then the wise men,
The skilled artisans constructing the Holy place, came to Moses again and again,
Each came from his work to say to Moses, "The people are bringing much more than we need
For the work of construction that the Lord has commanded so we may complete this deed."
So then Moses had this proclamation sent throughout the camp: "Let no woman or man
Expend any more work in the offering of gifts for the Holy place building plan."
So the people were stopped from bringing; the construction materials they brought before
Was enough for all of the construction work needed to build the Holy place, and more.

Then all those who were skilled among those who did work made the tabernacle from ten curtains
Of fine twisted linen, of blue, and of purple, and of crimson. The workers were certain
To include cherubim, skillfully worked according to the designer's craftsmanship.
The length of each one curtain was twenty-eight cubits, and the width of each four cubits.
And then five of the curtains were joined together, with each one being joined to the next,
And the other five curtains were also joined to one another, so they would connect.
They made loops of blue violet on the edge of one curtain at the end of the one set,
And did the same with the edge of the curtain that was on the end of the other set.
Fifty loops were made on the first curtain, and fifty loops were also made on the other,
On the edge of the other set's outermost curtain, so that the loops faced one another.
Then they made fifty clasps of gold, and joined the curtains to each other using the clasps,
So that the tabernacle-dwelling became one piece when all of these steps had elapsed.

Then the curtains of goats' hair were made to hang over the tabernacle, as a tent.
There were eleven tapestries there, the length of each one thirty cubits in extent,
And the width of each curtain was four cubits; All eleven curtains were the same size.
Five of the tapestries were joined separately, the other six to themselves were tied.
Then some loops were made, fifty of them, at the edge of one set's end-curtain, at the joint,
And fifty loops were made at the edge of the curtain that joined it, at its joining point.
Then bronze clasps were made, fifty of them, to join the tent together into one whole piece.
Then a covering for the tent was made of rams' skins dyed red, and above that same crease
Was a covering of tanned leather skins. And then boards were made for the Tabernacle
Of acacia wood, standing upright, with ten cubits as the length of each board in full,
And a cubit and a half, the width of each board, with two pegs, parallel to each other,
And so all the boards for the Tabernacle were made, with pegs across from each other.

Then the boards for the Tabernacle were made with twenty boards facing the Negev, south,
And forty silver sockets beneath twenty of the boards, two sockets serving as mouths

To catch the pegs beneath each board, and two sockets beneath each other board for its pegs.
And for the northern wall of the Tabernacle, twenty boards, with sockets to catch pegs,
With their forty silver sockets, two beneath each one board, two beneath each other board.
And for the rear of the Tabernacle, seawards, facing west, they constructed six boards.
And two boards were made for the back corners of the Tabernacle, apart at the base,
But then coupled together above at the top in one ring. With two boards, that took place,
So the two of them formed the two corners. Eight rear boards in all, with sixteen silver sockets,
Two sockets beneath each board, and two sockets beneath each other board, in place to lock it.

Then they made bars of acacia wood, five for boards on one side of the Tabernacle,
Five bars for the boards on the other side, and five bars for the rear, west towards the sea's pull.
And the middle bar was made halfway up the boards to run from end to end going through.
The boards were overlaid with gold, and their rings were made of gold, to put the bars into,
And the bars were overlaid with gold. They made a curtain of blue, purple, and crimson,
And fine twisted linen. It was made with cherubim in the skilled design that was done.
Then four pillars of acacia were made for it, overlaid with gold, their hooks of gold,
And four silver sockets were cast for the hooks. Then for the Tent's entrance and threshold
Was made a screen of blue, purple, crimson, and fine twisted linen, with embroidery;
And its five pillars with hooks, tops and bands overlaid with gold, five sockets bronze to be.

Exodus 37

> Bezalel made the ark, and the table of wood,
> Then the lampstand of gold with his tireless toil.
> He constructed the altar, done just as he should,
> And then made smoking incense and the holy oil.

Bezalel made the ark of acacia wood, with its length as two and a half cubits,
One and a half cubits was its height and one and a half cubits was also its width.
Then he overlaid it with pure gold, inside and out, and made a gold rim all around.
He cast four rings of gold for it, to be placed upon its four feet which stood on the ground,
With two rings on one side and two rings on the other. He made poles of acacia wood,
Overlaid them with gold, and inserted them into the rings which on the ark's sides stood,
So the ark could be carried by means of them. He made a penance-cover of pure gold,
Two and a half cubits long, and a cubit and a half wide (just as he had been told).
He made two cherubim of gold, made of hammered-work at the penance-cover's two ends,
One cherub at one end and one at the other end. From the cover they did extend,

So they were made from one piece with the cover, at the two ends, and their wings
    spread upwards,
With their wings sheltering the cover. The cover and each other was what they faced towards.

He made the table of acacia wood, two cubits in length, and one cubit in width,
And one and a half cubits in height. He overlaid it with pure gold, and made for it
A gold rim all around, and a border one hand's breadth wide, with a gold rim for its border
All around. He cast four gold rings for it and put the rings at the four edges (as ordered),
Where the table's four legs are. The rings were close to the rim, so that they could hold the poles
Which would carry the table. He made the poles of acacia wood, overlaid with gold,
So that they could carry the table. He made the implements to be put on the table:
Its dishes, and its jars and its jugs from which offerings were to be poured, and its ladles;
Of pure gold he made them. He made a lampstand of pure gold, of hammered-work,
    base and branches,
Its cups, its calyxes, its petals were made from it. And from its sides issued six branches,
Three branches from one side, three branches from the other side. On one branch there
    were three cups
Shaped like almond-blossoms, each with calyx and petals, and on the other branch going up,
Three cups like almond-blossoms, with calyx and petals, so for all six branches from the base
Of the lamp. And on the lampstand itself, four almond-cups, calyx and petals in place,
A calyx under two branches, all from the same piece, a calyx under a branch pair,
From the same piece, a calyx beneath two branches, all formed from this one lamp piece,
    with care,
And so on for all six of the lampstand's branches. Their calyxes and stems shall be from it,
All of hammered-work, all of pure gold, and all made of one piece, with all else being from it.
He made its lamps, seven of them, and its tongs and its trays of pure gold. From one ingot
Of pure gold he made it, with all its implements, from one ingot of pure gold he wrought.

He made the altar for burning incense, of acacia wood, with its length one cubit,
And a cubit its width, square, and two cubits its height. It had two horns coming from it.
He overlaid it all with pure gold, its top, and its sides all around, and its horns too.
He made a rim of gold for it all around, and two rings of gold for poles to go through.
The rings were to go under the rim on the two opposite sides, so that the poles could
Be held there, so the altar could be carried by them. He made them of acacia wood,
And he overlaid them with gold. He made the holy anointing oil as was intended,
And prepared the fragrant smoking incense, as a perfumer would make, expertly blended.

Exodus 38

> Then he made the great altar used for sacrifice,
> The bronze basin, the courtyard surrounding it all.
> A half-shekel from each man was the standard price,
> Bezalel had made everything, answered his call.

He made the offering altar of acacia wood, five cubits long, five cubits wide,
Square, and three cubits high. He made horns on its four corners which the altar could provide,
The horns were from it. He overlaid it with bronze. He made all the altar's implements:
Pans for removing its ashes, the scrapers, the basins, the flesh-hooks, the firepans—
All its implements he made of bronze. He made a lattice for the altar, like a grating,
Beneath the altar's ledge, reaching to the middle. And at the four corners of the grating,
He cast four rings to hold the poles. He made the poles of acacia wood, bronze overlaid,
Brought them through the rings on the altar's sides to carry it. Hollow, of boards, it was made.

He made the basin of bronze, its pedestal of bronze, with the mirrors of the women
In the working force who assembled to do the work at the Tent of Meeting's entrance.

He made the courtyard for the Tabernacle, on the Negev desert border, southward,
With the hangings of fine twisted linen, one hundred cubits long across the courtyard,
With its twenty posts and their twenty sockets of bronze, the hooks of the posts and
     their bandings
Of silver. And same with the northern border, lengthwise, one hundred cubits of hangings,
With its twenty posts and twenty sockets of bronze, and the posts' hooks and their
     bandings silver.
And along the courtyard's width on the west side, hangings of fifty cubits, on sea border,
With its ten posts and ten sockets. And along the courtyard's width on the east towards sunrise,
Fifty cubits: fifteen cubits of hangings with their three posts and sockets for one side,
And for the other side, fifteen cubits of hangings with their posts, three, and sockets, three.
All the hangings around the courtyard were of fine twisted linen. Additionally,
All the sockets for the posts were bronze, the hooks of the posts and their bandings were of silver,
And the overlay for their tops was silver, all the courtyard's posts were banded with silver.
The screen of the courtyard gate was done in blue, purple, and crimson, in embroidery,
With fine twisted linen, twenty cubits long, and five cubits high where the width would be,
Corresponding to the courtyard hangings, their four posts, their four sockets of bronze,
     their hooks,
Of silver, and the overlay for their tops and bandings, of silver. And if one looked,
All the pegs for the Tabernacle and the courtyard all around were bronze as could be.

These are the accountings of the Tabernacle, the Dwelling of the Testimony,
Accounted by Moses, for the service of the Levites, under the man Itamar,
Son of Aaron the priest. Now already Bezalel the son of Uri, son of Hur,
Of the tribe of Judah, had made all that the Lord had commanded Moses. And with him,
Oholiab son of Ahisamach, of the tribe of Dan, a designer of trim,
A carver, a craftsman, and embroiderer in blue, purple, and crimson, and fine linen.
All the gold that was used in the work of constructing the Holy place from the beginning
All the gold gathered up from the elevation offering totaled twenty-nine ingots
And seven hundred thirty shekels (sanctuary weight) as all the people did bring it.
And the silver brought in by the community totaled one hundred ingots in weight,
And a thousand and seven hundred and seventy five shekels (sanctuary rate),
A beka (or "split-piece") per head, a half-shekel (sanctuary weight) for each one counted,
From the age of twenty years and up, for each one in the community, which amounted
To all of the six hundred thousand and three thousand and five hundred and fifty men.
There were one hundred silver ingots for casting sockets of Holy-place and curtain,
One hundred sockets for one hundred ingots, an ingot per socket. As for the rest,
The one thousand, seven hundred and seventy-five shekels of silver, they were pressed
Into hooks for the posts, and overlaid their tops, and were banded around the posts too.
And the bronze from the elevation offering when it was added up all came to
Seventy ingots, and two thousand and four hundred shekels. And of all that, they made
The sockets for the entrance of the Tent of Meeting, the altar of bronze there displayed,
Its bronze grating, all the altar's implements, the sockets of courtyard all around,
Sockets of the gate, and all the pegs of the Tabernacle, and courtyard, all around.

Exodus 39

Then the garments were made, with the holy ephod,
And the breastplate, coat, and tunic to be displayed.
Then they made the gold plate that said, "Holy to God",
And all God had commanded, the people had made.

Now from the blue and purple and crimson yarns, they made the garments of office, to use
For attending at the Holy place. And they made Aaron's holy garments from the blues,
And the purples, and the crimsons, as the Lord commanded Moses. They made the ephod
Of gold, blue, purple, crimson, and fine twisted linen. Gold sheets were beat out thin and broad,

And then split into threads, to be woven through the blue, purple, crimson, fine twisted linen,
All worked in designs. They made shoulder-pieces for it, so together it could be fastened,
Joined at its two ends. The designed band of the ephod, on it, was like it, of one piece,
Of gold, blue, purple, crimson, and fine twisted linen, as the Lord commanded Moses.
They made the onyx stones, bordered with braids of gold, engraved as one would engrave signets,
With the names of the Children of Israel. On the ephod's shoulder-piece they were set,
As stones of remembrance for the Children of Israel, as the Lord commanded Moses.

Then the breastpiece was made skillfully worked in design, just like an ephod one composes;
Of gold, and of blue, and purple, and of crimson, and fine twisted linen. It was square,
They made the breastpiece doubled, a span as its length, and a span as its width, doubled there.
Then they set stones in it, mounted stones, until they had set four rows of three stones, in full.
The first row of stones contained a carnelian, and a topaz, and a carbuncle.
The second row: emerald, sapphire, and diamond. The third row: jacinth, agate, amethyst.
The fourth row: beryl, onyx, and jasper; All framed with gold braids where the settings exist.
The stones were one with the names of the Children of Israel, twelve as their names prescribe,
They were engraved like signet engravings, each one with its name, for names of the twelve tribes.

They made on the breastpiece braided chains of cord-work, of pure gold. They made two braids
    of gold,
And two rings of gold, and put the two rings on the two ends of the breastpiece, there to hold
The two chains of gold which they put in the two rings on the end of the breastpiece, and then
The two ends of the two chains they put on the two braids, and placed them on the two
    front ends
Of the shoulder-pieces of the ephod. They made two rings of gold, and those rings they placed
On the two ends of the breastpiece, on its edge across from the ephod, the inward face.
And they made two more gold rings and put them on the ephod's two shoulder-pieces, below,
Facing forward, across from its joint, above where the designed band of the ephod goes.
They tied the breastpiece from its rings to the rings of the ephod, with a cord of pure blue,
To be on the designed band of the ephod, attached so the breastpiece wouldn't come loose
From the ephod, as the Lord had commanded Moses. And then was made the ephod's robe,
All of blue, woven work. The head-opening was in the robe's middle, just like the o-
pening of armor, with a seam for its opening all around, so it wouldn't split.
They made on the robe's skirts blue, purple, crimson, and fine twisted linen pomegranates.
They made bells of pure gold and attached them between all the pomegranates all around
On the skirts of the robe between the pomegranates, attached so this pattern was found:
Bell and pomegranate, bell and pomegranate, all around the robe's skirts for attending,
As the Lord had commanded Moses. They made the coat of fine linen, of weaver's making,
For Aaron and his sons, and the headdress of fine linen, and the turbans of fine linen,
The breeches of fine linen, fine twisted linen, and the sash made of fine twisted linen,
Of blue, purple, and crimson, embroidered, as the Lord had commanded Moses to do.
They made the plate for the holy diadem, of pure gold, and on it inscribed and hewed

With signet engravings, inscribed with "Holiness for the Lord". And they tied a blue cord
To be put on the headdress from above, as Moses had been commanded by the Lord.

So all the work of construction was finished for the Tabernacle, the Tent of Meeting.
The Children of Israel made it according to all the Lord told Moses, thus heeding
All the Lord had commanded, so they did. And they brought the Tabernacle to Moses:
The tent and all its implements, it clasps, its beams, its bars, and its posts and its sockets,
The covering of rams' skins dyed red and the covering of tanned leather skins the other,
The curtain for the screen, the ark of Testimony and its poles, the penance-cover,
The table, all its implements and the Bread of the Presence (shewbread), the pure lampstand,
Its lamps (lamps for arranging), and all its implements, and the oil for lighting the lamps,
The altar of gold, and anointing oil and fragrant incense, screen for the Tent's entrance,
The altar of bronze and its bronze lattice as well, its poles and all of its implements,
The basin and its pedestal; the hangings of the courtyard, its posts and its sockets,
And the screen for the courtyard gate, its cords and pegs, and all the implements they did get,
For the work of constructing the Tabernacle, the Tent of Meeting; the office garments
For attending at the Holy place, the holy garments for Aaron the priest, and garments
For his sons to be priests in. According to all that the Lord had commanded Moses,
The Children of Israel had done so, all the work of construction and its service.

And when Moses saw all of the work, here: They had made it as the Lord commanded them,
As the Lord had commanded, so had they done, and they had made it. Then Moses blessed them.

Exodus 40

> God told Moses, "In the first month, on the first day,
> Build the dwelling, set up all the things you've constructed.
> From the tent and the ark to the shrine where you pray."
> Moses did it exactly as God had instructed.

Now the Lord spoke to Moses, saying, "On the first day of the first month, you shall erect
The Dwelling of the Tent of Meeting. Place there the ark of Testimony with respect,
And screen off the ark with the curtain. You shall bring in the table, set its arrangements,
You shall bring in the lampstand and light its lamps, you shall put the gold altar of incense
Before the ark of Testimony, and you shall place the Tabernacle's entrance screen.
Put the offering altar before the entrance of the Dwelling, the Tent of Meeting.
Place the basin between the Tent of Meeting and the altar, and put water in it.
You shall set up the courtyard all around, and put in place the screen for the courtyard gate.

You shall take the anointing oil and anoint the Tabernacle and all that's within,
You shall hallow it and all its implements so they become holy, pure implements.
You shall anoint the altar for burnt offerings and all its implements, by this deed,
You shall hallow and consecrate the altar so the altar may become most holy.
You shall anoint the basin and its pedestal, you shall consecrate it. You shall bring
Aaron and his sons up to the entrance of the Tent of Meeting, and begin washing
Them with water. You shall clothe Aaron in the holy garments, and anoint him as well,
You shall hallow him to serve Me as priest. And his sons you shall also bring near. You shall
Clothe them in tunics, and anoint them as you anointed their father, to priest for Me;
Their anointing shall be for them priesthood through their generations, for eternity."
Moses did so, according to all that the Lord had commanded him, so Moses did.

And on the first day of the first month of the second year, the Dwelling was erected.
Moses set up the Tabernacle, placed its sockets, set up its boards, put up its bars,
Raised its posts, spread out the tent over the Tabernacle, and he placed the tent's cover
Over above it, as the Lord had commanded Moses. He took the Testimony,
And placed it in the ark, placed the poles of the ark, and moved the penance-cover to be
On the ark. He brought the ark into the Tabernacle, and there he placed the screen-curtain,
And screened off the ark of Testimony, as the Lord commanded Moses to be certain.

He put the table in the Tent of Meeting, on the Tabernacle's side faced northward,
Outside the curtain. He arranged on it the shewbread, before the presence of the Lord,
As the Lord had commanded Moses. In the Tent of Meeting, Moses placed the lampstand,
Opposite the table, on the south side of the Tabernacle. He set up the lamps
Before the presence of the Lord, as the Lord had commanded Moses. And then he put
The altar of gold in the Tent of Meeting, before the curtain, and he burned on it
Fragrant incense, as the Lord had commanded Moses. He put in place the entrance screen
For the Dwelling. The altar of offering he placed at the entrance to the Dwelling
Of the Tent of Meeting, and burned offerings on it, and offered up grain offerings,
As the Lord had commanded Moses. He placed the basin between the Tent of Meeting
And the altar, and put water in it for washing, so Moses, Aaron, and his sons
Would wash their hands and feet with it; When they came into the Tent of Meeting,
    and would come
Near the altar, they would wash, as the Lord had commanded Moses. He raised the courtyard
All around the Dwelling and the altar, and set the screen for the gate of the courtyard.

And so Moses finished the work. And then the cloud covered the Tent of Meeting in full,
And the Presence of the Lord, this cloud, the Glory of the Lord filled the Tabernacle.
Moses could not come into the Tent of Meeting, for the cloud took up dwelling on it,
And the Glory of the Lord filled the Tabernacle. Whenever the cloud lifts from it,
The Children of Israel march on, on all their journeys. When the cloud does not go up,
They do not march, and they do not journey onwards, until such time as it does go up.

For the cloud of the Lord is over the Dwelling by day, and fire is in it by night,
Before the eyes of all the House of Israel, throughout all their journeys, in their sight.

LEVITICUS

Leviticus 1

> God called Moses, and said, "Tell the Israelites,
> When you bring Me an offering, from flock or herd,
> Make it unblemished. Then let the priest do the rites
> Before burning it, even if it is a bird.

[Vayikra]

Now the Lord called to Moses, and the Lord spoke to him from the Tent of Meeting, saying,
"Speak to the Children of Israel and say to them: When anyone among you brings
An offering for the Lord from your domestic animals; from the flock or the herd
You may bring near your offering. If his offering is an offering from the herd,
Then he shall offer up a male without blemish. Let him bring it near to the entrance
Of the Tent of Meeting, as an acceptance on his behalf, before the Lord's presence.
He shall lay his hand on the head of the offering to gain acceptance for himself,
And to serve as atonement for him. Before the Lord's presence he shall slaughter the bull;
And the priests, Aaron's sons, shall bring near the blood, dashing it all around on the altar
At the entrance of the Tent of Meeting. Then he is to flay what is being offered,
And to cut it up into sections. Now the sons of Aaron the priest are to put fire
On the altar, and arrange the wood on the fire. Aaron's sons, the priests, shall tend the pyre,
They shall arrange the sections, the head and the fat, on the wood on the fire on the altar,
And once the sections have been arranged, then its entrails and its legs he shall wash in water,
And the priest shall turn all of it to smoke upon the altar as a burnt offering,
An offering by fire of sweet savor for the Lord, with an odor that is pleasing.

If his offering is from the flock, a burnt offering of sheep or goats he provides,
He shall offer a male without blemish, and slay it upon the altar's northward side,
Before the presence of the Lord. And Aaron's sons, the priests, shall take its blood to be dashed
Against the altar, all around. Then he shall cut it in sections, the head and the fat,
And the priest shall arrange them on the wood on fire on the altar, and then wash in water
The entrails and legs, and the priest shall bring all of it near to be burned on the altar:
It is a burnt offering, an offering by fire of pleasing odor to the Lord.

If his burnt offering to the Lord is one of fowl, then he is to act in accord,

Offering turtledoves or pigeons as his offering. The priest shall then bring it near,
Offer it on the altar, and pinch off its head, turning it to smoke on the altar,
And its blood shall be drained out against the side of the altar. He shall remove its crop,
With its feathers, and toss it next to the altar on the eastward side where ashes drop.
He shall tear it open by its wings, but do so without severing it or dividing,
And the priest shall turn it into smoke on the altar, on the fire the wood is providing,
It is a burnt offering, an offering by fire of pleasing odor to the Lord.

Leviticus 2

> When an offering brought to the Lord is of grain,
> Two ingredients you must add can't be ignored.
> Make sure oil is something that your gift contains,
> And then top it with salt, covenant to the Lord.

When a person brings near an offering of meal, a grain-gift offering to the Lord,
His offering shall be of choice flour, he shall pour oil and frankincense upon it,
Then he shall bring it to Aaron's sons, the priests. And he shall scoop out a scoopful from it,
From the flour and its oil and its frankincense; the priest shall take this part of reminder
And turn it to smoke on the altar, a fire offering for the Lord, of sweet savor.
What remains of the grain offering is Aaron's and his sons', a portion most holy
From the Lord's fire-offerings. When you bring offering of grain oven-baked, it shall be
Of choice flour: unleavened ("matza") cakes mixed with oil , unleavened wafers spread with oil.
And if a grain-gift on a griddle is the offering you give, flour mixed with oil,
Unleavened. Crumble it into bits and pour oil on it, it is a grain offering.
And if a grain-gift from a frying pan is your offering that you've chosen to bring,
It shall be made of flour in oil. If you bring a grain-gift that is made in these ways
To the Lord, it shall be brought to the priest, and up to the altar the priest then conveys.
The priest shall set aside from the grain-gift a reminder-portion and turn it to smoke
On the altar, an offering of fire, of pleasing odor to the Lord from his folk.
And the remainder of the grain-gift is Aaron's and his sons', a portion most holy
From the fire-offerings of the Lord. Every grain-gift you bring to the Lord shall not be
Made leavened, for any fermentation and any honey, none of it you may turn
Into smoke as a fire-offering for the Lord. (For these imperfections can't be burned).
As an offering of first fruits you may bring them to the Lord, but they shall not placed
On the altar to offer up as a pleasant odor. (This is not to the Lord's taste.)
All your offerings of a grain gift you shall season with salt, you are not to omit
The salt of your God's covenant from atop your grain-gift. When you are offering it,

Atop all your offerings you shall offer salt. Now if you offer firstfruit grain-gifts
To the Lord, new grain, parched with fire, grits of fresh grain you shall bring as your firstfruit
    grain-gift.
You shall put oil and frankincense on it, it is a grain-gift. To smoke, the priest shall turn
The reminder-part, from its grits, oil, and frankincense, the Lord's fire-offering to burn.

Leviticus 3

> If the offering brought is of greeting and peace,
> Then the priests shall burn all of the kidneys and fat.
> All the fat is the Lord's, every single last piece;
> You shall eat no fat, or blood, or any of that.

If a man's offering is a sacrifice of shalom (a gift of peace, or greeting),
If he offers it from the herd, whether it be male or female, the man is to bring
His gift without blemish before the Lord's presence. The man shall lay his hand on its head,
And slay it at the entrance of the Tent of Meeting. And once his offering is dead,
Aaron's sons, the priests, shall dash the blood all around against the altar. Then he shall offer
From the offering of shalom, a fire-offering to the Lord: The fat that covers
The entrails, and all the fat around the entrails, the two kidneys and surrounding fat,
Fat on the tendons, and the extension on the liver—he shall remove all of that.
And the sons of Aaron shall turn it all to smoke on the altar, and the offering stored
On the wood on the fire—A fire-offering that is of pleasing odor to the Lord.
Now if his sacrifice of shalom to the Lord is from the flock, female or male,
He shall offer one without blemish. If he brings a sheep as offering with a tail,
He shall bring it before the presence of the Lord. He shall then lay his hand on its head,
And slay it at the entrance of the Tent of Meeting. And once his offering is dead,
Aaron's sons, the priests, shall dash the blood all around against the altar. And after that,
He shall offer from the shalom-offering, a fire-offering to the Lord, its fat:
The whole thick tail, which shall be removed close to the backbone, fat that covers the entrails,
And all the fat around the entrails, the two kidneys, and all of the fat that entails,
All the fat on the tendons, and the protrusion on the liver, all shall be removed,
Along with the kidneys. Then the priest shall turn it into smoke on the altar as food,
A fire-offering for the Lord. Now if his offering is a goat, he shall bring it
Close before the presence of the Lord. He shall lay his hand on its head and shall slay it
In front of the Tent of Meeting; And Aaron's sons shall dash its blood against the altar,
All around. Then he shall offer from it as his offering, an offering of fire

For the Lord: The fat that covers the entrails and the fat from around the entrails, all,
The two kidneys and all of the fat on them, fat from the tendons, and the liver's caul,
Along with the kidneys, he shall remove. The priest shall turn them to smoke on the altar,
As food, an offering by fire of pleasing odor. And all the fat is for the Lord,
It shall be a law for the ages, through your generations, through all your settlements:
Any fat or any blood you are not to eat, not even in the smallest extent.

Leviticus 4

> If a priest sins, then his people carry his sin.
> It's as if the community sinned; slay a bull.
> If a leader or one person has done akin,
> Then a goat must be slain for forgiveness in full.

The Lord spoke to Moses saying, "Speak to the Children of Israel, saying: Now when
Any person sins unintentionally against any of the Lord's commandments
About things which should not be done, by doing one of them... If the anointed priest sins,
Bringing guilt upon the people, then he is to offer for the sin which he has sinned,
A young bull of the herd without blemish, for the Lord, as a means of purification,
He shall bring the bull to the entrance of the Tent of Meeting to gain his expiation,
Before the Lord's presence, he shall lay his hand on the bull's head. And he shall slay the bull
Before the Lord's presence. Then the anointed priest shall take some of the blood of the bull,
And bring it into the Tent of Meeting; the priest shall dip his finger in the blood, and
Shall sprinkle of the blood seven times, before the Lord's presence, in front of the curtain
Of the Holy place. Then the priest shall put some of the blood on the horns of the altar
Of fragrant incense, before the Lord's presence, that is in the Tent of Meeting. As for
All the rest of the bull's blood, he shall pour it out at the burnt-offering altar's base
That is at the entrance of the Tent of Meeting. As for all the bull's fat in this case,
From the purification-offering, he shall remove all fat. Fat covering entrails,
All the fat around the entrails, and the two kidneys and all of the fat that entails,
All fat on the tendons, the liver's extension, shall be removed with the kidneys;
Just as it is removed from the ox of the sacrifice of shalom. And then the priest
Shall turn them into smoke on the offering altar. Now as for the bull's skin and flesh,
Along with its head, its shins, its entrails, and its dung, the priest is to take all the rest
Of the bull to a pure place outside of the camp, to the ash heap, and burn it on wood,
In the fire on the ash dump it shall be burned. Now if Israel's community should,
As a whole, commit error, and the matter is hidden from the assembly's eyes
So that they do any of the things which the Lord's commandments say should be otherwise

And not be done, then they have incurred guilt. When it becomes know that they're guilty of sin,
The assembly shall offer a young bull of the herd, purification-offering;
They shall bring it before the Tent of Meeting. And the community's elders shall lay
Their hands on the bull's head before the Lord's presence, and the bull, one of them is to slay
Before the Lord's presence. Then the anointed priest shall take some of the blood of the bull
And bring it into the Tent of Meeting, dip his finger in the blood, and shall sprinkle,
Sprinkle the blood seven times before the presence of the Lord, in front of the curtain.
And once the sprinkling of the blood seven times before the presence of the Lord is done,
Then some of the blood he shall put on the horns of the altar that is before the Lord
That is in the Tent of Meeting; As for all the rest of the blood, it is to be poured
At the base of the offering altar that is at the entrance of the Tent of Meeting.
As for all its fat, he shall remove it, and then turn it into smoke with fire-heating,
On the altar. He shall do with the bull just as he did with sin-offering bull,
He shall do the same with it. And so the priest shall make an atonement for them, in full,
And they shall be pardoned. He shall take the bull outside the camp, and then burn it shall he,
Just as he burned the first bull; it is the penance-offering for the assembly.

When a leader sins and does a thing which by the Lord's commandments ought not to be done,
Accidentally, and incurs guilt, when he learns that he sinned and is a guilty one,
He shall bring as his offering a male kid goat without blemish. He shall lay his hand
On the head of the goat, and it shall be slain where the offerings are slain in that land,
Before the Lord's presence; it is a sin-offering. The priest shall take with his finger
Some blood from the offering and put it on the horns of the burnt-offering altar;
He shall pour the rest of its blood at the base of the offering altar. All its fat,
He shall turn into smoke on the altar, like fat of the shalom sacrifice, and that
Is how the priest shall make expiation for him from his sin, and he shall be forgiven

Now if any one of the people of the land sins in error, does something forbidden
By the commandments of the Lord, and incurs guilt, or he comes to know that he has sinned:
He shall bring as his offering a female goat, without blemish, to pay for his sin.
He shall lay his hand on the sin-offering's head, at the offering-place to be slain.
The priest shall take some blood with his finger and put it on the altar's horns. What remains,
He shall pour out at the base of the altar of offering. As for all of its fat,
He shall remove it, as the fat was removed from the shalom sacrifice before that,
And the priest shall turn it into smoke on the altar, a soothing savor for the Lord;
So the priest shall attain expiation for him, and forgiveness shall be his reward.
If he brings a sheep to offer as a penance-offering, a female he shall bring,
Without blemish. He shall lay his hand on its head, and shall slay the penance-offering,
At the offering-place. The priest shall take some blood of the offering with his finger,
And put it on the horns of the offering altar. The rest of its blood he shall pour
At the base of the offering-altar. He shall remove all of its fat, just as he
Removed all of the fat of the sheep from the sacrifice of shalom, and then the priest

Shall turn them into smoke on the altar, along with the fire offerings of the Lord.
So the priest shall get expiation for his sin, and forgiveness shall be his reward.

Leviticus 5

> If a person sins, he bears the guilt for his deed,
> And shall bring a sheep to offer up to the Lord.
> If he can't afford sheep, two young birds he will need.
> Men who rob men must pay them back, with one fifth more.

When a person sins: If he has heard that the public is calling for testimony
And though he was a witness (seeing or knowing) he won't tell, he bears iniquity;
Or if a person touches anything unclean, like the carcass of an unclean beast,
Or the carcass of unclean cattle, or the carcass of unclean swarms, even the least,
And though he does not notice, he has become unclean, and thus he has become guilty;
Or if he touches human uncleanliness, any by which one can become unclean,
Even if the fact is hidden from him, but he later learns that he has incurred guilt;
Or when a person swears an oath rashly with his lips, to do good or to do evil,
Or whatever a man might say in swearing rashly, though guilt he is unaware of,
Later he realizes that he incurred guilt in any of these matters above:
When he incurs guilt in one of these ways, he shall confess that he sinned, and in which one.
Then he shall bring his penalty guilt-offering to the Lord, for the sin he has done:
A female from the flock, a lamb or kid to be a sin-offering. And then the priest
Shall make expiation for him from his sin, so that from his guilt he may be released.
If he cannot afford a sheep, then he shall bring as a guilt-offering for his sin
Either two turtledoves or two young pigeons for the Lord; One for a sin-offering,
And one for a burnt-offering. He shall bring them to the priest, the sin-offering first.
The priest shall pinch its head from its neck, but not sever it. Then its blood shall be dispersed,
With some sprinkled upon the side of the altar, and the rest drained at the altar's base,
It is a sin-offering. And the second one is to take the burnt-offering's place,
In accordance with regulations for burnt offerings, the priest shall seek expiation
On his behalf from the sin he sinned, and he shall be forgiven for his violation.
If he cannot afford even two turtledoves or two young pigeons, then he shall bring
A tenth of an ephah of choice flour (two omers, or sheaves) for a sin-offering.
He shall not put any oil or frankincense on it, for a sin-offering it is.
He shall bring it to the priest, and the priest shall scoop out a handful of it with his fist,
A token portion, and turn it to smoke on the altar, with the Lord's fire-offerings,
It is a sin-offering. So the priest shall make expiation for him for his sin,

In any of these cases, whichever he sinned, forgiveness for him will be attained.
And the remainder of the offering shall be for the priest, like the gift of the grain."

The Lord spoke to Moses, saying, "When a person breaks faith and sins accidentally
Regarding any of the Lord's holy things, he shall bring to the Lord as penalty
A ram without blemish from the flock, or its value in silver, sanctuary weight
By the shekel, as guilt-offering. He shall pay restitution and so compensate
For his sin involving holy things, he shall pay and add for the priest one fifth again,
Then with the ram of guilt-offering, the priest shall on his behalf make an atonement,
And he shall be forgiven. When a person sins, doing something that has been forbidden
By the Lord's commandments that are not to be done, even if his guilt from him is hidden,
He must bear his iniquity. He shall bring a ram from the flock, without blemish, whole,
Or its value in silver, as a guilt-offering, to the priest; The priest, in his role,
Shall make atonement for him for his error even if accidental. As reward,
He shall be forgiven. It is a guilt-offering; he incurred guilt before the Lord."

The Lord spoke to Moses, saying, "When a person sins and against the Lord does break faith
By denying his fellow's charges about a deposit placed with him to keep safe,
Or through robbery, or by withholding property from his fellow, or if he finds
A lost object and then denies it, or swears falsely about things one does of the kind
That would be sins to do—When a person has sinned such, and then realizes his guilt,
He shall return the robbed object that he robbed, or the withheld property he withheld,
Or the deposit that was deposited with him, or the lost object which he found,
Or any other thing about which he swore falsely, he is to repay this amount:
Its full principal, and a fifth more, he shall pay to the owner once guilt is acknowledged.
He shall bring for the Lord as a guilt-offering a ram from the flock, which is unblemished,
Or its value in silver, as guilt-offering, to the priest, who shall atone for him
Before the Lord's presence, and he shall be granted pardon for his guilt-incurring sin."

Leviticus 6

God commanded, "All offerings must heed this law:
The flame must be kept blazing, it must not go out.
The grain offerings shall be part in the priests' jaw,
And the portion that's holy shall be burned without.

[Tzav]

The Lord spoke to Moses, saying, "Command Aaron and his sons, say: This is the Instruction
For the burnt-offering: This is what goes on the altar's hearth until dawn's introduction,
All night, while the altar's fire is kept blazing on it. The priest shall dress in his raiment
Of linen, with linen breeches over his flesh. He shall then pick up the ash remnant
Of the burnt-offering on the altar which the fire consumed, and then he is to place them
Beside the altar. Then he shall take off his garments, and with other garments replace them,
And he shall bring the ashes outside of the camp, to a place that is both clean and pure.
And the fire on the altar shall be kept ablaze on it, its must not go out, be sure.
Every morning the priest shall stoke wood on it, and arrange the burnt offering on it,
And the priest is to turn the fat parts of the sacrifice of shalom to smoke on it.
So a regular fire is to be kept ablaze on the altar—it shall not go out.
Now this is the Instruction for the grain-gift: Aaron's sons must bring it near, round about,
Before the Lord's presence, in front of the altar. By the handful shall be set aside
Some of the flour and oil from the grain-gift, and the frankincense that on it resides,
And this token portion shall be turned to smoke on the altar as a soothing savor
To the Lord. What is left of it, Aaron and his sons shall eat, in an unleavened form,
In a holy place, in the courtyard of the Tent of Meeting is where they are to eat it.
It shall not be baked with leaven; As their portion from My fire-offerings I have ceded,
It is a holiest holy portion, like the sin-offering and guilt-offering.
Any male among the Children of Aaron may eat it, throughout your generations,
As an allotment for the ages, from the fire-offerings of the Lord, it shall be;
And whoever or whatever thing that should touch any of these shall become holy."

The Lord spoke to Moses, saying, "This is the offering of Aaron and of his sons,
That they shall offer to the Lord at the time of his anointment, (each one's occasion):
A tenth of an ephah of flour as a regular grain gift. Half in the morning,
And half in the evening. It shall be made on a griddle with oil. Well-baked you shall bring,
As baked slices of grain you are to offer it, as a soothing savor to the Lord.
So the priest anointed in his stead, from his sons, shall prepare it. It is for the Lord,
A law for the ages; it shall be completely turned to smoke. Each grain-gift of a priest
Shall be completely offered and turned into smoke. It shall not be eaten, not the least."

The Lord spoke to Moses, saying, "Say to Aaron and his sons: This is the Instruction
For the sin-offering: In the place where the slaying of the burnt-offering is done,
The sin-offering shall be slain, before the Lord's presence; it is a portion most holy.
The priest who sacrifices the sin-offering shall eat of it, in a place that's holy
It shall be eaten, in the Tent of Meeting's courtyard. And whatever touches its flesh
Shall become holy. And if some of its blood spatters on a garment, then you shall wash
The spot on which it spattered in a holy place. The earthen vessel in which it boiled
Shall be broken; if it boiled in a copper vessel, the vessel is to be de-soiled,

It shall be scrubbed and rinsed with water. Any male among the priestly line may eat it,
It is a holiest holy-portion. But any sin-offering, the blood from which
Is brought to the Tent of Meeting, to attain expiation in the Holy Shrine room,
Shall not be eaten, for any such shall be burned in the fire, and by it, consumed."

Leviticus 7

> From the holiest portion, the fat shall be burned.
> Eat no thing that has touched unclean meat, not the least.
> Though the fat is for God, let the breast be returned,
> Waved up high by Aaron and his sons, as the priests.

Now this is the Instruction for the guilt-offering; it is a most holy portion.
In the place where they slay the burnt offering, the guilt-offering's slaying shall be done,
And its blood shall be dashed against all sides of the altar. He shall offer all its fat:
The thick tail and the fat that covers the entrails, the two kidneys and fat that's on that,
And the fat on the tendons, the liver's extension, shall be removed with the kidneys.
The priest shall turn them into smoke on the altar, a fire-offering it is to be
For the Lord; it is a guilt-offering. Any male among the priestly line may eat it,
In a holy place it shall be eaten, it is a most holy portion, as such treat it.
Like the sin-offering is the guilt-offering, one Instruction applies to the two;
The priest who makes expiation through it, it shall belong to him. And so the priest who
Offers the burnt-offering of a layman shall keep the skin of the burnt offering
Which he offered. And any grain-gift oven-baked, or prepared in a pan of frying
Or on a griddle, shall belong to the priest who offered it. But any grain-gifts mixed
With oil, or dry, shall go to the sons of Aaron, to each brother as much as the next.

Now this is the Instruction for the sacrifice of shalom for the Lord one offers:
If he offers it for giving thanks, then along with the thanks sacrifice which occurs,
He shall offer matza cakes mixed with oil, matza wafers smeared with oil, and flour cakes
With oil mixed in. Along with this matza offering, cakes of leavened bread he shall take,
And his thanks-giving sacrifice of shalom. One of each kind he shall offer from it,
One of each offering as a contribution to the Lord. And then he shall remit
It to the priest that sprinkles the blood of the sacrifice of shalom, his it shall be.
As for the flesh of his thanksgiving sacrifice of shalom, on the same day that he
Offers it, it shall be eaten, none of it may be left until morning. Nonetheless,
If a vow-offering or a freewill-offering is his offering sacrifice,

On the day he offers his sacrifice it shall be eaten, and what's left the next day.
Only on the third day shall what's left of this flesh sacrifice be in fire burned away.

Now if on the third day, any flesh of his shalom sacrifice one should chance to eat,
It shall lose acceptance, not counting for he whom offered it. It shall be tainted meat,
And the person who eats of it shall bear iniquity. Flesh that touches the unclean
Shall not be eaten, but in fire it shall be burned. As for other flesh, anyone clean
May eat it. But the person who eats while unclean from the Lord's sacrifice of shalom
Shall be cut off from his kin. When a person touches anything unclean, from human
Uncleanliness to an unclean animal to unclean detestable swarming things,
And eats from the flesh of the Lord's shalom sacrifice, he shall be cut off from his kin."

The Lord spoke to Moses, saying, "Speak to the Children of Israel, say: You shall not
Eat any fat from an ox, a lamb, or a goat. Now fat from a carcass, or the fat
From an animal torn by beasts may be used for other use, but shall not be eaten.
For whoever eats fat from an animal from which one could make a fire-offering
To offer to the Lord, then the person who eats it is to be cut off from his kin.
And you shall not eat any blood, of bird or animal, throughout all your settlements.
Any person that eats any blood, that person shall be cut off from his kinspeople."

The Lord spoke to Moses, saying, "You are to say this to the Children of Israel:
He who offers shalom-sacrifice to the Lord shall bring his offering to the Lord,
From his shalom-sacrifice with his own hands he shall bring fire-offerings for the Lord.
He shall bring the fat with the breast, breast to be used as an elevation-offering,
Elevated before the Lord's presence (to show that it is God who now owns this thing).
And the priest shall turn the fat into smoke on the altar, and the breast shall be Aaron's
And his sons'. Now the right thigh you are to present to the priest as a contribution,
From your sacrifice of shalom. He among Aaron's sons who offers the blood and fat
Of the shalom-offerings, he shall receive as his portion the right thigh taken from that.
For the breast of the elevation-offering and the thigh of the contribution
I take from the Israelites, from their shalom-offerings, and give them to Aaron
The priest and his sons, as an allotment for all time, from the Children of Israel.
This is the anointed portion of Aaron and anointed-share of his sons as well
From the fire-offerings of the Lord, from the time the Lord brought them near to serve as priests,
Which the Lord commanded to be given them at the time he anointed them as priests,
From the Children of Israel, as a law for the ages, through their generations.

This is the Instruction for the burnt-offering, for the grain-gift, and offering of sin,
For the guilt-offering, ordination-offering, and the sacrifice of shalom,
The Instruction that the Lord commanded to Moses on Mount Sinai some time ago,
At the time when He commanded that the Children of Israel were all to bring nigh
And present and offer their offerings to the Lord in the wilderness of Sinai."

Leviticus 8

The Lord had Moses ready both Aaron and sons,
Dressing them, and anointing with oil their heads.
He slew animals, offered to the Lord each one,
But saved blood to make holy what the Lord had said.

The Lord spoke to Moses, saying, "Take Aaron and his sons with him, also the garments,
And the anointing oil, the bull for sin-offering (which one in hot hot flames presents),
The two rams, and the basket of unleavened bread; assemble the whole community
At the entrance of the Tent of Meeting." Moses did as the Lord had commanded he.
The community assembled at the Tent of Meeting's entrance, and then Moses said
To the community, "This is the thing which is to be done as God has commanded."
Moses brought Aaron and his sons near, washed them with water. He put the tunic on him,
Girded him with the sash, clothed him with the robe, put the ephod on him, and girded him
With the designed-band of the ephod, binding it to him. He placed on him the breastpiece,
Putting into the breastpiece the Urim and Tummim, the lights and perfections of each.
He placed the headdress on his head, in front of his face, and then he placed on the headdress,
The plate of gold, the holy diadem, just as the Lord had commanded to Moses.

Moses took the anointing oil and anointed the dwelling, and all that was in it,
Consecrating them. He sprinkled some of it on the altar, seven times sprinkled it,
Anointing the altar, all its vessels, the basin and pedestal, to consecrate them.
He poured some of the anointing oil on Aaron's head, anointing him, to consecrate him.
Moses brought Aaron's sons near, clothed them in robes, girded them with sashes, wound
    them turbans,
As the Lord had commanded Moses. He brought forward the bull of the sin offering,
And Aaron and his sons lay their hands on its head, and he slew it. Moses took the blood,
And put it on the horns of the altar, all around, with his finger, purging sin from
The altar, and decontaminating it. At the altar's base, he poured the blood out.
So he consecrated it to purge it of sin. Then he took all fat that was about
The entrails, the extension of the liver, the two kidneys, and their fat on and within,
And Moses turned them into smoke on the altar. The rest of the bull, dung, flesh, and skin,
He burned in fire, outside the camp, as the Lord commanded Moses. Then he presented
The ram for the burnt offering. Aaron and his sons lay their hands upon the ram's head,
And he slew it. Moses dashed the blood against the altar, all around. The ram he cut
Into sections, and Moses turned into smoke the head, the sections, and all the suet.

Now the entrails and shins he washed in water, and Moses turned the whole ram into smoke
On the altar. It was a burnt offering for soothing savor, as the Lord had spoke;

A fire-offering for the Lord, as the Lord had commanded Moses should be done.
Then he brought near the second ram, the ram of ordination. And Aaron and his sons
Laid their hands on the head of the ram, and he slew it. Moses took of its blood, and put
Some on the ridge of Aaron's right ear, his right hand's thumb, and the big toe of his right foot.

Then he brought near Aaron's sons, and Moses put some of it on the ridge of their right ear,
And on their right hand's thumb, and their right foot's big toe. Moses dashed the rest on the altar,
All around. He took the fat, the broad tail, all fat on the entrails, the liver's extension,
The two kidneys and their fat, and the right thigh. From the matzot basket earlier mentioned,
Before the Lord's presence, he took one cake of unleavened bread, and one cake of oil bread,
And one wafer, and put them on the fat-parts and the right thigh. These he deposited
On the palms of Aaron and his sons, and they raised them as elevation offering,
Before the Lord's presence. Then Moses took them from their palms, to burn with burnt offering
On the altar. They are ordination offerings, a soothing savor to create;
It is a fire-offering for the Lord. Then Moses took the breast to elevate
Elevating it as elevation-offering, before the Lord's presence, from ram
Of ordination—It was Moses's portion, as the Lord had gave Moses command.

Now Moses took some of the anointing oil and some of the blood upon the altar
And sprinkled it on Aaron, his garments, his sons, and the garments that all his sons wore;
So he consecrated Aaron, his garments, his sons, and with him all his sons' garments.
Moses said to Aaron and to his sons, "Boil the flesh at the Tent of Meeting's entrance,
There you shall eat it, along with the bread that is in the basket of ordination,
As I have commanded, saying: Aaron and his sons shall eat it; and when they are done,
What is left of the flesh and the bread you shall burn in fire. You shall not go outside
From the entrance of the Tent of Meeting for seven days. In courtyard, you must abide,
Until the days of your ordination are done. It will take seven days to be through;
Everything done today, the Lord commanded to be done, to make atonement for you.
At the entrance to the Tent of Meeting you are to stay, day and night, for seven days;
You are to keep the charge of the Lord, so that you do not die for straying from his ways,
For such is what I have been commanded." And Aaron and his sons followed the command,
Doing all of the things that the Lord had commanded through Moses, by Moses's hand.

Leviticus 9

After eight days of waiting outside of the Tent,
Moses had Aaron sacrifice, as God's command.
And God's fiery glory was seen, as it went
From His presence. The people fell down to the sand.

[Shemini]

Now on the eighth day, Moses called Aaron and his sons and the elders of Israel,
And he said to Aaron, "Take a calf of the herd as a sin offering, and as well,
Take an unblemished ram for burnt offering, which before the Lord's presence you shall bring.
And to the Children of Israel you shall say: Take a he-goat for sin offering
And a calf and a lamb, year-old ones unblemished, as a burnt offering, and also
An ox and a ram to sacrifice before the Lord as an offering of shalom,
And a grain-gift mixed with oil, for today the Lord shall appear to you." So they begun,
Brought what Moses commanded to the front of the Tent of Meeting. The congregation
Came near and stood before the Lord's presence. And Moses said, "This is the word of the Lord,
Which He has commanded that you do, so His Glory may appear to you." Afterward,
Moses said to Aaron, "Come near to the altar, and then offer your sin offering
And your burnt offering, and make atonement for yourself and for the people. And bring
Their offering as well, make atonement for them, as the Lord has commanded be done."
So Aaron approached the altar and killed the calf for his sin offering. Aaron's sons
Brought the blood near to him, he dipped his finger in it, and with it, the altar's horns touched.
Then he poured out the rest at the base of the altar. But the fat and kidneys and such
And the liver's extension from the sin offering, he burned it and turned it to smoke
On the altar, as the Lord had commanded Moses was to be done, just as he spoke.
The flesh and skin he burned in fire, outside the camp. Then Aaron slew the burnt offering,
And Aaron's sons brought him the blood. He dashed it all around the altar. And they did bring
The burnt offering to him, piece by piece, in sections, and the head. He burned both of them,
Turning them into smoke on the altar. Then he washed the entrails and legs, and burned them
With the burnt offering on the altar. Then he brought near the people's offering too,
And he took the he-goat of the sin offering for the people, and that goat he slew,
And offered it for sin, like the first offering, Then the burnt offering he brought near,
Sacrificing it according to regulation. And then the grain gift he brought near,
Taking a handful of it, and burning it, turning it into smoke on the altar
(Aside from the burnt offering of the morning, which was still later to be offered).
Then he killed the ox and the ram from the people's shalom-sacrifice; And Aaron's sons
Presented the blood to him, which he tossed against the altar (on all sides it was done),

Along with the fat of the ox and ram, the fat tail, the fat which the entrails possessed,
And the kidneys, and the extension of the liver. And they put the fat on the breasts,
And he burned the fat on the altar, but the breasts and the right thigh Aaron elevated,
As an elevation offering to the Lord, as the Lord (through Moses) had mandated.
Now Aaron lifted up his hands towards the people and he blessed them, then Aaron came down
From offering the sin offering, burnt offering, and the offering of shalom.
And Moses and Aaron went into the Tent of Meeting, and when they came out they blessed
The people. And the Glory of the Lord appeared, and by all the people was witnessed.
And fire came forth from the Lord's presence and consumed the burnt offering and bits of fat
On the altar; And when the people saw it, they shouted, and on their faces fell flat.

Leviticus 10

Nadab and Abihu had each taken their pan,
And burned incense God had not commanded they burn,
So they died. Moses called Mishael and Elzephan
To remove them. Then told Aaron's two sons in turn,
"As priests, you may not mourn, though all Israel weeps
For your brothers. And you must remain in the tent
While anointed with oil. Don't drink wine. This all keeps
Holiness separated as your allotment.

Now Aaron's sons, Nadab and Abihu, each took his fire-pan, placing fire in it,
And laid incense on it, and offered outside fire to the Lord (who was not pleased one bit);
So the two of them offered unholy fire such as the Lord had not commanded them.
And fire came forth from the presence of the Lord and then the fire consumed both of them,
And they died before the Lord's presence. Moses said to Aaron, "This is what the Lord meant
When He said: Through those near Me, I will show Myself holy, and before the full extent
Of the people, I will be accorded glory." Aaron held his peace and was silent.
Moses called Mishael and Elzaphan, sons of Uzziel, Aaron's uncle. (And they went).
Moses said to them, "Come near, carry your brothers from in front of the sanctuary
Outside the camp." They came near, and carried them by their tunics past the camp boundary,
As Moses had said. Moses said to Aaron, and Eleazar and Ithamar, his sons,
"Do not bare your heads, nor tear your clothes, lest you die, and wrath fall on the congregation;
But your kinsmen, all the House of Israel, shall weep over the burning the Lord burned.
And do not go out from the entrance of the Tent of Meeting, or you might die in turn;

For the Lord's anointing oil is on you." And they did as Moses's words told them to.

Now the Lord spoke to Aaron, saying, "Drink no wine nor strong drink, you nor your
    sons with you,
When you enter the Tent of Meeting, lest you die; a law throughout your generations.
There must be separation between the sacred and the profane, the unclean and clean.
You shall teach the Children of Israel all the laws the Lord spoke to them through Moses."
And Moses said to Aaron, and to Eleazar and Ithamar, his sons who were left,
"Take the grain gift remaining of the fire-offerings to the Lord, and then eat it,
Unleavened by the altar, (even though you mourn,) for a most holy portion is it.
You shall eat it in a holy place, because it is your due, and your children's due too,
From the offerings by fire to the Lord, for so have I been commanded you do.
But the breast of the elevation offering and the thigh of the contribution,
You shall eat in any clean place, you and your children with you, both your daughters and sons,
Because they are your due and your children's due too, given you from the sacrifices
Of shalom from the Children of Israel. The thigh of contribution and the breast
Of the elevation offering they shall bring, along with the fire-gifts of the fat,
To elevate as an elevation offering before the Lord. And after that,
It shall be both for you and your sons a due forever, as the Lord has commanded."

Moses then asked about the goat of sin offering, and it was already burn-ed!
He got furious with Eleazar and Ithamar, Aaron's sons still left behind,
Saying, "Why have you not eaten the sin-offering in the place of the Holy Shrine?
For it is a most holy thing, and He gave it to you to bear the iniquity
Of the congregation, to make atonement for them before the Lord's presence. Now see,
Its blood was not brought into the Holy Shrine, inside, where you ought to have eaten it,
In the Holy Shrine, as I commanded." But then Aaron said to Moses, "Wait one bit.
Here, today they offered their sin offering and their burnt offering before the Lord,
And yet such things (the death of my two sons) have befallen me, and cannot be ignored.
If I had eaten the sin offering today, would it have been good in the Lord's sight?"
Moses heeded the words of Aaron and approved; Moses was content that things were right.

Leviticus 11

God told Moses, "Eat only cud-chewing hooved beasts,
Don't eat things from the water without scales and fins.
Don't eat creatures at all unclean, not in the least,
Or drink from any vessel a dead mouse falls in.

The Lord spoke to Moses and to Aaron, saying, "Say to the Children of Israel,
'these are the living things which you may eat among all the animals that on earth dwell:
Any animal with a hoof, cloven-hooved, which brings up cud to chew, such you may eat.
However, among those that chew cud or have a hoof, these are the ones you shall not eat:
The camel, for it chews the cud, but it does not have a hoof, it is unclean for you;
The hyrax, for it chews the cud, but it does not have a hoof, it is unclean for you;
The hare, for although it chews the cud, it does not have a hoof, it is unclean for you;
The swine, for it has a cloven hoof, but does not chew the cud, it is unclean for you.
From their flesh you shall not eat, their carcasses you shall not touch, it is unclean for you.
These you may eat from all that are in the waters: Any one that has fins and scales too,
Whether in the seas or in the rivers, you may eat it. But those without scales and fins,
Whether in the seas or in the rivers, from all the water's swarming creatures within,
From all living beings in the waters, they shall be for you an abomination.
They shall remain an abomination to you; Of their flesh you shall not eat. Not one,
Even their carcasses you shall hold in abomination. All without scales or fins
That is in the waters is an abomination to you. (To eat it would be sin).

Now these you shall hold in abomination among the birds, they shall not be eaten,
They are an abomination: The eagle, vulture, osprey, the kite, and the falcon
According to its kind, every raven according to its kind, the ostrich, nighthawk,
The seagull, hawk according to its kind, the little owl, the cormorant with its squawk,
The great owl, the swan, and the pelican which holds its food in its bill like a vat.
The bustard, the stork, and the heron according to its kind, the hoopoe, and the bat.

Any winged swarming thing that goes on all fours shall be an abomination to you.
Yet among these winged swarming things that don't stand upright, there are a few that
    you may chew.
You may eat those which have jointed legs above their feet, with which they can leap
    on the ground.
And of them you may eat these: the locust according to its kind, wherever it's found,
The bald-locust according to its kind, the cricket according to its kind, and next,
The grasshopper according to its kind. But all other winged flying swarming insects

That have four legs shall be an abomination to you. And these shall make you unclean;
Whoever touches their carcass shall be unclean until sunset, until the evening,
And whoever carries any part of their carcass shall be unclean until evening,
Every animal with hooves uncloven, or which does not chew cud, for you is unclean.
Whoever touches them is unclean. And any one which on its four paws walks about
Is unclean for you. Whoever touches their carcass is unclean 'til the sun goes out;
He who carries their carcass shall wash his clothes and be unclean until the twilight's birth.
They are unclean for you. And these are the unclean ones for you of what swarms on the earth:
The weasel, and the mouse, and the great lizard according to its kind, and the gecko,
The land crocodile, lizard, sand lizard, and the chameleon that darts to and fro.
These are unclean to you among all that swarm; whoever touches them when they are dead
Shall be unclean until sunset, anything on which one of them falls when they are dead
Shall be unclean, be it wood or cloth, skin or sackcloth, any vessel that can be used,
It shall be dipped in water, remaining unclean until sunset, then pureness accrues.
And any earthen vessel in which one of them falls, all inside it shall be unclean,
And you shall break it. Any food that might be eaten touched by water shall be unclean,
And any drink one might drink, if in such a vessel, shall be unclean. And anything
On which their carcass falls shall be unclean, be it oven or stove, you must be breaking—
They are unclean, they shall remain unclean for you. Nevertheless, a spring or cistern
Holding water shall be clean, though one who touches the carcass, uncleanliness will earn.
If part of a carcass falls on an unsown seed, it is clean. But if water is placed
On the seed and a carcass falls on it, it is unclean for you, thus you may not taste.
If an animal that you may eat dies, one who touches its carcass shall be unclean
Until sunset. One who eats from its carcass must wash his clothes, until sunset unclean,
One who carries its carcass shall wash his clothes, unclean until the setting of the sun.

All the things that swarm on the earth are an abomination; they shall not be eaten.
Whatever goes on its belly, or on all fours, or on many legs, all swarming things
That swarm upon the earth, you are not to eat them, for they are abominable things.
Do not make yourselves or your throats abominable through any swarming thing that swarms;
Don't defile yourselves and make yourselves unclean, so you become unclean through the swarms.
For I am the Lord, your God: Therefore, you are to sanctify yourselves and be holy,
For I am holy. You shall not defile yourselves through any swarming thing that may be
Crawling on the earth. For I am the Lord, the one bringing you up out of Egypt's land,
To be your God; You shall therefore be holy, for I am holy.'" (That was his command.)

This is the Instruction concerning animals, birds, and all living creatures that stir
In the water, and every creature that swarms upon the earth, in order to insure
That there may be a separation and distinction between the unclean and the clean,
And between living creatures you may eat, and living creatures that shall not be eaten.

Leviticus 12

When a woman gives birth, she's unclean seven days,
And for thirty-three days she must be purified.
If the birth is a girl, for twice that long she stays.
And for offering, lamb or two birds she'll provide.

[Tazria]

The Lord spoke to Moses, saying, "Say to the Children of Israel: If a woman
Conceives and bears a male, she shall be unclean for seven days, as with her menstruation.
Like the days of her menstrual infirmity she shall be unclean; and on the eighth day,
The flesh of the boy's foreskin shall be circumcised. Then for thirty-three days she shall stay
In her period of her blood purification; she is to touch no hallowed thing,
Nor shall she enter the sanctuary until done with her days of purifying.
Now if she bears a female, she shall be unclean for two weeks, like her time of menstruation;
And for sixty-six days she is to stay for a period of blood purification.
And at the fulfilling of the days of her purification, for a son or daughter,
She shall bring a lamb in its first year to the priest as a burnt offering he can slaughter,
Along with a young pigeon or turtledove as a sin offering, to the entrance
Of the Tent of Meeting, to the priest. He shall there offer it before the Lord's presence,
And shall make an atonement on her behalf, then she will be clean and be purified
From the source and the flow of her blood. This is the Instruction which the Lord does provide
For one who bears a child, be it male or female. But if she cannot afford a lamb,
Then she is to take two young pigeons or two turtledoves, and offer them with her hand,
One for burnt offering and the other for sin offering, and the priest will make sure
That he makes expiation and atonement for her, and only then shall she be pure."

Leviticus 13

When a man's skin turns scaly, with swelling scab spots,
Then the priest looks at him to see if he's unclean.
He must leave the camp if plagued with leprosy's rot,
But the man may return once his pureness is seen.

The Lord spoke to Moses and to Aaron, saying, "When any person has on the skin
Of his body a swelling, a scab, or a shiny spot which becomes an affliction
Or a leprous disease on the skin of his body, then he shall be brought to Aaron,
The priest, or one of his sons, the priests. The priest then is to examine the affliction.
On the skin of the flesh. If the hair in the diseased spot has turned white, and the disease
Appears to be deeper than the skin of his body, then it is a leprous disease;
When the priest has examined him, he shall pronounce him unclean. But if the spot is white
On his skin, and the spot appears no deeper than the skin, and the hair has not turned white,
The priest shall shut up the diseased person for seven days. The priest on the seventh day
Shall examine him, and if it appears to him that the disease has spread in no way,
And remains unchanged, the priest shall shut him up seven days more. When the priest
    checks again,
On the seventh day, if the affliction has faded and it has not spread on the skin,
The priest shall pronounce him clean, it is just a scab; Once he washes his clothes, he is clean.
But if the scab should spread on the skin after the priest has looked at him to make him clean,
He shall have the priest look at him a second time. When the priest looks, and the scab has spread
On the skin, then the priest shall pronounce him unclean; it is leprosy. When afflicted
With leprosy, a person shall be brought to the priest. When the priest looks, if he finds there
That there is a white swelling on the skin and that it has somehow turned into white hair,
With a live patch of raw skin in the swelling, it is mature leprosy on the skin
Of his body. The priest shall pronounce him unclean, but not shut him up—he is unclean.
Now if the leprosy breaks out on the skin so that it covers the sick person's skin,
From his head to his feet, as far as the priest can see, he shall make examination,
And if the leprosy has covered all his flesh, he shall pronounce the diseased man clean;
It has all turned white, so he is clean. But if raw flesh appears on him, he is unclean.
When the priest sees the raw flesh, he shall pronounce him unclean, for the raw flesh is unclean;
It is leprosy. But when the raw flesh turns back to white, the priest shall see him again.
When the priest looks, if the affliction has turned back to white, the priest shall pronounce
    him clean,
He is clean. Now if there is a boil in the skin of one's body all healed and unseen,
But in place of the boil there is now a white swelling, or a reddish-white shiny spot,
He shall have the priest look at him. When the priest looks, if the hair has turned white on
    the spot,
And it is deeper than the skin, he shall pronounce him unclean; it's a leprous disease
That has broke out in the boil. But if the priest looks at the spot, and no white hair he sees,
And it is not lower than the rest of the skin, and has faded, then for seven days
The priest shall shut him up. And if it spreads, the priest shall pronounce him unclean in his gaze,
It's a disease. But if the spot remains in one place and does not spread, it is the scar
Of the boil, and the priest shall pronounce him clean. Or if the skin has a burn caused by fire,
And on the raw flesh of the burn appears a shiny spot, either reddish-white or white,
The priest shall look at it, and if it's deeper than the skin and the hair in it turned white,

Then it is leprosy, it broke out in the burn, and the priest shall pronounce him unclean,
It is a leprous disease. But if the priest examines it, and no white hair is seen
And it's no deeper than the skin, and faded, then for seven days he shall shut him in.
And when the priest examines him on the seventh day, if it is spreading on the skin,
Then the priest is to pronounce him unclean, for it is an affliction of leprosy.
But if the shiny spot stays in one place, not spreading, faded from where it used to be,
It is a swelling from the burn, the priest shall pronounce him clean, it's the scar of the burn.

Now if a man or woman has a disease on the head or the beard, the priest in turn
Shall examine the disease. And if it looks deeper than the skin, and has yellow hair,
Then the priest shall pronounce him unclean, it's a scall, leprosy of the head or the beard.
But if the priest examines the scall affliction and finds it no deeper than the skin,
And there is no black hair on it, for seven days the priest shall shut the diseased one in.
When the priest examines the disease on the seventh day, and finds the scall has not spread,
And there's no yellow hair in it, and it is not deeper than the skin once inspected,
He shall shave himself, but he shall not shave the scall, and the priest shall shut him up once more,
For seven more days. And on the seventh day, the priest shall look at the scall like before.
And if the scall has not spread on the skin, and the scall does not look deeper than the skin,
The priest shall pronounce him clean, once he washes his clothes, he is clean. But if on the skin,
The scall spreads after his cleansing, when the priest looks at him and sees the spread of the scall,
The priest need not examine him for yellow hair, he is clearly unclean after all.
Now if he sees the scall is in a standstill, and sprouting black hair, then the scall is healed,
He is clean, and the priest shall pronounce him clean. When a man or woman has spots revealed
On the skin of the body, white spots, when the priest looks and on their body's skin is seen
Shiny spots, faded or white, it is a rash that has sprouted on the skin; he is clean.

When a man's hair has fallen from his head, he is bald, but clean. If a man's hair should fall
From his forehead and temples, then he is bald-foreheaded, but is still clean after all.
But when there is a reddish-white spot on the bald head or forehead, it is leprosy
Breaking out on his bald head or his bald forehead. Then the priest shall examine to see,
And if the diseased swelling is reddish-white on his bald head or on his bald forehead,
Like the look of leprosy on the body's skin, he is a leprous man pronounced,
He is unclean, the priest must pronounce him unclean, for the affliction is on his head.
Now the one with the leprous affliction, his clothes must be torn, and he must bare his head,
And his upper lip shall be covered. He must cry out, "Unclean! Unclean!" He shall remain
Unclean as long as he has the disease. He is unclean, and so alone he shall stay,
Outside of the camp he must dwell. Now when there is a leprous disease in a garment,
Fungus or mold on a cloth of wool or a cloth of linen to the smallest extent,
Or in the woof or warp of the linen or of the wool, or in an animal skin,
Or in anything made of skin, if the disease is greenish or reddish on the skin,
Or the cloth, or the woof or the warp, or on any vessel of skin, it is diseased,
An affliction of leprosy. He shall have the priest examine it. When the priest sees

The affliction, he shall shut up the diseased item for seven days. Then when he looks
At the affliction on the seventh day, if it has spread on the cloth or warp or woof
Or the skin, whatever its use might be, malignant leprosy is the affliction,
It is unclean. It shall be burned, the cloth, or the woof or warp in the wool or linen,
Or anything of skin, for it is malignant leprosy, it shall be burned in fire
But if the priest looks and the disease's spread in the cloth's warp or woof has not transpired,
Nor in any vessel of skin, the priest shall command that they scrub that which is diseased,
And shut it up for seven days a second time. When the priest looks, once the thing diseased
Has been scrubbed, and the disease has not changed its color, and the affliction has not spread,
It is unclean, in fire you shall burn it, it is decay, on the cloth's front-side forehead,
Or its back-side bald-spot. But if the priest looks and the disease faded once it was washed,
He shall tear it from the cloth, skin, woof, or warp, and if it is seen again on the cloth,
Whether in the woof, or the warp, or in any vessel of skin, then it is spreading,
And in fire you must burn the diseased thing, anything in which there is the affliction.
But the cloth, woof or warp, or the vessel of skin that you washed to dissolve the disease,
When it is washed a second time, then it is clean. This is the Instruction for disease,
The affliction of leprosy in cloth of wool or linen, wherever it is seen,
Or the warp or the woof, or anything of skin, for declaring it clean or unclean."

Leviticus 14

   The Lord told Moses, "To have such men purified,
   The priest shall slay two birds and two lambs as the cure.
   If a house is afflicted, diseased all inside,
   Then it must be destroyed if it can't be made pure.

                      [Metzora]

The Lord said to Moses, "This shall be the Instruction for the one who has leprosy:
On the day of his cleansing he shall be brought to the priest, who shall leave the camp with he;
When the priest looks, if the leprous disease has been healed from the leper from what he's seen,
The priest shall command that they take for the one to be cleansed two birds, both living
  and clean,
And wood of cedar and worm-scarlet and hyssop. Then the priest shall command that they slay
One of the birds in an earthen vessel over "living water" (running, that's to say),
And the live bird he shall take, and the cedar wood, the worm-scarlet and the hyssop too,
And shall dip them and the live bird in the slain bird's blood, above water that's running through.

Then he shall sprinkle it seven times over the one to be cleansed, declaring him clean,
And send out the live bird into the open field. Now when the one who is being cleaned
Washes his clothes, shaves his whole head of hair, and washes in water, he is clean full well.
After that he shall come into the camp, but outside his tent seven days he shall dwell.
On the seventh day he shall shave off all his hair, from his head, beard, eyebrows, all his hair.
Then he is to wash his clothes, wash his body in water, and shall be clean; he is pure.
On the eighth day, he shall take two lambs, wholly-sound, and a yearling lamb without blemish,
And three tenths of a measure of flour to serve as a grain-gift, with oil to be mixed,
And one log-pint of oil. The priest who cleanses shall stand both the man to be cleansed and them
Before the Lord's presence, at the door of the Tent of Meeting. The priest shall take one lamb
And offer it as a guilt offering, with a log of oil, and shall elevate them
As an elevation offering, before the Lord's presence. Then he shall slay the lamb
In the place where one slays the sin offering and the burnt offering, the holy place,
For like the sin offering, the guilt offering is the priest's portion of holy grace.
Then the priest shall take some of the blood of the guilt offering, and that blood he shall put
On the right ear's ridge of the one to be cleansed, his right hand's thumb, big-toe of his right foot.
And the priest shall take some of the log of oil and shall pour it onto his own left palm,
Then the priest shall dip his right finger into some of the oil that is on his left palm,
And shall sprinkle some of the oil with his finger, seven times, before the Lord's presence.
The priest shall place some of the oil left in his palm upon the one who is being cleansed,
On the ridge of his right ear, the thumb of his right hand, and the big-toe of his right foot,
On top of the blood of the guilt offering. Then what remains of the oil, he shall put
On the head of the one being cleansed; then the priest is to make an atonement for him,
Before the presence of the Lord. Then the priest is to sacrifice the sin offering,
And make atonement for the one being cleansed from his uncleanliness, and then after,
The priest shall slay the burnt offering, offering it and the grain-gift on the altar,
And so the priest will make an atonement for him, and then he shall be cleansed; he is clean.
But if he is poor and cannot afford the sacrifice due to insufficient means,
He shall take one lamb as a guilt offering, for elevating, to make atonement
For himself, and a tenth of a measure of flour, mixed with oil, as grain-gift to present,
And a log of oil; also two turtledoves or two young pigeons, as he can afford;
One shall be a sin offering and the other a burnt offering, both to the Lord.
On the eighth day of his cleansing he shall bring them to the priest, at the Tent of Meeting,
At the entrance before the Lord's presence. The priest shall take the lamb of guilt offering,
And the log of oil, and elevate them as elevation offering to the Lord.
And he shall slay the lamb of the guilt offering, and take some of the blood that it poured,
And put it on the ridge of the right ear of he who is to be cleansed, and on the thumb
Of his right hand, and on the big toe of his right foot. And then the priest is to pour some
Of the oil into the palm of his own left hand, and then with his right finger, sprinkle
Some of the oil from his palm before the presence of the Lord, seven times. Then he shall
Place some of the oil from his palm on the ridge of the right ear of the one being cleansed,
And on the thumb of his right hand, and big toe of his right foot, atop where the blood lands,

The blood that was put there from the guilt offering. What remains of the oil on his palm,
The priest shall place on the head of the one being cleansed, to make an atonement for him,
Before the Lord's presence. Then he shall sacrifice one of the turtledoves or pigeons,
Such as he can afford, one he can afford for sin offering, and the other one
For a burnt offering, along with a grain gift, and the priest is to make atonement
Before the Lord for the one who is being cleansed. This is the Instruction I present
For he who has a leprous disease, and cannot afford means for purification."

The Lord spoke to Moses and to Aaron, saying, "When you enter the land of Canaan,
Which I give you as a possession, and I place a leprous affliction on a house
In the land of your possession, an eruptive plague, then the person who owns the house
Shall come and tell the priest, 'something like an affliction on my house has been seen by me!'
Then the priest shall command that the house be cleaned before the priest enters to look and see
The affliction, so that nothing in the house becomes unclean. After that, the priest may
Enter to look at the house. When he looks at the affliction, if it shows in the way
Of greenish or reddish eruptions on the walls of the house, deeper than the surface,
The priest shall leave from the house, to the door of the house, and shut it up for seven days.
On the seventh day, when he returns and looks, if the disease has spread, with rot or mold,
On the house's walls, he shall command that they pull out the stones where the disease took hold,
And throw them outside the city, in an unclean place. The house's inside shall be scraped
All around, and the plaster scraped off they shall dump outside the city, an unclean place.
They shall take other stones and bring them in place of those stones, they shall bring other plaster,
And replaster the house. Now if the affliction of leprous mold or rot should recur
After one has pulled out the stones, scraped out the inside, and even replastered the house,
Then the priest shall enter. And when he looks, if he sees the disease has spread in the house,
It is a malignant leprosy in the house, it is unclean; It must be demolished.
He must tear down the house, all its stones, all its wood, all its plaster, and all of its polish,
And one shall take it outside the town to an unclean place. Furthermore, one entering
The house during the days when it is shut up is to remain unclean until evening.
He who lies down in the house shall wash his clothes; he who eats in the house shall
     wash his clothes.
Now if the priest should enter and look, and sees the disease did not spread as one supposed
Once the house was replastered, the priest shall declare the house clean; the disease has
     then healed.
He shall take to decontaminate the house: two birds, cedar wood, scarlet of worm's yield,
And hyssop. He shall slay one bird in an earthen vessel, over living (running) water,
Then he shall take the cedar wood, hyssop, and worm-scarlet, and the bird he did not slaughter,
And dip them in the blood of the slain bird and the running water, and shall sprinkle it
On the house seven times. So he shall decontaminate the house, and purge and cleanse it
With the blood of the bird, living water, the live bird, cedar wood, scarlet of worm's yield,
And hyssop. Then he shall send the live bird free, outside the city, toward the open field.

Once he makes this purgation and atonement for the house, then it shall be pure and clean.
Now this is the Instruction for any affliction of leprosy, scalls, mold that's green,
For a leprosy of cloth or house, for scabs or spots, for swelling, so that you may see
When it is unclean and when it is clean. This is the Instruction for all leprosy."

Leviticus 15

When a man or a woman has discharge of flow,
They are unclean, as are those who sit where they sat.
All that touch them must be scrubbed, and all this is so
They not dirty God's Dwelling, for they'd die from that.

The Lord spoke to Moses and to Aaron, saying, "Tell the Children of Israel this:
When any man has a discharge from his flesh, his discharge is unclean. And this is his
Own uncleanness, whether his flesh runs with his discharge, or is stopped by his discharge,
This is his law of uncleanness: Any place for lying down where the one with discharge
Lies upon becomes unclean, and anything on which he sits also becomes unclean.
A man that touches his bed shall wash his clothes and bathe in water, remaining unclean
Until sunset. One who sits where the one with discharge sits shall wash his clothes, and then wash
Himself in water, remaining unclean until sunset. And one who touches the flesh
Of the one with discharge shall wash his clothes and bathe in water, unclean until sunset.
Now if one with discharge spits on one who is clean, he shall wash his clothes (of unclean spit),
And bathe in water, and will remain unclean until sunset. Any means for riding,
Like a saddle, which one with discharge mounts is unclean. Whoever touches anything
That was under him shall be unclean until sunset; and anyone who carries them
Shall wash his clothes and bathe in water, remaining unclean until sunset. Anyone
Whom the one with discharge touches, not having rinsed his hands in water, must
    wash his clothes
And bathe in water, and shall remain unclean until sunset. If the one with the flows
Of discharge touches an earthen vessel, it must be broken. If a vessel of wood,
It must be rinsed in water. Now when the one with discharge is cleansed of discharge for good,
He shall count for himself seven days for his cleansing, and wash his clothes, and wash his flesh
In living water, then he shall be clean. On the eighth day he is to take for himself
Two young pigeons or two turtledoves, and he shall come before the presence of the Lord,
At the entrance to the Tent of Meeting, and shall give them to the priest, who in accord
Shall sacrifice them, one as a sin offering and the other as burnt offering;
And the priest shall make atonement for him before the Lord, for his discharge and flowing.

When a man has an emission of semen, he shall wash all of his flesh in water,
And will remain unclean until sunset. And every garment, of cloth or of leather,
On which there is an emission of semen shall be washed in water and is unclean
Until sunset. And a woman with whom a man lies with an emission of semen,
Both of them shall wash themselves in water, and they shall both be unclean until sunset.

When a woman has a discharge, and her flow of discharge is one of blood from her flesh,
She shall be in her impurity seven days, whoever touches her is unclean
Until sunset. Anything she lies upon during her impurity is unclean;
Anything that she sits upon shall be unclean. And anyone who touches her bed
Is to wash his clothes and wash himself in water, and will be unclean until sunset.

Anyone who touches any object that she sat upon is to then wash his clothes
And wash in water, he shall be unclean until sunset. Whether it is one of those
Things she sat on, or her bed, upon touching it, he shall be unclean until sunset.
And if a man lies with her, her impurity is upon him, transferred in the bed,
He shall be unclean for seven days, during which time where he lies shall become unclean.
If a woman has a discharge of blood for many days, not from her impurity,
Or if she has a discharge beyond the time of her impurity, for all those days
She shall remain unclean, as during the days of her impurity, unclean she stays.
Any bed where she lies, all the days of her discharge, shall be for her just like the bed
During impurity, and anything which she sits on shall likewise be affected,
Being unclean like the uncleanness of her impurity. Whoever touches these
Becomes unclean, and shall wash his clothes and wash himself in water, remaining unclean
Until sunset. Now when she is cleansed of her discharge, she shall count days for herself, seven,
After which she is clean. And on the eighth day she shall take two turtledoves or two pigeons
And bring them to the priest, to the entrance of the Tent of Meeting. The priest at the tent
Shall offer one as sin-offering, the other as burnt-offering, make atonement
For the woman before the presence of the Lord, for her unclean discharge flow gone by.
You shall have the Children of Israel avoid their uncleanness, so they do not die
From their uncleanness by making unclean and defiled My dwelling which is in their midst."

This is the Instruction for he who has a discharge and he whom from semen emits,
So becoming unclean, and for she who has menstrual impurity, and anyone
Who has a discharge, male or female, and for a man that lies with an unclean woman.

Leviticus 16

The Lord told Moses, "Aaron can't enter My Shrine
Unless he is dressed properly, with sacrifices.
He shall slay a bull, in the way I assign,
And bring two goats, just one of which he slays and slices.
The other goat, he'll lay his hands on its head,
And confess all the sins that Israel may hold,
Then the goat shall run off, so the sin will have fled."
Moses spoke this to Aaron, just as he was told.

[Acharei]

Now the Lord spoke to Moses after the death of the two sons of Aaron, who came near
Before the presence of the Lord, and died. The Lord said to Moses, "You are to make clear
To your brother Aaron that he shall not at just any time enter the Holy Shrine,
Inside the curtain, facing the penance cover on the ark, so that he does not die;
For I shall appear in a cloud over the penance-cover. Aaron is to enter
Only like so: With a bull, a young of the herd, for a sin-offering to offer,
And a ram for a burnt-offering. He shall dress in a holy tunic of linen,
Linen breeches shall be on his flesh, and he shall be girded with a sash of linen,
He shall wear a linen turban; these are the garments of the Holy Shrine. And once he
Has washed his body in water, he may dress in them. And then from the community
Of the Children of Israel he shall take two hairy goats for a sin offering,
And one ram for burnt-offering. Aaron shall offer the bull as a sin offering
For himself, to atone on behalf of himself and his household. Then he shall take more,
Aaron shall take the two hairy goats and stand them before the Lord's presence at the door
Of the Tent of Meeting. Aaron shall cast lots on the two goats, with one lot for the Lord,
And the other lot for Azazel. And the goat on which came up the lot for the Lord,
Aaron shall offer as a sin-offering. But the goat on which the other lot fell
Shall be brought alive before the Lord to make atonement over it. To Azazel
It shall be sent, escaped goat which carries the sins, to the demon of the wilderness.
Aaron shall present his bull of sin offering to atone for his house and himself;
He shall slay his bull of sin offering, and shall take a panful of fiery coals
From atop the altar, from before the presence of the Lord, and also two handfuls
Of fragrant incense, finely-ground, and shall bring it behind the curtain. Then he shall place
The incense on the fire before the presence of the Lord, so the cloud the incense makes

Covers the penance-cover on top of the ark, so that he does not die. And then he
Shall take some of the blood from the bull with his finger, and sprinkle it on top of the
Penance-cover, eastward. And in front of the cover he shall sprinkle with his finger
The bull's blood, seven times. Then he shall slay the goat of the sin offering to offer
For the people, and bring its blood inside the curtain, doing with its blood what he did
With the bull's blood; he shall sprinkle it on the penance cover, and in front of the lid.
So he shall make atonement, purgation for the Holy Shrine from all the pollutions
Of the Children of Israel, for all of their sins, and from all of their transgressions,
And so shall he do with the Tent of Meeting, which dwells and abides with them in the midst
Of their pollutions. No human shall be in the Tent of Meeting when he enters it
To make atonement in the Holy Shrine, until he goes out. He shall make atonement
On behalf of himself, his household, and all Israel's assembly to its full extent.
Then he is to go out to the altar before the presence of the Lord and purge it,
He shall take some of the blood of the bull and some of the blood of the goat, and place it
On the horns of the altar, all around. And the rest of the blood he is to sprinkle
On the altar with his finger, seven times. He shall hallow it and cleanse it in full
From the pollutions of the Children of Israel. And when he has finished purging
For the Holy Shrine, the Tent of Meeting, and also the altar, then he is to bring
The live goat. Aaron shall lay his two hands on the head of the live goat, and then confess
Over it all the iniquities of the Children of Israel to be redressed,
All of their transgressions, and all of their sins. He shall lay them all upon the goat's head
And send it into the wilderness, by the hand of a man for this task selected.
The goat shall bear on itself all of their iniquities, to a cut-off land vacant;
He shall send the goat free into the wilderness. Then Aaron is to enter the Tent
Of Meeting, and shall strip off the linen garments which he dressed in to enter the Shrine,
And shall leave them there. He shall wash his flesh in water, in a place holy and divine,
And dress in his clothes. He shall go out and sacrifice his burnt-offering, and the one
Of the people, so atonement on his own behalf and for the people will be done.
And the fat of the sin offering Aaron shall turn into smoke upon the altar.
The one who sent the goat to Azazel shall wash his clothes and wash his flesh in water;
After that he may reenter the camp. And the bull and goat of the sin offering
Whose blood was brought in to purge the Holy Shrine and atone for it, someone is to bring
Outside of the camp. And their hides, their flesh, their dung, shall completely be burned
    in the fire.
And each one who burns them shall wash his clothes and wash his flesh in water. Once
    that transpires,
He may reenter the camp. And it shall be a law for you for all time to obey:
In the seventh month, on the tenth day of the month, you shall afflict yourselves on that day.
You shall do no work, neither the native nor the sojourner who sojourns in your midst,
For on this day shall atonement be made for you, so to purge you from all of your sins.
Before the presence of the Lord, you shall be clean. It is a Sabbath of solemn rest,
Sabbath-Ceasing for you, you shall afflict yourselves, and forever this law is to last.

The priest who is anointed and hallowed as priest in his father's place then shall atone,
Wearing the linen garments, the holy and sacred linen garments, he shall atone
For the Tent of Meeting, and atone for the altar, and the holy sanctuary.
And he shall make atonement for the priests and all of the people of the assembly.
This shall be for you a law for the ages, that once a year you shall make atonement
For the Children of Israel from all their sins." Moses followed the Lord's commandment.

Leviticus 17

> Any man who may slaughter an ox, sheep, or goat
> And does not bring it as offering to the Lord
> Shall be cut off from his kin. You all must take note:
> The blood ransoms your life, this cannot be ignored.

The Lord said to Moses, "Say to Aaron and his sons and all the Children of Israel:
This is the word that the Lord has commanded. If any man of the House of Israel
Slays an ox or a sheep or a goat in the camp, or who slays it outside of the camp,
And does not bring it to the door of the Tent of Meeting to offer it as a grant,
A gift to the Lord before the Tabernacle of the Lord, bloodguilt shall be reckoned
To that man; He has shed blood, and so that man is to be cut off from amidst his kin.
In order that the Children of Israel may bring their sacrifices which they slay
In the open field, in order that they may bring them to the Lord, to the priest who stays
At the door of the Tent of Meeting, and slaughter them as sacrifices of shalom
To the Lord. The priest shall dash their blood against the altar of the Lord, which has its home
At the entrance of the Tent of Meeting, and shall burn the fat for a soothing savor
To the Lord. So that they may no longer slay their sacrifices for hairy satyrs,
After whom they go whoring. This shall be a law for the ages, forever to them,
Throughout their generations. And to them you shall also say: Any man, any man
Of the House of Israel or of the sojourners who are sojourning in your midst
Who offers any kind of sacrifice and to the Tent of Meeting does not bring it,
To offer to the Lord; that man shall be cut of from his kinspeople. And any man,
Any man of the House of Israel or of the sojourners who are in their land
Who eats any blood: I will set My face against the one who eats the blood; I will cut
Him off from amidst his kinspeople. Because the life of the flesh, it is in the blood.
I Myself have given it to you on the altar, to make atonement for your lives,
For the blood, it makes ransom for life. Therefore I say to all of the Israelites:
No person among you shall eat blood, nor shall the sojourner who sojourns in your midst.
And any man of the Children of Israel or of the sojourners in your midst

Who hunts any beast or a bird that may be eaten shall pour out its blood once it's dead,
And cover it with dust. For the life of all flesh—its blood is its life. Therefore I said
To the Children of Israel: The blood of all flesh you are not to eat, for the life
Of all flesh—it is its blood, and whoever eats it shall be cut off. Its blood, its life.
And any person that eats an animal that has died, or one that by beasts was torn,
Regardless of whether the person was a sojourner or one of the native-born,
When he washes his clothes and flesh in water, unclean until sunset, then he is clean.
But if he does not wash his clothes and wash his flesh, then he still bears his iniquity."

Leviticus 18

God told Moses, "Tell Israel: I am your God!
Don't expose naked flesh of any of your kin.
Don't do what Egypt did, all their practices odd,
Or you will be unclean, and that would be a sin.

And the Lord spoke to Moses, saying, "You are to say to the Children of Israel:
I am the Lord your God. What is done in the land of Egypt, wherein you once did dwell,
You shall not do. And what is done in the land of Canaan to which I am bringing you,
You shall not do; You are not to walk by their laws. My regulations you are to do,
My laws you shall keep, walking by them; I am the Lord your God. You are to keep My laws
And My regulations, which by observing them, man shall live. I am the Lord your God.
None of you shall approach any kin of his own flesh to uncover their nakedness.
I am the Lord. The nakedness of your father and also your mother's nakedness,
You shall not uncover. She is your mother—you shall not uncover her nakedness.
The nakedness of your father's wife, you shall not uncover. She is the nakedness
Of your father. The nakedness of your sister, the daughter of your father or mother,
Whether born in the house or outside the house, their nakedness you are not to uncover.
The nakedness of your son's or daughter's daughter—their nakedness you shall not uncover.
For they are your nakedness. The nakedness of the daughter of the wife of your father,
Born to your father's household—she is your sister. You shall not expose her naked skin
The nakedness of your father's sister you shall not expose. She is your father's kin.
The nakedness of your mother's sister, you shall not expose. She is kin of your mother.
The nakedness of your father's brother you shall not expose. His wife, do not approach.
She is your aunt. (And since a man and wife share one flesh, his nakedness you would expose.)
The nakedness of your daughter-in-law, you shall not uncover. She is your son's wife.
So you are not to uncover her nakedness. The nakedness of your brother's wife,

You shall not uncover. She is the nakedness of your brother. If you uncover
The nakedness of a woman, you shall not expose the nakedness of her daughter,
Nor shall you take her son's or daughter's daughter in marriage, exposing their nakedness,
For they are kindred, kin to the woman; And so to do such things would be wickedness.
You shall not take a woman and her sister in marriage, producing a rivalry,
And uncover her nakedness while her sister still lives. (This would produce jealousy).
You shall not approach a woman during her period of menstrual impurity,
Uncovering her nakedness. With your neighbor's wife you are not to lie carnally,
So defiling yourself and becoming unclean through her (and through the path that you trod).
Do not give your offspring to be offered to Molech, profaning the name of your God.
I am the Lord. You are not to lie down with a male as with a woman one would lie.
It is an abomination. You shall not lie down with any animal, thereby
Becoming unclean through it. Nor shall any woman give herself to an animal,
Mating with it; it is a perversion. You shall not make yourselves unclean and defiled
By any of these things. For through all of them, the nations that I cast out before you
Have defiled themselves. So the land became unclean, which is why I do what I do.
I have punished it for its iniquity, so its inhabitants it has spewed out.
But you shall keep My laws and My regulations, and also keep yourselves quite devout,
Not doing any of these abominations, native or sojourner in your midst,
(For all these things were done by the men of the land before you, and unclean they made it,)
So the land does not vomit you out for making it unclean, as it spewed out the nation
That came before you. For whoever does any one of these things, these abominations,
Those persons that do them shall be cut off from their kin. So keep My charge never to do
Any of the abominable customs that were done by the people before you,
Nor to engage in any of their abhorrent practices, abominations flawed,
So you do not defile yourselves and become unclean through them. I am the Lord your God."

Leviticus 19

Now tell Israel: Be holy, since I am too.
Keep the Sabbath, hold both of your parents in awe.
Do not worship false gods, Harvest not your land through,
But leave some for the sojourner. This is the law.
Do not steal, rob, or swear falsely using My name,
Don't corrupt justice, love your neighbor as your own.
When a man takes a handmaid, a ram clears the blame.
And treat strangers well. Only use fair weighing-stones.

[Kedoshim]

The Lord spoke to Moses, saying, "Speak to the entire Israelite community,
And say to all of them: You are to be holy, for I, the Lord your God, am holy.
Each man shall revere his mother and father, keep My Sabbaths; I am the Lord your God.
Do not turn to false idols, or make molten gods for yourselves; I am the Lord your God.
Now when you slay an offering of shalom to the Lord, so it may be accepted,
You shall slaughter it. And then the sacrifice shall be eaten on the day that you did,
And on the next day too, but what remains by the third day is to be consumed in fire.
If it is eaten on the third day, it is tainted, and no acceptance will transpire.
He who eats it must bear his iniquity, for the Lord's holy thing he has profaned,
That person shall be cut off from his kin. Now when you harvest the harvest of your land,
You shall not harvest to the edge of your field, nor gather your harvest's full gathering;
Your shall not pick your vineyard bare, nor gather fallen fruits. Rather, for those sojourning
And those poor and afflicted, you shall leave them. I am the Lord your God. You shall not steal,
You shall not lie, You shall not deal falsely with each other nor use deceit in your deals.
You shall not swear by My name falsely, and profane the name of your God. I am the Lord.
You shall not withhold property from your neighbor, nor are you to rob him of his hoard.
You shall not hold the wages of hired-hands overnight until morn; pay him on time.
You shall not insult the deaf, nor are you to place stumbling blocks in front of the blind.
Rather, you shall hold your God in awe; I am the Lord. You shall not commit corruption
In justice; You shall not favor the poor, nor defer to the great in your decisions.
You shall judge your fellows even-handedly. You shall not spread slander amongst your kin.
You shall not stand against the blood of your neighbor, I am the Lord. When you look within,
Do not hate your brother in your heart, but rebuke and reprove your fellow openly,
So you do not bear sin because of him (For not to tell him would be iniquity.)

You shall not take vengeance, you shall not bear a grudge against the sons of your kinspeople,
But love your neighbor as one like yourself, I am the Lord. My laws, you shall keep in full:
You shall not let your animal mate in two kinds (cattle can't mate with a different breed),
You shall not sow your field with two kinds (you can't have two crops; use all the same kind
    of seed),
And clothing of two kinds, of material mixed, shall not go on you. Now when a man
Lies with a woman, emitting seed, and she is a slave destined for another man,
And she has not been redeemed or given her freedom, then there is to be compensation;
They shall not be put to death because she has not been freed. But as a remuneration,
He shall bring as guilt offering to the Lord, to the entrance of the Tent of Meeting
A ram for guilt offering. The priest shall atone for him with ram of guilt-offering,
Before the Lord's presence, for the sin that he sinned, and he shall be pardoned for his sin.
When you enter the land and plant any kind of tree for food, count its fruit as foreskinned.
For three years it shall be foreskinned, forbidden to you. By you it must not be eaten
And in the fourth year all its fruit shall be a holy portion, for a jubilation
Before the Lord. In the fifth year, you may eat its fruit, so its yield for you will increase;
I am the Lord your God. You shall not eat anything with its blood. Don't make prophecies
With witchcraft or augury. You shall not practice divination, or practice soothsaying.
You shall not round off the edge-growth on your head, nor trim the edges your beard
    is displaying;
You shall not make incisions in your flesh for the dead, nor cut marks into your own skin.
I am the Lord. You shall not profane your daughter by making her a whore (that's a sin),
Otherwise the land will go whoring, and will be filled with depravity and harlots.
My Sabbaths you shall keep, My sanctuary you shall keep, I am the Lord. You shall not
Turn your faces to ghosts, don't seek out wizards, or inquire of spirits familiar,
To become unclean through them. I am the Lord your God. You shall rise when faced
    with gray hair,
You shall honor the face of the elderly, and hold your God in awe. I am the Lord.
Now when a sojourner sojourns with you in your land, respect to him you shall accord.
You shall not maltreat him or deal unfairly with him; you shall treat him as a native,
You shall love him as yourself, for you yourselves were once strangers in the land of Egypt,
I am the Lord your God. You shall not judge falsely measured length, weight, or capacity.
You shall have just scales, just weights, a just ephah, and a just hin, measured with equity.
I am the Lord your God, who brought you out of the land of Egypt, where you had been moored.
You shall keep all My laws and all My regulations, and observe them. I am the Lord."

Leviticus 20

> The Lord said, "Tell the Israelites: Any man
> Who gives his children over to false gods will die.
> Those ignoring him, I shall curse them and their clan.
> No man shall with the wife of another man lie,
> Nor the wife of his father, his daughter or sister,
> Or other man, or any beast they may see.
> They've committed a sin if they did more than kissed her.
> You must keep My laws; you are holy to Me.

The Lord spoke to Moses, saying, "And to the Children of Israel you are to say:
Any man of the Children of Israel, or sojourner that in Israel stays
That gives any of his children to Molech (in sacrifice) is to be put to death;
The people of the land are to pelt him with stones until he can no longer draw breath.
As for Me, I will set My face against that man, and cut him off from amidst his kin,
Since he gave of his seed to the Molech and so has made My sanctuary unclean
And profanes My holy name. Now if the people of the land hide their eyes from that man
When he gives of his seed to the Molech, and do not put him to death by My command,
I will set My face against that man and his clan, and cut them off from amidst their kin,
Him and all those who go whoring with him and follow the Molech, so committing sin.
If a person turns his face to ghosts or wizards to go whoring after them, then I,
I will set My face against that person and cut him off from amidst his kin, to die.
So you are to hallow yourselves, you are to be holy, for I the Lord am your God.
You shall keep My laws and observe them, I the Lord am the one who hallows you, your God.
Any man who curses his father or his mother is to be put to death, yes, death,
For his has cursed his father or his mother, and so his bloodguilt is upon himself.

If a man adulters with the wife of another man, with the wife of his neighbor,
The two of them shall be put to death, both the adulteress and the adulterer.
If a man lies with the wife of his father, he has exposed his father's nakedness,
The two of them shall be put to death, and their bloodguilt is on themselves since
    they transgressed.
If a man lies with his daughter-in-law, the two of them are both to be put to death,
They have committed an abomination, and so it is on themselves their bloodguilt rests.
If a man lies with a male as one lies with a woman, they've done an abomination,
They shall be put to death, and their bloodguilt lies upon themselves for this bad situation.

If a man takes in marriage a woman and her mother, it is insidiousness.

All three of them shall be burned in fire, so that no such wickedness will be in your midst.

A man who lies with a beast shall be put to death, and the beast you are also to slay.

A woman who approaches a beast to mate with it, you shall deal with in the same way;

You shall kill the woman and the beast, they shall be put to death, their own bloodguilt they bear.

If a man marries his sister, daughter of his father or daughter of his mother,

So that he sees her nakedness and she sees his nakedness, it is a shameful thing,

They shall be cut off before the eyes of their people, cut off in the sight of their kin,

For he has exposed the nakedness of his sister, he shall bear his iniquity.

If a man lies with a woman, exposing her nakedness, in her infirmity,

He has laid naked her fountain of blood, and as for her, she has exposed her fountain;

The two of them shall be cut off from amidst their kinspeople for this transgression.

You shall not expose the nakedness of your mother's sister or your father's sister,

For that is laying naked your own kin, and so their iniquity they are to bear.

If a man lies with his aunt, his uncle's wife, he has exposed his uncle's nakedness,

They shall bear their sin, and they shall die in shame, they shall die accursed and childless.

If a man marries his brother's wife, it is an unclean thing and is indecency,

He has exposed the nakedness of his brother, accursed and childless they will be.

You shall keep all My laws and all My regulations, and observe them so that the land

Where I am bringing you to settle does not spew you out. You shall follow My command.

You shall not follow the customs of the nations which I am driving out before you,

For they did all these things, and therefore I abhorred them, so I say to you: It is you

Who will possess their soil, I Myself will give it to you, to take possession of it,

A land flowing with milk and honey. I am the Lord your God who has made separate

You and other peoples, I have made a distinction. So you shall separate between

The clean animals and the unclean ones, and between the clean birds and the ones unclean,

So you do not make yourselves detestable through animal or bird or anything

With which the soil stirs, that I have separated for you to regard as unclean.

You shall be holy to Me, for holy am I, the Lord; I have separated you

From the other peoples so that you should be Mine. Any man or any woman who

Has a ghost or a familiar spirit, or who is a wizard or medium,

They shall be put to death, you shall pelt them with stones, and their bloodguilt shall be
    upon them."

Leviticus 21

God told Moses, "Say to the priests: When there are dead,
Do not make yourself unclean unless they're your kin.
Do not trim your beards, cut your flesh, or shave your head.
They are holy to God, and so they must not sin.
Now the high priest shall not mourn by tearing his clothes,
Nor approach the dead, even if his parents die.
Men with defects (blind, lame, scabby, any of those),
Shall not enter the Shrine; they'd profane it thereby.

[Emor]

The Lord spoke to Moses, saying, "Speak to the priests, the sons of Aaron, and say to them:
None of shall defile himself for the dead among his kin, except for those closest to him,
For his mother, his father, his son or his daughter, his brother, or virgin sister,
Who is closest to him since she had no husband, he may make himself unclean for her.
He shall not make himself unclean as a (non-priestly) husband among his people does,
To profane himself. They shall not make bald spots on their head, or shave off any beard fuzz,
Nor make cuts in their flesh. They shall be holy to their God, they shall not profane the name
Of their God; For the fire-offerings of the Lord, their God's food, they offer to his claim,
So they shall be holy. A woman who is a whore, one profaned, they shall not marry,
A woman divorced from her husband they shall not marry; to his God he is holy
And you are to treat him as holy, for he brings near the food-offerings of your God;
He shall be holy for you, for holy am I, the Lord, the one who hallows you, God.
And the daughter of a man who is a priest, when she profanes herself by harlotry,
It is her father that she profanes by her actions, and so burned in fire she must be.
Now the high priest among his brothers, who has had the anointing oil poured on his head
And has been ordained to wear the holy garments: Of his head he shall not bare one shred,
His garments he not tear; the presence of any dead persons he is not to enter,
He shall not defile himself or make himself unclean even for his father or mother,
From the sanctuary he shall not go out, so he won't profane the sanctuary
Of his God, for the sacred anointing oil is upon him, I am the Lord. And he,
Only a virgin woman may he marry. Widows, divorcees, and women defiled
And profaned by whoring, these he shall not marry. Rather, a virgin from his people
He shall take as a wife, so that his children among his people he does not profane,
For I am the Lord, the one who has consecrated him." The Lord spoke to Moses, saying,

"Speak to Aaron, and say to him: No man of your seed, throughout all their generations,
Who has a defect shall come near to offer the food of his God. Defects mean these ones:
Any man who has a blemish shall not come near, any man blind, lame, or mutilated,
Any man with a broken leg, or broken arm, or one whose limbs are too elongated,
Or a hunchback, or a dwarf, or one with a growth in his eye, one with a scab or scar,
Or with eruptions or crushed testes. Any man with any defects mentioned so far,
From the seed of Aaron the priest, shall not approach to offer the Lord's fire offerings,
A defect is in him, he is not to approach with the food of the Lord, near to bring.
The food offerings of his God he may eat from the most holy and holy portions;
But he has a defect, so he shall not approach the altar or enter the curtain,
He shall not profane my sanctuaries, for I am the Lord, the one who hallows them."
So spoke Moses to Aaron and to his sons and to all the Children of Israel.

Leviticus 22

The Lord told Moses, "Tell Aaron, and his sons too,
That no man unclean shall touch My holy donations.
A priest's daughter, once married, this food can't chew,
But if single and childless, skips this regulation.
The animals you bring to offer to Me
Must be whole, without blemish, not blind, scabbed, or scored,
For I won't accept defects in any degree.
You shall keep My commandments, for I am the Lord."

The Lord spoke to Moses, saying, "Speak to Aaron and his sons, so they may be careful
When they are dealing with all the holy donations of the Children of Israel
Which they consecrate to Me, so they do not profane My holy name, I am the Lord.
And say to them: If throughout your generations any person comes near—of your horde—
To the holy donations that the Children of Israel consecrate to the Lord,
With his uncleanness upon him, he shall be cut off from My presence, I am the Lord.
Any man of the line of Aaron, if he has leprosy or if he has a flow,
He may not eat of the holy donations until he is as pure as driven snow.
Whoever touches anything that has been made unclean by way of a dead person,
Or whoever has a discharge of seed, a man who has an emission of semen,
Or a man who touches any swarming thing through which he becomes unclean, or if he
Touches a human through which he becomes unclean, whatever his uncleanness may be,

The person who touched it shall remain unclean until sunset, and he is not to eat
Of the holy donations, unless he washes his flesh in water, from head to feet;
When the sun comes in, then he is pure, after which he may eat of the holy donations,
For they are his food. He shall not eat a carcass or beasts which have suffered mutilation,
To become unclean by means of them. I am the Lord. And therefore they shall keep my charge
So they do not bear sin for it and die because of it, when they profane it at large;
I am the Lord, who makes them holy. An outsider shall not eat the holy donation;
A sojourner or hired-hand of the priests is also subject to this regulation.
But when a priest buys a slave with money, as his property, the slave may eat of it;
And those that are born into his household, they may eat of his food and share in a bit.
A priest's daughter who marries an outsider shall not eat of the raised holy donations.
But a priest's daughter who is a widow or who has divorced from her marriage relations
And has no children—When she returns to her father's house, as time in her youth was spent,
Then she may eat her father's food; no outsider may eat it. But if by accident,
A layman eats a holy donation, he shall add to it one fifth of its value,
And give the holy donation to the priest; as compensation this shall be his due.
The priests shall not profane the holy donations which the Children of Israel bring
That they set aside for the Lord, making them bear sin requiring a guilt offering,
By eating their holy donations, for I am the Lord, the one who makes you holy."

The Lord spoke to Moses, saying, "Speak to Aaron and to his sons, and to all of the
Children of Israel, and say to them: When any man of the House of Israel
Or of the sojourners in Israel brings his offering, offerings of free will
Or offerings in payments for vows, any offered to the Lord as burnt offering:
For your acceptance, they must be wholly sound, with no blemish on the offer you bring,
A male from among the cattle, the sheep, or the goats. Any one which has a defect,
You shall not offer, for such will not be accepted for you, not in any respect.
When a man brings a sacrifice of shalom to the Lord, be it to fulfill a vow
Or an offering of freewill, from among the herd or flock, be it bull, goat, or cow,
It must be unblemished for acceptance, and there must not be any defect in it.
Animals blind or broken, disabled or mutilated, with a scar, scab, or itch,
You shall not offer these to the Lord, you shall not burn them in fire on the Lord's altar,
But an ox or a sheep with limbs too long or short, you may voluntarily offer,
Though it will not be accepted as a vow offering, only offers of free will.
You shall not offer to the Lord animals which have been damaged in the testicles.
Be they bruised, smashed, crushed, bashed, torn up, or cut out, these may not be sacrificed in
  your land.
And you shall not offer the food of your God from those obtained through a foreigner's hand,
For their ruin is in them, a defect is in them, they won't be accepted for you."

The Lord said to Moses, "When an ox, goat, or sheep is born (from a cow, she-goat, or ewe),

It shall stay seven days under its mother, and only from the eighth day and forward
Will it be accepted as a near offering, as a fire offering to the Lord.
Be the mother a cow or a ewe, you shall not kill both her and her young in one day.
When you slay offerings of thanksgiving to the Lord for your acceptance, you shall slay
The animal, and eat it on that day; You shall leave none until morning to be stored,
I am the Lord. You are to keep My commandments and shall observe them; I am the Lord.
You shall not profane My holy name, so that I may be hallowed amidst and all through
The people and the Children of Israel. I am the Lord, the one who hallows you,
Who is bringing you out of the land of Egypt, land of bondage where you were once moored,
I have brought you out of the land of Egypt to be a God for you. I am the Lord."

Leviticus 23

"Tell the Children of Israel: All the set feasts
Of the Lord you'll proclaim as days holy to you.
You shall rest on the Sabbath, not work in the least,
And on Passover, eat matzoh for one week through.
When you harvest the land where I bring you, that day,
Offer up sheaf and sheep. On the seventh New Moon,
The tenth day is a day of Atonement to pray,
Then a seven day feast of booths will happen soon.

The Lord spoke to Moses, saying, "Speak to the Children of Israel, and say to them:
The appointed feasts of the Lord which you are to proclaim as holy convocations,
My festivals are these: For six days, work may be done, but then upon the seventh day
Is the Sabbath, a Sabbath of rest, a holy convocation; no work shall you make.
You shall not do any kind of work; It is Sabbath to the Lord, through all your dwellings.
These are the set feasts of the Lord, holy convocations, which you shall be proclaiming
At their set times: In the first month, on the fourteenth day after the new moon, at twilight
Is Passover to the Lord. And on the fifteenth day after this new moon sheds its light
Is the feast of matzot to the Lord: For seven days, you are to eat unleavened bread.
On the first day there shall be a holy convocation for you, no strain exerted,
You shall not do any kind of heavy labor, nor work servile in any way.
You shall offer a fire-offering to the Lord, for seven days. On the seventh day
Is a holy convocation, you shall not do servile heavy labor by your hand."

The Lord said to Moses, "Say to the Children of Israel: When you enter the land

That I am giving you, and you harvest its harvest, you shall bring that harvest's first sheaf
To the priest; And the sheaf will be elevated before the Lord's presence by the priest,
To gain acceptance for you; On the morrow of the Sabbath he shall elevate it.
You shall offer a sacrifice on the day you elevate the sheaf, this shall be it:
An unblemished sheep, one year old, as a burnt offering to the Lord. And as grain gift,
Two tenth-measures of flour mixed with oil, a fire-offering to the Lord, which shall lift
A soothing savor up to Him; And a libation of wine, one quarter of a hin.
You shall not eat bread, fresh grain, or parched grain until you have brought your
     God this offering;
It is a law for the ages, throughout your generations, through all of your dwellings.
Now you shall number for yourselves, from the morrow of the Sabbath, from the day you bring
The elevated sheaf, seven Sabbaths of days (meaning seven weeks you are to count),
Until the morrow of the seventh Sabbath, so fifty days will be the full amount.
Then you shall offer a grain gift of new crops to the Lord, bringing from your settlements
Bread as an elevation offering, two loaves made of measures of flour, two tenths.
You shall bake them leavened, as first fruits to the Lord. And you shall bring along with the bread
Seven unblemished sheep, a year old, and one bull, young of the herd, and two rams, well bred.
They shall be a burnt offering to the Lord, with their grain gift and with their libations,
A fire-offering of soothing savor to the Lord. You shall offer in addition:
One he-goat as a sin offering, and two yearling sheep, as a shalom sacrifice.
The priest shall elevate them, along with the bread made from firstfruits of your grains and rice
As an elevation offering before the Lord's presence, along with the two sheep;
They are to be a holy portion for the Lord, holiness to the Lord for the priest.
And you shall hold a celebration on that day, a holy convocation for you,
You shall not do any heavy labor, a law for the ages, all your dwellings through,
Throughout your generations. When it comes time for you to reap the harvest of your land,
You shall not harvest your field all the way to its border, nor glean what falls in the sand;
You shall leave some for the afflicted and for the sojourner, I am the Lord your God."
The Lord spoke to Moses, saying, "Say to the Children of Israel this, from your God:
On the seventh month, on the first day of the month, you shall have a day of Sabbath rest,
A memorial proclaimed by blasting of horns, a proclamation of holiness.
You shall do no heavy labor; You are to offer a fire-offering to the Lord."

The Lord spoke to Moses, saying, "Mark the tenth day, once the seventh month's new
     moon is scored,
It is the Day of Atonement, and it shall be a holy convocation for you.
You shall afflict yourselves, and you shall sacrifice a fire-offering to the Lord too.
On that day you shall not do any kind of work, for it is the Day of Atonement,
To effect atonement and gain acceptance for you, before the Lord your God's presence.
For whoever does not afflict himself on that day is to be cut off from his kin,
And whoever does work on that day, I shall cause him to perish from amidst his kin.

You shall not do any kind of work—a law for the ages, through your generations,
In all of your dwellings. It is Sabbath, Sabbath-ceasing for you, no work may be done;
You shall afflict yourselves. On the ninth day of the month at sunset, from one to the next,
You shall keep your Sabbath, both ceasing and afflicting yourself." The Lord said to Moses,
"Speak to the Children of Israel, saying: On the fifteenth day of this seventh month
Is the pilgrimage-festival of Sukkot, for seven days, to the Lord. Feast of Huts.
On the first day is a holy convocation, do no work servile in any way.
For seven days you shall offer a fire-offering to the Lord; and on the eighth day,
There shall be a holy convocation for you; offer fire-offerings to the Lord.
It is a day of solemn assembly, no servile work by you is to be endured.
These are the appointed times of the Lord, which you shall proclaim as holy convocations,
To offer fire-offerings to the Lord, burnt, grain-gifts, sacrifices, and libations,
Each on its proper day, in addition to the Sabbaths of the Lord and your presents,
In addition to all your offerings to the Lord for vows, or of free will's intent.
Mark the fifteenth day of the seventh month, once you've gathered in the produce of the land,
You shall keep the feast of the Lord for seven days: On the first day a Sabbath is planned,
And also a Sabbath of rest on the eighth day. On the first day, you shall take of those,
Fruits of beautiful trees, branches of palm trees, boughs of thick leafy trees, and brook willows.
And then you are to rejoice before the presence of the Lord your God for seven days,
You shall celebrate it as a pilgrimage feast to the Lord, every year, seven days,
A law for the ages, through your generations, you shall keep it in the seventh month.
You shall dwell in huts for seven days, every native in Israel shall dwell in huts,
So that your generations may know that in huts I had the Children of Israel
Stay when I brought them out of the land of Egypt. I am the Lord your God, mark it well."
So Moses declared the appointed feasts of the Lord to the Children of Israel.

Leviticus 24

God told Moses, "Tell all of the Israelites
That you need to put lamps up inside of the tent.
You shall offer up bread. These are the Sabbath rites,
And for all of the priests shall be an allotment.
If a man curses God, he shall be put to death.
One who injures another, let that be his own,
Break for break, eye for eye, tooth for tooth, bone for bone.
But those who curse the Lord shall be pelted with stones.

The Lord spoke to Moses, saying, "You are to command all the Children of Israel

That they bring you pure oil from beaten olives so the light may burn regularly.
Aaron shall arrange it in the Tent of Meeting, outside the veil of Testimony,
From sunset to sunrise, before the Lord's presence regularly, this is My command;
A law for the ages, through your generations. He shall arrange on the pure lampstand
The lampwicks, before the Lord's presence, regularly. You shall take fine flour and bake,
Bake it into twelve loaves, with two tenths of an ephah of flour for use in each cake.
You shall put them in two rows, six per row, upon the table before the Lord's presence.
And you shall place on each row, as memorial-portion for the bread, clear frankincense,
A fire-offering to the Lord. Sabbath day by Sabbath day, Aaron shall arrange it
Before the presence of the Lord, regularly, to be an eternal covenant
For the Children of Israel. And the bread shall belong to Aaron and to his sons;
They shall eat it in a holy place, since for him it shall be a most holy portion,
From the fire-offerings of the Lord, an allotment for all time, eternally due."

Now the son of an Israelite woman, who was the son of an Egyptian too,
Went out among the Children of Israel, and had a scuffle with an Israelite,
For the half-Israelite had cursed the Name of God, the other knew this was not right,
So they brought him to Moses. (His mother was named Shelomit, the daughter of Divri,
Of the tribe of Dan) And until the Lord could clarify, they put him in custody.

Then the Lord spoke to Moses, saying, "Take outside the camp the one who spoke blasphemy,
Let all those who heard the curse lay their hands on his head, and let the whole community
Pelt him with stones. And to the Children of Israel you shall speak, saying: Any man,
Any man who insults his god shall bear his sin. But whoever curses the Lord's Name
Shall be put to death. The whole community shall stone him, both native and sojourner,
When he curses the Lord's Name he shall be put to death. He who kills a man shall endure
Being put to death. One who kills an animal shall pay for it, life in place of life.
And when a man disfigures his neighbor, the same shall be done to he whom caused the strife,
A break for a break, an eye for an eye, a tooth for a tooth, punishment shall be grim;
However he has disfigured another human, the same thing shall be done to him.
He who kills a beast shall pay for it, while he who kills a human shall be put to death.
One standard of judgment there shall be for you, native and sojourner, all in one breath,
One law shall apply to you all, stranger and citizen, for I the Lord am your God."

That is what Moses said to the Children of Israel, speaking the words of their God.
They brought the one who had cursed the Lord's Name outside the camp, and they pelted him
    with stones;
So the Children of Israel did as the Lord had commanded Moses should be done.

Leviticus 25

"Work the land for six years, then the seventh year, rest.
For the land gets a Sabbath where it can rest free.
After seven times these seven years have progressed,
Blow the trumpet; it's a Homebringing Jubilee.
Men return to their holdings and gain them anew.
But don't mistreat your fellow man when selling land,
Price it based on the time left. When men come to you
Needing work, don't make them slaves, but just hired hands.

[Behar]

The Lord spoke to Moses at Mount Sinai, saying, "Speak to the Children of Israel,
And say to them: When you enter the land that I am giving to you, the land itself
Shall rest, observing a Sabbath-ceasing to the Lord. For six years you shall sow your field,
For six years you are to prune your vineyard, and then you are to gather in all its yield,
But in the seventh year there shall be a Sabbath of Sabbath-ceasing rest for the land,
A Sabbath to the Lord. You shall not sow your field, nor prune your vineyard, by My command.
You shall not harvest the aftergrowth of your harvest, nor the grapes of your untrimmed vines,
It shall be a Sabbath of Sabbath-ceasing rest which the land shall observe at that time.
Now whatever the land produces by itself during the Sabbath year, you may eat,
It is food for you, your servants, handmaids, hired-hands, strangers with you, your
     household complete,
And for your cattle, and even for all the wild animals that roam throughout your land,
All its yield shall be for them to eat. Now when seven weeks of years you count by your hand,
Seven years seven times, so the time of the seven Sabbath-cycles of years is through,
Then you shall have a total of forty-nine years. Once they end, this is what you must do:
You shall blow the shofar, on the tenth day of the seventh month, the Day of Atonement,
You shall send forth a mighty blast on the shofar, throughout all your land, all its extent.
You shall hallow the fiftieth year, proclaiming liberty throughout all of the land
And to all its inhabitants. It shall be a ram's horn jubilee for you, and grand;
A home-bringing where each man among you shall return to his clan and his property
It is home-bringing, the fiftieth year, and so for you it shall be a jubilee;
You shall not sow, nor reap of the aftergrowth, nor gather grapes from any untrimmed vine,
For it is jubilee, it shall be holy for you. What the field grows during that time
By itself without any work from a man's hand, is the only produce you may eat.
In this Year of Homebringing Jubilee you shall return, each man to his property.

Now if you should sell property to your fellow, or purchase property from your brother,
No one is to take advantage of his neighbor, you are not to maltreat one another.
You shall purchase it from your fellow by the number of years that passed since Jubilee,
And according to the number of years until the next one, he shall set you your fee:
Many years left means that the price may be raised, while few years left means that the
    price must fall,
Since what he is selling to you is a certain number of years' harvests, after all.
So no man shall wrong his fellow man, but rather you are all to hold your God in awe,
For I, the Lord, am your God. You shall keep My regulations, you shall observe My laws,

So that you may dwell in the land with security, so the land may give forth its fruit,
And you may eat your fill and be settled securely in it. Now if you should dispute,
And ask yourselves, 'What shall we eat in the seventh year, if we can't sow or gather crops?'
I shall dispatch my blessing for you during the sixth year, so for three years it won't stop,
Bringing forth produce. You may sow the eighth year's yield, but you must eat of the last
    year's yield
Until the ninth year when the new produce comes in, you must it what is old from the field.
The land shall not be sold permanently beyond reclaim, for the land belongs to Me;
For you are sojourners and strangers with Me. And throughout all land of your property,
You shall grant a redemption of the land, so that it can stay within the family.
When your brother sinks down in poverty and is forced to sell some of his property,
His redeemer, (his nearest in kin who aids him) shall come and redeem what has been sold.
Now if a man has no redeemer, but can afford the price, be it cattle or gold,
He shall reckon the years since the sale, and return the surplus to the man he sold to,
And the land shall return to his holding. But if adequate means he cannot accrue,
What he sold shall remain in the hands of the one who bought it, until the Jubilee,
It shall be released in the Year of Homebringing, and then return to his property.
If a man sells a residential house in a walled town, its period of redemption
Shall be until the end of the year of its sale, one year full of days with no exemption.

If it is not redeemed within one full year, the house in the walled town is established,
And shall evermore belong to him who bought it, property for the one who purchased,
Through his generations; it shall not even be released in the Year of Jubilee.
But houses in cities with no walls around them shall be reckoned as open country,
They may be redeemed, and released in the Year of Jubilee. Now the towns of Levites,
For the houses in towns of their possession, they are to retain full redemption rights
For the ages. And that redeemed from the Levites, in their cities if a house is sold,
It shall be released during the Jubilee Year. For houses in towns which Levites hold
Are their holdings among the Children of Israel. But open land near their city,
Pastures and fields near their towns shall not be sold, for it is their holding eternally.

Now when your brother sinks down in poverty and he cannot afford means to survive,
You shall strengthen him, as though he is a sojourner, by your side he shall stay alive.
Do not take any profit or biting interest from his plight, but hold your God in awe,
So that your brother may live beside you. Do not maltreat your fellow; this is My law.
You shall not lend him money with interest, nor charge him interest when giving him your food.
I the Lord am your God who has brought you out of the land of Egypt, to give to you
The land of Canaan, and to be your God. And if your brother sinks down in poverty,
So much that he sells himself to you, an indentured servant he is never to be.
You are not to make him serve the servitude of a slave; he shall be a hired-hand,
As a resident-settler and sojourner he is to serve beside you on your land,
And he shall only serve beside you until the year of Homebringing, then shall go free.
Along with his children, he shall return to his clan, and to his fathers' property.
For they are My servants, whom I brought out of Egypt's land, they shall not be sold as slaves.
You shall not rule over him with harsh labor, but hold your God in awe. Your slaves and maids
Shall be gotten from nations surrounding you, from them you may purchase maids and servants.
You may also buy from the sons of those who sojourn beside you, from those residents,
Or from their clans beside you who were born in your land, and they shall become your holdings.
You may leave them as inheritance for your children, for them to possess as holdings;
For the ages you may make them serve you. But as for your brothers the Israelites,
No one shall hold dominion over the other with harsh labor, for such is not right.

If a sojourner with you becomes rich while your brother is sinking in poverty,
So that he sells himself to the sojourner, or one in the sojourner's family,
Even after he has sold himself, he may still be redeemed, by one of his brethren,
Or his uncle or the son of his uncle, or of a clansman who is of his kin,
Or if he can afford it, he may redeem himself. He is to reckon faithfully
With his buyer, from the year that he was sold to him until the Year of Jubilee;

The price of the sale shall be according to the number of years, like a hired-hand.
If there are many years left, he shall refund for his redemption an amount that's grand;
He shall pay according to the years. And if few years remain until the Jubilee,
He shall reckon it to him; according to the years of service owed shall be the fee.
Like a hired hand paid by the year, he shall be with him, not exerting dominion
Over him like a slave with harsh labor before your eyes. But, when all is said and done,
If he has not been redeemed in any of these ways, then he is still to be set free
In the Year of Homebringing, he and his children with him, in the Year of Jubilee.
For it is to Me that the Children of Israel are servants, of Me they are awed,
They are My servants, whom I brought out of the land of Egypt; I am the Lord your God.

Leviticus 26

"You shall not make false idols to which you bow low.
If you keep My laws, I will give peace through your land.
You will have plenty, reaping more than you can sow,
And your foes in the hundreds fall down 'neath your hand.
But if you do not heed Me and follow My law,
Then your fields will be barren, your foes will all win.
You will suffer from hunger, and beasts with great maws.
Though I'll take you back, if you atone for your sin.

You shall not make idols for yourselves, nor erect graven images or stone pillars,
Nor shall you place any decorated stone in your land to prostrate yourselves before,
For I am the Lord your God. You shall keep My Sabbaths and honor My sanctuary,
I am the Lord.

[Bechukotai]

If you follow My laws and you observe My commandments faithfully,
Then I will give you your rains, in due season, so that the land will give forth its increase,
And the trees of the field shall yield their fruit. Until vintage comes, the threshing will not cease,
And the vintage shall last until the time of sowing. You shall eat your food to your fill,
And dwell in security in your land. I will give peace throughout the land, so you will
Lie down with none to make you afraid. I shall give the land a respite from vicious beasts,
And the sword shall not cross through your land. You shall pursue your enemies, down
    to the least,
And they will fall before you to the sword. Five of you shall chase a hundred of their horde,
And a hundred of you shall chase a myriad, your foes falling to you by the sword.
I shall turn My face toward you with favor, to make you fruitful and to multiply you.
You will eat old grain, long-stored, which will last so long, you must clear it out to store the new.
I shall place My Dwelling in your midst, and I shall not spurn you. I shall walk in your midst,
I will be your God, and you yourselves shall be My people, for as long as you exist.
I the Lord am your God, who brought you out of Egypt's land, so you would not be their slaves.
I broke the bars of your yoke and then allowed you to walk upright; By Me you were saved.

But if you do not heed Me, and do not observe these commandments, if My laws you spurn,
And My rules, so you will not do My commandments, but break My covenant, I in turn

Shall do this to you: I shall mete out to you shock, fever, and consumption, causing pain,
Wearing out the eyes and exhausting your breath, so all the seed that you sow is in vain,
For your enemies shall eat it. And I will set My face against you, plagued you will be
Before your enemies. Those who hate you will have dominion over you; you shall flee
Although no one pursues you. Now if you do not heed Me, even after all of this,
I will go on to discipline you sevenfold for your sins—I will break your hubris.
I will make your skies like iron and make your earth like bronze, so your strength is spent in vain,
Your land will not give forth its yield, nor shall the trees give forth fruit if found on your terrain.
Now if you walk against Me, and still will not heed Me, I shall plague you sevenfold more,
Continuing to rain blows upon you, to discipline you for your sins, like before.
I will loose against you vicious beasts of the field, so they bereave you of your children,
So they decimate your cattle, so that they make you few, and your roads become barren.

Now if you do not turn to Me, but you still walk against Me after this discipline,
I Myself shall walk against you, and I Myself will strike you sevenfold for your sins.
I will bring an avenging sword against you to take revenge for breaking covenant,
And if you gather yourselves into you cities, I shall send among you pestilence,
And you shall be delivered into the hand of your foes. When I break your 'staff of bread',
If ten women bake your bread in one oven, you can eat it, and still won't be well-fed.
Even if they bring you your own weight in bread, and you eat it, content you will not be.

And if in spite of this you will not heed Me, but still walk in opposition to Me,
I will walk against you in fury, and will discipline you sevenfold for your sins.
You shall eat the flesh of your sons, and you shall eat the flesh of your daughters for your sins.
I will decimate your high places, I will cut down your cult-stands and your pagan shrines,
I will place your dead bodies atop the corpses of the idols you thought were divine;
I will spurn you. I will make your cities a wasteland, your sanctuaries desolate,
And I will not savor your soothing savors. And the land, I Myself will devastate,
So that your enemies that settle in it will be astonished at the devastation.
And I will unsheathe the sword against you, and I will scatter you among all the nations.
So your land becomes a desolation and all of your cities become a wasteland.
Then the land will atone for its Sabbath years, throughout all the time of its desolation,
When you are in the land of your enemies, then the land will enjoy rest and cessation,
And the land shall atone for its Sabbaths. All the days of desolation it shall rest,
Since it did not rest during its Sabbaths when you lived upon it (as was My request).
As for those among you who remain, I shall make their hearts faint in their enemies' lands,
They shall flee from the sound of a leaf blown about, as if they were pursued by brigands,
And they will fall, though no one pursues them. They will stumble on each other, all around,
As if faced with a sword, though there is none. And you will not be able to stand your ground
Before your enemies, but shall perish among nations; your foes' lands shall consume you.
Those remaining among you will rot away in their foes' lands for their sins, as is due.

Yes, because of the iniquities of their fathers, with them they shall all rot away.
Now if they should confess their iniquity and the sins of their fathers in their day,
By their treachery in breaking faith with Me, yes, since they have indeed walked against Me,
Then I Myself shall walk against them and bring them into the land of their enemies.
And if their stubborn heart should then humble itself, and they accept their sins' punishment,
Then I will bear in mind My covenant with Jacob, and with Issac My covenant,
And My covenant with Abraham I will bear in mind, and bear the land in mind too.
The land will have to be left behind by them, gaining acceptance and atoning through
Its Sabbaths by being desolate of them, while they atone for their iniquity,
Because they have spurned My regulations and My laws, and they have repelled My decrees.
Yet, when they are in the land of their enemies, I will not spurn them, not even then.
I will not repel them to destroy them and so leave My covenant with them broken,
For I, the Lord, am their God. I will bear in mind, for their sake, covenant between Me
And the ancients, whom I freed from Egypt's land, to be their God, where all nations could see.
I am the Lord." These are the laws, regulations, and instructions the Lord established
Between Him and the Children of Israel, at Mount Sinai, by the hand of Moses.

Leviticus 27

"When a man makes a vow, you shall give valuation,
And charge them, in shekels, appropriate price.
More for men than for women, and if of low station
And poor, then the priest will charge less, being nice.
If you hallow your house or your land to the Lord,
Then the time to the Jubilee year you must count.
With the twenty-grain shekel, you'll be in accord,
And the tithes that you pay shall all use this amount.

The Lord spoke to Moses, saying, "Say to the Children of Israel: When any man
Makes a vow offering to the Lord, in the assessed equivalent of a human,
Your assessment shall be: For a male from age twenty to sixty, sanctuary weight,
Fifty silver shekels. And for a female of that age, thirty shekels is the rate.
If the age is from five up to twenty years, twenty shekels is the rate for a male,
And ten for a female. If the age is from one month to five years, the rate for a male
Is five silver shekels, and three silver shekels for a female. If sixty or higher,
Fifteen shekels is the rate for a male, ten shekels the rate a female will require.

If one is too poor to afford the assessment, then he shall be brought before the priest,
And the priest shall assess an amount for him based on his means. If it concerns a beast,
Or an animal that can be brought as an offering to the Lord, then all of it
That a man gives to the Lord is holy. He shall not exchange or substitute for it,
Neither good for bad, nor bad for good. And if he tries to exchange a beast for a beast,
Both the first one and the one exchanged with it are holy. His duty is not released.
And if it is an unclean beast from which there may be an offering brought to the Lord,
Then it shall be stood before the priest, who shall make an assessment, being in accord
With whether it is good or bad, and the assessment he makes is binding arbitration.
If one wishes to redeem the animal, he must add one-fifth to the valuation.

When a man consecrates his house as holy to the Lord, the priest shall make assessment
Between good and bad; And what the priest assesses is to be the worth, with no dissent.
If the one who hallowed it wants to redeem it, he must add a fifth to the money
Set as the house's value, then it shall remain his. If a man from his property
Consecrates part of his field to the Lord, the assessment shall be according to seed;
Fifty shekels of silver per homer of barley. If he does his hallowing deed
In the Homebringing Year, it shall stand at your valuation. But if he dedicates
His field after a Jubilee Year, then the priest is to figure out the value rate
According to the number of years until the next Year of Jubilee will occur,
And that amount shall be subtracted from your valuation. Now if the land donor
Wants to redeem the field, he must add one fifth to the sum at which the land was assessed,
And it shall be his. But if he does not, or if by another man it is purchased,
It cannot be redeemed any more. And when the field is released in the Jubilee,
It shall be holy to the Lord, like a field devoted, it is the priest's property.

If he dedicates to the Lord a field he bought, and not one of his inheritance,
The priest shall compute the assessed value for him, until the Jubilee does commence.
And the man shall give that assessed value, on that day, to the Lord as holy portion.
In the Jubilee year, the field shall return to the one who had sold his possession,
The one whose property it is. All your assessments shall be by sanctuary weight,
Twenty grains to the shekel. Now a firstborn animal assigned to the Lord by fate,
As the Lord's firstling, no man may dedicate it. Whether ox or sheep, it is the Lord's.
Now if it is an unclean beast, he shall buy it back at the assessment you accord,
Adding one fifth to it. And if it is not redeemed, it shall be sold at your value.
However, nothing a man devotes to the Lord, from anything which he has accrued,
Be it of man, of beast, or his inherited field, it shall not be sold or redeemed.
Everything devoted in this way is holy to the Lord. And any person deemed
To be specially devoted to destruction for the Lord is not to be ransomed;
He shall be put to death. All tithes from the land, whether from the trees or the
    ground they come,

Are the Lord's. If a man wants to redeem any of his tithes, one fifth more he must add.
And all tithes of herds or of flocks, every tenth animal passing 'neath the herdsman's rod,
Shall be holy for the Lord. He shall not search for good or bad, or make a substitution,
But if he substitutes, then both new animal and his original contribution
Shall be holy to the Lord and can't be redeemed." These are the commandments from on high
That the Lord commanded Moses for the Children of Israel upon Mount Sinai.

NUMBERS

Numbers 1

The Lord told Moses, "Take up a head count by clan,
Of all army-aged men of the Israelites.
Every tribe has divisions and has a head man,
But there is one exception, and that's the Levites.

[Bamidbar]

The Lord spoke to Moses in the wilderness of Sinai, inside of the Tent of Meeting,
On the first day of the second month, in the second year, after successfully fleeing
From the land of Egypt, saying, "Take up a head-count of the Children of Israel,
By clans, by fathers' houses, according to the number of names, and include each male;
From the age of twenty years and upward, all those eligible for the military:
You are to count them to prepare for battle, according to their forces, you and Aaron.
And there shall be with you a man from each tribe, each one the head of his ancestral home.
(These heads of their fathers' houses will help you count, so you don't have to do it alone.)
Now these are the names of the men who shall stand with you: From Reuben, Elizur the son
Of Shedeur. From Shimon, Shelumiel son of Zurishaddai. From Judah, Nashon
Son of Amminadab. From Issachar, Nethanel son of Zuar. From Zebulun,
Eliab son of Helon. From Joseph's sons: From Ephraim, Elishama the son
Of Ammihud, and from Manasseh, Gamaliel son of Pedahzur. From Benjamin,
Abidan son of Gideoni. From Dan, Ahiezer who possesses as kin
His father Ammishaddai. From Asher, Pagiel son of Okhran. And then from Gad,
Eliasaph son of Deuel. From Naftali, Ahira who has Einan as a dad."
These were the ones chosen by the community, the leaders of their congregation,
Chieftains of their ancestral tribes, and now also the heads of Israel's divisions.

Moses and Aaron took these men who were named, and assembled the whole community
On the first day of the second month; they registered themselves by clan and family,
According to the number of names, from age twenty and up, every one and no less.
As the Lord commanded Moses, he counted them for battle in Sinai's wilderness.

So they were: The sons of Reuben, firstborn of Israel, their generations by clan,
By their ancestral houses, as numbered by name, head by head, each eligible man

From the age of twenty years and upward, those who could go forth to war, their full amount,
From the tribe of Reuben: Forty-six thousand and five hundred men was their final count.

From the sons of Shimon: All their generations in their ancestral homes and their clans,
By the count of Moses, as numbered by name, per capita, each eligible man
From the age of twenty years and upward, those who could go forth to war, their full amount,
From the tribe of Shimon: Fifty-nine thousand and three hundred men was their final count.

From the sons of Gad: All of their generations in their ancestral homes and their clans,
By their fathers' house, as numbered by name, per capita, every eligible man
From the age of twenty years and upward, those who could go forth to war, their full amount,
From the tribe of Gad: Forty-five thousand, three hundred and fifty was their final count.

From the sons of Judah: All their generations in their ancestral homes and their clans,
By their fathers' house, as numbered by name, per capita, every eligible man
From the age of twenty years and upward, those who could go forth to war, their full amount,
From the tribe of Judah: Seventy-four thousand and six hundred was their final count.

From the sons of Issachar: All their generations in their ancestral homes and clans,
By their fathers' house, as numbered by name, per capita, every eligible man
From the age of twenty years and upward, those who could go forth to war, their full amount,
From the tribe of Issachar: Fifty-four thousand, and four hundred was their final count.

From the sons of Zebulun: All their generations in their ancestral homes and clans,
By their fathers' house, as numbered by name, per capita, every eligible man
From the age of twenty years and upward, those who could go forth to war, their full amount,
From the tribe of Zebulun: Fifty-seven thousand, four hundred was their final count.

From Joseph's sons: From the sons of Ephraim: All of their generations by their clans,
By their ancestral homes, as numbered by name, per capita, each eligible man
From the age of twenty years and upward, those who could go forth to war, their full amount,
From the tribe of Ephraim: Forty thousand and five hundred men was their final count.
From the sons of Manasseh: All their generations in their ancestral homes and clans,
By their fathers' house, as numbered by name, per capita, every eligible man
From the age of twenty years and upward, those who could go forth to war, their full amount,
From the tribe of Manasseh: Thirty-two thousand and two hundred was their final count.

From the sons of Benjamin: All their generations in their ancestral homes and clans,
By their fathers' house, as numbered by name, per capita, every eligible man
From the age of twenty years and upward, those who could go forth to war, their full amount,
From the tribe of Benjamin: Thirty-five thousand and four hundred was their final count.

From the sons of Dan: All of their generations in their ancestral homes and their clans,
By their fathers' house, as numbered by name, per capita, every eligible man
From the age of twenty years and upward, those who could go forth to war, their full amount,
From the tribe of Dan: Sixty-two thousand and seven hundred men was their final count.

From the sons of Asher: All their generations in their ancestral homes and their clans,
By their fathers' house, as numbered by name, per capita, every eligible man
From the age of twenty years and upward, those who could go forth to war, their full amount,
From the tribe of Asher: Forty-one thousand and five hundred men was their final count.

From the sons of Naftali: All their generations in their ancestral homes and clans,
By their fathers' house, as numbered by name, per capita, every eligible man
From the age of twenty years and upward, those who could go forth to war, their full amount,
From the tribe of Naftali: Fifty-three thousand and four hundred was their final count.

Those are the enrollments numbered by Moses and Aaron, and by Israel's leaders,
The twelve men, each who represented his ancestral home. So the entire number
Of all those accounted from the Children of Israel by fathers' house and by clan,
From twenty years and up, all those eligible for war in Israel, every man,
Their full number was six hundred and three thousand, five hundred and fifty in the horde.
But the Levites, by the tribe of their fathers, were not counted in their midst. For the Lord
Spoke to Moses, saying, "You shall not count the tribe of Levi, do not take their head-count
When taking census of the Children of Israel. But you shall hold them to account
For the Tabernacle of the Testimony, implements, all that belongs to it:
They shall carry the Tabernacle and all its implements, they shall attend to it,
And they are to camp around the Tabernacle. When the Tabernacle must embark,
The Levites shall take it down, and when it must be set up, Levites shall set up the Ark;

Any outsider who comes near is to be put to death! The Children of Israel
Are to camp, each one according to encampment, under his own banner he shall dwell.
But the Levites shall camp around the Tabernacle of Testimony, so no wrath
Comes against the community of the Children of Israel (for leaving God's path),
And the Levites shall keep charge of the Tabernacle of Testimony." So God bid,
And the Children of Israel did all the Lord had commanded Moses, so they did.

Numbers 2

> The Lord told Moses, "Have them encamp on all sides,"
> And then gave him a list, where to set each camp's corps.
> The clans marched by the words that the Lord did provide,
> But the Levites did not, they were not meant for war.

The Lord spoke to Moses and to Aaron, saying, "Every man of the Israelites
Shall encamp under the banner of his ancestral home, to the left and to the right,
At a distance, on every side, facing the Tent of Meeting. Those encamped to the east
Toward the sunrise shall be: The contingent of the camp of Judah, and their companies.
Now the leader of the children of Judah shall be Nashon, son of Amminadab;
His force seventy-four thousand, six hundred. Camped next to him, the tribe of Issachar.
The leader of Issachar shall be Nethanel, son of Zuar. His troops in number
Fifty-four thousand, four hundred men. The tribe of Zebulun shall have as a leader
Eliab son of Helon; his force fifty-seven thousand, four hundred in amount.
So Judah's forces are one hundred and eighty-six thousand, four hundred in full count;
They shall march first. Then on the south side, the banner of the camp of Reuben, and
    their troops:
The leader of the children of Reuben: Elizur, son of Shedeur, with his troops
Numbering Forty-six thousand, five hundred men. Camped beside them, the tribe of Shimon,
The leader of the sons of Shimon is to be Shelumiel, ZurishaddaI's son.
His force is fifty-nine thousand, three hundred men. And the tribe of Gad, their tribe's chieftain:
Elyasaph son of Reuel, his force forty-five thousand, six hundred and fifty men.
So the camp of Reuben has one hundred and fifty-one thousand, four hundred fifty,
With all their troops; They shall march second. Then shall march the Tent of Meeting,
    camp of Levi,
In the midst of the camps, the Levites shall march as they encamp, with each one in position,
By their banners. On the west side shall be the banner and camp of Ephrayim's division.
The leader of Ephraim: Elishama, son of Ammihud. His forces' number
Forty thousand, five hundred. And beside them the tribe of Menasseh, with their leader
Gamaliel, son of Pedahzur; His force's count thirty-two thousand and two hundred.
And the tribe of Benjamin, their leader Avidon, who by Gideoni was bred.
Their troop count shall be thirty-five thousand, four hundred. So all of Ephraim's camp's force
Shall come to one hundred and eight thousand, one hundred. And they shall march
    third in the course.

On the north side, there shall be the banner of Dan, and their forces. The leader of Dan
Shall be Ahiezer, son of Ammishaddai, with his forces counting every man

As full sixty-two thousand, seven hundred. And camped beside him, the tribe of Asher.
The leader of Asher: Pagiel, son of Okhran. The count of troops he will have there
Shall be forty-one thousand, five hundred men. And the tribe of Naftali, their leader
Of the sons of Naftali: Ahira, son of Einan. His troops in their full number
Shall be fifty-three thousand, four hundred. So the full enrollment of the camp of Dan
One hundred fifty-seven thousand, six hundred. They shall march last, by banner and man."

These are the enrollments of the Children of Israel, in camps by ancestral clan,
The troops numbered six hundred and three thousand, five hundred and fifty, counting each man,
Except for the Levites, who were not counted for battle amidst the Israelites,
As the Lord had commanded Moses. And the Children of Israel did (as was right)
According to all that the Lord commanded Moses, so they each camped by their banners,
And they marched, every man with his ancestral clan, alongside the house of his fathers.

Numbers 3

> The Lord told Moses, "Bring near the tribe of Levi,
> They shall serve under Aaron and his sons as priests.
> Any outsider breaching the Tent, he will die.
> All the firstborn are Mine, every man, every beast.
> Count the Levites, by their Father's House and by clan,
> So they may do the duty that's due in the Tent.
> Every Levite a month old or more, if a man,
> You shall count them. They shall fulfill My commandment.

These are the generations of Aaron and Moses, at the time when the Lord spoke to
Moses on Mount Sinai. These are the names of Aaron's sons: Firstborn Nadab, Abihu,
Eleazar, and Ithamar. These are the names of the sons of Aaron, anointed priests
Whom he had ordained to minister as priests. But Nadab and Abihu's lives both ceased
Before the Lord, when they offered unholy fire before the Lord in the wilderness
Of Sinai. Eleazar and Ithamar were made priests, (for both dead boys were childless),
In the lifetime of Aaron their father. The Lord spoke to Moses, saying, "Bring the tribe
Of Levi, and have them stand in Aaron's presence, attending to him as he prescribes.
They are to perform duties for him, and the whole congregation, in front of the Tent
Of Meeting, doing work for the Tabernacle. They shall be in charge of implements
For the Tent of Meeting, and attend to the duties of the Children of Israel,
As they minister and perform all the duties to be done at the Tabernacle.

You shall give the Levites to Aaron and his sons, commissioned from the Israelites.
And Aaron and his sons shall be appointed to keep the priesthood, all duties and rites;
Any outsider who comes near shall be put to death." The Lord spoke to Moses and said,
"Now behold, I hereby take the Levites from among all children Israel has bred,
In place of each firstborn, of each breacher of womb that the Children of Israel birth,
The Levites shall be Mine. For all firstborn are Mine, every breacher of womb on the Earth.
On the day I struck down every firstborn in Egypt, I hallowed to Me all firstborn
In Israel, both of man and of beast, every firstborn shall be Mine. I am the Lord."

Now the Lord said to Moses in the wilderness of Sinai, "Count the sons of Levi,
By their Fathers' house, by their clans, from those age one month and up, you shall
    count every guy."
So Moses counted them by the order of the Lord, as he was commanded be done.
These were the sons of Levi according to their names: Merari, Kehat, and Gershon.
And these were the names of the sons of Gershon by their families: Livni and Shimi.
And Kehat's sons by their clans: Amram, Izhar, Hebron, and Uzziel. Sons of Merari,
By their clans: Mahli and Mushi. These, by their Fathers' houses, are the clans of Levites:
From Gershon: The Livnite clan and the Shimite clan, these are the clans of the Gershonites.
Their number, counting all males age one month and up, was seven thousand and five hundred.
The Gershonite clans shall encamp behind the Tabernacle to the west, near sea-bed.
As the leader of the Father's house of the Gershonites: Elyasaph, son of Lael.
The charge of the Sons of Gershon at the Tent of Meeting was both the Tabernacle
And the Tent of Meeting, with its covering, the screen of its entrance, courtyard hangings,
Entrance screen to the courtyard of the Tabernacle and altar, cords—all of those things,
And the service connected with them. From Kehat: The Amramite clan, the Izharites,
The Hebronite clan and the Uzzielite clan. Those are the families of the Kehatites.
Their number, counting every male one month and up, was eight thousand and six hundred men,
Keepers of the charge of the sanctuary. The families of the Sons of Kehat then
Shall camp on the south flank of the Tabernacle, with Elizaphan, Uzziel's son
As head of the Fathers' house of the families of the Kehatites. Their charge to be done
Is the ark, the table, the lampstand, and the altars, and implements of holiness
That are used in conjunction with those holy things, and the screen that serves to encompass,
And all service required for these. Eleazar was the chief leader of the Levites,
Son of Aaron the priest, in charge of those in charge of the sanctuary and its rites.

From Merari: The Mahlite clan and the Mushite clan, these two are the Merarite clans.
Their number, counting every male one month and up, was six thousand and two hundred mans.
And the leader of the Fathers' house of the clan of the Merarites was Zuriel,
Son of Abihail. They shall camp to the north, on the north flank of the Tabernacle.
The charge of the Sons of Merari is as follows: The Tabernacle's bars and boards,
Its posts and its sockets, all of its implements, all its service (since it is the Lord's),

The posts of the courtyard, all around, and their sockets, their pegs and their cords and their ties.
Now those to camp in front of the Tabernacle, to the east, towards where the sun would rise,
In front of the Tent of Meeting, were Moses and Aaron and his sons, all to have charge
Of the sanctuary and its services for the Children of Israel at large;
The outsider who comes near shall be put to death. All those numbered among the Levites,
Whom Moses and Aaron counted by the Lord's order, by their clans, all males in their sight,
From the age of one month and upward numbered twenty-two thousand Levite males in all.

The Lord spoke to Moses, saying, "Count each firstborn male of the Children of Israel,
From the age of one month and upward, you shall take their number by their names.
     And you shall
Take the Levites aside for me in place of every firstborn of the Israelites,
And in place of every firstborn cattle of theirs, you shall take cattle of the Levites,
I am the Lord." Moses counted, as the Lord commanded to him, every firstborn child
Of the Israelites. The names of all firstborn males age one month and up were compiled,
And the full count was twenty-two thousand, two hundred and seventy-three. And the Lord
Said to Moses, "Take aside the Levites, in place of all the Israelite firstborn,
Along with the cattle of the Levites, in place of their cattle; the Levites shall be
Mine, for I am the Lord! And for the redemption of the two hundred seventy-three
First-born of the Children of Israel who are above the number of the Levites,
You shall take five shekels (sanctuary weight, twenty grains) per capita to make right,
And give the silver to Aaron and his sons as redemption price for those in excess."
Moses took the redemption silver from their number (since the Levites' number was less),
Five shekels for each one of the two hundred seventy-three in excess, so the rate
Was one thousand, three hundred and sixty-five shekels in all, at sanctuary weight.
Moses gave the silver for redemption to Aaron and his sons for each in excess,
By the order of the Lord, and so Moses did as the Lord had commanded Moses.

Numbers 4

God told Moses and Aaron, "Take up the head count
From each clan of Levi, those the right age to serve,
All from thirty to fifty." The total amount
Was eight thousand, five hundred and eighty observed.

The Lord said to Moses and Aaron, "Take a count of the sons of Kehat from among
The sons of Levi, by their clans and ancestral homes, from the age of thirty years young,

To the age of fifty years old; all who can enter the workforce to work in the Tent
Of Meeting. This is the service of the Kehatites: The holiest of implements
In the Tent of Meeting. When the camp marches out, Aaron and his sons shall enter it,
And take down the curtain of the screen and cover the Ark of Testimony with it.
They shall cover it with a goatskin, and spread over that a blue cloth, and place its poles.
On the Table of Presence, they are to spread a blue cloth, and shall place on it the bowls,
The ladles, the jars and jugs for libations, and the shewbread shall remain on the cloth.
They shall then spread a scarlet cloth over these, and use a goatskin to cover that cloth,
Putting its poles in place. They shall take a blue cloth and cover the lampstand for the light,
Its lamps, its tongs, its fire-pans, and all the implements for oil used with it for rites.
They shall place it and all of its implements in a goatskin covering, on a frame.
And over the gold altar they shall spread a blue cloth, with goatskin, cover it the same,
Putting its poles in place. They shall take all the implements to tend the sanctuary
And put them in blue cloth, cover them with goatskin, and put them on a frame to carry.
They shall take the ashes away from the altar, and spread a purple cloth over it,
They shall place on it all of its implements used for the service that takes place on it:
The fire-pans, flesh-hooks, scrapers, and bowls, all the implements of the altar, every one.
They shall spread a goatskin covering over it, putting its poles in place. When Aaron
And his sons finish covering the holy things and all sanctuary implements,
When the camp marches on, only then may the sons of Kehat come and enter the Tent
To carry the holy-things, which they may not touch, so they do not die. These are the things
Which the sons of Kehat shall carry from the sanctuary and the Tent of Meeting.
Eleazar son of Aaron the priest shall have charge of the oil for the light, the incense,
The grain-gift, and the oil for anointing—the Tabernacle and all of its contents,
Be they holy things or implements." The Lord spoke to Moses and to Aaron saying,
"Do not cut of the tribe of the clans of Kehat from the Levites. Instead, do this thing,
So that they may live and not die when they come near to the most holy of holy things:
Aaron and his sons shall enter and assign them, each man, a service of carrying.
But they shall not enter and see the holy things dismantled, for one blink of an eye,
For if they look upon the dismantling of the sanctuary, they will surely die."

[Naso]

The Lord said to Moses, "Take a count of the sons of Gershon, they as well, by their clans
And their ancestral homes, all men age thirty years up to every fifty year old man,
All who enter to join forces with those who work and service in the Tent of Meeting,
This is the service of the Gershonite clans: Services of packing and carrying.
They shall carry the curtains of the Tabernacle, Tent of Meeting and its cover,
The goatskin covering atop it, and the screen for the Tent of Meeting's entrance door,
The hangings and the gate's entrance screen of the courtyard that surrounds the Tabernacle
And the altar, as well as their cords, and all the equipment for their service in full.

Whatever needs to be done with them, they shall do it. The duties of the Gershonites,
All their carrying and packing service, shall be done as Aaron and his sons see right;
You shall make them accountable for all the carrying. This is the task of the clans
Of the sons of the Gershonites in the Tent of Meeting, and their charge under the hand
Of Ithamar, son of Aaron the priest. You are to number the sons of Merari,
By clan and by ancestral home, from the age of thirty up to the age of fifty,
You shall count every one that may enter the working force, serving at the Tent of Meeting.
This is their charge of carrying, all the packing they must do for the Tent of Meeting:
The boards of the Tabernacle, its bars, its columns, its sockets; and for the courtyard,
Its columns, sockets, pegs, and cords, including all implements for the service they guard;
You by name shall assign all the objects they must carry. That's the service of the clans
Of Merari's sons, all their service in the Tent of Meeting under Ithamar's hand."

So Moses, Aaron, and the community leaders counted all the sons of Kehat,
By their clans and ancestral homes, from age thirty to age fifty, every person that
Entered the workforce for serving in the Tent of Meeting. The full count of every man
Was two thousand, seven hundred fifty. That is the count of all the Kehatite clans,
Everyone that was serving in the Tent of Meeting, whom Moses and Aaron did count
By the order of the Lord, by the hand of Moses, that number was the full amount.

The number of the sons of Gershon, by their clans and ancestral homes, from age thirty
Up to age fifty, all who were doing service in the Tent of Meeting, or could be,
They were counted by clan and ancestral home: two thousand, six hundred and thirty men.
These are the accountings of the sons of Gershon, all who could serve in the Meeting Tent,
Whom Moses and Aaron counted as the Lord had commanded. And those who were enrolled
From the sons of Merari, by their clans and ancestral homes, from age thirty years old

Up to fifty years old, everyone in the workforce to serve in the Tent of Meeting,
Their number, by their clan, came to three thousand, two hundred. And that was the accounting
Of the clans of the sons of Merari, whom Moses and Aaron counted by command
Of the Lord, who had ordered Moses and Aaron to count them, all through Moses's hand.

All the Levites, whom Moses and Aaron and all of the leaders of Israel counted,
By their clans and ancestral homes, from age thirty to age fifty, counting every head,
Everyone that could serve in the Tent of Meeting to carry or to serve as a porter,
Their number was eight thousand, five hundred and eighty. They were counted by the
    Lord's order,
By the hand of Moses, each man to his task, be it of carrying or of service,
Each was counted and held to account for his task, as the Lord had commanded Moses.

Numbers 5

God told Moses, "All unclean, by corpse or by flow,
You shall send from the camp. When a man commits sin
And breaks faith with the Lord, and their own guilt they know,
Once confessing, they must pay back, add one fifth in.
A man's wife gone astray to lie with other men
Shall be brought to the priest, bitter water brought near.
If she's guilty, it brings bitter bane to her, then
She will suffer. If innocent, she's in the clear.

The Lord spoke to Moses, saying, "Command the Children of Israel to send away
From the camp each one with leprosy, a discharge, or defiled by a corpse in some way.
Male and female alike you shall send away, outside the camp, so they do not defile
Their camp, in the midst of which I keep a dwelling." And so the Children of Israel
Did so, driving them all outside of the camp, just as the Lord had spoken to Moses.
The Lord said to Moses, "Tell the Children of Israel: If man or woman commits
A sin that humans commit by breaking faith with the Lord, and that person is guilty,
He shall confess the sin which he has committed, and then pay a restitution fee
Of the full amount plus one fifth, and shall give it to the one to whom he did the wrong.
Now if the man has no kinsman whom he can pay to make restitution for his wrong,
The guilt-payment shall go to the Lord, for the priest, along with the ram of atonement,
With which atonement shall be made for him. And any contributions beneficent,
Or holy offerings of the Children of Israel that they bring near for the priest,
Shall be his. Whatever any man gives the priest shall be his, from the greatest to least."

The Lord spoke to Moses, saying, "Speak to the Children of Israel and say to them:
Any man whose wife goes astray and trespasses against him, so breaking faith with him,
If a man lies with her carnally, and the act remains hidden from the husband's view,
And she hides the fact that she has been defiled, and was not caught doing what she did do,
And the spirit of jealously comes on the man, and he feels jealousy towards his wife
For defiling herself, or if she did not, but the suspicion of such brings him strife,
The man shall bring his wife to the priest. And he shall bring an offering of barley meal,
One tenth of an ephah, with no oil poured on it, and no frankincense put on the meal,
For it is a grain-gift of jealousy, a grain-gift to remember iniquity.
The priest shall bring her near and have her stand before the Lord, take water that is holy
From an earthen vessel, and take some dirt from the floor of the Tabernacle, and then
Place some dirt from the floor of the Tabernacle in some of the holy water. When

The priest has had the woman stand before the Lord, he shall loosen the hair on her head
And shall place the grain-gift of remembrance on the palms of her hands, which jealousy fed.
And in the hand of the priest is to be the 'Water of Bitterness Bringing the Bane'.
The priest shall have her swear, saying to the woman, 'If it is true that no man has lain
With you, and if you did not stray, defiling yourself, from your husband's authority,
Then from the curse of this water of bitterness bringing the bane, you are to be free.
But if you strayed from under your husband's authority, and you made yourself unclean,
And a man other than your husband has lain with you, and that man gave to you his seed,'
(The priest shall have the woman swear the oath of curse, and the priest shall say to the woman,
'May the Lord make you a curse and cause for oath among your people and among your kin,
When the Lord makes your thigh fall and your belly flood, may this water of bitterness bane
Enter your innards, causing your belly to flood and thigh to fall.' She shall say, 'Amen!'.
The woman shall say, 'Amen! Amen!' Then on a document the priest is to inscribe
The curse, and wash it into the Water of Bitterness, which the woman must imbibe.
The priest shall make the woman drink from the water of the bitterness bringing the bane,
So the bane-bringing water may enter her, bringing her bitterness, bringing her pain.
Then the priest shall take the grain gift of jealousy from the hand of the woman and he
Shall raise it to the Lord, bring it to the altar, and from the grain-gift of jealousy
He shall take a handful as reminder-portion and turn it to smoke on the altar.
After that he shall make the woman drink the water, and once it has been drunk by her,
If she made herself unclean and broke faith with her husband, the water bringing the bane
Shall enter her for bitterness, her belly shall flood, her thigh shall fall, she shall feel pain,
And the woman shall become a curse among her people. But if she has not defiled
Herself, and she is pure, she shall be cleared, and she shall be permitted to bear a child.
This is the law for jealousy, when a woman strays from her husband's authority
And defiles herself, or when a man feels a jealous rush and becomes jealous of she,
He shall have her stand before the Lord, and the priest shall perform all this law upon her.
The man shall be clear of iniquity, but that woman's iniquity she must bear."

Numbers 6

"When a woman or man takes the Nazarite vow
To be holy, and hairy, and not drink of wine,
They shall not touch the dead, they shall not shave their brow,
For in those days, they are holy to the divine.
Now the Nazarite's Ritual on the last day
Is to shave their head, offer their hair in the fire.
Now tell Aaron to bless the Israelites: 'May
The Lord bless you, and bring you the peace you desire.'"

The Lord spoke to Moses, saying, "Speak to the Children of Israel, and say to them:
If a man or woman makes the Nazarite's vow, to set oneself aside for Hashem,
One must separate oneself from wine and strong drink, any which may cause intoxication,
One shall consecrate oneself and not even drink vinegar made through wine fermentation.
One shall drink no juice made of grapes, and eat no grapes, be they fresh or dried.
    Throughout the time
Of one's separation, one is not to eat anything that is made from the grapevine,
From seeds to skin. All the days of one's separation, no razor shall touch on one's head,
Until the time of consecration to the Lord is complete, one shall not shave one shred.
One shall be holy, letting the locks of one's hair grow loose. All the days one consecrates
Oneself to the Lord, one shall not come near a dead person, parents or sisters or mates.
One shall not make oneself unclean, because hair consecrated to God is on one's head.
All the days of one's consecration, one is holy to God. If a man becomes dead
Suddenly, near one consecrated, and one's head is defiled by the corpse in some way,
One must shave one's head on the day of cleansing, and on the seventh day. On the eighth day,
One shall bring two young pigeons or two turtledoves to the priest at the Tent of Meeting.
He shall sacrifice one for a sin offering, the other for a burnt-offering,
And atone for the one who was contaminated by contact with the dead person.
One shall make one's head holy again on that day, and undergo reconsecration
To the Lord for one's days being consecrated, and bring a yearling lamb to offer
As a guilt offering, since the former days were nullified when one became impure.

Now this is the Instruction for the Nazarite, the one who has been consecrated:
On the day one completes the term of consecration, that one is to be transported
To the entrance of the Tent of Meeting; and offer to the Lord as an offering:
One yearling male lamb, unblemished, as a burnt-offering. And as a sin-offering,

One yearling ewe lamb, unblemished. And as a shalom-sacrifice, one ram, wholly sound;
A basket of matzot made of flour, flour cakes mixed with oil in loaves that are round,
Unleavened wafers spread with oil, along with a grain-gift and also a poured libation.
The priest shall come before the Lord, offer the sin-offering and the lamb as oblation,
And he shall slay the ram as shalom-sacrifice and sacrifice the unleavened bread.
Then the priest shall offer the grain-gift and libation. The Nazarite shall shave his head
At the entrance of the Tent of Meeting, and from one's consecrated head take the hair
And put it on the fire which is under the sacrifice of shalom, to burn it there.
The priest shall take the shoulder of the ram, boiled, and from the basket one unleavened cake,
And one unleavened wafer, to put upon the Nazarite's palms, for the Lord to take,
After the consecrated one has been shaven of all one's hair that was consecrated,
Then as elevation offering before the Lord, the priest shall have them elevated.
It is a holy offering for the priest, along with the breast and the offered thigh,
And after that the consecrated one may drink wine, his set-apart term now gone by.
This is the Instruction for the Nazarite who takes a vow above his consecration,
His offering to the Lord must match his vow, beyond that one's Nazarite obligation,
Apart from what else one can afford: According to one's vow, one must do what is right,
And so this must be filled in addition to what is required of all Nazarites."

The Lord spoke to Moses, and these are the instructions for blessing he gave to Moses,
Saying, "Speak to Aaron and to his sons, saying to them: This is how you are to bless
The Children of Israel—say to them: 'May the Lord bless you and may the Lord keep you!
May the Lord shine His face upon you and be gracious to you, may the Lord favor you!
May the Lord lift His face toward you and grant you peace!' So the people are to put My name
Upon the Children of Israel, so that I may bless them; I Myself will bless them."

Numbers 7

At the time Moses finished the great preparation
Of the tabernacle, the dwelling of God,
Each clan's leaders, one per day, brought forth their donation
Just inside of the Tent of Meeting's facade.
First from Judah, then Issachar, then Zebulun,
Fourth was Reuben, Shimon fifth, and sixth there was Gad.
Then Ephraim, Mannasseh, and ninth, Benjamin,
Then Dan, Asher, and last, from Naphtali, a lad.

On the day that Moses finished setting up the Tabernacle, he anointed it
And hallowed it, with all its implements, and the altar, with all utensils for it.
Then the leaders of Israel, heads of their ancestral houses, the tribal chieftains
Who were set over those who were numbered, brought their offerings before the Lord's presence:
Six covered wagons and twelve oxen, an ox for each leader, a wagon for each two.
They brought them to the Tabernacle. The Lord said to Moses, "This is what you shall do:
Take these from them, to use for service of the Tent of Meeting; give them to the Levites,
Each man for his service." Moses gave the carts and oxen to them. To the Gershonites,
He gave two wagons and four cattle, as their service required. To Merarl's Sons,
He gave four wagons and eight cattle, as their service required, with the direction
Of Ithamar, son of Aaron the priest. But to the Kehatites he did not give any,
For their service was transporting holy things, which they must shoulder to carry the many.
The leaders offered offerings for dedicating the altar when it was anointed.
Now when they offered their offerings before the altar, the Lord to Moses appointed,
"One leader per day, one leader each day shall offer their offering for dedication
And anointing of the altar." So the one who offered an offering on day one

Was Nashon, son of Amminadab, of the tribe of Judah. He brought his offering:
A plate of silver, one hundred and thirty shekels in weight, and a silver basin,
Seventy shekels in weight, by the weight of the sanctuary, and both of them filled
With flour mixed with oil, for a grain-gift; one ladle made of gold that weighed ten shekels,
Filled with incense; one young bull; one ram; one male lamb in its first year as burnt offering;
One he-goat as sin-offering; and as a sacrifice of shalom Nashon did bring:
Two oxen and five rams, and five he-goats as well, along with five lambs in their first year.
That was the offering to the Lord which Nashon son of Amminadab did bring near.

On day two, Netanel son of Tzuar, leader of Issachar brought his offering:
A plate of silver, one hundred and thirty shekels in weight, and a silver basin,
Seventy shekels in weight, by the weight of the sanctuary, and both of them filled
With flour mixed with oil, for a grain-gift; one ladle made of gold that weighed ten shekels,
Filled with incense; one young bull; one ram; one male lamb in its first year as burnt offering;
One he-goat as sin-offering; and as a shalom-sacrifice Netanel did bring:
Two oxen and five rams, and five he-goats as well, along with five lambs in their first year.
That was the offering to the Lord which Netanel the son of Tzuar did bring near.

On the third day, Eliab son of Helon, the leader of the sons of Zebulun
Offered a silver plate one hundred and thirty shekels in weight, and a silver basin,
Seventy shekels in weight, by the weight of the sanctuary, and both of them filled
With flour mixed with oil, for a grain-gift; one ladle made of gold that weighed ten shekels,
Filled with incense; one young bull; one ram; one male lamb in its first year as burnt offering;
One he-goat as sin-offering; and as a shalom-sacrifice Eliab did bring:

Two oxen and five rams, and five he-goats as well, along with five lambs in their first year.
That was the offering to the Lord which Eliab the son of Helon did bring near.

On the fourth day, Elitzur son of Shedeur, the leader of the Sons of Reuben
Offered a silver plate, one hundred thirty shekels in weight, and a silver basin,
Seventy shekels in weight, by the weight of the sanctuary, and both of them filled
With flour mixed with oil, for a grain-gift; one ladle made of gold that weighed ten shekels,
Filled with incense; one young bull; one ram; one male lamb in its first year as burnt offering;
One he-goat as sin-offering; and as a shalom-sacrifice Elitzur did bring:
Two oxen and five rams, and five he-goats as well, along with five lambs in their first year.
That was the offering to the Lord which Elitzur son of Shedeur did bring near.

On day five, the leader of the Sons of Shimon, Shelumiel, Zurishaddaï's son
Offered a silver plate, one hundred thirty shekels in weight, and a silver basin,
Seventy shekels in weight, by the weight of the sanctuary, and both of them filled
With flour mixed with oil, for a grain-gift; one ladle made of gold that weighed ten shekels,
Filled with incense; one young bull; one ram; one male lamb in its first year as burnt offering;
One he-goat as sin-offering; and as shalom-sacrifice Shelumiel did bring:
Two oxen and five rams, and five he-goats as well, along with five lambs in their first year.
That was the offering which Shelumiel the son of Zurishaddai did bring near.

On day six, the leader of the Sons of Gad, Elyasaph son of Deuel's offering:
A plate of silver, one hundred and thirty shekels in weight, and a silver basin,
Seventy shekels in weight, by the weight of the sanctuary, and both of them filled
With flour mixed with oil, for a grain-gift; one ladle made of gold that weighed ten shekels,
Filled with incense; one young bull; one ram; one male lamb in its first year as burnt offering;
One he-goat as a sin-offering; and as shalom-sacrifice Elyasaph did bring:
Two oxen and five rams, and five he-goats as well, along with five lambs in their first year.
That was the offering to the Lord which Elyasaph the son of Deuel did bring near.

On day seven, leader of the Sons of Efrayim, Elishama, Ammihud's son
Offered a silver plate, one hundred thirty shekels in weight, and a silver basin,
Seventy shekels in weight, by the weight of the sanctuary, and both of them filled
With flour mixed with oil, for a grain-gift; one ladle made of gold that weighed ten shekels,
Filled with incense; one young bull; one ram; one male lamb in its first year as burnt offering;
One he-goat as sin-offering; and as shalom-sacrifice Elishama did bring:
Two oxen and five rams, and five he-goats as well, along with five lambs in their first year.
That was the offering to the Lord, Elishama son of Ammihud did bring near.

On day eight, the leader of the Sons of Menasseh, Gamliel son of Pedahzur
Offered a silver plate, one hundred thirty shekels weight, and a basin of silver,

Seventy shekels in weight, by the weight of the sanctuary, and both of them filled
With flour mixed with oil, for a grain-gift; one ladle made of gold that weighed ten shekels,
Filled with incense; one young bull; one ram; one male lamb in its first year as burnt offering;
One he-goat as sin-offering; and as a shalom-sacrifice Gamliel did bring:
Two oxen and five rams, and five he-goats as well, along with five lambs in their first year.
That was the offering to the Lord which Gamliel son of Pedahzur did bring near.

On day nine, Avidan son of Gidoni, the leader of the Sons of Benjamin
Offered a silver plate, one hundred thirty shekels in weight, and a silver basin,
Seventy shekels in weight, by the weight of the sanctuary, and both of them filled
With flour mixed with oil, for a grain-gift; one ladle made of gold that weighed ten shekels,
Filled with incense; one young bull; one ram; one male lamb in its first year as burnt offering;
One he-goat as sin-offering; and as a shalom-sacrifice Avidan did bring:
Two oxen and five rams, and five he-goats as well, along with five lambs in their first year.
That was the offering to the Lord which Avidon son of Gidoni did bring near.

On the tenth day, the leader of the Sons of Dan, AmmishaddaI's son Ahiezer
Offered a silver plate silver, one hundred thirty shekels weight, and a basin of silver,
Seventy shekels in weight, by the weight of the sanctuary, and both of them filled
With flour mixed with oil, for a grain-gift; one ladle made of gold that weighed ten shekels,
Filled with incense; one young bull; one ram; one male lamb in its first year as burnt offering;
One he-goat as sin-offering; and as shalom-sacrifice Ahiezer did bring:
Two oxen and five rams, and five he-goats as well, along with five lambs in their first year.
That was the offering which Ahiezer the son of Ammishaddai did bring near.

On the eleventh day, Pagiel son of Okhran, leader of the Sons of Asher,
Offered a silver plate, one hundred thirty shekels weight, and a basin of silver,
Seventy shekels in weight, by the weight of the sanctuary, and both of them filled
With flour mixed with oil, for a grain-gift; one ladle made of gold that weighed ten shekels,
Filled with incense; one young bull; one ram; one male lamb in its first year as burnt offering;
One he-goat as sin-offering; and as a shalom-sacrifice Pagiel did bring:
Two oxen and five rams, and five he-goats as well, along with five lambs in their first year.
That was the offering to the Lord which Pagiel the son of Okhran did bring near.

On the twelfth day, the leader of the sons of Naftali, Ahira son of Einan
Offered a silver plate, one hundred thirty shekels in weight, and a silver basin,
Seventy shekels in weight, by the weight of the sanctuary, and both of them filled
With flour mixed with oil, for a grain-gift; one ladle made of gold that weighed ten shekels,
Filled with incense; one young bull; one ram; one male lamb in its first year as burnt offering;
One he-goat as sin-offering; and as a shalom-sacrifice Ahira did bring:
Two oxen and five rams, and five he-goats as well, along with five lambs in their first year.
That was the offering to the Lord which Ahira the son of Einan did bring near.

This was the offering of dedication for the altar, from Israel's leaders,
On the day it was anointed: Twelve gold ladles, twelve bowls and dishes, each of silver,
One hundred thirty shekels the weight of each silver dish, seventy shekels per bowl,
All the silver weighed two thousand four hundred sanctuary-weight shekels as a whole.
Twelve gold ladles filled with incense, ten sanctuary shekels the weight of each ladle,
All the gold of the ladles weight one hundred and twenty shekels. And all the cattle
For the burnt offerings: Twelve bulls, twelve rams, twelve firstling lambs, with their grain-gift;
    Twelve he-goats
For the sin-offering. And all the cattle used for the sacrifices of shalom:
Twenty-four bulls, the rams sixty, the he-goats sixty, and sixty of the lambs, firstlings.
This was the dedication offering to the altar, following its anointing.

Now when Moses would come into the Tent of Meeting to speak with Him, Moses would hear
The voice speaking to him from above the penance-cover that was atop the coffer
Of the Testimony. From the mercy seat atop the ark between two cherubim,
From between those two winged-sphinxes, Moses would hear a voice, and there He would speak
    to him.

Numbers 8

>   God told Moses, "Tell Aaron, when lampwicks you draw,
>   Light the seven to light the front." Aaron did so.
>   "The Levites must be purified, without a flaw;
>   Shave and wash, then take two bulls, and flour also.
>   Let the Israelites lay hands on the Levites,
>   And the Levites lay hands on the heads of each bull.
>   All firstborn shall be mine from the Israelites."
>   The Levites, purified, could then all serve in full.

[Behaalotecha]

The Lord said to Moses, "Speak to Aaron and tell him: When you set up the lamps aglow,
Let the seven lamps give their light towards the front of the lampstand." And Aaron did so;
He set up the lamps to give light in front of the lampstand, just as the Lord did command
To Moses. Hammered-work of gold, from base to petal, was the making of the lampstand.

According to the vision the Lord had shown Moses, the lampstand was made in his sight.

Now the Lord spoke to Moses, saying, "Take the Levites from amidst the Israelites,
And cleanse them. This is how you shall cleanse them: sprinkle on them the purifying water,
And scrub their clothes. Then they shall shave their whole body, and go over it with a razor.
Then they shall be cleansed. They shall take a young bull, and as a grain-gift, flour with
oil mixed in,
And a second bull, also young of the herd, you shall take as an offering of sin.
You shall have the Levites approach the Tent of Meeting, assemble the community
Of all the Children of Israel. Presented before the Lord, the Levites shall be.
And the Children of Israel shall lay their hands upon the Levites. And then Aaron
Shall raise the Levites to the Lord, raising them as an offering of elevation,
On behalf of the Children of Israel, so the service of the Lord they may do.
Then the Levites shall lay their hands on the heads of the bulls, and as sin-offering you
Shall offer one of the bulls, the other bull you shall offer as a burnt offering
To the Lord, as a ransom for the Levites, the bulls are to serve as an atoning.
So you shall have the Levites stand before Aaron and his sons. You shall elevate them
As an elevation offering to the Lord. And so you are to separate them
Separate the Levites from the midst of the Israelites, for Mine they are to be.
After that the Levites may enter into service for the Tent of Meeting, for Me,
Once you have cleansed them and elevated them, then to Me they shall be given over
From the midst of the Children of Israel, in place of every firstborn womb-breacher,
The firstborn of every one of the Children of Israel; For Myself I take them.
For all firstborn among the Children of Israel, of man or of beast, are mine. When,
At the time I struck down every firstborn in Egypt, for Myself I made them holy.
Now I take the Levites in place of all firstborn the Children of Israel will see,
And I give the Levites to be given over to Aaron and his sons from the midst
Of the Children of Israel to serve in the Tent of Meeting and do the service
Of the Children of Israel, and to make ransom for the Israelite firstborn,
So if the Israelites encroach on the sanctuary, no plague by them is borne."

Moses, Aaron, and all of Israel's community acted so with the Levites,
Just as the Lord commanded Moses about the Levites, so did the Israelites.
The Levites purified themselves and scrubbed their clothes, Aaron offered them, raised,
    to the Lord;
And Aaron made atonement for them, to cleanse them. After that, all the Levites entered
To do their service in the Tent of Meeting, in the presence of Aaron and his sons.
As the Lord had commanded Moses with regard to the Levites, just so was it done.

The Lord spoke to Moses, saying, "This is what shall be done with regard to the Levites:
From the age of twenty-five and upward, they shall enter the working force to do rites

And do tasks of service in the Tent of Meeting. And once they reach the age fifty years,
They shall retire from the force of doing service, and serve no more as like their peers.
They may attend upon their brothers in the Tent of Meeting, to do maintenance at large,
But no heavy labor shall they serve. This is how you shall assign the Levites their charge."

Numbers 9

God told Moses, "Have Passover at its set time."
And Moses told the Israelites what to do.
Those unclean by corpse couldn't sacrifice the sublime,
So allowance was made to let them offer too.
When the Tabernacle was set up, it was covered
By cloud, that would hang from the night to the dawn.
By God's orders, they'd all stay camped while the cloud hovered,
And when the cloud lifted, then they would move on.

The Lord spoke to Moses in Sinai's wilderness, in the first month of the second year
After they had come out of the land of Egypt, saying, "Let the Israelites here
Offer the Passover sacrifice at its appointed time, on this month's fourteenth day,
In the evening, between sunset and total darkness. You shall offer it in this way
At the appointed time. According to all its laws and to all its regulations,
You shall sacrifice it." So Moses told the Children of Israel God's instructions,
To offer the Passover sacrifice. And they offered the Passover sacrifice
On the fourteenth day of the first month, between sunset and total darkness, at twilight,
In Sinai's wilderness. According to all the Lord commanded Moses, so they did.
But there were some men who, because of a dead person, had become contaminated,
And so, being unclean, they could not offer a Passover sacrifice on that day.
They came before Moses and Aaron, on that same day, and to Moses those men did say,
"We are unclean through touching a dead body, but why should we lose our privileged rights,
And not be allowed to present the Lord's offering from amidst the Israelites,
At its appointed time?" Moses told them, "Wait here, and I shall hear what the Lord commands
About you." The Lord spoke to Moses, saying, "Say to the Israelites: Any man
Among you or your descendants who is unclean because he has touched a dead body
Or is off on a journey, and he gives a Passover sacrifice to the Lord, he
Shall sacrifice it on the fourteenth day of the second month, when twilight has alit,
Along with matza and bitter herbs they shall eat it. They shall not leave any of it

Until morning. No bone shall be broken from it, according to the Passover law,
They shall sacrifice it. But a man who is clean and has not been journeying afar,
Yet refrains from the Passover sacrifice, that person shall be cut off from his kin,
For he has not brought the Passover sacrifice to the Lord; that man shall bear his sin.
Now when a stranger sojourns with you, offering Passover sacrifice to the Lord,
According to the law of Passover sacrifice, he shall offer it in accord.
There shall be one law for you, both sojourner and native, one law shall serve you in full."

Now at the time the Tabernacle was set up, the cloud covered the Tabernacle
Over the Tent of Testimony, and after sunset, like the appearance of fire,
It remained over the Tabernacle until daybreak. So did it always transpire:
The cloud would cover the Tabernacle by day, an appearance of fire by night.
Now whenever the cloud would lift up from the tent, then set out all the Israelites,
And wherever the cloud settled down, there the Children of Israel would make camp too.
By the Lord's command, the Israelites would march, and as the Lord commanded they do,
They would encamp. When the cloud stayed over the Tabernacle, in camp they would remain.
When the cloud stayed over the Tabernacle many days, Israelites would maintain
Their guard duty, and keep the charge of the Lord, and the Israelites would not march on.
Sometimes the cloud stayed over the Tabernacle many days before it would be gone,
And they would stay in camp by the Lord's order, and march on by the Lord's order as well.
Sometimes the cloud stayed from sunset until sunrise, when it lifted from where they did dwell,
Then they would march on. Whether by day or by night, when the cloud from the Dwelling
     was raised,
They would march on. Whether it was for two days, or for a month, or a year full of days,
When the cloud camped over the Tabernacle, the Israelites remained encamped too;
They would not march on. Only when the cloud was lifted up, would they march and continue.
By the order of the Lord they would encamp, and by the Lord's command they would progress;
They would keep the charge of the Lord, by the command of the Lord, through the hand
     of Moses.

Numbers 10

God told Moses, "Make two silver trumpets. They are
For the calling-together of the congregation.
When sounding them, let them come from near and far,
All to gather at the Tent of Meeting's location.
When the long trumpet blasts sound, let people convene.
When the shorter blasts sound, You shall march with your horde.
When the cloud went up, all of the tribes could be seen
Marching in order. Moses would say, "Rise, O Lord!"

The Lord said to Moses, "Make for yourself two trumpets, make them hammered work, of silver;
You shall use them to summon the congregation, and to have them march from where they were.
When you blow long blasts on both of them, the whole community shall gather before you,
At the entrance of the Tent of Meeting. If only one trumpet is blown, and not two,
Then the leaders, the heads of the tribes of Israel before you shall gather together.
But if you trill short blasts of alarm, the east camps shall set out (regardless of the weather).
And when you blow an alarm the second time, the camps that are on the south shall set out.
Alarms shall be blown whenever they need to march forward, a clear signal with no doubt.
But to gather the assembly, don't blow short alarm trills, but long blasts of assembly.
So the sons of Aaron, the priests, shall blow the trumpets. And to you, the trumpets shall be
A law for the ages, through your generations. And when you go to war in your land
Against an aggressor who attacks you, you shall sound the alarm on your trumpets, and
You will be remembered by the Lord your God, and be delivered from your enemies.
And on the days of your rejoicing, the first days of your months, and your appointed-feasts,
You shall blow your trumpets over your burnt offerings and sacrifices of shalom.
They shall serve as a reminder before your God—I am the Lord your God, I alone."

In the second year, in the second month, on the day before that month's twentieth night,
The cloud lifted from the Tabernacle of Testimony, and the Israelites
Marched by stages from the wilderness of Sinai. The cloud settled in the wilderness
Of Paran. They set out for the first time by the Lord's order, through the hand of Moses:
The contingent of the camp of Judah marched first, troop by troop, and set over their force
Was Nashon son of Amminadab. And set over all the tribe of Issachar's force
Was Netanel son of Zuar. And over Zebulun's tribal force was Helon's son
Eliab. Once the Tabernacle was taken down, then on marched the sons of Gershon
And the sons of Merari, who carried the Tabernacle. There marched Reuben's tribe group,
By their forces. Over them was Elitzur son of Shedeur. And over the troops

Of the tribe of Shimon was Shelumiel son of Zurishaddai. Over the force
Of the tribe of Gad was Elyasaph son of Deuel. The Kehatites then marched that course,
Carriers of the holy things. The Tabernacle was set up when they would arrive.
There marched the force of Ephrayim's camp, troop by troop. Over them to make sure
  that they thrived
Was Elishama son of Ammihud. And over the force of the tribe of Menasseh
Was Gamliel son of Pedahzur. And serving as the tribe of Benjamin's troop master
Was Avidan son of Gideoni. Then marched the contingent of the camp of Dan,
Acting as the rear-guard for all of the camps, and they all marched troop by troop, man by man;
Over their forces was Ahiezer son of Ammishaddai. And over the troops
Of the tribe of Asher was Pagiel son of Okhran. And over all of the troops
Of the tribe of Naftali was Ahira son of Einan. These were the marching groups
Of the Children of Israel by their deployed forces, when they set out, by their troops.

Moses told Hobab son of Reuel the Midyanite, the father-in-law of Moses,
"We are marching to the place of which the Lord said: I will give it to you. Come with us,
And we will do you good, for the Lord has promised good to Israel." He said to him,
"I will not go. Instead, I will depart to my own land, and I will go to my kin."
He replied, "Pray, don't leave us, for you know our best place to camp out in the wilderness,
You shall serve as our eyes. And if you go with us, whatever good the Lord does to us,
We will do that good for you." They marched from the mountain of the Lord for three
  days' journey,
With the ark of the Lord's covenant marching before them, on that same three-day journey,
To scout out a resting place for them. Now the cloud of the Lord was over them by day,
When they marched on from camp. Now whenever the ark was to move on, then
  Moses would say,
"Arise, O Lord, may Your enemies scatter, and Your foes flee from before You as well."
And when it rested, he said, "Return, O Lord, to Your many thousands of Israel."

Numbers 11

Now the people complained, "In Egypt, we had meat,
But there's nothing but manna for us to consume."
Moses asked the Lord, "What will I give them to eat?"
God said, "If they want meat, then let meat be their doom.
I will give them so much meat, a month it will last,
'till it comes out their nostrils and spills on the ground."
Moses asked, "Does Earth have the meat for this repast?"
God said, "I am the Lord." Meat appeared, all around.

Now the people complained bitterly in the ears of the Lord about their misfortunes.
When the Lord heard them, his anger flared up, and then a fire of the Lord blazed up among
The people, and it ate up the edge of the camp. Then to Moses, the people cried out.
And Moses interceded to the Lord, and the fire abated and finally went out.
So they named that place Tavera ("Blaze") because there the Lord's fire blazed up against them.
Now the rabble among them possessed a craving, and the Israelites wept again,
Saying, "Who will give us meat to eat? We remember the fish that we ate in Egypt,
Fish for free, the cucumbers, the watermelons, the leeks, the onions, and the garlic!
But now our throats are dry, and there's nothing aside from this manna in front of our eyes."
Now the manna was like coriander seed, colored like bdellium, little in size.
The people would roam around and gather it, grind it in millstones or crush it in mortars,
Boil it in a pot, and make it into cakes which tasted like rich oiled cakes from a larder.
And when the dew fell on the camp at night, the manna would come down on top of it more.
Moses heard the people weeping by their clans, each man at the entrance to his tent door.
Now the Lord's anger flared up exceedingly, and it was bad in the eyes of Moses.
Moses asked the Lord, "Why have You dealt badly with Your servant, why do I not possess
Favor in Your eyes, that You lay the burden of this entire people upon me?
Did I conceive this whole people? Did I give birth to them, so that You should say to me,
'Carry them in your bosom as a nurse carries a child', to the land which You did swear
To their fathers? Where should I get meat to give this people, who whine at me and declare:
'Give us meat so we may eat!' I can't carry this people alone, it's too much for me.
If You'd do this to me, please kill me instead, I beg You, so I do not have to see
My ill fortune!" Then the Lord said to Moses, "Gather for me a full seventy men
Of the elders of Israel, whom you know as officers to be experienced,
And take them to the Tent of Meeting, setting them there with you. I shall come down and speak
With you there, I will extend from the spirit upon you and put it upon their cheek;

Then they, along with you, shall bear the people's burden, so you need not do it alone.
Now to the people, you shall say: 'Hallow yourselves for the morrow, and let it be known,
So you may eat meat; for you have wept in the Lord's hearing, "Who will give us meat to eat?
For it went better for us when we were in Egypt." Therefore the Lord shall give you meat.
Yes, the Lord shall give you meat to eat, and you shall eat it. You shall not eat just one day,
Not for two days, nor five days, nor ten days, nor twenty days, but for a monthful of days,
Until it comes out of your nostrils, and becomes for you something you find nauseating,
Because you have spurned the Lord who is among you, by weeping at him and remonstrating,
Saying, "Why did we leave Egypt?"'". Moses said, "These fighting people whom I am among
Number six hundred thousand on foot, yet You say: 'I will give meat to them for a month'?
Are there flocks and herds that may be slain for them, so that there will be enough food for each?
Or shall all the fish in the sea be caught for them, so that amount of meat can be reached?"
The Lord said to Moses, "Is the Lord's arm too short? By My power, all things can be got.
Very soon you shall see whether what I have spoken is to come true for you or not."

Moses went out and told the people the words of the Lord, and gathered seventy men
From the elders of the people, and stationed all seventy of them around the tent.
Then the Lord came down in a cloud and spoke to him, and took some of the spirit on him
And put it upon the seventy elders. And when the spirit rested upon them,
They acted like prophets, and did not stop the trance while imbued with the spirit of God.

Now two men remained in the camp, one named Eldad, and the other one was named Medad.
And the spirit rested on them, they were among those registered, but had not progressed
To the Tent, and they acted like prophets in the camp. A young lad ran and told Moses,
"Eldad and Medad are acting like prophets in the camp." Then Joshua son of Nun,
Moses's attendant from his youth, spoke up and he said, "My lord Moses, contain them!"
But Moses said to him, "Are you jealous for my sake? I wish that all the Lord's people
Were prophets, that the Lord would put his spirit on them." And the elders of Israel,
Along with Moses, returned to the camp. And then from the Lord a great wind issued forth,
Sweeping in quails from the sea, and letting them fall near the camp, one day's walk to the north,
And as far as one day's walk south, one day's journey all around the camp, fell the meat hail;
It was two cubits deep all around on the ground. The people set to gathering quail,
They rose all that day, all that night, all the next day, gathering quail. He who gathered least
Still got ten homers worth. They spread it out to dry. While the meat was still between
    their teeth,
Before it was chewed, the Lord's anger flared up against the people, and then the Lord smote
The people with an exceedingly great plague, so they called the name of that place "Kivrot
Ha-Taava" ("Burial Places of the Craving") For it was there they buried in droves
People with the craving. From there they marched to Hazeroth, and remained in Hazeroth.

Numbers 12

Now both Aaron and Miriam spoke against Moses,
"Is it just through him that the Lord God will speak?
Does the Lord speak through us too, or do you suppose His
Word's only through Moses?" These words raised God's pique,
And He said, "I trust Moses, I speak to him clearly.
Why did you dare speak against him a critique?"
God struck Miriam, and scales afflicted her dearly,
The price for her sin, which she paid for a week.

Miriam and Aaron spoke against Moses, because he had taken a Cushite wife,
And they said, "Is it only through Moses that the Lord has spoken for all of our life?
Is it not also through us that He speaks?" And the Lord heard. Now Moses was very meek,
And exceedingly humble, more than any man on earth. Suddenly, the Lord did speak,
And said to Moses, Aaron, and Miriam, "Go out, you three, to the Tent of Meeting!"
The three of them went out. The Lord came down in a pillar of cloud and then was standing
At the entrance to the Tent, where He called out, "Aaron and Miriam!" The two went out.
He said, "Hear my words: If there is a prophet of the Lord among you, then have no doubt,
In a vision to him I shall make Myself known, and I shall speak to him in a dream.
But this is not the case with My servant Moses, most trusted in all My house, is he.
I speak with him mouth to mouth, in plain sight, not riddles, and he sees the form of the Lord.
So why weren't you afraid to speak against My servant Moses?" The anger of the Lord
Was kindled against them, and He went off. When the cloud was lifted from over the Tent,
Behold, Miriam was leprous, white as snow! Aaron faced her and saw its full extent:
She was leprous! Aaron said to Moses, "Please, my lord, do not punish us for a sin
Which we committed in foolishness. Let her not be like one of those half-dead children,
One which when it emerges from its mother's womb, eaten away is half of its flesh!"
Moses cried out to the Lord, "Heal her, O God, I pray you!" The Lord said to Moses,
"If her father spat in her face, would she not be shamed for seven days, at minimum?
Let her be shut up outside the camp seven days, then readmitted." So Miriam
Was shut out of the camp seven days. Until she was brought back, the camp did not march on.
Only then did they set our from Hazeroth, camping in the wilderness of Paran.

Numbers 13

God told Moses, "Send men to scout out Canaan's land."
And so Moses sent forth spies, one man from each tribe.
He said, "Find out who lives there, what arms are at hand,
Where they live. Are there trees? Then come back and describe
What you've seen." They went out, and came back with this tale,
"It flows with milk and honey, but we can't advance,
For fierce men live there." Caleb said, "We can prevail!"
Others said, "No, they were giants, we are just ants."

[Shlach]

The Lord spoke to Moses, saying, "Send men, so that they may spy out the land of Canaan
That I give to the Children of Israel. From each ancestral tribe send out one man,
Every one a leader among them." So Moses sent them out from Paran's wilderness,
By the order of the Lord, all of them men who were the Children of Israel's heads.
These were their names: From the tribe of Reuben: Shammua son of Zakkur.
From Shimon's tribe:
Shafat son of Hori. From Judah's tribe: Caleb, Jephunneh's son. From Issachar's tribe:
Igal son of Joseph. From Ephraim's tribe: Hoshea, Nun's son. From Benjamin's tribe:
Palti son of Rafu. From Zebulun's tribe: Gaddiel, SodI's son. From Joseph's tribe,
(Also known as the tribe of Menasseh): Gaddi, SusI's son. While from the tribe of Dan:
It was Ammiel, GemallI's son. From Asher's tribe: Setur son of Mikhael was the man.
From NaftalI's tribe: Nahbi son of Vofsi. From Gad's tribe: Geuel son of Makhi.
These were the names of the men whom Moses sent to scout the land and see what they could see.

Now Moses called Hoshea the son of Nun: "Joshua". Moses sent them out to spy
On the land of Canaan, and said to them, "Go up through the Negev desert, then up high
To the hill country, and survey the land—what it is like, and the people in those towns,
Are they strong or weak, are they few or many, and as for the land where they've settled down,
Is it good or bad, and what are the towns like where they settled, like camps or castle walls,
And what the land is like, is the soil rich or poor, and are there trees or not? Now, you all,
Exert yourselves, and take from the fruit of the land." (These were the days of the
    first ripe-grapes).
So they went up and scouted the land, from Zin's wilderness to Rehob, the path one takes
Coming towards Hamath. They went up through the Negev, and came to Hebron. And Ahiman,
Sheshai, and Talmai, the descendants of the Anakite giants were there. (Now Hebron

Had been built seven years before Zoan in Egypt.) They came to a valley and brook
Called the Wadi of Eshkol (or "Clusters"), and from that place, one cluster of grapes they took,
And a branch, both cut down, which then had to be carried on a pole between two of them,
And some pomegranates and some figs. That place was called "The Wadi of Eshkol" by them,
Due to the cluster that the Children of Israel had cut down there. Now they returned
From scouting out the land at the end of forty days. They came to Moses, and Aaron,
And the whole community of the Israelites, in the wilderness of Paran,
At Kadesh; they brought word to them and the community, showing the fruit of the land.

Now they told him, "We came to the land you sent us to, it is flowing with milk and honey,
And this is its fruit. But the people settled in the land are very fierce, and are many,
Their cities are well-fortified, very large, and we saw the descendants of Anak!
Amalek dwells in the Negev, while those of Hittite, Amorite, and Jebusite stock
Are settled in the hill-country, the Canaanites dwell by the sea, and on the Jordan's banks."

But Caleb hushed the people before Moses, and said, "Let us go up there, in our ranks,
And possess it, for we can triumph over it!" But the men who went up with him said,
"We can't go up against those people, they are stronger than us, and we might end up dead!"
So they gave a false report of the land they scouted to the Children of Israel,
Saying, "This land we crossed through to scout is a land which devours all those who there dwell;
And all the people that we saw in the midst of that land, were men of massive stature,
We saw the giants there, Nephilim—for in them the Children of Anak have their birth,
And when faced with these giants, these Children of Anak who had such an enormous size,
We seemed like grasshoppers to ourselves, and that is also how we appeared in their eyes."

Numbers 14

> People grumbled, "I wish we were back in Egypt,
> For out here, all our children will die by the sword."
> Caleb and Joshua said, "No, we're well-equipped,
> We will triumph, but only if we heed the Lord."
> But the people just wanted to stone them, until
> God appeared and said, "Those who complained against Me
> Shall die here in the wilderness. They never will
> See the land Caleb and Joshua shall soon see.

The whole community raised up a loud cry, and then the people wept that night as well.
And they grumbled against Moses and against Aaron, all the Children of Israel.
The whole community said to the two of them, "Would that we had died in Egypt's land!
Or that we had died in this wilderness! Now why is the Lord bringing us to this land,
To fall by the sword? Our wives and little ones will become prey! So would it not be better
For us all if we were to return to Egypt?" So then they all said to one another,
"Let's choose a new leader and head back to Egypt!" Moses and Aaron fell on their faces
Before the whole assembled community of Israel, when they heard these disgraces.
Only Joshua son of Nun and Caleb son of Jephunneh, among all the scouts,
Ripped their clothes and expressed to the whole Israelite community all of their doubts,
Saying, "The land we crossed through to scout out, that land is good, it is exceedingly good!
If the Lord is pleased with us, he will bring us to this land and give it to us he would,
A land flowing with milk and honey. But do not rebel against the Lord. And also,
Do not fear the people of the land, they are our prey. Their protector and their shadow
Has turned away from them, and the Lord is with us. Do not fear them, for they are alone!"
But the whole community of Israel ignored them and thought to pelt them with stones,
When the glory of the Lord appeared at the Tent of Meeting to all Israelites.
The Lord said to Moses, "How long will this people scorn Me, and not trust in Me, despite
All the signs I have worked among them? Let Me strike them down with pestilence and plague,
And I shall make of you a nation which is greater, bigger, and mightier than they!"

But Moses said to the Lord, "The Egyptians shall hear that you have destroyed Israel,
For you brought up this people with Your power from among their land. And then they will tell
The inhabitants of this land. They have heard that You, the Lord, among this people dwell.
You were seen face to face, O Lord, Your column of cloud before them by day, and as well,
In a column of fire by night. So if this entire people You decide to kill,
Then the nations that have heard of You will say, 'It was because the Lord was lacking skill
To bring this people to the land He swore to them, that He slew them in the wilderness.'
So now, pray let the power of the Lord be great, as you once long ago did express,
'the Lord, slow to anger, and of great loyalty, bearing iniquity and transgression,
Yet not clearing the guilty, visiting the father's sins on sons through four generations.'
Pardon the iniquity of this people, I pray You, as Your steadfast love is great,
And just as You have been bearing sin for this people, from Egypt to the present date."

The Lord said, "I grant pardon, by your words, but as I live and My glory fills the earth:
All the men who have seen My glory and signs which in Egypt and wilderness I worked
Yet have tested Me these many times by not heeding My voice, they shall not see the land
Which I swore to their fathers. Yes, none of those who have scorned Me will ever see that land.
But My servant Caleb had the spirit of courage in him, and followed Me fully,
So I shall bring him into the land where he went, and it shall be possessed by his seed.
Now the Amalekites and the Canaanites dwell in the valleys, so on the morrow,
Turn about and set out for the wilderness, facing to march out by the Red Sea road."

The Lord said to Moses and Aaron, "How much longer shall that wicked community
Grumble against Me? The grumblings of the Children of Israel, grumbled against Me,
I have heard. Say to them: 'As I live,' says the Lord, 'I will do to you what you have said.
Your carcasses will fall in this wilderness, all of your number shall soon end up dead,
All those counted from the age of twenty and up, all you that have grumbled against Me!
To the land which I raised my hand over and swore you would dwell in, you won't gain entry,
Except Caleb son of Jephunneh and Joshua the son of Nun. Your little-ones,
Whom you said would become prey, I shall let them enter, they shall know the land
        you have shunned.
But your corpses shall fall in this wilderness, where your children shall roam for forty years.
So they shall pay for your faithlessness, until your corpses fall in the wilderness here.
According to the number of days which you scouted out the land, a year for each day,
You shall bear your iniquity for forty years, and feel my displeasure with your ways.'
I am the Lord, I have spoken: I will to this to the whole wicked community
That have gathered together against Me. In this wilderness their finals days will be,
They will come to an end, and die there." So the men whom Moses sent to scout out the land,
Who returned, and made the community grumble against him with false news of the land,
Those men died, those who brought ill reports of the land, in a plague before the Lord's presence.
But Joshua son of Nun and Caleb son of Jephunneh stayed alive, from those men
That had gone to scout out the land. Now when Moses spoke all this to the Israelites,
The people mourned exceedingly. And early in the morning, they went up to the heights
Of the hill country, saying, "Here we are, let us go attack the place the Lord promised,
For we have sinned." But Moses said, "Why are you now transgressing the Lord's command
        with this?
It will not succeed! Do not go up, for the Lord is not with you, and without the Lord,
You will die. The Amalekite and Canaanite shall face you, you shall fall by the sword.
Since you turned away from following the Lord, the Lord will not be there with your offense."
But they stormed recklessly up to the hill-tops, though both the Ark of the Lord's Covenant
And Moses did not move from the campsite. The Amalekite and the Canaanite bands
Who were settled in those hill-tops came down and crushed them, pursuing them to
        Hormah's lands.

Numbers 15

God told Moses, "Tell them: When you enter the land
I am giving to you, and you make sacrifice,
The sojourner's hand shall do the same as your hand.
Of your bread, you shall give some to God. And the price
If you err in not following these rules I've set
Shall be one bull and one goat to pardon your sin.
But if you break rules willingly, with no regret,
Then you shall be cut off from among all your kin.

The Lord said to Moses, "Speak to the Israelites, and say to them: When you enter
The land of your settlements that I give to you, and make an offering by fire
To the Lord, whether from the herd or from the flock, be it burnt-offering, sacrifice,
A vow-offering, an offering of free will, or an appointed feast sacrifice,
To offer soothing savor to the Lord, the one bringing his offering to the Lord
Shall offer as a grain-gift a tenth-measure of flour, in which has been mixed and poured
A fourth of a hin of oil, and a quarter-hin of wine, to serve as a libation.
You shall sacrifice it with the burnt-offering or sacrifice for each lamb, each one,
Or for each ram, you shall make as a grain-gift: Two tenth-measures of flour mixed with oil,
One third of a hin, and one third of a hin of wine, as a libation from one loyal;
This is the soothing savor you shall offer to the Lord. When you slay one of the herd,
A bull, as burnt offering, vow-offering, peace-offering, sacrifice to the Lord,
You shall offer with the bull a grain gift: Three tenth-measures of flour, with oil mixed,
Half a hin. And you shall pour half a hin of wine as libation, (this amount is fixed),
A fire-offering of soothing savor for the Lord. This is how it is to be done
With each ox, or each ram, or each lamb from the flock or from the herd, so that for each one,
According to the number you sacrifice, you shall do this for each of their number.
Every native shall sacrifice in this way, bringing fire-offerings of sweet savor
To the Lord. Now when a sojourner sojourns with you, or one has remained in your midst,
Through your generations, and a fire-offering of sweet savor he sacrifices
To the Lord, he shall sacrifice it as you sacrifice it. And for the assembly,
There shall be one law for you and the sojourner who sojourns with you, eternally:
As it is for you, so shall it be for the sojourner before the Lord. As you do,
So shall he do. There shall be one law and instruction for the sojourner and for you."

The Lord spoke to Moses, saying, "Speak to the Children of Israel and say to them:
When you enter the land that I am bringing you to, and eat the bread of the land, then

You shall set aside a contribution to the Lord: The first yield of your baking,
You shall offer a loaf as a contribution, just like the threshing-floor's offering,
Is how you shall present it. From the first yield of your baking, you shall give to the Lord,
Through your generations. Now if you should err, and these commandments you by
    chance ignore—
Any commandment which the Lord commanded you through the hand of Moses, from the day
That the Lord commanded him, onward through your generations—If it was done away
From the eyes of the community, in error, the whole community will offer
One bull, young of the herd, for a burnt offering to the Lord, as a soothing savor,
With its grain-gift and libation, by regulation, and one he-goat sin offering.
The priest shall atone for the whole Israelite community, and so by doing,
They shall gain forgiveness, for their sin was in error, and their offering they have brought,
A fire-offering of soothing savor for the Lord, and their sin offering hot hot
Before the Lord's presence, because of their error. So there shall be granting of pardon
For the whole Israelite community, and sojourners with them, for it was done
By the entire people in error. Now if one person should mistakenly sin,
He shall offer a yearling she-goat, as sin-offering. And to make expiation,
The priest shall atone for the one who commits error and sins before the Lord's presence,
To atone for him so he may be forgiven. For the Israelite citizen,
And the sojourner in your midst, there shall be one law for he who does something in error.
But the person who does anything defiantly, be he native-born or sojourner,
It is the Lord that he blasphemes, and that person shall be cut off from among his kin,
For he has despised the word of the Lord, and has violated the Lord's commandment.
That soul shall be utterly cut off, his iniquity shall be upon him to bear.

While the Israelites were in the wilderness, they found a man gathering wood there
On the Sabbath day. And those who found him picking wood brought him to Moses and Aaron,
And the whole community. They put him in custody, not knowing what should be done,
For there was no ruling for him. The Lord said to Moses, "The man shall be put to death;
The whole community shall pelt him with stones outside the camp 'til he no more draws breath."
And the entire community brought him outside the camp, where at him, stones they threw,
And they pelted him with stones, so he died, as the Lord had commanded Moses to do.

The Lord spoke to Moses, saying, "Speak to the Children of Israel and say to them
That they should make tassels on the corners of their garments, throughout their generations,
And on the corner tassel, they shall put a blue thread. It shall be a tassel for you,
So you may look at it and remember all the commandments of the Lord you must do,
And observe them, so that you do not follow after your heart or after your own eyes,
Which you are inclined to follow wantonly. So you shall remember and realize
And observe all My commandments, and be holy to your God. I am the Lord your God,
Who took you out of the land of Egypt, to be God for you. I am the Lord your God."

Numbers 16

Now Korah and Dathan rose to Moses and said,
"You have taken too much on yourself, gone too far."
Moses said, "Sons of Levi, I ask this instead:
Is it too little that God made you what you are?
Now come offer to God." But they said, "We'll not go!
First you bring us from good land to here, now your goal
Is to lord over us?" And then Moses said, "No,
God shall make His will known." They were sent to Sheol.

[Korach]

Now Korah son of Izhar son of Kohath son of Levi took himself, and Dathan
And Abiram, sons of Eliab son of Pallu and On son of Pelet, the sons
Of Reuben, to rise up before Moses, with many of the Children of Israel—
Two-hundred and fifty community leaders, chosen in the assembly as well,
Well-known men. They assembled against Moses and against Aaron, and complained to them,
"You have gone too far! Now the whole community is holy, every last one of them,
And the Lord is among them. So why do you raise yourselves above the Lord's congregation?"
Now when Moses heard this, he fell on his face, and then made the following proclamation
To Korah and his whole community. "At daybreak, the Lord will make known who is His,
And who is holy, and will grant him access to Himself. The one who the Lord chooses,
He will bring near to Him. Do this: Take fire-pans, Korah and your whole community,
And put fire in them, placing incense on them, before the Lord, tomorrow. It shall be,
That the man the Lord chooses is the holy one. *You* have gone too far, Sons of Levi!"
And Moses said to Korah, "Hear this, Sons of Levi: Is it not enough in your eyes
That the God of Israel sets you apart from the community of Israel,
To bring you near to Him, and to serve tasks in the Tabernacle wherein the Lord dwells,
To stand before the community, and to tend to them? He has brought you all near to Him,
Both you and all your brethren, the Sons of Levi, yet you still seek the priesthood from Him?
Truly you and your community have gathered against the Lord. What has Aaron done,
That you grumble against him?" Moses sent for Dathan and Abiram, Eliab's sons,
But they said, "We will not go up! Is it not enough that you've brought us out of a land
Flowing with milk and honey to kill us in the wilderness, that you must take command
And make yourself a prince over us? You've not brought us to lands where milk and honey flow,
Nor given us possession of fields or vineyards. Will your lies blind us? We will not go!"

Then Moses became very upset, and said to the Lord, "Don't favor their offering.
I have not taken one donkey of theirs, nor done harm to them, I've not done one ill thing."
Moses said to Korah, "Tomorrow, you and your company, appear before the Lord,
You and they, and Aaron. And each man shall take his fire-pan, and of incense, a cord,
Bringing the pans of smoking incense before the Lord's presence. One pan brought for each man,
Two hundred fifty pans, and you, and Aaron too, each man his pan." Each man brought his pan,
Placing fire and incense on them, and they stood at the entrance to the Tent of Meeting,
As did Moses and Aaron. Now Korah and all of the community he was leading

Assembled against them at the entrance to the Tent of Meeting. And then the Lord's Glory
Was seen by the whole community, and the Lord said to Moses and Aaron, "Now hurry,
Separate yourselves from this community, that I may consume them in an instant!"
They fell on their faces and said, "O God of the spirits of all flesh, when one man sins,
Will You be angry with the whole community?" The Lord said to Moses, "Then tell them,
Tell the community, 'Get away from the dwelling of Korah, Dathan, Abiram!'"
Moses rose and went to Dathan and Abiram, Israel's elders followed him there.
And he said to the community, "Turn away from these wicked men's tents, and beware,
Do not touch anything that is theirs, otherwise you will be swept away for their sins."
So they all went up from the dwellings which Korah, Dathan, and Abiram were within.
Now Dathan and Abiram had come out, and were stationed at the entrance of their tents,
With their wives, their children, and their little ones. Moses said: "Now you shall know I am sent
By the Lord to do these things, and not by my own mind. If these men die a normal death,
Like all humans would die, suffering the fate of all mankind, as they stop drawing breath,
It is not the Lord who has sent me. But if the Lord creates a new unseen creation,
And the ground opens its mouth and swallows them up, and also swallows all their possessions,
And they go down alive into Sheol, then you will know that these men have scorned the Lord."
No sooner had Moses finished speaking these words, then the ground opened up in accord.
The earth beneath them opened its mouth and swallowed them up as Moses said it would be,
Swallowed their households too, all the people that belonged to Korah, and all property.
So they went down, they and theirs, to Sheol, alive; and the earth closed itself over them,
And they perished from the midst of the assembly. All Israel that was around them
Fled at the sound of their shrieks, saying, "What if the earth swallows us?" Now from the
    Lord's presence
Went out fire that consumed the two hundred and fifty men, those who had brought near
    the incense.

Numbers 17

God told Moses, "The pans of the sinners who died,
Make them plates." But the people all grumbled next day.
"Moses and Aaron, you killed God's people!", they cried.
God came down in a cloud, told Moses, "Go away
From the people, for I will destroy them right now!"
Aaron prayed to God, that he stop his deadly power.
Each tribe leader put staffs in the Tent, to allow
God to choose one, and Aaron's staff bloomed and bore flowers.

Then the Lord said to Moses, "Speak to Eleazar, son of Aaron the priest, so that he
Will take the censers from the blaze and charred remains, for those fire-pans have become holy,
And to scatter the coals far and near. The pans of those who sinned at the cost of their lives,
Let them be beaten into plates as covering for the altar, for the slaughter-site.
They were offered before the Lord, and so have become holy. Let them serve as a sign
For the Children of Israel." So Eleazar the priest took the pans of bronze design
That the burned men had offered, and they were hammered out into an altar covering,
A reminder for the Children of Israel, that no man but Aaron's line may bring
Incense before the Lord to burn, lest he end up like Korah and his congregation,
As the Lord had spoken to him through Moses. But at the dawning of the next day's sun,
The Children of Israel grumbled against Moses and Aaron, saying, "It is you
Who have killed the people of the Lord." But as more grumbling was about to ensue,
It was then when the community had assembled against Moses and against Aaron,
That they turned toward the Tent of Meeting, and behold, in the sky that was formerly barren,
The cloud now covered it, and the Lord's glory appeared. Moses and Aaron then arrived
At the front of the Tent of Meeting. And the Lord spoke to Moses, saying, "Move aside
From the midst of this community, so that I may consume them all in an instant!"
They flung themselves on their faces. Then Moses said to Aaron, "Take up your fire-pan,
And put fire on it from the altar, and incense. Go quickly to the community,
And atone for them, for wrath has gone out from the Lord's presence, and still goes out fury;
The plague has begun!" Aaron took it, as Moses said, and to the assembly he ran.
And behold, the plague had already begun among the people! So he took the pan,
And put incense in it and atoned for the people: He stood between living and dead,
And the plague was held back. Those who died by the plague were fourteen thousand
    seven hundred,
(Not including those who died in the situation with Korah). Then Aaron came back
To Moses, at the entrance of the Tent of Meeting, because the plague had been held back.

Now the Lord said to Moses, "Speak to the Children of Israel, take from them a staff,
One staff each for each ancestral home, from all their leaders, for their tribal house: Twelve staffs,
And write each man's name upon his staff. And write Aaron's name upon the staff of Levi.
There shall be one staff for each tribal head. You shall put them in the Tent of Meeting by
The testimony, before the Ark of Testimony, where I have meetings with you.
Now it shall be that the man I choose, his staff shall sprout. And so by this thing that I do,
I will cause to cease the grumbling of the Children of Israel against both of you."
Moses spoke to the Children of Israel, the leaders did as they were told to do,
They gave him a staff, one staff for each leader, for their ancestral home and tribe, twelve staffs,
With the staff of Aaron in the midst of their staffs. And then Moses laid out all the staffs
Before the Lord's presence, in the Tent of the Testimony, to quell all who had doubted.
And the next day, when Moses entered the Tent of the Testimony, here: it had sprouted!
The staff of Aaron, of the house of Levi, it had sprouted and produced sprouting buds,
It had blossomed a blossom, and flowered a flower, and even had ripened almonds!
Moses brought out all the staffs from the Lord's presence to all the Children of Israel;
They saw them, and each man took his staff. The Lord said to Moses, "Take the staff of Aaron,
Put it back before the Testimony, kept safe as a sign for rebellious ones,
So their grumbling against Me may be finished once and for all, so that they do not die"
Moses did it, according to all the Lord commanded him, he did it and complied.

But the Children of Israel said to Moses, "Here, we're perishing, we're all expiring!
Anyone who gets anywhere near the Lord's Dwelling will die. Are we all doomed to dying?"

Numbers 18

> All the Levites shall act in attending the Tent,
> Doing service in order that they do not die.
> Of each contribution, priests shall get a percent,
> All first sacrifices are their piece of the pie.
> Aaron and the priests shall not receive any land,
> For God is their inheritance, portion by rights.
> And the tithes that are given from each person's hand
> Shall serve as the inheritance of the Levites.

The Lord said to Aaron, "You, your sons, and your father's house shall bear all iniquity
Connected with the sanctuary, and you and your sons shall bear all iniquity

Connected to your priesthood. And bring your brothers, the tribe of Levi, your father's tribe,
So they may join you and attend you and your sons at the Tent of Meeting, as prescribed.
They shall attend to you and attend to all duties of the Tent, but shall not approach
The holy implements, nor come near the altar, lest they and you die when they encroach.
They shall be joined to you and keep charge of the Tent of Meeting, and all duties related.
No outsider shall come near you. You shall keep charge of the sanctuary consecrated,
And the duties of the altar, so no more wrath comes against the Children of Israel.
Now I hereby take your brethren the Levites from among all the Children of Israel,
They are a gift to you, given to the Lord, to do service in the Tent of Meeting.
And you and your sons with you shall attend to your priesthood in all matters concerning
The altar and all inside the curtain, and you shall serve. Special service in this breadth
I give your priesthood as a gift. Any outsider who comes near shall be put to death."

The Lord said to Aaron, "Now I hereby give you the charge of all my contributions,
All the sacred donations of the Children of Israel, I give you as portion,
And to your sons, as an allotment for the ages. This shall be yours, of the holy
Sacrifices from the fire, all offerings (grain, sin, and guilt) that they offer to Me,
It is a most holy portion, for you and your sons. Eat it in a most holy place,
Every male may eat it, it shall be holy for you. And also for you from My grace,
I give you their gift offering, all elevated offerings of the Israelites;
I give them to you, and your sons and daughters with you, as a perpetual right.
Everyone clean in your house may eat it. All your choicest oil, choicest wine, choicest grain,
The first fruits of what they give to the Lord, I give to you. First fruits of all on their plain,
That they bring to the Lord, it is for you. And all who are clean in your house may partake.
Everything specially devoted in Israel shall be yours. Firstborn of all makes,
Each breacher of a womb of all flesh, man or beast, offered to the Lord, shall be for you.
But you shall redeem the firstborn of humans, and firstborn of unclean animals too.
And its redemption price (which you shall pay at one month old) is to be at a fixed rate:
Five shekels of silver, which is twenty gerahs (or grains) by the sanctuary weight.

However, you shall not redeem the firstborn of oxen, firstborn of sheep, or of goats.
They are already holy, their blood you shall dash on the altar, turn their fat to smoke,
As a fire-offering of soothing savor for the Lord. And their meat shall be for you,
Like the breast of the elevation offering, like the right thigh, it shall be your due.
All the holy contributions that the Children of Israel offer to the Lord,
I give to you and your sons and daughters with you, to be a perpetual reward.
It is a covenant of salt for the ages, and like salt, is to be eternal,
A covenant before the Lord's presence, for you and your offspring after you as well."
The Lord said to Aaron, "In their land you shall have no inheritance nor land portion
Among them. I am your portion and inheritance in the midst of Israel's sons.
And to the Levites, here, I give all tithes in Israel, inheritance in exchange
For their service, serving duties in the Tent of Meeting, all things that need be arranged.

The Children of Israel shall no more approach the Tent of Meeting, to sin, to die.
The Levites alone shall serve the duties of the Tent of Meeting, and also thereby
It is they who shall bear their iniquity, a law throughout all their generations:
In the midst of the Children of Israel they shall inherit no inheritance.
For the tithing of the Children of Israel which they give as a gift to the Lord,
I have given to the Levites as an inheritance. Therefore of them I declared:
They shall inherit no portion of territory amidst the Children of Israel."

The Lord said to Moses, "Say to the Levites: When you take from the Children of Israel
The tithe I give you from them, your inherited-share, you shall set aside for the Lord
A tenth of that tithe: It shall count as your contribution, like grain from the threshing-floor,
Like well-fermented grapes from the vat. So you shall offer to the Lord a contribution
From all your tithes you take from the Children of Israel, this shall be an institution.
You shall give the Lord's tithe to Aaron the priest. From all your gifts, you are to set aside
The cream of the crop, all the choicest holy parts, to be given to the Lord as tithe.
And you shall tell them: When you tithe the choice parts from it, the rest shall be for the Levites,
Like the produce of the threshing-floor, like the produce of the vat. You may take a bite,
And eat it in any place, you and your household, for it is a recompense for you,
A payment in exchange for your service in the Tent of Meeting and all that you do.
You will not bear any sin because of it, once all of its choicest parts have been tithed,
But you must not profane the holy offerings of the Israelites, lest you die."

Numbers 19

The Lord told Moses, "This is the ritual law:
Take a red cow, and then by the priest have it slain.
The cow can't have been yoked, and it can't have a flaw.
Then its blood shall be sprinkled again and again
On the Tent, seven times. Burn the cow, keep the ash,
Mixed in water for cleansing. Those who touch the dead
Must be cleansed with that water, so give them a splash,
Otherwise they remain unclean from foot to head.

[Chukat]

The Lord said to Moses, "This is the ritual law which the Lord commands you respect:
Tell the Children of Israel to bring you a red cow, unblemished, without defect,

One that has not yet yielded to a yoke. And you shall give it to Eleazar the priest,
It shall be brought forth, outside the camp, slaughtered in his presence. Then Eleazar the priest
Shall take some of its blood with his finger and sprinkle it towards the Tent of Meeting,
Towards the front of the tent, seven times. Then the cow shall be burned in his sight, with its skin,
And its hide, and its blood, along with its dung shall be burned. The priest shall take cedar wood,
Along with hyssop and worm-scarlet, (all three of those things red, like the cow, and like blood),
And throw them into the midst of the cow burning. Then the priest is to scrub his garments
And wash his body in water. Then he may enter the camp after all these events,
But the priest shall remain unclean until sunset. And the one who performed the burning
Shall scrub his garments and wash his body in water, until sunset being unclean.
And a clean man shall gather the ashes of the cow, deposit them in a pure place
Outside of the camp. It shall be for the Israelite community, there kept safe
For the water of separation for the impurity, for the cleansing of sin.
The collector of the cow's ashes shall wash his clothes, until sunset staying unclean.
It shall be for the Children of Israel and sojourner who sojourns among them
A perpetual law: He who touches a corpse of any human being now dead,
Shall be unclean for seven days. If he decontaminates himself on the third day
With the water and ashes, and also the seventh day, he is made clean in that way.
But if he does not cleanse himself with the water on the third day and the seventh day,
He is not clean. Anyone who touches a corpse of a man who died in any way,
And does not decontaminate himself, then he has defiled the Lord's Tabernacle.
He shall be cut off from Israel, for the cleansing ash and water was not sprinkled
Upon him, so he is unclean, and his uncleanness stays with him. This is the Instruction:
When a man dies in his tent, anyone who enters or is inside the tent's construction
Shall be unclean for seven days. And any open vessel which does not have a cover
Is unclean. Anyone who touches on the field one slain by sword, or corpse of another,
Or bones of a human, or a grave, shall be unclean for seven days. They are to take
For the unclean some dust of the sin offering, added to running water to make
A solution in a vessel. He shall take hyssop and dip it into the water,
The clean man, and shall sprinkle it on the tent and implements, and all people who were
In the tent, and the one who touched the bones or the slain-one or the dead man or the grave.
Then the clean man shall sprinkle it on the unclean one on the third day and seventh day,
Thereby cleansing him on the seventh day. Then he shall wash with water his clothes and self,
And be cleansed after sunset. Now a man who becomes unclean and does not cleanse himself
Shall be cut off from amidst the assembly, for he has defiled the sanctuary
Of the Lord, and the waters of impurity were not dashed on him; he is unclean.
It is an eternal law for you: He who sprinkles the water of impurity
Shall wash his clothes, and he who touches the water until sunset shall remain unclean.
And whatever the unclean person touches becomes unclean, and if one touches it,
Then the person that touches it becomes unclean too, remaining so until sunset."

Numbers 20

> There was no water, so then to Moses, God spoke:
> "Take this staff, tell the boulder to make water flow."
> Moses took the staff, then gave the boulder a poke,
> And the water came forth. But God said to him, "No!
> I said talk, I did not tell you: 'Go hit the rock'.
> You lack faith. So the land Israel has in store,
> You are never to reach." They went on with their walk,
> From Kadesh, and left Aaron on top of Mount Hor.

Now the Children of Israel, the whole congregation, came to the Zin wilderness,
In the first month. The people stayed in Kadesh, where Miriam died and was laid to rest.
Now there was no water for the community, so all of them assembled together
Against Moses and Aaron. And they quarreled with Moses, saying, "It would have been better
If we had died when our brethren died before the Lord. Why did you bring the assembly
Of the Lord into this wilderness, so that we would die here, both our cattle and we?
Why did you make us go up from Egypt to bring us to this evil place that is cursed?
Not a place of seeds and figs, vines and pomegranates, and no water to quench our thirst."

Moses and Aaron left the assembly and went to the entrance of the Tent of Meeting,
Where they fell on their faces, and the glory of the Lord appeared to them. And in greeting,
The Lord spoke to Moses, saying, "Take the staff and then assemble the community,
Both you and Aaron your brother. Then you shall speak to the boulder where they all can see
So it gives forth water. So you shall bring water for them from the rock, on My behalf,
So that you can give drink to the assembly and to their cattle." Moses took the staff
From before the Lord's presence, as He had commanded him. Moses and Aaron gathered
The assembly to face the boulder. He said to them, "Here, you rebels, from this boulder
Shall we bring you water?" And Moses raised his hand, and struck the boulder with
    his staff, twice.
And abundant water came out, and the assembly and their cattle drank, it sufficed.

But the Lord said to Moses and Aaron, "Because you did not trust and believe in Me,
And did not sanctify Me in the sight of the Children of Israel, it will be:
That you two shall not bring this assembly into the land that I am giving to them."
Those were the waters of Meribah ("Quarreling") where the Israelites did contend
With the Lord, and He was sanctified through them. Now Moses sent messengers from Kadesh
To the king of Edom, "Your brother Israel says: You know what hardships have found us,

That our fathers went down to Egypt and we stayed in the land of Egypt many years,
And Egypt dealt harshly with us and with our fathers. We cried to the Lord, and He hears,
He heard our voice and sent a messenger, and brought us out from Egypt. Now here we are,
At Kadesh, the town at the border of your territory. Our passage, do not bar.
Pray, let us cross through your land. We will not cross through field or orchard, or drink
    from your wells,
We will march on the King's Road, not turning from it, until we've passed the land
    where you dwell."
But Edom said to him, "You shall not cross through me, or I'll come after you with my sword."
The Children of Israel said to him, "On the highway we will go up, we implore,
If we drink your water, my livestock and I, I will pay you the full value of it,
Just let us cross on foot, this is of little matter." But Edom replied, "Not one bit!
You shall not cross!" And Edom went out to meet them, with a strong force and with many men.
So Edom wouldn't let Israel cross through his land, and Israel turned away from him.

They marched on from Kadesh, and the Children of Israel, the entire congregation
Came to Mount Hor ("The Hill of Hill"). Now at Mount Hor the Lord said to Moses and Aaron,
By the border of the Land of Edom, "Let Aaron be gathered to his kin people,
For he shall not enter the land that I am giving to the Children of Israel,
Since you both rebelled against my orders at the Waters of Meribah. Take Aaron
And Eleazar his son, bring them up on Mount Hor. Take Aaron's clothes, put them on his son.
Aaron shall be gathered to his people, and die there." Moses followed the Lord's command:
They went up Mount Hor in sight of the entire community. Then Moses with his hand
Stripped Aaron of his garments and put them on Eleazar his son. So Aaron died there,
Atop the hill. When Moses and Eleazar came down, the whole assembly was aware
That Aaron had expired. The entire community saw that he died on the hill,
And they wept for Aaron for a full thirty days, the entire House of Israel.

Numbers 21

> Now the Canaanites warred with the Israelites, who
> Vowed to God, "If You'll please help us conquer our foe,
> We'll destroy all their towns, and devote them to You."
> So God heeded them. But as they marched to and fro,
> They complained against Moses, so God sent down snakes.
> And the people said, "Moses, please pardon our sin!
> Intercede with the Lord; we admit our mistakes!"
> And they sang, and they battled, and God helped them win.

When the Canaanite, the king of Arad who ruled in the Negev, heard that Israel
Was coming by the Atharim road, he fought them, and took some of them captive as well.
Then Israel vowed this vow to the Lord, "If You will give this people into our hand,
We will utterly destroy their cities, devoting to You all that is in their land."
Now the Lord heeded the voice of Israel, and so he gave to them the Canaanites,
Whom they utterly destroyed, along with their cities, and devoted to the Lord's might.
So the place was named Horma ("Destruction"), because of the destruction wrought on that day.

They marched from Mount Hor by the Reed Sea Road, to go around Edom's land. And
     on the way,
The people became short-tempered. The people spoke against God, and spoke against Moses,
Complaining, "Why did you bring us up from Egypt only to die in this wilderness?
There is no food and there is no water, and our throats all loathe this despicable food!"
So the Lord sent vipers among the people, burning snakes, who bit many of their brood,
And many of the Israelites died. The people came to Moses, said, "We have sinned,
For we spoke against the Lord and spoke against you. Pray to the Lord, remove the serpents."
So Moses interceded on their behalf. And the Lord said to Moses, "You shall make
A burning snake and put it on a pole. And all who are bitten, when they see this snake,
They shall live." So Moses made a viper of copper, and set it up atop a pole.
And if a snake bit anyone, he would look at the copper viper, and remain whole.

The Children of Israel marched on and encamped at Oboth. From there they mobilized,
Encamping at Iye-Abarim, in the wilderness that faces Moab, toward sunrise.
From there they marched on to encamp at the Wadi of Zered, and from there they embarked,
Encamping across the Arnon in the wilderness, where Amorite boundaries are marked
(For the Arnon is the border of Moav, between the Moav and the Amorites).
And therefore is it said in the Book of the Wars of the Lord, in this text where one writes:

"Vahev in Sufa, and the wadis of the Arnon, along with its canyon wadis,
   That stretch along the settled country of Ar, and touch the edge of Moab territory."

From there to the Beer Well, the well of which the Lord said to Moses, "Gather the people,
And I will give them water." Then this song was sung by all the people of Israel:
   "Spring up, O well, sing in chorus to it, the well that was dug out by princes so brave,
   The well that was excavated by people's nobles, with their scepters, and their own staves."

Now from the wilderness they went to Mattana, and then from Mattana to Nahliel.
And from Nahliel to Bamot ("The Heights"), and from there to the valley that lies in the field
In the open country of Moab, at the peak of Pisga ("the Summit"), which looks down
On the face of the wasteland. Now Israel sent messengers to the one with the crown,
Sihon king of the Amorites. They said, "Let us cross your land, we'll not step in your fields,
Nor in your vineyards. We shall not drink from your wells, nor take anything of your land's yield.
We shall march only on the King's Highway until we have passed through your territory."
But Sihon would not let Israel pass through his land. And Sihon gathered his army,
And went out to fight Israel in the wilderness. He came to Yahaz and waged war
Against Israel, but Israel defeated him, slew him with the edge of the sword,
And took possession of his land, from the Arnon to the Jabbok, to the Ammonites,
(But not past that border, for the Ammonites were strong, and they wanted no other fight).
Israel took all these cities and settled in the Amorite cities, like Heshbon,
And all its villages. For Heshbon was the city of the Amorite king Sihon.
He had made war on a former king of Moab, and had taken his land, to Arnon.
Therefore bards say,
   "Come to Heshbon, let it be built, and establish the town of Sihon!
   For fire went forth from Heshbon, and flame from the city of Sihon, thus devouring
   Ar of Moab, the inhabitants of the Arnon heights. Woe to you, Moab and king!
   You have perished, people of Kemosh! He made his sons fugitives, his daughters captives
   To an Amorite king, Sihon. We shot them, as far as Divon, Heshbon no more lives.
   We laid waste to them as far as Nofah, and the fires of destruction spread to Medeva."

So Israel settled in the Amorite land, and Moses sent men to scout out Jezer.
They took its villages, and they dispossessed the Amorites that were there. Then they turned
And went up the Bashan Road. Og king of Bashan went out to meet them, with all his herd,
All his fighting men, ready for war, at Edrei. The Lord told Moses, "Do not fear him,
For I give him into your hand, him and his people and land. And you will do to him
As you did to Sihon, Amorite king who ruled in Heshbon." They followed this command,
And slew him, his sons, all his people, until not one was left him. Then they took his land.

Numbers 22

    Now Balak, King of Moab, sent Bilam this call:
    "Put a curse on the people who enter my land."
    But the Lord told Bilam, "You can't curse them at all,
    They are blessed." Bilam said, "I can't cross God's command."
    Balak sent for Bilam. Bilam would not depart
    Until God gave His leave for Bilam to take flight.
    Bilam came to Balak, who decided to start
    Slaying oxen and sheep. They ascended Baal's heights.

And the Children of Israel marched on and camped on the plains of Moab, by the shore
Of the Jordan River, across from Jericho.

[Balak]

                                      Now Balak, who was son of Zippor,
Saw all Israel had done to the Amorites, so Moab was overcome with fear
Because they were so many. Moab feared the Children of Israel, and caught the ear
Of the elders of Midyan. Moab told them, "Look, this horde will lick clean all things around,
Everything that's around us they will lick up, like an ox licks up grass from the field's ground."
Now Balak son of Zippor was king of Moab at the time, so he sent messengers
To Balaam, the son of Beor, who was at Pethor, beside the Euphrates River
In the land of Amaw, of his kinsfolk, to tell him, "Here, a people came from Egypt,
And they cover the face of the land. They are settled near me; I fear I'll be outstripped.
Pray, go curse this people for me, since they are too numerous and too mighty for me.
Perhaps I can defeat them like this and drive them from the land, for I know it to be
That whomever you bless is blessed, and whom you curse is cursed." The elders of Moab's land
And the elders of Midyan departed, with the payment for divination in hand.
They came to Balaam and spoke Balak's words to him. He told them, "Spend the night
    here tonight,
I will speak to you as the Lord tells me." Moab's nobles spent the evening at that site,
With Balaam. Now God came to Balaam and said, "Who are these men with you?"
    Balaam replied,
"Balak, son of Zippor, king of Moab, sent to me, 'this people from Egypt I've spied,
And they cover the face of the land. Please go curse them for me, and perhaps then I can
Make war on them and drive them away.'" But God said to Balaam, "You shall not go with them,

You shall not curse that people, for they are blessed." Balaam rose in the morning and decreed
To Balak's nobles, "Go to your land, for the Lord will not let me follow where you lead."
The nobles from Moab arose, came to Balak, and said, "Balaam will not go with us."
So Balak sent nobles again, this time more numerous and honored then previous.

They came to Balaam and said to him, "Balak son of Zippor says: Pray, do not refrain
From joining me. Indeed, I will honor you greatly, and over myself, grant you reign,
If you'll only go curse this people for me." Balaam responded to Balak's servants,
"If Balak gave me his house filled with silver and gold, I can't do what the Lord prevents.
I cannot go against the command of the Lord my God, or do one thing contrary.
So please, stay here for this night as well, so I may know what more the Lord may say to me."
And God came to Balaam at night and said to him, "Since the men have all come to call you,
Rise and go with them. But, only the word I speak to you, only those things may you do."

Balaam rose in the morning, and saddled his donkey, and went with the Moab nobles.
But the Lord's anger flared up because he was going, so the Lord's messenger angel
Stationed himself in the way as an adversary to Balaam, who rode his she-ass.
Balaam had his two servants with him, and the donkey saw the angel blocking the pass,
The Lord's messenger standing in the way, his sword in his hand, so the ass turned away,
And went into the field. But Balaam struck the ass, guiding her back, and made her obey.
Then the Lord's messenger stood in a narrow path, in the vineyards, a fence on each side.
Now the ass saw the Lord's messenger, so she pressed herself against the wall. And her ride,
Balaam's foot was also pressed against the wall. And once again Balaam struck the she-ass.
But the Lord's messenger crossed to a narrow place, where one could not turn off of the pass.
Now the she-ass again saw the Lord's messenger, so she lay down underneath Balaam.
And Balaam's anger flared, and he struck the ass with his staff, losing the last of his calm.

Then the Lord opened the mouth of the ass, who said to Balaam, "What have I done to you,
That you've struck me these three times?" And Balaam replied, "You have mocked me. And
    if it were true
That I had a sword, by now I would have killed you." The ass said, "Am I not your donkey
Upon whom you have ridden your whole life until today? And have you ever known me
To do something like this to you?" Balaam said, "No." Then the Lord uncovered Balaam's eyes,
And he saw the Lord's messenger standing there, drawn sword in his hand, to Balaam's surprise.
He bowed his head and fell to his face. The Lord's messenger said to him, "Why did you hit
Your donkey three times? Here, I have come forth to withstand you, because of your errand. It
Is perverse to me; and the ass saw me, so she turned away those three times in the past.
Had she not turned from me, by now I would have killed you, allowing to live just the ass."
Balaam said to the messenger of the Lord, "I have sinned, for I did not know that you
Were standing in the road to be an adversary against me. But now that I do,
If it is evil in your eyes, I will head back." The Lord's messenger said to Balaam,
"Go with the men, but only the word I speak to you may you speak." So Balaam went on,

With Balak's nobles. When Balak heard that Balaam was coming, he went out to meet him,
To the town of Moab, by the border formed by the Arnon, at the boundary's rim.
And Balak said to Balaam, "Did I not send for you? So why did you not come to me?
Am I not able to honor you?" Balaam said to Balak, "I have come to you, but see,
Am I able to speak anything myself? The word God puts in my mouth, I may speak,
And those words alone." Balaam went with Balak, to Kiriath-Huzoth ("Village of Streets").
Balak sacrificed oxen and sheep, sending them to Balaam and the nearby nobles.
The next morn, Balak took Balaam up Bamoth-Ba'al, from where he saw some of the people.

Numbers 23

Balak built seven altars, at Bilam's instruction.
They slaughtered on each. To Bilam, the Lord said,
"Tell Balak: Israel shall not meet with destruction,
But with prosperity they shall be blessed instead."
Balak said, "What have you done? I asked you to curse,
But you bless them!" Bilam said, "It isn't my choice.
When the Lord has me say good, I can say no worse,
For I told you, I only can follow God's voice."

Balaam said to Balak, "Build me here seven altars, provide for me here seven rams
And seven bulls." Balak did as Balaam had spoken to him, then Balak and Balaam
Offered one bull and one ram on each altar. Balaam said to Balak, "Stand over there
Beside your offering, and I will go; perhaps the Lord will come meet me. I will share
Whatever He lets me see with you; I will bring you reports." He went off to the heights
By himself. God met Balaam, and Balaam said to Him, "I set up seven slaughter sites,
And have offered a bull and a ram on each altar." The Lord put words in Balaam's mouth,
And said, "Return to Balak, and this is what you shall speak." Balaam returned, to the south,
Where Balak and all the nobles of Moab were standing beside Balak's offering.
Balaam took up his parable and said, "I have been led from Aram by Moab's king,
Balak, from the hills of Kedem: 'Come curse Jacob for me, and come denounce Israel!'
How can I curse whom God has not cursed, how can I revile those the Lord has not reviled?
Indeed, from the mountaintops I behold him. From the hills I can see him, and have done.
Here, a people dwelling alone in security, not reckoned among the nations.
Who can measure the dust of Jacob, or the fourth-part of the dust-clouds of Israel?
May I die the death of the righteous, and may my future end up like Jacob's as well."

Balak said to Balaam, "Why have you done this to me, with all of the things you have said?
I took you on to curse and revile my foes, and here you went and blessed them instead!"
Balaam answered, "Is it not whatever words the Lord puts in my mouth that I must speak?"
Balak said to him, "Come with me to somewhere else, where a new perspective we will seek,
Somewhere that you can see only the nearest of them, but still cannot see all of them.
Curse them for me from there." So Balak took him to Sedeh-Zophim ("The Field of Watchmen"),
To the top of the summit. He built seven altars, offered a ram and bull on each.
Then he said to Balak, "Stand here, by your offering, while I go there, the Lord to meet."
And the Lord met Balaam, put words in his mouth, and said, "Return to Balak, and speak so."
He returned to Balak, who was standing by his offering, Moab's nobles also.
Balak said to him, "What did the Lord say?" Balaam took up his parable and replied,
"Arise, Balak, and heed. Hear me, O son of Zippor. God is no man, that He should lie,
Or a human being, that He should change his mind. Would He say something and not do it?
Or promise and not fulfill? I was commanded to bless, He blessed; I can't revoke it.
He has not beheld misfortune in Jacob, nor has he seen trouble in Israel.
The Lord their God is with them, and shouts of fanfare for a king are among them as well.
God who freed them from Egypt, He is like the horns of a wild-ox they are possessing.
For against Jacob there is no enchantment, against Israel there is no divining;
At once it is told to Jacob, to Israel, what God intends and what God has wrought.
Here, a people arises like a lion, lifts itself up as a king of beasts ought,
It does not lie down 'til it devours its prey, and 'til it drinks the blood of the slain."

Balak said to Balaam, "If you cannot curse them, then don't, but at least don't bless their name."
Balaam said to Balak, "Did I not tell you: Whatever the Lord speaks, that I must do?"
Balak said to Balaam, "Come, I will take you somewhere else, and perhaps seen from that view,
It will be right in God's eyes that you curse them for me from there." So Balak took Balaam
To the top of Peor overlooking the wasteland. And then to Balak said Balaam,
"Build for me seven altars here, and prepare for me here seven bulls and seven rams."
So Balak did as Balaam had said, and on each altar offered a bull and a ram.

Numbers 24

Bilam saw that the Lord preferred Israel blessed,
And said, "Bless Israel, crushing your foes like mice."
Balak's anger was kindled. He said, "I protest!
I had called you to curse my foes, you've blessed them thrice!
So now, please go away; you don't do what you're told."
Bilam said, "Though I told you before, you ignored;
I said: Even if you give me silver and gold,
I can not contradict a command of the Lord."

When Balaam saw that it was good in the Lord's eyes to bless Israel, he did not go
To search for omens, as he had previous times. He turned to the wilderness below.
And Balaam lifted his eyes and saw Israel, dwelling and encamping tribe by tribe,
And the Spirit of God came upon him, and he took up his parable and described:
"So speaks Balaam the son of Beor, these are the words of the man of the open eye,
The words of him who hears the words of God, and one who beholds visions of God Shaddai,
Bowing prostrate, but with eyes uncovered: How fair are your tents, O Jacob, your dwellings
O Israel! Like valleys stretching afar, like gardens beside a river running,
Like aloes planted by the Lord, like cedars beside the waters, and water will flow
From their boughs, their seed in many waters. Their king will be higher than Agag, and so
Their kingdom will be exalted. God who brought them from Egypt, like the horns of an ox.
They shall eat up the enemy nations, crush their bones, destroy their arrows, all the stocks.
They crouch, they lie down like a lion, like the king of beasts, who then will dare to rouse them?
Every one who blesses you shall be blessed, and every one who damns you, they shall be damned."

Balak's anger flared up against Balaam, he struck his hands together, and Balak said
To Balaam, "I called you to curse my enemies, and here you went and blessed them instead,
And three times! So now, go back to your place. I had said before that 'I will honor you,'
But now the Lord has denied you honor." Balaam said to Balak, "Now is it not true
That I told the messengers you sent me, 'Even if Balak gave a house full of gold
And of silver to me, I cannot go against words that by the Lord I have been told,
I could not do one thing good or bad of my own will, for what the Lord speaks in my ear,
That alone is what I may speak.' What the Lord says, that is what I too must say. Now here,
I will advise you as to what this people will do to your people in days to come."
And Balaam then proceeded to do so, taking up his parable which he spoke from:

"So speaks Balaam the son of Beor, these are the words of the man of the open eye,
The words of him who hears the words of God, and one who knows the knowledge of
    the Most High,
Who sees the vision of the Almighty, bowing, but with eyes uncovered. I see it,
But not now. I behold it, but not soon. A star will go forth which Jacob does emit,
A meteor arises from Israel, and smashes the pate of Moab, the crown
Of all the sons of Sheth. Edom shall be dispossessed, and Seir too shall be brought down
To become a possession of its enemies, while Israel does valiantly.
From Jacob will come one with dominion, destroying what's left of Ir and the cities."
Then Balaam looked upon Amalek, so he once more took up his parable and said,
"Amalek is the first of nations, but its fate is oblivion, all will be dead."
He saw the Kenites, and took up his parable, saying, "Your dwelling is secure, true,
Your nests of kin are set in the clefts, but Kain will lie in flames when Ashur captures you."
And he took up his parable and said, "Alas, when God does this, who can stay alive?
Who can survive whom God has condemned? Ships come from the Kittite shore and though
    now they thrive,
They afflict Ashur, they afflict Eber, but they too shall come to destruction one day."
Then Balaam rose and went, returning to his place, and Balak also went on his way.

Numbers 25

    Israel started whoring with the Moabites,
    And bowed down to their god called the Baal of Peor.
    The Lord's anger was kindled when He saw these rites,
    And God told Moses, "They shall all die, by the score!"
    But then Phineas saw whoring start to commence,
    And with spear, stabbed two people, and made them both cease.
    God said, "Thanks to this man, now My anger relents,
    So to Phineas, I give My covenant of peace."

While Israel dwelled in Shittim they whored themselves with the women of the Moabites,
Who invited the people to sacrifice to their gods. The people took the invite,
Partook and bowed to their gods. So Israel yoked themselves to the Baal of Peor.
And the anger of the Lord flared up against Israel. So to Moses said the Lord,
"Take the heads of all of the people, and impale them to the Lord, all facing the sun,
So the flaming anger of the Lord may turn away from Israel when it is done."

Moses said to the judges of Israel, "Let each man kill those men who took the yoke,
And joined themselves to Baal of Peor." And just after this command Moses had spoke,
One of the Israelites came and brought a Midianite woman to his family,
In sight of Moses, and in sight of the Children of Israel's whole community,
While they were weeping at the entrance of the Tent of Meeting. And when this was witnessed
By Phineas son of Eleazar son of Aaron the priest, he arose from the midst
Of the community. Taking up a spear, he went after the man, with spear in hand,
Into the private chamber, where he thrust it through both of them—the Israelite man,
And the woman, in her belly. The plague was held back from the Children of Israel.
Nonetheless, many died in the plague, from which a total of twenty-four thousand fell.

[Pinchas]

Now the Lord said to Moses, "Phineas son of Eleazar son of Aaron the priest
Has turned My wrath from the Israelites because of the jealousy he has released,
By displaying his passion for Me in the middle of all of the Israelites,
So I did not destroy them in My wrath. Therefore, say: Since this man has done what is right,
Here, I grant him My covenant of peace. It shall be for him and his seed after him
A covenant of eternal priesthood because for his God he was zealous with vim,
And atoned for the Children of Israel." Now the name of the Israelite man,
The one killed with the Midianite woman, was Zimri son of Salu, of the clan
Of the Simeonites, where he led an ancestral home. The Midianite woman's name
Was Kozbi daughter of Zur, who is head of the ancestral home of Midian's fame.

Now the Lord spoke to Moses, saying, "Attack the Midianites, strike them to the core,
For they attacked you with their craftiness and beguiled you in the matter of Peor,
In the matter of Kozbi, the daughter of the leader of Midian, their sister,
The one who was struck dead on the day of the plague, on account of the Peor matter."

Numbers 26

God told Moses and Eleazar (Aaron's son),
"Of the Israelites, you shall take a head count.
Each man twenty and up who can war, every one,
By their ancestral houses. Get the full amount."
So a census they took, of each man of each tribe,
Making Six hundred one thousand, seven hundred
Thirty. Those who'd lived through the wilderness, aside
From Joshua and Caleb, were already dead.

After the plague, the Lord said to Moses and to Eleazar son of Aaron the priest,
"Take the head count of the entire community of Israelites who are at least
Twenty years old, and upward, by their fathers' houses, all in Israel who can bear arms."
Moses and Eleazar the priest, on the plains of Moab, spoke to the Israelite swarms,
By the Jordan at Jericho, saying, "For those twenty years and up..." As God did command
To Moses. And the Children of Israel, those had had been brought forth from Egypt's land:
Reuben, firstborn of Israel. The sons of Reuben: Of Enoch, the Enochite clan,
Of Pallu, the Pallite clan, of Hezron, the Hezronites, of Karmi, the Karmite clan.
These are the Reubenite clans, forty-three thousand, seven hundred and thirty in all.
Pallu's son: Eliab. The sons of Eliab: Abiram, Dathan, and Nemuel.
(That is the Dathan and Abiram whom the community chose from the congregation,
Who argued against Moses and Aaron, along with Korah, during the situation
When Korah's congregation had struggled against the Lord, and the earth opened its mouth
To swallow them and Korah, when that company died, and into the ground all went south.
At the death of the community, when the fire consumed two hundred and fifty men.
They became a sign of warning. Notwithstanding, the sons of Korah did not die then.

The sons of Shimon by their clans: Of Nemuel, the Nemuelite clan, of Yamin,
The Yaminite clan, of Yakhin, the Yakhinite clan, of Zerah, the Zerahite kin,
Of Shaul, the Shaulite clan. These are the Shimonite clans, the full count to a man,
Twenty two thousand two hundred men. These are the sons of Gad according to their clans:
Of Tzefon, the Tzefonite clan, of Haggi, the Haggite clan, of Shuni, the Shunites,
Of Ozni, the Oznite clan, of Eri, the Erite clan, of Arod, the Arodites,
Of Areli, the Arelite clan. These are the clans of the sons of Gad by their count:
According to their number, Forty thousand five hundred men was the total amount.

The sons of Judah: Er and Onan, but Er and Onan died in the land of Canaan.
Now the sons of Judah, according to their clans, were: Of Shela, the Shelanite clans,
Of Perez, the Perezite clan, of Zerah, the Zerahite clan. The sons of Perez:
Of Hezron, the Hezronite clan, of Hamul, the Hamulite clan. And so all of these
Are the clans of Judah, by their count: Seventy-six thousand five hundred, to the man.

The sons of Issachar, each according to their clan: Of Tola, the Tolaite clan,
Of Puvva, the Puvvites, of Jashub, the Jashubites, of Shimron, the Shimronite clan.
These are the clans of Issachar numbered: Sixty-four thousand three hundred, to the man.

The sons of Zebulun, by clan: Of Sered, the Sardites, of Elon, the Elonites,
Of Jahleel, the Jahleelite clan. These are the count of the clans of the Zebulunites:
Sixty thousand, five hundred. The sons of Joseph by their clans: Menasseh and Efrayim.
The sons of Menasseh: Of Makhir, the Makhirite clan. Makhir's son who was born by him
Was Gilad. Of Gilad, the Giladite clan. These are the sons of Gilad: Of Iezer,
The Iezerite clan, of Helek, the Helekite clan, of Asriel, were the Asr-
Ielite clan, of Shekhem, the Shekhemite clan, of Shemida, the Shemidaites,
Of Hefer, the Heferite clan. Now Tzelof son of Hefer had no sons for birthright,
Only daughters. The names of his daughters were: Mahla, Noa, Hogla, Milka, and Tirtza.
These are Menasseh's, fifty two thousand seven hundred the full count of Menasseh.
These are the sons of Efrayim, by their clans: Of Shutelah, the Shutelahite clan,
Of Bekher, the family of the Bekherites, and of Tahan, the Tahanite clan.
These are the sons of Shutelah: Of Eiran, the Eiranite clan. And these are the clans
Of the sons of Efrayim: Thirty two thousand and five hundred, counted to the man.
These are the sons of Joseph, by their clans. Now the sons of Benjamin, all by their clans:
Of Bela, the Balites, of Ashbel, Ashbelites, of Ahiram, Ahiramite clan,
Of Shefufam, the family of the Shufamites, of Hufam, the Hufamite clan.
The sons of Bela were named Ard and Naaman. Of Ard, the Ardite clan, and of Naaman,
The Naamite clan. These are the sons of Benjamin, the full count according to their clans:
Forty-five thousand and six hundred. These are the sons of Dan by their clans: Of Shuham,
The Shuhamite clan. These are the clans of Dan, by their clans. All of the Shuhamite clans,
By their accountings: sixty-four thousand, four hundred. The sons of Asher, by their clans:
Of Yimna, the Yimnite clan, of Ishvi, the Ishvite clan, of Beriah, the Beriites.
For the sons of Beria, of Hever, the Hevite clan, of Malkeil, the Malkeilites.
Now the name of Asher's daughter was Serah. These are the clans of the sons of Asher,
According to their count: Fifty-three thousand, four hundred. The sons Naftali did bear,
According to their clans: Of Jahzeel, the Jahzeelite clan, of Guni, the Gunite clan,
Of Jezer, the Jezerite clan, of Shillem, the Shillemite clan. And these are the clans
Of Naftali, by their clans, and their accountings: Forty-five thousand and four hundred.
This is the count of the Israelites: Six hundred and one thousand, seven hundred
And thirty. The Lord spoke to Moses, saying, "To these the land is to be divided
And apportioned out as an inheritance to the names which were enumerated:

To the many, you shall give much as their inheritance, and give little to the few,
Each tribe shall be given inheritance, according to its population, by you.
However, the land shall be apportioned by lot; by the listings of ancestral tribes
Each one shall inherit land. It shall all be done by lot, between the tribes of all size.

And these are the accountings of the Levites, by their clans: Of Gershon, the Gershonites,
Of Kehat, the family of Kehatites, of Merari, the family of Merarites.

These are the clans of Levi: The Livnite clan, the Hebronite clan, and the Mahlite clan,
The Mushite clan, and the Korhite clan. Now Kehat fathered Amram. The wife of Amram
Was Jochebed the daughter of Levi, and it was in Egypt that he fathered her.
She bore sons to Amram, both Aaron and Moses, and also Miriam their sister.

To Aaron there were born four sons: Nadab, and Abihu, Eleazar and Ithamar.
Nadab and Abihu had died when they offered unholy fire before the Lord.
And their count was: Twenty-three thousand. All the males from the age of one month
    up to more,
For they had not been counted amidst the Children of Israel in their count before,
For they were not given an inheritance in the midst of the Children of Israel.

These are those counted by Moses and Eleazar the priest, of the Children of Israel
Whom they counted in the plains of Moab, beside Jericho, by the Jordan River.
Among these there was not one man counted by Moses and Aaron the priest when
    they numbered
The Children of Israel in the Wilderness of Sinai. For the Lord said to them,
"They shall die in the wilderness." And there will not be one man that shall remain of them,
Except for Caleb son of Jephunneh and Joshua son of Nun.

Numbers 27

> Now Zelophehad died, but no sons he had left.
> So his daughters said, "Our father died for his sin,
> But because we are girls, should his clan be bereft?
> Give us his land." God told Moses, "True, they're his kin."
> And the Lord said to Moses, "These mountains, ascend,
> So the land that I give your people, you may view.
> Since you broke my command in Sin, your life will end,
> But take Joshua, who will lead on after you."

Now there came near
The Daughters of Zelophehad son of Hepher son of Gilead son of Makhir
Son of Menasseh, of the clan of Menasseh son of Joseph, and these are the names
Of his daughters: Mahla, Noah, Hoglah, Miclah, and Tirtza. They all stood where they came,
Before Moses and Eleazar the priest, the leaders and the whole community wide,
At the entrance to the Tent of Meeting, saying, "In the wilderness our father died.
He was not one of the community of Korah that had gathered against the Lord,
But he died for his own sin, and had no sons. Now why should our father's name be ignored,
And taken from his family just because he has no son? Give to us a possession
In the midst of our father's brethren. Moses brought near their case before the Lord's discretion.
And the Lord said to Moses, "The daughters of Zelophehad have quite justly spoken.
You are to give to them an inheritance in the midst of all their father's brethren,
You shall transfer their father's inheritance to them. And to the Israelites, say:
When a man dies, and has no son, you shall transfer his inheritance in the same way
To his daughter. If he has no daughter, you shall give the inheritance to his brothers.
And if he has no brothers, you are to give the inheritance to his father's brothers.
If his father has no brothers, you shall give his inheritance to his next of kin,
From his clan, whoever is nearest to him, shall of his property gain possession.
It shall be for the Israelites a law and statute, as the Lord commanded Moses."

The Lord said to Moses, "Go up these mountains of "Avarim" (or "The Region Across")
And see the land that I am giving to the Children of Israel. When you have seen,
You will be gathered to your kin, you will be gathered as your brother Aaron had been,
Since you rebelled against My order in the wilderness of Syn when the congregation
Was in strife, and you did not sanctify Me through water in their sight at that location."
Those are the waters of Meribah ("Quarreling") at Kadesh, in the Syn wilderness.
Then Moses spoke to the Lord, and said, "Let the Lord, the God of the spirits of all flesh,

Appoint a man over the community, who will go out and come back before them,
Who will lead them out and bring them back, so the Lord's congregation will not be like lambs
Who have no shepherd." The Lord said to Moses, "Take yourself Joshua the son of Nun,
A man in whom the spirit is, and lay your hand upon him. And then when you are done,
You shall have him stand before Eleazar the priest and before the whole community,
And you shall commission him before their eyes, and give him some of your authority,
So that the whole Israelite community will pay heed. And then he is to stand
Before Eleazar the priest, who will seek judgment for him with the Urim at hand,
The oracular Urim which lies in the ephod, before the presence of the Lord.
By his order he will go out, and by his order he will come back, he and the horde
Of the Children of Israel." Moses did just as the Lord had given his command.
As commanded, he took Joshua, and before Eleazar the priest had him stand,
And also before the whole community of the Israelites who would witness
As he lay his hands on him and commissioned him, as the Lord commanded through Moses.

Numbers 28

God told Moses, "Now tell all the Israelites:
Bring me two lambs a day that you'll burn to the Lord.
On the Sabbath, two more. And for first New Moon rites,
Two bulls, seven lambs, one ram, and offerings poured.
Fourteenth day of the first month is Passover time,
And to celebrate, for one week, you'll eat matzot.
On the Feast of Weeks, when the firstfruits reach their prime,
Do no hard labor, but sacrifice one male goat."

The Lord spoke to Moses, saying, "Command the Children of Israel, and say to them:
Of My offering, My food, My fire-offerings, and My soothing savor, all of them,
You shall be in charge, offering them to Me in their due seasons." And say furthermore
To the Israelites, "This is the fire-offering you shall offer to the Lord:
Two male lambs, a year old, without blemish, two per day, as continual offering.
The first lamb you shall sacrifice in the morning, the second lamb, offer at evening;
And a tenth of an ephah of flour, as grain gift, mixed with one quarter-hin beaten oil
(The offering regularly sacrificed at Mount Sinai by all those who were loyal)
As a soothing savor, a fire-offering for the Lord. And its libation shall be
One fourth of a hin for the first lamb, which you are to pour out in the sanctuary

As a libation of strong drink for the Lord. And the second lamb you shall sacrifice
In the evening, and do as with the morning grain-gift and libation, thus giving twice
A fire-offering of soothing savor for the Lord. And offer on the Sabbath day,
Two yearling lambs, unblemished, and two tenth-measures of flour, for a grain-gift the same way,
Mixed with oil, and its proper libation, the Sabbath offering on its Sabbath,
And also the regular offering and its libation that it should be offered with.

At the beginnings of New Moons, you shall bring an offering to the Lord: Two young bulls,
One ram, seven lambs of one year in age, unblemished and wholly-sound. And for each bull,
Three tenth-measures of flour as a grain-gift, mixed with oil. For the ram, two tenth-measures,
Mixed with oil. For each lamb, one tenth-measure, mixed with oil, to offer as soothing savor,
A fire-offering for the Lord, with their libations: For each bull shall be half a hin,
A third of a hin for each ram, and for each lamb shall be a fourth of a hin of wine.
That is the monthly offering on the New Moon for each new moon in the year's rotation.
And one goat as sin offering to the Lord, plus the standard offering, and libation.

On the fourteenth day of the first month is the Lord's Passover. And on the fifteenth day
Of that month is a pilgrimage festival. Matzot shall be eaten for seven days:
On the first day there shall be a holy convocation, no heavy work shall you do.
You shall offer a fire-offering as an offering-up for the Lord: Young bulls, two,
And one ram, and seven lambs one year in age. They shall be unblemished—see that they are.
And their grain-gift: You shall offer flour mixed with oil, for each bull three tenth-measures,
And two tenth-measures for the ram. And for each lamb, you are also to offer a tenth,
For the seven lambs, and one goat as a sin offering to gain yourself atonement,
Along with the regular morning offering, you shall sacrifice these in accord.
You shall offer in this way for seven days, offerings of soothing savor for the Lord,
Along with the regular offering-up you shall sacrifice it and its libation.
Now on the seventh day, you shall do no heavy work, it is a holy convocation.

And on the day of the first fruits, when you offer a grain-gift of new grain for the Lord
At your feast of weeks, you shall have a holy convocation; heavy work shall be barred.
You shall offer an offering, soothing savor for the Lord: Two young bulls of the herd,
One ram, and seven yearling lambs, and their grain-gift, flour mixed with oil. Three
    tenth-measures
For each bull, two tenth-measures of flour for the ram, and one tenth-measure for each lamb,
One for each of the seven lambs, plus one male goat to gain atonement, in addition
To the regular offering and its grain-gift which you shall sacrifice all week round,
Which you shall offer with their libations. And you shall make sure that they are wholly-sound."

Numbers 29

"In the seventh new moon (seventh month), the first day
Is a sacred occasion; do no heavy work,
But give sacrifice. All these rules, you must obey.
On the tenth day, every type of work, you shall shirk.
On the fifteenth day, for one full week you'll observe
Festival to the Lord. On each day, sacrifice.
On the eighth day, no heavy labor shall you serve;
Seven lambs, one bull, one ram, your offering price."

"On the first day of the seventh month, there shall be a holy convocation for you.
It shall be a day of trumpet blasts for you, and no heavy labor are you to do.
You shall sacrifice an offering as a soothing savor for the Lord: One young bull,
One ram, and seven yearling lambs, wholly sound, and their grain-gift, flour mixed with oil:
Three tenth-measures of flour for each bull, and two tenth-measures of flour for the ram,
And one tenth-measure of flour for each lamb, one tenth-measure for each of seven lambs,
And one male goat as sin-offering, to gain yourself atonement. And this all aside
From the new moon offering and grain-gift, and regular offering you would provide,
With their libations, by regulation, a soothing savor, offerings for the Lord.

On the tenth day of this seventh month shall be a holy convocation for your horde,
You shall afflict yourselves, and do no kind of work. You shall sacrifice an offering
As a soothing savor for the Lord: One young bull, and one ram, and yearling lambs, seven.
Be sure that they are unblemished, and their grain-gift, flour mixed with oil—three tenth-measures
For each bull, two tenth-measures for the ram, and for each of seven lambs a tenth-measure,
One male goat as a sin-offering, aside from the sin-offering of atonement,
And the regular offering, its grain-gift, and their libations to the full extent.

On the fifteenth day of the seventh month, there is a holy convocation for you,
You shall not do any heavy labor. You shall keep a feast to the Lord, as is due,
Keep a festival to the Lord for seven days. And you shall offer an offering,
A fire-offering of soothing savor to the Lord: Bulls, young ones of the herd, thirteen,
Two rams, and fourteen yearling lambs, all wholly-sound. And their grain-gift, flour mixed with oil:
Three tenth-measures for each of thirteen bulls, two tenth-measures for each of two rams unspoiled,

And one tenth-measure for each of the fourteen lambs, and one male goat as sin-offering,
Beside the regular burnt-offering, its grain-gift, and its libation offerings.

On the second day, twelve young bulls, two rams, and fourteen male lambs a year old
    wholly sound,
With the grain gift and libation for the bulls, for the rams, for the lambs, counted as found
According to the regulation. And one male goat to serve as a sin-offering,
Beside the regular burnt offering, its grain-gift, and its libation offerings.

On the third day, eleven young bulls, two rams, and fourteen male lambs a year old wholly sound,
With the grain gift and libation for the bulls, for the rams, for the lambs, counted as found
According to the regulation. And one male goat to serve as a sin-offering,
Beside the regular burnt offering, its grain-gift, and its libation offerings.

On the fourth day, ten young bulls, two rams, and fourteen male lambs one year in age,
    wholly sound,
With the grain gift and libation for the bulls, for the rams, for the lambs, counted as found
According to the regulation. And one male goat to serve as a sin-offering,
Beside the regular burnt offering, its grain-gift, and its libation offerings.

On the fifth day, nine young bulls, two rams, and fourteen male lambs one year in age,
    wholly sound,
With the grain gift and libation for the bulls, for the rams, for the lambs, counted as found
According to the regulation. And one male goat to serve as a sin-offering,
Beside the regular burnt offering, its grain-gift, and its libation offerings.

On the sixth day, eight young bulls, two rams, and fourteen male lambs one year in age,
    wholly sound,
With the grain gift and libation for the bulls, for the rams, for the lambs, counted as found
According to the regulation. And one male goat to serve as a sin-offering,
Beside the regular burnt offering, its grain-gift, and its libation offerings.

On the seventh day, seven young bulls, two rams, and fourteen male yearling lambs, wholly sound,
With the grain gift and libation for the bulls, for the rams, for the lambs, counted as found
According to the regulation. And one male goat to serve as a sin-offering,
Beside the regular burnt offering, its grain-gift, and its libation offerings.

On the eighth day, there shall be restraint for you, no kind of heavy labor shall you do.
You shall offer a fire-offering of soothing savor for the Lord. This is His due:
One bull, one ram, and seven lambs one year in age, all without blemish and wholly-sound,
With the grain gift and libation for the bulls, for the rams, for the lambs, counted as found

According to the regulation. And one male goat to serve as a sin-offering,
Beside the regular burnt offering, its grain-gift, and its libation offerings.

These you shall sacrifice to the Lord at your feasts, beside vow and freewill offerings,
For your burnt-offerings and your grain-gifts, for your libations and shalom offerings."

Numbers 30

> Moses told all the Israelites, "When a man
> Or a woman does vow to the Lord a sworn-oath,
> They are bound by their word, they must follow that plan,
> For the vow is binding obligation for both.
> If a woman does vow, but her own father hears,
> And restrains her that instant, the vow does not stand.
> If her husband restrains her, the vow disappears,
> But if either waits long, then the vow's her command.

So Moses told to the Children of Israel all that the Lord commanded Moses.

[Matot]

Now Moses spoke to the heads of the tribes of the Children of Israel, saying, "This,
This is the word that the Lord has commanded: Any man who vows a vow to the Lord
Or swears an oath to bind himself by a pledge, that man is not to violate his word,
He shall act according to all that has come out of his mouth, doing as he has said.
And a woman, when she vows a vow to the Lord or binds herself by making a pledge
While in her father's house, in her youth, and her father hears of her pledge or of her vow
And says nothing to her, then her vows will stand, and she shall be bound by all she vowed.
But if her father restrains her when he hears it, he has annulled the vow she has made,
The pledge she bound herself by is void, the Lord will forgive her what her father forbade.
Now the vow of a widow or divorced woman, anything she has vowed on her own,
It shall bind her. And if she vowed or pledged in her husband's house, and to him it was known,
Yet he did not tell her or oppose her, then all the vows and pledges she made shall stand.
But if he annulled them upon hearing it, all of the vows she had spoken and planned,
They shall not be upheld. Her husband has annulled them, and the Lord shall grant her pardon.
Every vow and pledge by which she binds herself, her husband may uphold or void each one.

But if her husband says nothing to her from one day to the next, her vows are upheld,
He has upheld her vows and pledges that bind her, by not speaking to make them annulled
At the time when he heard it. Now if her husband should annul it after hearing it,
Then he is to bear his wife's iniquity, he shall inherit her sin, every bit."

These are the laws that the Lord commanded Moses shall stand between a man and his wife,
And between a father and his daughter, in her father's house, in the youth of her life.

Numbers 31

God told Moses, "Revenge, on the Midianites,
Draft one thousand from each tribe to join the attack."
So twelve thousand were mustered to go on these fights.
All the menfolk, they killed. All the goods, they brought back.
Moses, angry, said, "You left the women alive!
Kill all those who have slept with a man, and their fruit."
Then the spoils were divided, so both camps could thrive;
Both the army and community split the loot.

The Lord said to Moses, "Avenge the Children of Israel on the Midianites,
After which you shall be gathered to your kinsfolk." Moses said to the Israelites,
"Pick men from among you for an attack-force, send them against Midian, to exact
The Lord's vengeance upon Midian. You shall send one thousand from each tribe to attack."
So one thousand from each tribe of Israel were mustered from Israel's divisions,
Twelve thousand men drafted for the attack. Moses sent them out, from each tribe a thousand
To the attack-force, along with Pinhas son of Eleazar, the priest of the armed-force,
With the holy implements and trumpets for sounding the alarm in his hand, of course.
They warred against Midian, as the Lord had commanded Moses, and they killed every male,
The kings of Midian slain with the rest: Evi, Rekem, Tzur, Hur, and Reba were impaled,
The five kings of Midian. And Bilam son of Beor they also had killed with the sword.
And the Children of Israel captured the women of Midian, and all their horde.
All their children, their animals, all of their wealth and all their goods, they took as plunder.
And all their towns, among their settlements and all their villages, they burned with fire.

They took all the plunder and all the captives, men with beasts, and then they brought to Moses,
To Eleazar the priest, and the Israelite community, all that they now possessed.

All the captives and plunder and spoils to the camp, to the Moab plains by the Jordan,
Near Jericho. Moses and Eleazar the priest and the heads of the congregation
Came to meet them outside the camp. And Moses was furious with the army's commanders,
Who returned from the war. He said to them, "You've left alive all of the female gender!
Here, these women were the cause (through the word of Balaam) of the Children of Israel
Turning away from the Lord and breaking faith in the Peor matter, as you know well,
So a plague came against the Lord's community. So, now kill all males of the children,
And kill every woman who has lain with a man. But the younger among the women
Who have not lain with a man, you may keep alive for yourselves. Now, encamp seven days
Outside of the camp, everyone who killed a person or touched a corpse in any way.
Purify yourselves on the third day and on the seventh day, you and your captives too.
Every garment, all things made of skin, goat's hair, or wood are to be purified by you."

Eleazar the priest said to the men of the armed force who now had returned from the war,
"This is the statute of the law which the Lord commanded Moses: All gold and silver,
Bronze, iron, tin, and lead, anything that can stand fire, shall be put through fire to become pure.
However, it shall be purified with the water of separation, to be sure.
Everything that cannot pass through fire, you shall pass through water. You shall then
    wash your clothes
On the seventh day, then you will be purified. Then, back into the camp you may go."
The Lord said to Moses, "Take count of the plunder that was taken, of man and of beast,
You, along with the family heads of the community, and Eleazar the priest.
You shall halve the plunder equally between those wielding swords skillfully in the war
Who went out to the army, and the whole community. Raise a levy for the Lord
From the men of war who went out to the army: One item out of each five hundred,
From humans and cattle, from donkeys and from sheep. From their half-share shall be provided
To Eleazar the priest a contribution for the Lord. And you are also to keep
From the Israelite half-share, one of each fifty, humans, cattle, donkeys, and sheep,
And you shall give them to the Levites, those who have been given charge of the Lord's Dwelling."
Moses and Eleazar did as the Lord commanded Moses. Now the loot remaining
From the spoils that the men of war took was: Six hundred and seventy-five thousand sheep,
Seventy-two thousand cattle, sixty-one thousand donkeys, women who did not sleep
With a man, the full number of persons captured in that way was thirty-two thousand.
And the half-share, the portion of those going out to the war given into their hand:
From the sheep, three hundred thirty-seven thousand, five hundred, of which the Lord's tribute,
Was six hundred seventy-five sheep. Thirty-six thousand cattle their share of the loot,
Of which the Lord's tribute was seventy-two. Their donkeys, thirty thousand five hundred,
Of which their tribute to the Lord was sixty one. Of women who touched no man in bed,
Their share was sixteen thousand persons, of which the tribute to the Lord was thirty-two.
Moses gave the Lord's tribute to Eleazar the priest, as the Lord commanded he do.

Now from the half-share of the Israelites Moses split from what the warring men keep,
The community share, there were three hundred thirty-seven thousand five hundred sheep,
And thirty-six thousand cattle, thirty thousand five hundred donkeys, and of persons,
Sixteen thousand women. Moses took from the Israelite share. For each fifty, one,
One for each fifty of man and beast. And then he gave them to the Levites to possess,
The Levites charged with keeping the Dwelling of the Lord, as the Lord commanded Moses.

Then the commanders of the army, officers over thousands and hundred divisions
Approached Moses and told him, "Your servants have counted our armies, as was your provision,
And not one man has gone uncounted. We have brought the Lord's offering, what
    each man found—
Gold things, armlets and bracelets, rings, earrings, and ornaments, to atone as we are bound,
To atone for ourselves before the Lord's presence." So Moses and Eleazar the priest
Took the gold from them, all crafted articles and jewels, from the greatest to the least.
Now the total of all of the gold of the contribution they offered to the Lord,
Offered by the officers of thousands and those who commanded hundreds as a horde,
Was sixteen thousand seven hundred fifty shekels. (And the men of the armed forces
Had taken plunder, and each man kept for himself the plunder that was his.) So Moses
And Eleazar the priest took the gold from officers of thousands and of hundred hordes,
And brought it to the Tent of Meeting, to remind the Israelites, before the Lord.

Numbers 32

All the Sons of Reuben, also the Sons of Gad,

Had a whole lot of livestock, abundance of cattle.

They said, "Let us have this land in Gilead,

Don't make us cross the Jordan and join in the battle."

But Moses said, "God told all men that can war

To cross over. If you don't, you'll bring ruin to all.

But do so, and the land that you spoke of before

shall be yours, if you'll join us and answer God's call."

Now the Sons of Gad and the Sons of Reuben had livestock, a very great multitude,
And they saw the lands of Jazer and Gilead, fit for livestock to graze and find food.
So the Sons of Reuben and the Sons of Gad came, and said to Moses and Eleazar
The priest, and to the leaders of the community, "Atarot, Divon, and Jazer,

Nimra, Heshbon, and Elaleh, Sebam, Nebo, and Beon, the lands which the Lord struck
Before the community of Israel—it is a land very fit for livestock,
And your servants have livestock." And they said, "If we have found grace in your sight, let this land
Be given to your servants as a holding, don't make us cross the Jordan with our band."

Moses said to the Sons of Gad and the Sons of Reuben, "Shall your brothers go to war,
While you stay here? Why would you discourage the Israelites from crossing to the fore
Of the land which the Lord has given them? That is what your fathers did previously,
When I sent them out of Kadesh Barnea to see the land. They went to the wadi
Of Eshcol, and they saw the land, then they discouraged the heart of the Israelites,
Thus preventing them from going into the land which the Lord gave to them as a right.
And the anger of the Lord flared up on that day, and He swore, 'Not a one of these men
Who came out of Egypt, Twenty years and up, shall see the land I swore to Abraham,
To Issac and to Jacob. For they have not been loyal to Me, not a single one
Except for Caleb son of Jephunneh the Kenizzite, and Joshua son of Nun,
For they were loyal to the Lord.' And the anger of the Lord flared against Israel,
And He had them wander in the wilderness for forty years, until finally fell
The whole generation that had done ill in the eyes of the Lord; it came to an end.
Now here, you have arisen in place of your fathers, another brood of sinful men,
To add more to the Lord's flaming wrath against Israel. If you turn away from him,
He will abandon them in the wilderness once again; you will bring them to ruin."

They came closer to him and said, "We will build sheep fences here for our flocks, and cities
For our children, and we shall go armed before the Children of Israel, all readied
Until we have brought them to their place. But our children shall stay in cities fortified
Against this land's inhabitants. We shall not come back to our houses on our own side
Until the Children of Israel have each inherited their own inheritance.
For we will not inherit with them across the Jordan, or past the Jordan's extent,
Because our inheritance has come to us on the east side of the Jordan River."
Moses said to them, "If you do this thing, if you mobilize before the Lord for war,
And you cross the Jordan, every armed man, before the Lord, until He has driven out
All His enemies from before Him, and the land is subdued before Him without doubt,
After that you may return free of obligation before the Lord and Israel,
This land will be a possession for you before the Lord, a holding where you may dwell.
But if you do not do this, you will have sinned against the Lord, and be sure that your sin
Will find you out. Build cities for your children and sheep fences to keep your livestock in,
And then do what you have promised." The Sons of Gad and Sons of Reuben said to Moses,
"Your servants will do as my lord commands. Our children, wives, and all livestock we possess,
And our animals will stay in the towns of Gilead. Your servants will cross over,
Every man armed for war, before the Lord to battle, as my lord has given orders."

So Moses commanded Eleazar the priest about them, and Joshua son of Nun,
And the heads of the ancestral homes of the Israelites, and Moses told each one,
"If the Sons of Gad and the Sons of Reuben cross over the Jordan River with you,
Every man armed for battle, before the Lord, and before you all the land is subdued,
You may give them the land of Gilead as an inheritance. But if their armed bands
Do not cross over with you, they shall receive possessions among you in Canaan's land."
The Sons of Gad and the Sons of Reuben answered, "What the Lord has said to your servants,
So shall we do: We shall cross over, armed, before the Lord, into the land of Canaan,
And the possession of our inheritance shall remain with us beyond the Jordan."
So Moses gave to them, both to the Sons of Gad, and also to the Sons of Reuben,
And to the half-tribe of Menasseh the son of Joseph, the kingdom of king Sihon,
King of the Amorites, and the kingdom of Og, (who at that time was king of Bashan),
And the land and its cities with their territories, the towns of the surrounding land.
And the Sons of Gad rebuilt Divon, Atarot, Aroer, and Aterot Shofan,
Jazer, Jogbehah, Bet Nimra, and Bet Haran, as fortified cities and sheep fences.
The Sons of Reuben rebuilt Heshbon and Elalei and Kirtatayim's residences,
And Nevo and Baal Meon (some names being changed) and Sibma, and they gave other names
To the cities they built. Then the Sons of Makhir son of Menasseh went out to claim
The land of Gilead. They conquered it and drove out the resident Amorites.
And Moses gave Gilead to Makhir son of Menasseh, the whole land and full rights,
And he settled there. Jair son of Menasseh marched out and conquered their villages,
And he called them Havvot Jair ("Jair's Fortified Villages", for they were now his).
And Novah went out, and Novah conquered Kenat, and its villages and daughter-towns,
And he renamed it Novah, after his own name (for he presumably liked the sound).

Numbers 33

Now the Israelites marched from border to border
From Egypt to Canaan, with all of their force.
Moses wrote down each marching stage, by the Lord's order,
Recording each place they went through on their course.
Aaron died on Mount Hor. The Lord gave this command,
"When you reach Canaan, smash all the idols you view,
Dispossess all the people who live in the land;
If you don't take from them, I will dispossess you."

[Masei]

These are the stages of marching of the Children of Israel that they journeyed on
From the land of Egypt, with their forces, led through by the hand of Moses and Aaron.
Moses wrote down their departures, their marches stage by stage, by the order of the Lord.
Now these are the stages of their march, by place of departure, which Moses did record:
They marched from Ramses in the first month, on the fifteenth day of the month; on the morrow
Of Passover, the Children of Israel left in triumph where all Egypt would know,
In the sight of all Egypt, while Egypt was burying those that the Lord had struck dead—
All their firstborn—and the Lord had executed judgment upon all of their gods' heads.

So the Children of Israel marched on from Ramses, and camped at Sukkot to take rest.
They marched on from Sukkot and camped at Etham, which is at the edge of the wilderness.
They marched on from Etham and turned toward Pi-Hahiroth, which lies east of Baal-Zephon,
And camped before Migdol. They set out from before Pi-Hahiroth, and then they marched on,
Crossing in the midst of the sea into the wilderness, and marching on three days' length
Journeying into the Wilderness of Etham, camping at Mara to regain strength.
They marched on from Mara and came to Elim. At Elim, there were twelve springs of water
And seventy palm trees, and they encamped there. Then they marched on from Elim
     where they were
And encamped by the Sea of Reeds (Red Sea) They marched on from the Sea of Reeds
     and encamped
In the Wilderness of Syn. They marched on from the Wilderness of Syn, and then encamped
In Dofka. They marched on from Dofka and encamped at Alush. They marched on from Alush
And camped at Rephidim, but there was no water there for people to drink, no springs gushed.
They marched on from Rephidim and camped in the Wilderness of Sinai, then they Marched on
From the Wilderness of Sinai and encamped at Kivrot Hatavva. Then they marched on
From Kivrot Hatavva and encamped at Hazeroth. They marched on from Hazeroth and
Camped at Ritma. They marched on from Ritma and encamped at Rimmon Peretz
     with their band.
They marched on from Rimmon Peretz and they encamped at Livna. They marched on
     from Livna
And camped at Rissa. They marched on from Rissa and then they encamped at Kehelata.
They marched on from Kehelata and encamped at Mount Shefer. They marched on
     from the Mount,
Mount Shefer, and encamped at Harada. They marched on from Harada with their full count
And encamped at Makhelot. They marched on from Makhelot and they encamped at Tahat.
They marched on from Tahat and encamped at Terah. They marched on from Terah,
     from that spot,
And camped at Mitka. They marched on from Mitka and camped at Hashmona (as Moses wrote).
They marched on from Hashmona and encamped at Moserot. They marched on from Moserot

And camped at Benei Yakan. They marched on from Benei Yakan, and camped
    near the mountain
At Hor Hagidgad ("The Pass of Hagidgad"). They marched on from Hor Hagidgad and then
They encamped at Yotvata. They marched on from Yotvata and at Avrona they camped.
They marched on from Avrona and camped at Etzion Gever. They marched on from their camp
At Etzion Gever and camped in the Wilderness of Syn (As "Kadesh", it is known).
They marched on from Kadesh and encamped at Mount Hor, at the edge of the land of Edom.

Now Aaron the priest went up on Mount Hor, by the Lord's order, and there he met his end,
In the fortieth year after the Children of Israel went out of Egypt's land,
In the fifth month, on the first day of that month, atop Hill's Hill as ordered by the Lord.
And Aaron was a full one hundred and twenty three years old when he died at Mount Hor.

Now the Canaanite, the king of Arad who ruled over the Negev in Canaan's land,
Heard of the coming of the Children of Israel. They marched from Mount Hor with their band
And encamped at Zalmona. They marched on from Zalmona and they encamped at Punon.
They marched on from Punon and encamped at Ovot. They set out from Ovot and marched on
And encamped at Iyyei Ha-Avarim, which is in the territory of Moab.
They marched on from Iyyim (of the Avarim Mountains) and then encamped at Divon Gad.
They marched from Divon Gad and camped at Almon Divlatayim. They marched on and did go
From Almon Divlatayim and camped in the mountains of Avarim, facing Nevo.
They marched on from the Avarim mountains and camped in the Moab Plains, by Jericho
And the Jordan. They camped on the Jordan, from Bet Yeshimot to Acacia Meadow
(or "Avel Shittim") in the Moab plains. The Lord spoke to Moses in the Moab Plains,
By the Jordan at Jericho, saying, "Speak to all the Children of Israel, saying:
When you cross the Jordan into the Canaan's land, you shall drive out all the inhabitants
Of the land from before you. You shall destroy all of their figured stones (which represent
Other gods). You shall destroy all their molten images, demolish all their cult sites,
So you may take possession of the land and settle in it. It is yours as a right,
For I have given the land to you, to possess it. You shall arrange inheritance
Of the land by lot, according to your clans. Large clans shall get a large inheritance,
And small tribes shall get a small inheritance. Wherever the lot falls for any man,
That shall be what he gets; by your fathers' tribes you shall gain inheritance in this land.
But if you do not drive out the inhabitants of the land before you, and abide,
Those of them who you leave will be like barbs in your eyes, they will be like thorns in your side.
They will assault you on the land that you are settling in, and then it will come true:
That what I had been planning to do to all of them, instead I will do it to you!"

Numbers 34

> God told Moses, "Tell all of the Israelites:
> When you enter the land, Canaan, that you'll possess,
> Your south border shall reach as far as Azmon's heights,
> From the place where it starts in the Sin wilderness.
> Your west border shall be the coast of the Great Sea,
> To the north, the line drawn from Hamath to Zedad.
> The Sea of Salt shall serve as the east boundary."
> And that's how it was measured, the land that they had.

The Lord said to Moses, "Command the Children of Israel and say to all of them:
When you enter the land of Canaan, the land that shall fall to you as inheritance,
The land of Canaan with all its borders: The Southern region from the Syn Wilderness
Alongside Edom, and your southern border from the Sea of Salt (Dead Sea) on the east,
The border shall extend for you, turning to the south of the ascent of Akrabim
(Which means "Scorpion's Pass"), crossing to Zin, the south of Kadesh Barnea its extreme,
Then turning towards Hazar Addar and crossing on to Azmon. Then the border shall bend
From Azmon toward the Wadi of Egypt, and at the sea shall be the boundary's end."

For the Western border, you shall have the Great Sea (Mediterranean) and its coast,
This shall be your western border. And this will be your northern border: You are to post
And mark your line from the Great Sea to Mount Hor. From Mount Hor a line
shall be demarcated
Going to Hamath, and the edge of the border you mark at Zedad shall be located.
Then the border will go out to Zifrom, and its boundaries shall be Hazar Einan;
This shall be the northern border for you. And you shall mark out your boundary eastern,
From Hazar Einan to Shefam, and the border will go down from Shefam to Rivla
On the east side of Ayin ("The Spring"), then the border will go down and brush the shoulder
Of the Sea of Kinneret (or "Galilee") eastward. And then the border will go down
Along the Jordan, ending at the Dead Sea. This will be your land, its borders all round.

Moses commanded the Children of Israel, "This is the land which you shall inherit
By lot, which the Lord has commanded to give to the nine tribes and half-tribe; they shall share it.
For the tribe of the Sons of Reuben, by ancestral house, and tribe of the Sons of Gad,
By ancestral house, and half of the tribe of Menasseh, their land they've already grabbed.
They have already taken their inheritance, the two tribes and also the half-tribe,
They have taken it across from the Jordan at Jericho, to the east, toward sunrise."

The Lord spoke to Moses, saying, "These are the names of the men who shall divide the land
Among you for your inheritance: Eleazar the priest and Joshua son of Nun,
And one leader, you shall take one leader per tribe to arrange the land inheritance.
These are the names of the men: From the tribe of Judah, Caleb the son of Jephunneh.
From the tribe of the Sons of Shimon, Shemuel the son of Ammihud. From the tribe
Of Benjamin, Elidad son of Kislon. From the Sons of Dan, leader for the tribe,
Bukki son of Jogli. From the Sons of Joseph: From the tribe of the Sons of Menasseh,
A leader, Hanniel son of Ephod. From the tribe of the Sons of Ephraim, land-master,
Kemiel son of Shiftan. And the leader from the tribe of the Sons of Zebulun,
Elizafan son of Parnach. And the leader out of the tribe of Issachar's Sons,
Paltiel son of Azzan. From the tribe of the Sons of Asher, leader Ahihud
Son of Shelomi. From the tribe of Naftali's Sons, Pedahel son of Ammihud
As a leader. And these are the names of the men to whom the Lord had given command
To parcel out the inheritance for the Children of Israel, in Canaan's land."

Numbers 35

> God told Moses, "The Levites shall be given land.
> When the Jordan you cross, a few cities you'll choose
> As asylum, so those who have killed men unplanned
> May have somewhere to flee from the ones who accuse.
> If by accident, man stopped another man's breath,
> He shall live. But he dies if he struck with a knife.
> With two witnesses, charged man can be put to death,
> And if guilty, no ransom shall stand for his life.

The Lord said to Moses, in the Plains of Moab by the Jordan nearby Jericho,
"Command the Children of Israel to give, from the inherited lands of their own,
Towns to settle in for the Levites, and pasture land around the towns, give the Levites.
The towns shall be theirs to settle in, and the pasture land for their cattle as a right,
Their pasture land for their property and all their animals. The pastures of the towns
That you give to the Levites shall be from the walls out, one thousand cubits all around.
You shall measure outside the city, the eastern limit shall be two thousand cubits,
The south side, two thousand cubits, the east side, two thousand cubits, the northern limit,
Two thousand cubits, with the town in the middle. This shall serve as the towns' pasture land.
Of the towns you give to the Levites, there shall be six towns of refuge and asylum

Where you shall permit the accidental man-slaughterer to flee, and forty-two more.
So you shall give to the Levites forty-eight towns in total, with their pasture land stores.
And the cities that you give to them from the holdings of the Children of Israel,
You shall take many from the tribes that have many, take few from those that have few as well.
Each in proportion to their inheritance which they inherit, shall give the Levites
Of their cities and towns." The Lord spoke to Moses, saying, "Say to the Israelites:
When you cross over the Jordan, into the land of Canaan, than you shall select towns
To be cities of refuge for you, where accidental man-slaughterers can bed down,
Safe for those to flee to whom have struck down a life in error, without any intent.
The towns shall be refuge from avengers, so the murderer not die before judgment
Can be given, when he comes before the community. And the towns that you provide
Shall be your six towns of refuge. Three shall be across the Jordan, and three on this side
In the land of Canaan. They shall be towns of refuge for the Children of Israel,
For the sojourner, and for the stranger, six towns of refuge to flee to and to dwell
For anyone who strikes down a person in error. But if with an iron instrument
He struck him down so that he died, he is a murderer (since it would imply intent),
And the murderer must be put to death. And if he struck him with a stone in the hand,
By which a man can die, and he died, he is a murderer. You shall heed the command
That the murderer must be put to death. And if he struck with a large wood instrument
By which a man can die, and struck him so he died, then he had a murderous intent.
He is a murderer, and the murderer must be put to death. As for the avenger,
The avenger of blood shall put the murderer to death if they should have an encounter.
Now if he stabbed him in hatred or threw something at him, lying in wait, so he died,
Or struck him with his hand in enmity, so he died, then that action was homicide,
And the one who struck must be put to death, for he is a murderer. And the avenger,
The redeemer of blood shall put the murderer to death if they should have an encounter.

But if he without enmity stabbed him suddenly, without any previous hate,
Or if he had thrown an object at him, some instrument, but was not lying in wait,
Or struck him with a stone without seeing him, dropping it upon him so that he died,
And he was not his enemy, did not wish him ill, the community shall decide.
The community shall judge between the striker and the avenger using these rules,
And the community shall rescue the man-slayer from the avenger who would be cruel,
And the community shall return him to his town of asylum, from which he fled.
He shall stay in it until the high priest anointed with the holy oil is dead.
But if the murderer leaves the borders of the town of asylum that he fled to,
And the blood avenger finds him, outside the border of that town, then it becomes true
That the blood avenger may murder the manslayer, and still no bloodguilt on him lies.
For the manslayer must remain in his town of asylum until the high priest dies.

After the death of the high priest, the manslayer may return to the land of his holding.
These shall be procedural laws for you throughout your generations, in all your dwellings.

If any person should kill another person, only on the word of witnesses
Shall the murderer be put to death, and on the testimony of just one witness
No person shall be put to death. You shall accept no ransom for a murderer's life,
Since he is guilty of death, deserving of death, you shall put him to death, end his life.
And you shall accept no ransom for anyone who has fled to his town of refuge
For him to return and settle in the land until the high priest dies; You must refuse.
You shall not in that way corrupt the land that you are in, for blood would pollute the land,
And the land will not be purged of blood shed on it except through the blood of the same man
Who first shed blood. You shall not pollute the land in which you settle, in whose midst I dwell,
For I am the Lord, the dweller who dwells in the midst of the people of Israel."

Numbers 36

> Then the family heads of the Gilead clan
> Came to Moses and said, "It is by God's command
> That Zelophehad, since he gave birth to no man,
> Would have his daughters inherit his share of land.
> But what if they become married outside our tribe,
> And our inheritance ends up taken away?"
> Moses said by God's word, "It's true, what you describe,
> So from now on, within each tribe, their land shall stay."

The heads of the fathers' houses of the clan of the Sons of Gilead son of Makhir
Son of Menasseh, of the clans of the Sons of Joseph, those family heads came near,
And spoke before Moses and the leaders, the family heads of the Israelites.
They said, "The Lord commanded my lord to give out the land as an inheritance right,
By lot, to the Children of Israel, and my lord has been commanded by the Lord
To give our brother Zelophehad's inheritance to his daughters as an award.
Now if they should be married to men from another tribe among the Israelites,
Their inheritance will be taken away from our fathers' inheritance by right,
And be added to the inheritance of the tribe of whomever they're marrying;
It will be taken from our allotted portion! And when next there is a Homebringing
For the Children of Israel, their inheritance shall add to the share of the tribe
To which they now belong, and their inheritance shall be taken from our fathers' tribe."

So Moses commanded the Children of Israel, by order of the Lord, and said,
"The tribe of the Sons of Joseph has spoken justly. This is what the Lord commanded

About the daughters of Zelophehad: Let them marry whomever suits them most well,
But they must marry within a clan of their father. For the Children of Israel,
Their inheritance shall not go around from tribe to tribe, but each one is to stay bound
To the inheritance of the tribe of his father (that birthright cannot move around).
And every daughter who inherits possession of inheritance among the tribes
Of the Israelites must choose a man from her father's tribe when she becomes a bride,
And serve as his wife, so that each man of the Children of Israel stays in possession
Of the inheritance of his fathers. No tribe's inheritance shall go on procession
From one tribe to another, but each one shall hold his inheritance among the tribes
Of the Children of Israel." The daughters of Zelophehad did as was described,
As the Lord commanded Moses. Mahla, Tirtza, Hogla, Milka, and Noa, all five,
The daughters of Zelophehad married sons of their uncles, staying in the same tribe,
Into the clans of the Sons of Menasseh son of Joseph they married and were wives,
So that their inheritance remained in a tribe which was one of their father's clan's tribes.

These are the commandments and regulations that the Lord commanded, through Moses, to
The Children of Israel in the plains of Moab, by the Jordan at Jericho.

DEUTERONOMY

Deuteronomy 1

Moses said, "The Lord told us: March down to the land
That I swore to your fathers. I had realized
I couldn't solve all your problems with just my own hand,
So I picked some wise judges. And then we sent spies
To the land we would enter. They said it was great,
But you would not trust God, and you stayed back, in fear.
Thus aside from Caleb and Joshua, your fate
Was to never set foot over that land's frontier."

[Devarim]

These are the words that Moses spoke to all Israel in the land across the Jordan
In the Wilderness, in the plains near Suph, 'tween Paran and Tophel, Hazeroth, Laban,
And Dizahab. It is eleven days' journey from Horeb, by the route of Mount Seir,
To Kadesh Barnea (the base camp for their wanderings). And in the fortieth year,
On the first day of the eleventh month, Moses spoke to the Children of Israel
According to all that the Lord had commanded him about them, after he had felled
Both Sihon king of the Amorites, who ruled in Heshbon, and Og the king of Bashan,
Who ruled in Ashtaroth and also ruled in Edrei. In the land across the Jordan,
In the land of Moab, Moses set about to explain this law's instruction and said:

The Lord our God said to us at Horeb, "You've stayed long enough on this mountain. Instead,
Turn and take your journey to the hill country of the Amorites, and all their neighbors
In the plains, in the hill-country and the lowlands, in the desert and in the sea-shore,
The land of the Canaanites and the Lebanon, as far as Euphrates the great river.
Behold, I set the land before you, enter, take possession of the land I deliver,
Which the Lord swore to your fathers, to Abraham, to Isaac, and to Jacob to give
To them, and also to their offspring which come after them, all their descendants that live."
Now I said to you then, "I cannot carry you alone; the Lord your God multiplied you,
And today you are many like the stars in heaven. May the Lord, God of your fathers do
As He did before, increasing your number a thousand fold, and give you His blessing,
As He promised you. How can I alone carry you, your burden, and your quarreling?

Choose wise men, understanding and experienced, for your tribes, I'll appoint them as heads

Over you." And you answered me, saying, "What you propose is good, we like what you said."

So I took the heads of your tribes, wise and experienced men, and set them over you

As heads, commanders of thousands, of hundreds, of fifties, of tens, officers too,

Throughout your tribes. And I charged your judges then, "Hear out disputes between your
    fellow men,

Judge righteously between any man and his brother, or a sojourning alien.

You shall not be partial in judgment, hear the small and great alike, and fear no man's face,

For the judgment is God's. And any case too hard for you, bring to me, I'll hear the case."

And I commanded you at that time concerning all of the matters that you should do.

We set out from Horeb, and went through all the great and fearsome wilderness you did view,

By the Amorite hill-country route, as the Lord our God commanded us, and came we

As far as Kadesh Barnea. And I said to you, "You have come to the hill-country

Of the Amorites, which the Lord our God gives us. Behold, the Lord your God sets this land

Before you, go up and take possession of it, which God has given into your hand,

As the Lord the God of your fathers promised you. Do not be afraid, don't be dismayed."

Then you all came near me and said, "Let us send men before us, to see how things are laid

In the land, so that they may explore the land for us, and then bring us word of what route

We should use to go up against it, and information on the towns we will come to."

This all seemed good to me, so I took twelve men from among you, twelve men, one
    from each tribe.

They turned and went up into the hill country up to the Wadi of Eshcol, and spied.

Then they took in their hands some of the fruit of the land with them, and they brought it
    down to us,

And returned, bringing us word. They said, "It is a good land that the Lord our God gives us."

Yet you would not go up, but instead rebelled against the command of the Lord your God.

And you muttered in your tents, "Because the Lord hated us, he took us from Egypt's sod,

To give us into the hand of the Amorites, to destroy us! Where do we go up?

Our brothers made our hearts melt and said, 'People there are much greater with heads higher up,

With great towns fortified to the skies, and we have even seen Sons of Anakim there.'"

Then I said to you, "Do not have dread or be afraid of them. With God, you need not fear.

The Lord your God who goes before you will wage war for you, just as he did in Egypt,

Before your eyes, and in the wilderness where you saw how the Lord your God was equipped

To bear you as a man carries his son, all the way from there until you reached this place."

Yet despite this, you have shown no faith in the Lord your God, who proceeds you in each case,

To seek you out a place to pitch your tents, in fire by night, and to have you see the way

That you should go, and in cloud by day. When the Lord heard the sound of the words
    you did say,

He was angered! He swore, "Not one of these men of this evil generation shall see

The good land which I swore to give to their fathers. Only Caleb, Jephunneh's son, he,

He shall see it, to him and his children I shall give the land that he has tread upon.

For he has wholly followed the Lord." And the Lord was angry with me for what went on,

Because of you, he said, "You also shall not enter there. Joshua the son of Nun,
Who stands before you, he shall enter. Encourage him, because Joshua son of Nun
Shall allot it as inheritance to Israel. Now your little ones who you said
Would be taken for plunder, and your children who don't yet know good or ill in their heads,
They shall enter there, and I shall give it to them, and the shall possess it. As for you,
Turn and journey into the wilderness in the direction towards the Red Sea route."
But you spoke up and answered me, "We have sinned against the Lord, we will go up and fight,
Just as the Lord our God commanded us." And each man girded on his war-weapons tight,
And recklessly set off for the hill country. But God said me, "Warn them, do not go,
For I am not in your midst, and you would be routed by your enemies, and brought low."
So I spoke to you, but you would not heed, and rebelled against the command of the Lord,
Brazenly going up in the hills. Then the Amorites who lived there, with all their hordes,
Came out to fight you. They chased you like bees do and crushed you as far as Horma, at Seir.
When you returned, you wept before the Lord's presence, but the Lord did not give you His ear,
The Lord did not pay heed to the cries of your voice. So it was in Kadesh that you stayed,
You remained at Kadesh for many days, all that long time you remained there, many days.

Deuteronomy 2

> "Then God told me: Leave Esau and Moab alone,
> I have given them land; Cross the Wadi Zered.
> So we crossed through the wadi into Moab's zone,
> But we left them alone, just as the Lord had said.
> Then God told me: March on, cross the Wadi Arnon,
> And reach Sihon; you may take his land in a war.
> We sent peace messengers, but they were frowned upon,
> So God gave us a victory, just as He swore."

Then we turned and journeyed into the wilderness in the direction of the Red Sea,
As the Lord had told me, we circled Mount Seir for many days. Now the Lord said to me,
"You have gone around this hill country long enough! Turn northward, and command the people,
You shall soon pass through the territory where your brethren the sons of Esau have pull.
They live in Seir, and though they are afraid of you, take much care and with them do not fight,
For I will not give you any of their land, not even where one foot's sole would alight,
For I gave Mount Seir to Esau as a possession. You shall buy food from them for money,
So you may eat. And so you may drink, you are also to buy water from them for money.

For the Lord your God has blessed you in all the work of your hands, He knows you
    travel through
This great wilderness. You lacked nothing these forty years the Lord your God has been with you."
So we crossed by, away from our brethren the sons of Esau who live in Seir, away
From the Arabah road, from Eilat and Ezion Geber, we turned the other way,
And went in the direction of the wilderness of Moab. And the Lord said to me,
"Do not harass Moab or engage them in battle, for I will not give you any
Of their land as a possession, because to the Children of Lot I have given Ar
As a possession." (The Emites (frightful-ones) formerly lived there, a people who are
Great and many, as tall as the Anakim. And like them, they are called "Rephaim" (shades),
But the Moabites call them Emites. Now in Seir the Horites had formerly stayed,
But the sons of Esau dispossessed them, destroying them and settling in their place,
Just as Israel did to the land of their possession, which the Lord gave them, in grace.)
"Now rise up, cross the Wadi Zered!" So we crossed the Wadi Zered. And all the time
That we traveled from Kadesh Barnea until we crossed the Wadi Zered on our climb
Totaled thirty-eight years, until the entire generation, that is, the men of war
Had perished from the camp, just as the Lord had sworn would occur concerning them before.
Yes, the Lord's hand was against them, to destroy them from the camp until they were all dead.
When all the men of war had died from amidst the people, the Lord spoke to me, and said,
"Today you shall cross the territory of Moab, through Ar, near to the Ammonites.
When you approach their territory, be sure not to harass them or start any fights,
For I will not give you any of the land of the sons of Ammon as a possession,
Because I have already given all this land to the sons of Lot as a possession."
(It too is known as a land of Rephaim, Rephaim settled there in former dates,
But the Ammonites call them "Zamzummites" (barbarians), a people many and great,
Tall like the Anakim, yet the Lord wiped them out, and the Ammonites dispossessed them,
And settled in their place, as He did for the sons of Esau who live in Seir. For them,
He destroyed the Horites before them, and they dispossessed them, and settled in their stead,
Until this very day. And as for the Avvites who were all settled in villages
As far as Gaza, Caphtorites from Caphtor (Crete) destroyed them and settled in their place.)
"Now rise up, march and cross the Wadi Arnon. Behold, I give into your hand by grace
Sihon the Amorite, king of Heshbon, and his land. Now start! Start to take possession,
And wage war against him. This day I will put a dread of you and fear of you upon
The peoples that are under the heaven, who shall hear reports of you and feel anguish,
And writhe in fear because of you." Then I sent messengers from Kedemoth's wilderness
To Sihon the king of Heshbon, with words of peace, saying, "Let me pass through your country.
I will stay on the highway, not turning aside right or left. Food you shall sell to me
For money, so I may eat. And so I may drink, you shall sell me water for money,
Just let me pass through on foot, as the sons of Esau who settled in Seir did for me,
As did the Moabites who are settled in Ar, until I cross over the Jordan
Into the land which the Lord our God gives to us." But Sihon, who was king of Heshbon,

Was not willing to let us pass by him, for the Lord your god had hardened his spirit
And stiffened his heart, in order to give him into your hand, as this day shall be fit.
And the Lord said to me, "Behold, I have begun to give Sihon and his land to you,
Start to take possession of it, so you may possess his land." Then Sihon and his crew
Came out to meet us, he and all his warriors, to battle at Jahaz. And the Lord
Our God delivered him before us, and we defeated him, and his sons, and his horde.
We conquered all his towns at that time, and every town we devoted to destruction,
We destroyed all the men, all the women, and the little ones, to remain we left none.
Only the cattle did we plunder for ourselves, and the booty of the conquered cities.
From Aroer, on the bank of the Wadi Arnon, and the city in the Wadi,
As far as Gilead, there was not a city among them that was too high for us,
All of them the Lord our God delivered into our hands, he gave them all before us.
Only the land of the Ammonites you did not approach, to the banks of the Wadi
Jabbok, and the towns of the hill country, where the Lord God had commanded we not be.

Deuteronomy 3

"We went up to face Og, in the land of Bashan,
And God gave us a victory over each town.
We destroyed them, like Sihon who ruled in Heshbon,
Every city we conquered, and then struck it down.
Then I told you: God gives you this land where you go.
And I wanted to enter, so to God I prayed.
God said: Don't ask again, I've already said no,
But train Joshua to. Near Bet Peor we stayed.

Then we turned and went up the route to Bashan, and Og king of Bashan came out to fight,
He and all his warriors, to face us at Edrei. And the Lord told me, "Have no fright
Of him, for into your hand I give him and all of his people and all of his land,
And you shall do to him as you did to Sihon king of the Amorites at Heshbon."
And the Lord our God also gave into our hand Og, king of Bashan, and all his men,
We struck him until not one survivor was left. We conquered all his cities, and then
There was no city we did not take from them. Sixty cities, the whole of Argob's region,
The kingdom of Og in Bashan. All these were fortified towns, with high walls by the legions,
And barred gates, besides the many unwalled cities. And we devoted them to destruction,
As we had done to Sihon king of Heshbon, destroying all as was the Lord's instruction,

Every city, men, women, and children. But cattle and plunder we took as our right.
So at that time we took the land out of the hand of the two kings of the Amorites,
Who were in the land beyond the Jordan, from the Wadi of Arnon to Mount Hermon,
(Which the Amorites called Senir, though the Sidonians called it Hermon Sirion),
All the towns of the plateau and all Gilead, and all Bashan, as far as Salcah
And Edrei, cities of the kingdom of Og in Bashan. (For there remained only Og
King of Bashan from all the Rephaim. Behold, his bedstead was an iron bedstead,
And is now in Rabba (Amman) of the Ammonites, nine cubits length, four cubits breadth,
By a standard man's arm length cubit.) And at that time we took possession of this land,
From Aroer by the Wadi Arnon, half Mount Gilead I gave into the hand
Of the Reubenites and the Gadites, along with its towns. All Gilead that remains,
And all of Bashan, Og's kingdom, I give to the half-tribe Menasseh, All Argob's plains,
Including all of Bashan (Which is called the land of the Rephaim). Jair, the son
Of Menasseh, took all of the territory of Argob, as far as the region
Of the Geshurites and the Maacathites, and called them (the Bashan towns) by his name,
"Havvot-Jair" ("Tent Villages of Jair"), and until this day it has stayed the same.
Now to Makhir I gave Gilead, and to the Reubenites and the Gadites as well
I gave from Gilead, as far as Wadi Arnon, the boundary of where they dwell
Marked by the middle of the Wadi, as far as the Wadi Jabbok, the boundary
Of the Ammonites, and the Arabah to the Jordan, from the Sea of Galilee
(The Kinneret) to the Sea of Arabah, the Sea of Salt (Dead Sea) under the hills
Of the Pisgah range to the east. And I commanded you at that time with the Lord's will,
Saying, "The Lord your God has given you this land to possess. All your war-ready men
Must go armed in front of your brethren, the Children of Israel. Your wives and children,
And your livestock (I know you have many livestock) shall remain in the towns I give you,
Until the Lord gives rest to your brethren as you have, and they have gained possession too
Of the land that the Lord gives them beyond the Jordan, each man shall return to his land,
And his possession that I give you." Now at that time I gave Joshua this command,
"Your eyes have seen all that the Lord your God has done to these two kings (both
    Og and Sihon),
And so will the Lord do to all the kingdoms whose land you go over to walk upon.
You shall not fear them, for it is the Lord your God who will fight for you."

[Va'etchanan]

Now I implored
The Lord then, "My Lord God, You have begun to show Your servant the greatness of the Lord,
Your greatness and Your strong hand, for what god in heaven and earth can do what
You have done,
Who has power like Yours? Pray let me cross over to see the good land past the Jordan,
That good hill country, and the Lebanon." But the Lord was cross with me on your account,
And He would not heed me. The Lord told me, "Enough for you! Speak no more to Me about

This matter. Go up to the top of the Pisgah range, and look around. Lift up your eyes
To the west toward the sea, to the north, and to the south, and to the west toward the sunrise,
See it with your eyes, for you will not cross the Jordan. But charge Joshua, make him strong
And encourage him, for he will cross over ahead of these people in not too long,
And he will put them in possession of this land you see, and make them inherit it,
All the land which you shall see." And we stayed in the valley, with Bet Peor opposite.

Deuteronomy 4

> "Now, O Israel, heed all the laws that I teach,
> And the rules God commanded that I command you.
> When at Horeb, the Lord's presence spoke to you each,
> Saying: Don't pray to idols, whatever you do.
> So take care, as you enter the land, heed this law.
> For when you get old, if to false idols you pray,
> You shall suffer. For who else has seen what you saw,
> All the glory of God. Keep his rules, do not stray."

"And now, O Israel, heed the laws and instructions I am teaching you to observe,
So that you may live to enter and take possession of the land the Lord has preserved,
The land the Lord, the God of your fathers, is giving to you. To my word, do not add
To the things I command you. And do not subtract from it either (that is just as bad).
Keep the commandments of the Lord your God that I command you. You saw with
     your own eyes
What the Lord did at Baal-peor, every man among you the Lord God pulverized,
All who followed Baal-peor. But those who held fast to the Lord your God live today.
Behold, I have taught you the laws and instructions as the Lord God commanded I say,
That you should follow in the land you enter to posses. Keep and observe all these words,
For that will be your wisdom and understanding in the sight of peoples. When they've heard
All these laws, they will say, 'surely this great nation are people understanding and wise,
For what nation is so great that gods are as near to it as the Lord our God resides,
Near to us whenever we call upon Him? What great nation has instructions and laws
As righteous and perfect as the ones I have set before you this day, which you all saw?

But take heed, and take care of your lives diligently, lest you forget what you have seen,
So these things do not fade from your mind while you live. Make them known to children
     of your genes,

And your children's children: The day you stood at Horeb before the Lord your God, the Lord
Said to me, 'Gather the people to Me so they may hear My words, and they in accord
Shall learn to revere Me all the days that they live on the earth, and teach their children so.'
And you came near and stood at the foot of the mountain, which burned with a fiery glow,
Fires burning to the heart of heaven, in fog-clouded darkness. The Lord spoke to you,
From the midst of the fire; you heard the sound of words, but there was no form you could view,
Just a voice. He declared to you His covenant, which He commanded you to observe,
The Ten Commandments; And He inscribed them upon two stone tablets to keep
    them preserved.
At that time the Lord commanded me to teach you the laws and instructions to live by,
So that you would observe them in the land that you are going over to occupy.

Now take care for yourselves, for you saw no form on the day the Lord spoke to you from fire
At Horeb: 'Beware, lest you act wickedly and sculpt yourself an idol to admire,
In the form of any figure, likeness of male or female, the form of any beast
That is on the earth, the form of any winged bird in the sky, or the form of the least

Of the things that crawl on the ground, the form of any fish living in underground seas.
And beware lest you raise your eyes up to the heavens, and the sun, moon, and stars you see,
And on seeing the host of the heavens you are drawn away to worship and serve them,
Which the Lord has allotted for all of the peoples everywhere under the heavens.
But the Lord took and brought you out of Egypt, out of that iron blast furnace, to be
His people, as you are this day. Now, because of your words, the Lord was angry with me
And He swore that I should not cross the Jordan, and should not enter into the good land
Which the Lord your God is giving you as inheritance. For I must die in this land,
I shall not cross the Jordan; but you shall cross over and of that good land take possession.
So take care not to forget the covenant the Lord your God cut with you, lest transgression
Be committed by making a carved image, anything the Lord forbade you should fashion.
For the Lord your God is a devouring fire, a jealous God who is impassioned.

When you bear children, and your children have born children, and you have grown old
    in the land,
If you act corruptly by making a carved image in any form God did command
That you not make, thus doing ill in the Lord's sight, causing him displeasure and vexation,
I call heaven and earth this day to witness against you, you shall face annihilation.
You shall perish from the land you cross the Jordan to possess, you shall not long endure,
But will be utterly destroyed. The Lord will scatter you among the peoples, ensure
That only a scant few of your men remain among the nations where God scatters you.
And there you will serve gods man-made of wood and stone, who do not see, hear, eat,
    or smell. You
Will be driven to this, but if from there you search for the Lord your God, He you will find,
If you search after him with all of your heart, with all of your soul, and all of your mind.

When you are in distress because all of these things have befallen you in later days,
You shall return to the Lord your God and heed His voice. For the Lord your God in his ways
Is a merciful God, a compassionate God. He will not forsake or destroy you,
He will not forget the covenant with your fathers that He made an oath and swore to.

For ask now of past days before you, from the day that God created mankind on earth,
And ask from one end of heaven to the other, if there ever has been given birth
To such a great thing as the Lord created. Has its like ever been known to transpire?
Did any people ever hear the voice of a god speaking from the midst of the fire,
As you have, and survived? Or has any God ventured to come and take himself a nation
From the midst of another, with signs, portents, wonders, and war, as in your situation,
With a strong hand and outstretched arm, and awesome power, as God in Egypt did for you
Before your eyes? You have been shown that the Lord is God, and none beside Him. This is true.
From the heavens He let you hear His voice to discipline you. On earth he let you see
His great fire, and you heard his words from the midst of the fire. And now because He
Loved your fathers, He chose their offspring after them, and He Himself with his awesome might
Brought you out of Egypt, to drive from your path nations stronger than you (so they'd
    take flight),
To bring you into their land and give it to you as inheritance, as is today.
So know this day and keep in it your mind and heart that the Lord is God in every way,
In the heavens above and the earth below, there is no other. Therefore, you shall keep
His laws and commandments I command you today, so that in the future you may reap
Good fortune, and things will go well for you and your children after you, you will all thrive
And prolong your time on the land the Lord God gives to you for all days yet to arrive."

Then Moses set apart three cities on the east of the Jordan, to which a manslayer
Could flee if he killed his neighbor with no malice aforethought, no hatred did he bear
Towards him in the past. He could flee to one of these three cities and thus stay alive:
Bezer, in the wilderness of the Tableland plateaus owned by the Reubenite tribe,
Ramoth, in Gilead of the Gadites, and Golan, in Bashan of the Manassites.

This is the law and instruction which Moses set before all of the Israelites,
These are the precepts, laws, and regulations Moses spoke to the children of Israel
When they came out of Egypt, past the Jordan, across from where Bet Peor was revealed,
In a valley in the land of Sihon, the Amorite king, who ruled Heshbon with clout,
Whom Moses and the Children of Israel defeated, when from Egypt they came out.
And they took possession of his land, and also the land of Og, the king of Bashan,
The two kings of the Amorites who were on the east of the Jordan, now their land was gone.
The Israelites took possession of the land from Aroer which was near Arnon,
On the banks of the Wadi, as far as the peak of Mount Sion (now known as Hermon),
And all of the plains of Arabah on the east side of the Jordan, all of the plains
From that point to the Sea of Arabah, which lay beneath the slopes of the Pisgah range.

Deuteronomy 5

Moses said, "God made this covenant with us all,
Saying: I am the Lord, have no gods before Me,
Don't make idols, don't pray to a graven carved doll,
Don't take My name in vain, keep the Sabbath holy,
Honor your parents; don't murder, adulter, steal,
Bear false witness, or covet your neighbor's possessions.
So you heard all this word that the Lord did reveal,
And God told me you'll live, if you follow these lessons."

Moses summoned all Israel and said to them, "Hear, O Israel, all of the laws
And instructions I speak in your ears this day. You shall learn them and observe them because
The Lord our God cut a covenant with us at Horeb, not our fathers far away,
But the Lord made the covenant with us, we who are living, and are all here today.

Face to face the Lord spoke to you on the mountain from the midst of the fire, while I
Stood between the Lord and you to report the Lord's word to you; for you were terrified
Of the fire, so you did not go up the mountain. But the Lord spoke to you and said:
'I am the Lord your God, who brought you out of the land of Egypt, the house of bondage.
You shall have no other gods before me. You shall not make for yourself carved idols, no,
Nor any likeness of any thing in the heavens above or on earth down below,
Or in the waters under the earth. You shall not bow down to them, or serve them, for I
The Lord your God am a jealous God, visiting the guilt of the fathers from on high
Upon their sons to the third and fourth generations of those who have rejected Me,
But showing steadfast love to the thousands that love Me and keep My commandments. Keep the
Sabbath day, keep it holy, as the Lord your God commanded you. For six days labor,
And do all of your work, but the seventh day shall be a Sabbath of your God the Lord.
You shall not do any work on that day, not you, nor your son, nor your daughter, nor slave,
Nor your ox, nor your donkey, nor any of your cattle, nor strangers in your enclave,
So your slaves and maidservants shall rest just like you. For remember that in Egypt's land,
You were a slave, and the Lord your God brought you out with an outstretched arm and
    mighty hand.
Therefore the Lord your God commands you to keep the Sabbath day. Honor your mom and dad,
As the Lord your God commanded you, so you may long endure, and fare well (and not bad)
In the land the Lord your God gives you. You shall not kill. You shall not commit adultery.
You shall not steal. You shall not bear false witness against your neighbor. Don't let jealousy

Cause you to covet your neighbor's wife; You shall not desire to possess your neighbor's house,
Nor his field, his slave, his maidservant, his ox, his donkey—do not covet his spouse,
Nor any other thing of your neighbor's.' These words the Lord spoke to your whole assembly
At the mountain from the midst of the fire and fog-clouded darkness, with a loud voice. He
Added no more, but wrote them upon two tablets of stone, which He gave to me. And when
You heard the voice from the darkness, while the mountain burned with fire, and all of your men,
All your tribal leaders and your elders approached me, and said, 'the Lord our God has shown
Us His Glory and greatness, we heard His voice from out of the fire, let it be known
That this day we have seen that God can speak to humans and that they can remain alive!
But let us not die, for if we hear the Lord our God's voice longer, we shall not survive,
And this fearsome fire will consume us. For what mortal has heard the voice of a live God,
From the midst of the fire, as we have, and lived? You go closer where we dare not trod,
And you hear all the Lord our God says, and you tell us what the Lord our God speaks to you.
And once you tell us everything the Lord our God has said, that's what we will hear, and do.'

And the Lord heard the voice of your words, when you spoke to me, and then the Lord
    said to me,
'I have heard the voice of this people's words, that they spoke to you, and they spoke correctly.
Would that their hearts would always make them hold Me in awe, and keep all of My
    commandments,
So 'twill go well for them and their children forever. Go tell them, "Return to your tents."
But you, stand here by Me, and I'll tell you all the commandments, statutes, and instruction
Which you shall teach them, so they can observe them in the land I give for their possession.'
You shall take care to do as the Lord your God has commanded; you shall not turn aside
To the right or the left. Walk in ways by which the Lord your God commanded you abide,
In order that you may continue to live, and it may go well for you, and be blessed
So that you may prolong the days of your life in the land you are going to possess.

Deuteronomy 6

> "Now this is the commandment which God has commanded
> I teach you, your children, and their children too.
> The Lord our God is One, and these words shall be branded
> On your heart, your doorposts, and all that you do.
> When God brings you to enter the land that He swore
> To your fathers, take care that the Lord you still serve.
> Do not serve other gods, as you did once before
> At Massah, or God's wrath will be what you deserve."

Now this is the commandment, the laws and instructions the Lord your God commanded me
To teach you to observe in the land you will cross over to possess, so it may be
That you may hold the Lord your God in awe, keeping all His commandments I tell to you,
You, and your child, and your child's child, all the days of your life, so many days you'll accrue.
Hear, O Israel, and take care to observe them, so that you may multiply greatly,
And so that things may go well for you, in a land that is flowing with milk and honey,
As the Lord, the God of your fathers, promised you. Hear, O Israel, the Lord our God,
The Lord is One. You shall with all your heart, all your mind, all your soul love the
    Lord your God.
Take to heart these instructions with which I charge you this day, teach them well to
    your children.
You shall talk of them when you sit in your house and when you are walking away, and when
You are lying down and when you rise. Bind them as a sign on your hand, and frontlet plates
Between your eyes. And you shall inscribe them on the doorposts of your house, and on
    your gates.

When the Lord your God brings you into the land which he swore to your fathers, Abraham,
Isaac, and Jacob, to give you—with good and great towns of which you did not build a gram,
Houses filled with good things you did not fill, and wells dug that you did not dig, olive trees
And vineyards that you did not plant—And when you eat and are full, be sure that you take heed
That you do not forget the Lord who freed you from Egypt's land, a house of bondage low.
You shall fear the Lord your God, and serve him, and swear by His name. You are not to follow
Other gods, any gods of the peoples around you (for the Lord your God in your midst
Is a jealous God), lest the Lord's anger be kindled against you and you not exist
When He destroys you from the face of the earth. Do not test the Lord your God as you did
At Massah. Be sure to keep the commandments of the Lord your God, all the laws He bid

That you follow. Do what is good and right in the Lord's sight, so it may go well for you,
And you may go in and take possession of the land which the Lord swore he would give to
Your fathers, by pushing out your enemies from before you, as the Lord has promised.
When your child asks you in time to come, 'What mean all the rules, statutes, and laws in the list
Which the Lord our God commanded you?' You shall say to the child, 'In Egypt we were slaves
To the Pharaoh, and the Lord brought us out of Egypt, by His mighty hand we were saved.

The Lord worked portents and wonders, both great and grievous against Egypt, on Pharaoh
And all his house, before our eyes. He brought us out of there, so He could take us to show
Us and give us the land that he swore to our fathers. The Lord commanded we observe
All these laws and statutes, to hold the Lord our God in awe, so that we may be preserved
And have things go well for us, as is now the case. 'Twill be merit to God, and righteous
Before the Lord our God to observe these laws in good faith as He has commanded us.

Deuteronomy 7

"When God brings you into the land you will invade
And dislodges the nations that stand in your path,
Show no mercy to them, let no marriage be made,
Lest they turn you from God, and incur the Lord's wrath.
You are God's treasured people, you're holy to God,
So keep all of these rules I command you today.
Do not fear all your foes, though a numerous squad,
For with God on your side, none can stand in your way.

When the Lord your God brings you into the land you enter to possess, and with His might,
He dislodges great nations before you - the Hittites, the Girgishites, the Amorites,
Canaanites, Perizzites, Hivites, and Jebusites, seven nations much larger than you -
And the Lord your God delivers them to you and you destroy them, then what you must do
Is doom them to destruction. Grant them no terms, show them no mercy. Do not intermarry,
You shall not give your daughters to their sons, nor take their daughters for your sons. To so tarry
Would cause them to turn your children away from Me, and serve other gods. Then the anger
Of the Lord would be kindled against you, and swiftly destroy you. So you should be sure
To do this to them: Tear down their altars, smash their pillars, cut their sacred trees to shreds,
Burn their carved images with fire! To the Lord God, you are a people consecrated.
The Lord your God has chosen you to be His treasured people. Not because you are many
Has the Lord set His heart on you and chosen you, (Are nations smaller than you? Not any!)

But because the Lord loves you, and keeps the oath he swore with your fathers. He brought
    you out
With a mighty hand, and redeemed you from a house of bondage, where the Pharaoh held clout
As the King of Egypt. Know therefore that the Lord your God is God, and a faithful one
Who keeps His covenant of loyalty and mercy to the thousandth generation
Of those who love Him and keep His commandments. Those who hate Him, He will
    swiftly repay
To their face by destroying them; those who reject Him he will punish without delay.
 So observe faithfully the commandment, the laws and instructions that I command you
On this day.

[Eikev]

        And because you obey these commandments as ones to observe and to do,
The Lord your God will keep the covenant He swore with your fathers. He will love and bless
You and multiply you, bless the fruit of your body, and the fruit of your soil. Yes,
He will bless your grain and your wine and your oil, increase your cattle, the young of your flock,
In the land He swore to your fathers to give you. And so among all of your livestock,
There will be no barren animals, male or female. And you shall be blessed above all,
The Lord will remove all sickness from you, on you none of Egypt's diseases will fall,
But he will inflict them on your enemies. You shall destroy all the peoples the Lord
Your God delivers to you, showing them no pity. Their gods are all to be ignored,
Do not worship them and let them snare you. If you say to yourselves, "These nations for sure
Are much larger than us, how can we dispossess them?" You need not fear them. Remember
What the Lord your God did to Pharaoh and all Egypt, the great trials that your eyes saw,
The portents and the wonders, the mighty hand and outstretched arm that you all held in awe,
By which the Lord your God brought you out. He will do the same to all the peoples you fear.
The Lord your God will send a stinging plague among them, until all those who disappeared
Into hiding have all perished. Do not dread them, for the Lord your God is among you,
A great and awesome God. The Lord your God will dislodge these nations, take them few by few,
You may not finish them off all at once, lest the scavenging beasts reach such a profusion
That they overwhelm you. The Lord your God will deliver them to you, causing confusion
And panic in their ranks, until they are destroyed. He will give their kings into your hand,
So that you will obliterate their name from under the heavens. Not one man will stand
Up to you, until you have destroyed them. The carved-images of their gods burn with fire,
Do not covet the silver or gold that is on them, nor take it to fill your desire,
Lest you be ensnared by it, for it is an abomination to the Lord your God,
Nor shall you bring an abomination into your house, for if this path you do trod,
You shall become an accursed abomination just like it. So you must abhor
It as an abomination, for it shall be an accursed thing forever more.

Deuteronomy 8

> "Observe all the commandments I'm telling to you.
> Now, when God made you wander, your foot did not swell.
> Your clothes never wore out, all the forty years through,
> For because of the Lord, everything will go well.
> So take care that the Lord your God you don't forget,
> Don't say, "God didn't help me, my gain is my choice."
> If you do, or serve other gods, this you'll regret
> When you perish, for failing to heed the Lord's voice."

All the commandment that I command you today, you shall take care to observe and do,
So you may live and multiply, going in to possess the land the Lord promised to
Your fathers. And you shall remember the long way that the Lord your God led you to go
During these forty years in the wilderness, testing you with many hardships to know
What was in your hearts, whether you would keep His commandments or not. He subjected you
To afflictions of hunger, then fed you with manna which not you nor your fathers knew,
So that you might learn that man does not live by bread alone but all that leaves the
        Lord's mouth;
By all that the Lord orders does man stay alive. The clothing on you did not wear out,
Nor did your feet swell, these forty years. Know in your heart that the Lord gives you discipline
As a father disciplines his son. So keep the commandments of the Lord God. Walk in
The Lord's ways, and hold Him in awe. For the Lord your God brings you into a good land,
        with springs,
Streams of water, and fountains that flow from the valleys and hills. Land where wheat is growing,
And barley, vines, figs, and pomegranates, a land of oil, and honey, and olive trees,
A land where you will eat bread without running out, you will lack nothing for scarcity,
A land whose stones are iron and from whose hills you can mine copper. When you eat and chew,
And have had your fill, you shall bless the Lord your God for the good land He has given you.
Take care, lest you forget the Lord your God and fail to keep His commandments, all his laws
And his instructions, which I command you this day. When you have eaten to fill your jaws,
And have built fine houses to live in, and when your flocks have multiplied, as have your herds,
And your silver and gold have all multiplied, as have all things that you own, all prospered,
Beware lest your heart rise to be haughty, forgetting the Lord your God who brought you out
From the land of Egypt, the house of bondage, who led you through the wilderness of drought,
A great and terrible wilderness with burning snakes and scorpions, and thirsty ground
where there was no water, who brought you water out of the flinty rock where none was found,

Who fed you in the wilderness with manna which your fathers had never known, to test
You and humble you briefly in order to do you good in the future. Beware, lest
You say to yourselves, "My power and my own mighty hand have produced this wealth for me."
You shall bear in mind the Lord your God for it is He who gave you the power and He
Who lets you produce wealth, to establish His covenant that He swore with your fathers,
As is still the case. If you forget the Lord your God, and follow other gods to serve
And worship, I warn you today that you will perish. Just like the nations that the Lord
Will destroy before you, so shall you be destroyed, for not obeying your God the Lord.

Deuteronomy 9

"Hear O Israel: When the Lord gives you this land,
It is not because you are so righteous or great,
But because of your fathers. Your own foolish hand
Melted gold for an idol you worked to create,
And this sin made the Lord fill with anger and ire;
He would have destroyed you if I had not said:
'My Lord, please do not kill all your people with fire,
Remember your servants, and don't leave them dead.'"

Hear O Israel! You shall cross the Jordan this day to enter and to dispossess
Nations stronger and larger than you, great cities fortified to the heavens, no less.
A people great and tall, the Children of the Anakites, of whom you know; you have heard
People say, 'Who can stand before the Children of Anak?' But on this day be assured
That the Lord your God is the one crossing over before you, a devouring fire.
He will destroy them and subdue them before you, so that you can cause them to expire,
And swiftly drive them out, as the Lord promised you. Once the Lord has cleared them
    from your way,
Do not say, 'It is due to my righteousness the Lord let me possess this land today,'
For it is since these nations were wicked that the Lord is driving them out before you.
Not because of any righteous merit on your part, or because of your own virtue,
But due to the wickedness of these nations the Lord your God drives them off in a pack,
And so He may confirm the word He swore to your fathers, to Abraham, and Isaac,
And to Jacob. Know, then, that the Lord your God does not give you this good land to possess
Due to your righteous virtue, for you are a stiff-necked stubborn people that have been blessed.
Bear in mind and do not forget how in the wilderness you provoked the Lord God's wrath,
From the day you were brought out of Egypt's land until your coming here, all through the path,

You have been rebellious against the Lord. And at Horeb, you made Him so angry,
He was angered enough with you to destroy you! When I climbed the mountain to receive
The stone tablets, the tablets of the covenant that the Lord made with you, I remained
Forty days and forty nights on the mountain, I did not drink water, I ate no grain.
And the Lord gave me the two stone tablets inscribed with the finger of God, and on them
Were all the words the Lord had spoken with you out of the fire's midst on the mountain
On the day of the Assembly. At the end of those forty nights and those forty days,
The Lord gave me two stone tablets, the Tablets of the Covenant. To me He did say,
'rise and quickly go down from here, for your people which you have brought forth from
    Egypt's land
Have corrupted themselves, they have turned aside quickly away from what I did command.
They have made themselves a molten image.' And the Lord continued, 'this people I've seen,
And behold, they are a stiff-necked people. Let me be, so I may destroy them and clean
Them off the earth, blot out their name from under heaven, and then make a nation of you
Far greater and more numerous than they.' So I turned and down the mountain I withdrew,
And the mountain was burning with fire, but I went down the mountain and in my two hands
I held the two tablets of the covenant. And I saw you ignored the Lord's command,
You were sinning against the Lord your God, I saw that you made yourself a molten calf,
You were quick to straying from the path the Lord commanded you. So the two tablets I grasped,
And threw them from my two hands, and smashed them before your eyes. And then once more I
    lay prostrate
Before the Lord, for forty days and forty nights, no water I drank, no bread I ate,
Because of all the sins you committed, doing what was bad in the eyes of the Lord,
Angering him. For I was in dread of the Lord's fierce anger against you, since the Lord
Was ready to destroy you, but the Lord gave heed to me then. (As He did with Aaron;
The Lord was so angry with him, He was ready to destroy him. I prayed for Aaron,
And interceded for him also.) Then I took that sinful object that you had made,
That calf, I took it and burned it with fire, I broke it to bits, ground it 'til it would fade
Into small pieces as fine as dust. Then I threw the dust into the brook that descends
From the mountain. But you still provoked the Lord's anger again and again and again:
You had kindled His wrath at Taberah, at Massah His patience you put to the test,
At Kivrot Ha-Ta'ava you made Him crave your burial! And when sent on a quest
By the Lord from Kadesh-Barnea, saying, 'Go up to possess the land I give you,'
You rebelled against the command of the Lord your God, did not believe His word was true,
And did not heed His voice. You have rebelled against the Lord for as long as I've known you.

So I lay prostrate before the Lord for forty days and forty nights, when He planned to
Destroy you, I prayed to the Lord, 'My Lord God, do not annihilate Your own people,
And Your inheritance whom you redeemed with Your greatness, whom from Egypt You did pull
With a mighty hand. Remember Your servants Abraham, Isaac, and Jacob, all blessed.
Pay no heed to the stubbornness of this people, their wickedness, or their sinfulness.

Else the people of the land from which You brought us out will say, "It is because the Lord
Was unable to bring them into the land He promised them, He hated their whole horde,
So He brought them out to have them die in the wilderness." These are Your people, don't harm,
They are Your inheritance who You brought out with Your great power and Your
    outstretched arm.

Deuteronomy 10

"Then the Lord told me: Take two more stones like before,
And then make a wood ark where they both can reside.
So He wrote the commandments on tablets once more.
I climbed down to the ark, and I put them inside.
Now, O Israel, all that the Lord God demands
Is that you walk in His ways, and serve Him with love.
For as seventy, your fathers reached Egypt's lands,
But the Lord made you many, like stars up above."

Then the Lord said to me, 'Carve yourself two stone tablets like the first, and come up to Me
On the mountain, and make an ark of wood. I will write on the tablets so all can see,
The words that were on the first tablets which you broke. Then, put them in the ark to be stored.'
So I made an ark of acacia wood, and carved two tablets out of stone, like before,
And I went up, on the mountain, with the two tablets in my hands. And then the Lord wrote
On the tablets (as He did the first time) The Ten Commandments. The same ones, you will note,
That he told you on the mountain from the midst of the fire on the Day of Assembly,
And the Lord gave them to me. I turned and came down from the mountain, then as He decreed,
I placed the tablets in the ark I had made. There they are, as the Lord commanded me.

And the Children of Israel marched from the Wells of Bene-Ja'akan and journeyed
To Mosera. There Aaron died, and there was buried. And so Eleazar his son
Served as priest in his stead. From there they marched to Gudgoda, then to Jotbath, a region
Of running brooks of water. At that time, the Lord separated the tribe of Levi
To carry the ark of the Lord's covenant, stand before the Lord's presence to supply
Ministration, and give blessings in His name, to this day. And that is why the Levites
Do not have a portion of inheritance like their kinsmen. Their inheritance rights
Are the Lord, as the Lord your God said to them. I stayed on the mountain, like the first time,
Forty days and forty nights, and the Lord gave heed to me, so agreed that at that time,
He would not destroy you. And the Lord said to me, 'rise, take your march before the people,

So they may enter and possess the land I swore to their fathers I'd give them in full.'

And now, O Israel, what does the Lord your God ask of you? Just this: Hold Him in awe,
Walk in all His ways, love Him, serve the Lord your God with all your heart and soul,
    and His law,
You must keep the Lord's commandments and his laws which I command you today,
    for your good.
Behold, the heavens and heavens above are the Lord your God's, as Earth and all that stood
On its soil or water, all things on Earth at all. Yet of all this, the Lord gave His love
To your fathers, and choosing their descendants after them (that means you) to hold above
All other peoples, as it is to this day. Circumcise, therefore, the skin of your heart
That keeps it hardened against the Lord. Do not be stiff-necked, let your stubbornness depart.
For the Lord your God is the God of gods and Lord of lords supreme, great and powerful,
An awesome God who shows no favor and takes no bribes, but provides justice impartial
For orphans and for widows, loving the sojourner, by giving him food and clothing.
So you shall love the sojourner, for you were once strangers in Egypt's land, sojourning.
You shall hold the Lord your God in awe, you shall serve Him and cleave to Him. Swear
    by His name.
He is your praise, He is your God, who did for you these great and terrible deeds that came
To be seen by your own eyes. Your ancestors entered Egypt as just seventy men,
But now the Lord your God has made you as numerous as all the stars in the heavens.

Deuteronomy 11

> "Keep the Lord God's commandments, for you have all seen
> The Lord's greatness, the power of His mighty hand.
> He made waters part, then catch Egyptians between.
> With your own eyes you saw this, so keep His command.
> If you do, you will prosper, your land will be strong.
> If you don't, then the land will grow barren, and worse!
> So I give you a choice today: Do right or wrong.
> Heed the Lord, it's a blessing. If not, it's a curse."

Therefore, love the Lord your God and keep His charge, His laws, His statutes, and
    His commandments,
For all time. You shall know today—not your children, who have not seen or experienced

The discipline of the Lord your God, His greatness, His outstretched arm and His mighty hand,
His wonders and the deeds He performed in Egypt, to Pharaoh the king of Egypt's land,
And all his territory, to Egypt's army with its horses and charioteers,
How He caused the Red Sea's waters to roll back on them when they pursued you from the rear,
So that the Lord destroyed them to this day, and what He did to you in the wilderness
Before you arrived in this place, what he did with Dathan and Abiram who transgressed,
(Those two sons of Eliab son of Reuben), how the earth opened its mouth to swallow
Both of them, their households, their tents, all things in Israel that followed them, gone below—
But you, who have seen with your own eyes the great works of the Lord that He has done.
        Therefore,
Keep all the commandment I command you today, so you may have the strength to enter
And possess the land you are about to cross into and occupy, and to be sure
That you may prolong your days on the land the Lord swore to give your fathers and their seed,
A land flowing with milk and honey. For the land you cross over to possess indeed
Is not like the land of Egypt from which you have come. In Egypt, seed had to be sown,
And be watered by work from your own feet, as if a vegetable garden of your own.
But the land you enter to possess is a land of hills and valleys, which drinks water
From the heavens above, a land which the Lord your God cares for and its welfare ensures,
The eyes of the Lord your God are always upon it, from the year's beginning to end.
And if you obey the commandments I command you today, and this rule you don't bend,
To love the Lord your God with all your heart and soul, then He will give the rain for your land
In due seasons, both early and late rain, so you may gather your new grain and your hand
May gather wine and shining oil. He will provide grass in the field your cattle can eat,
And you will eat and have your fill. But take care not to be lured away by ill deceit
To serve other gods and worship them, for the Lord's anger will be kindled against you,
And He will shut the heavens so no rain will fall, and the ground will withhold its fruit too,
And you will quickly perish from the good land that the Lord gives you. So please understand,
You must place these words of mine upon your heart and soul, bind them as a sign on your hand,
And let them serve as frontlets between your eyes, a symbol on your forehead. Then instruct,
Teach them to your children, speaking of them when home and away, when in bed you are tucked,
And when you arise. Inscribe them on the doorposts of your house, and on your gates besides,
So that your and your children's days may be prolonged on the land the Lord swore to provide
To your fathers, to give them as long as the heavens hang over the earth. Now if you
Will obey the commandments faithfully that on this day I have commanded you do,
Loving the Lord your God, walking in all His ways, and holding fast to Him, then the Lord
Will dislodge all these nations mightier than you from before you (that is your reward).
Every place that the sole of your foot treads shall be yours, extending from the wilderness
To the Lebanon, and from the Euphrates River to the greatest Sea in the west,
To the Mediterranean Sea. No man will stand against you, for the Lord your God
Will (as He promised) put the dread and fear of you over the whole land in which you trod.

Behold, I set before you this day a blessing and a curse. Which it is, you shall say.
A blessing if you obey the Lord your God's commandments that I command you today,
And a curse if you do not obey the Lord your God's commandments, but are turned aside
From the path I command you today, walking after other gods who you've not seen tried.
Now when the Lord your God brings you into the land you are crossing over to possess,
You shall give the blessing on Mount Gerizim and the curse on Mount Eval. Bear witness,
They are both on the other side of the Jordan, past the western road where the sun falls
Which lies in the land of the Canaanites who live in the Arabah plains, near Gilgal,
The stone circle by the Oaks of Moreh. For you are crossing over the Jordan to
Enter into that land and possess it, the land which the Lord your God is giving you.
When you have occupied it and are settled in it, take care to observe in all ways
All of the laws, the instructions, and the statutes that I have placed before you this day.

Deuteronomy 12

> "These are all of the statutes that you must observe
> In the land that the Lord now gives you to possess.
> So no more shall each man simply follow his nerve,
> But you all shall heed God's law. You shall not transgress.
> Dispossess those who live there, don't let them sway you.
> You may eat any animal within your gates.
> Don't say, "How do they serve their gods? I'll do that too."
> For they burn their own children, and this the Lord hates."

These are the laws and the regulations that you shall take care to follow in the land
That the Lord, the God of your fathers, has given as a possession into your hands,
For as long as you live on the earth. You must demolish and destroy all of the places
Where the nations you dispossess served their gods, on hills and high mountains, and
    in the spaces
Beneath luxuriant green trees. You shall tear down their altars, their pillars you shall smash,
Their sacred Asherim poles you shall burn with fire until nothing remains except Ash,
You shall cut the carved-images of their gods to shreds, erasing their name from that site.
Do not do so to the Lord your God, but instead seek the place that is good in His sight,
That He shall choose from among all your tribes to put His name there and to have it there dwell,
You shall go there, and bring your burnt-offerings there, your tithes and sacrifices as well,

All your vowed offerings, offerings you give of free will, all offerings you present,
Plus the firstborn of your herds and flocks. You shall eat there, before the Lord your
    God's presence.
You shall rejoice in all you set your hand to, you and your households, with which you've
    been blessed
By the Lord your God. Now what you shall not do, and I want to make sure this point is stressed,
Is to do what we've been doing up to this day: Each man does what seems right in his eyes,
Causing chaos. (From now on, we must do what is right by the commandments God supplies.)
For you have yet to come to the rest and inheritance the Lord your God gives to you.
But when you cross the Jordan and settle in the land that the Lord your God gives to you
As inheritance, and when He gives you rest so from surrounding foes you are protected
And you live in safety, then you must bring all things I command you to the site selected,
Where the Lord God will choose to establish His name. There you shall bring your
    burnt-offerings,
Sacrifices and tithings, freewill and vowed offerings to the Lord, all that you bring.
And you shall rejoice before the Lord's presence, with your sons and daughters, maids
    and servants,
And the Levite within your gates, for with you he has no portion or inheritance.
Take care that you don't offer your burnt offerings at just random place you see,
But only in the place that the Lord chooses in one of your tribal territories.
There you shall sacrifice your burnt offerings, and there you shall do all I command you.
However, in your own settlements, you may slaughter and eat all the meat you want to,
As much meat as your appetite craves, according to the blessing of the Lord your God
Which he has granted you. The unclean and clean both may eat it, the gazelle and the hart.
Only the blood you shall not eat, instead you must pour it out like water on the ground.
You may not eat the tithe of your grain or of your wine or of your oil within your towns,
Nor the firstlings of your herd or flock, nor any offerings you make, vowed or freewill,
Nor your contributions from your hand. Instead, before the Lord God you will eat your fill
In the place the Lord your God selects. You will eat, you and your daughters and your sons too,
Your servants and your maids, and the Levite in your towns, rejoicing in all things that you
Set your hand to. Be sure not to forsake the Levite, as long as you live in your land.
When the Lord broadens your territory, as He promised you He would make it expand,
And you say, 'I will eat meat' because you crave meat, you may eat as much meat as you like.
If the place where the Lord your God chooses to establish His name is too far a hike,
You may slaughter any of the animals among your herd or flock the Lord gives you,
As I commanded you, and in your towns you may eat whatever you've appetite to.
However, eat it as the gazelle or hart are eaten, clean and unclean both may eat.
But be sure not to eat the blood, for blood is life; you shall not eat the life with the meat!
You must not eat it, but pour it out on the ground like water. You must not eat one bite,
So that all may go well with you and your children after you, when you do what is right
In the eyes of the Lord. But your holy and vowed offerings you shall pick up and bring
To the site the Lord chooses. You shall offer both flesh and blood there, your burnt offering,

On the altar of the Lord your God. The blood of your sacrifices shall be poured out
On the altar of the Lord your God, but the meat you may eat. Take heed to be devout
And observe these words with which I command you, so that it may go well not just with you,
But your descendants after you as well, forever, when you do what is good to do,
And what is right in the sight of the Lord your God. Now when the Lord your God has cut down
All the nations before you where you enter to dispossess them, and you take their towns
And settle in their land, take care that you are not lured or snared into following them.
Once they have been destroyed from before you, do not ask about their gods which I condemn,
Saying, 'How did these nations serve their gods? Tell me, so I may follow this practice too.'
You are not to act in this way toward the Lord your God, that is not what you shall do.
For all things abhorrent to the Lord, which He hates, are the things that they do with their gods,
Yes, they even burn their sons and their daughters with fire to offer them up to their gods.

Everything that I command you, you shall take care to observe, and not change it one bit.
You shall not add to what I have commanded you, nor are you to diminish from it.

Deuteronomy 13

> "Observe all I command you, no less and no more.
> When a prophet arises and gives you a sign,
> Don't say, "Let's go serve other gods." This I abhor.
> Those who lure you away from the Lord by design
> Shall be put to death. Even if it is your brother,
> Your daughter, your son, or your very own wife,
> If they say, "Don't serve God, let us go find another,"
> Then show them no mercy, you shall take their life."

Everything that I command you, you shall take care to observe, and not change it one bit.
You shall not add to what I have commanded you, nor are you to diminish from it.

If from your midst arises a prophet or dreamer of dreams, and he gives you a sign
Or a wondrous portent, and that sign or portent comes to pass, and then he opines,
"Let us follow and worship other gods," gods whom you do not know, you shall not pay heed.
Do not listen to the words of that prophet or dreamer, though his predictions succeed,
The Lord your God is just testing you, to know if you love Him with all your heart and soul.
You shall walk after the Lord your God, hold Him in awe, and keep all His
    commandments whole.

You shall obey His voice, you shall serve Him and cleave to Him. (Ignore what prophets
    might say.)
As for that prophet, he shall be put to death, for his words have tried to turn you away
From the Lord your God - the one who brought you out of Egypt's land, the one who
    redeemed you
From a house of serfs - by leading you astray from the path the Lord commands you pursue.
So shall you burn out the evil among you. If your brother (yes, your own mother's son)
Or your son or your daughter or dear wife or neighbor so close it seems you two are one
Comes to lure you in secret, and says, 'let us serve other gods, gods whom you have not known,
Nor your fathers before you, but gods of the people around you, in near or far zones,
From one edge of the earth to the other,' You shall not pay heed to him or give consent,
Your eye shall hold no pity for him, offer him no shield nor mercy from punishment.
You shall kill him, let your hand be the first against him to put him to death, after which
Shall come the hand of all the people. Stone him to death with stones, for he asked you to switch
Away from the Lord your God, the one who brought you out of Egypt's land, a house of serfs.
Now all Israel will hear, and fear, and be awed, so they never again have the nerves
To do more of this wickedness in your midst. If you hear in one of your settlements
That the Lord your God gives you to settle in, that some base scoundrels from among your tents
Have subverted the inhabitants of their town, saying, 'let us go serve other gods,'
(Whom you have not known), then you must investigate and examine behind all facades.
If your inquiries show that the claim is established as true, and such abomination
Was done in your midst, strike down the settlers of that town with your sword,
    causing devastation,
Destroying utterly the whole city, its settlers, even its cattle, with your sword.
Gather all the spoils in the square, and burn them with the town, an offering to the Lord.
It shall be a mound of ruin for the ages, not to be rebuilt. And let nothing
That has been devoted to destruction cling to your hand, so the Lord from the burning
Of His anger may turn, and show compassion to you. And in His compassion, what's more,
He will multiply you and make you many, just as the oath to your fathers He swore.
For you will be heeding the Lord your God's voice, keeping all of his commandments which I
Command you on this day, doing what is right in the Lord's sight, in the Lord your God's eyes.

Deuteronomy 14

> "You are children of God! You shall keep this routine:
> Only eat animals that chew cud, with cleft feet.
> Only eat fish with fins, only birds that are clean.
> Any thing dying natural death, you shall not eat.
> Do not boil a kid in the milk of its mother.
> Each year, you shall tithe to the Lord from your land.
> And give some to the Levite, for he has no other.
> Then God will bless all to which you set your hand."

You are children of the Lord your God. You shall not gash yourselves nor shave off a bald spot
Between your eyes to mourn for the dead, for you are a people holy to the Lord God;
The Lord your God chose you from among all people on earth to be His treasured people.
You shall not eat any abominable thing. These are beasts you may eat and be full:
The ox, sheep, goat, deer, gazelle, roebuck, wild goat, ibex, antelope, and mountain-sheep too,
Along with any other beast that has hooves cloven in two, and brings up cud to chew,
You may eat those. However, if they only have hooves split in two or just chew the cud,
You shall not eat them. Like the hare, camel, and daman, for although they do bring up cud,
They do not have split hooves, and therefore are unclean for you. Also unclean is the swine,
For though it has split hooves, it does not chew cud, hence is a thing on which you should
    not dine,
It is unclean for you, you shall not eat their flesh or touch their carcasses; (it's a sin).
This is what you can eat from the waters: You can eat whatever has both scales and fins.
But whatever does not have fins and scales, do not eat. For you it is unclean, impure.
You may eat any clean bird. But these are birds you shall not eat: The eagle, the vulture,
The osprey, the falcon, the buzzard and the raven, each of any kind, nor the kite,
The ostrich, the seagull, nighthawk, the hawk of any kind, the owl (great, little, or white),
The bustard, pelican, and the cormorant, the stork, the heron, the hoopoe, the bat.
And all things with wings that swarm are unclean for you, you are not to eat any of that.

You may only eat clean winged creatures. You shall not eat things that die of natural cause,
Give any such thing to the stranger in your gates, sell it to a foreigner, because
You are a holy people to the Lord your God. Don't boil a kid in its mother's milk.
You shall tithe all the produce of your seed, the yield of your field, one tenth of all that ilk.
You shall eat the tithe from your grain, your wine, your oil, and the firstlings from your herd
    and flock,
So you may learn to fear the Lord your God always. And if the way is too far to walk,

And you are unable to bring the tithe, for the place the Lord God chose to set His name
Is too far, the Lord your God will bless you. You can sell the tithe and give money the same.
Turn the tithe into money, which you will bind up in your hand, and then take it and go
To the place the Lord your God has chosen, and there spend it as you feel is apropos.
Buy whatever you desire, oxen or sheep, wine or strong drink, all that's craved by your soul,
And you shall eat it there before the Lord your God and rejoice, both you and your household.
And you shall not forsake the Levite within your gates, for he does not have a portion
Or inheritance with you. At the end of every three years, this is what shall be done:
You shall bring forth the tithe of your produce that year, and within your gates, leave it to stand.
Then the Levite (who has no inheritance portion with you), the stranger in your land,
The fatherless, and the widow within your gates will all eat until they eat their fill,
So the Lord your God may bless you in everything you set your hand to, just as He willed.

Deuteronomy 15

> "Every seven years, you are to grant a remission
> Of all debts. And don't think this means not to lend.
> You will sin if you find yourself in that position;
> The needy will be with you, till the world's end,
> So give freely to them. When a serf is sold you,
> And he serves you six years, then you must set him free.
> And not empty of hand, you shall give him gifts too.
> (For in Egypt's land, you were all serfs once, you see?)"

At the end of each seventh year, you shall grant a release. This is the nature of it:
Every creditor that has lent to his neighbor, the debt that is owed he shall remit.
He shall not exact it from his neighbor or brother, for the Lord's release is proclaimed.
If a foreigner owes you, you may exact pay, but your neighbor's debt shall not be claimed.
You shall release him. Now, there would be none in need among you (because the Lord will bless
You in the land that the Lord your God is giving you as inheritance to possess),
If only you would heed the voice of the Lord your God, doing as He tells you to do
And obeying these commandments I command you today. The Lord your God will bless you,
As He promised you, and you shall lend to many nations but you shall borrow from none.
You shall rule over many nations, but no nation shall rule over you, not a one.

If there is a poor man among you, one of your kinsmen, anywhere within your gates
In the land the Lord your God gives you, you shall not harden your heart to his dire straits,

Nor shall you shut your hand against your needy brother. Instead, open your hand to him,
And lend him enough for whatever he needs. Beware, lest some part of your heart grow dim
And the base thought arise, 'the seventh year is near, the Release year where debt is remitted,'
So that you see to do evil to your needy kinsman, and your kind loan is omitted.
If you give him nothing, and he cries out to the Lord against you, you have done a sin.
You shall give to him freely, not begrudging him your loan, and due to this you will win
Blessings from the Lord God in all you set your hand to. The poor shall remain in the land,
There shall always be some, which is why I command you with this: You shall open your hand
To your kinsmen, the poor, and the needy in the land. If your kinsman is sold to you,
A fellow Hebrew man or Hebrew woman, and serves you for six years, what you must do
Is to let him go free in the seventh year. And when you give him freedom to walk,
You shall not set him free empty-handed. You shall furnish him with goods from your own flock,
From your threshing floor, and from your wine press. For everything the Lord your God
    gave to you
And blessed you with, you must give to him. Remember, long ago you were a servant too,
In Egypt's land, then the Lord your God redeemed you, therefore I command you this today.
Now if he says to you, 'I will not go away from you,' and he would prefer to stay
Because he loves you, and your household, and fares well with you, then you shall pick up an awl
And put it through his ear, into the door, and he shall forevermore serve as your thrall;
(Do the same for a maidservant.) Don't let it seem hard to you when you let him go free,
For he served you six years with twice the service of a hired hand, so accept it calmly.
Then the Lord will bless you in all things that you do. Every firstling male born to your flock
Or your herd, you shall consecrate to the Lord your God. With the firstling of your bullock,
You are not to work, nor shall you shear the firstling of your sheep. You shall eat them instead,
You and your household, before the Lord your God's presence, in the place He has selected.
Now if there is a defect, be it lameness, blindness, or illness to any extent,
You shall not sacrifice it to the Lord your God. You shall eat it in your settlements,
Both the clean and the unclean may eat it, just like a gazelle or deer that you had slaughtered.
Only its blood you are not to eat, but instead, pour it out on the ground just like water.

Deuteronomy 16

> "Keep the month of Aviv, Passover to the Lord.
> Offer where the Lord chooses to have His name dwell.
> Seven weeks after sickle first touches grain cord,
> Have a festival of weeks to the Lord as well.
> And the feast of Sukkot booths, you shall keep also.
> These the three festivals to the Lord you must note.
> Provide judges who favor no man, high or low.
> Take no bribes, for true justice you are to promote."

Observe the month of Aviv, and keep the Passover to the Lord your God, doing right.
For in the ripe month of Aviv, the Lord your God brought you out of Egypt's land, at night.
You shall offer the Passover sacrifice to the Lord your God, from the herd and flock,
In the place the Lord chooses to have His name dwell. You shall eat no bread of leavened stock,
But for seven days you will just eat matzot with it, the unleavened bread of affliction
(For you fearfully flew out of Egypt's land) so you will remember all of the friction
On the day you came out of Egypt's land for the rest of your life. And for seven days
No leavened bread shall be seen in all of your land, nor shall meat from the sacrifice stay
Overnight until morning if you sacrificed it the first night. Do not sacrifice
The Passover offering within any of your towns to which the Lord gives you rights,
But only at the place where the Lord chooses to have His name dwell; there it shall be done.
And you shall offer the Passover sacrifice there, at the time of the setting sun,
The same time when you came out of Egypt. You shall boil it and shall eat it in the space
That the Lord your God will choose. Then in the morning, turn and go back to your
    tenting place.
For six days you shall eat unleavened bread. On the seventh day hold solemn assembly
For the Lord your God, doing no work on that day. Then count seven weeks from when you see
The sickle first get put to the standing grain. Count seven weeks, then you shall keep a feast,
A Feast of Weeks for the Lord. By your hand an offering of freewill shall be released,
And you shall give to the Lord according to what the Lord blessed you with. You shall rejoice
Before the Lord's presence in the place the Lord establishes His name, His place of choice.
You shall rejoice—You, your son and your daughter, and your servant and your maidservant too,
Along with the Levite within your gates, the stranger, orphan, and widow among you.
You shall remember that you were a slave in Egypt, and take care to follow these laws.
After the fall harvest from your threshing floor and wine vat, for one more feast you shall pause:
The Feast of Booths you shall hold for seven days. You shall rejoice in your feast, and your son,
And your daughter, your servant, your maid, the Levite, the sojourner, the fatherless one,

And the widow within your gates. For seven days you shall observe a feast to the Lord
In the place the Lord chooses, for the Lord your God has blessed you with abundant reward
In all your produce and all you set your hand to, so that you will have cause to rejoice.
Three times a year, all your men shall appear before the Lord God at the place of His choice:
On the feast of unleavened bread, on the feast of weeks, and the feast of booths in addition.
No man shall appear before the Lord empty handed, but give as befits his position,
According to the blessing that the Lord your God has given to you.

[Shoftim]

You will provide
Judges and officials in all your towns the Lord your God gives you. Throughout all your tribes,
They will judge people with righteous judgment. You shall not judge unfairly in any way,
You shall not be partial to some over others, nor shall bribery hold any sway
(For a bribe blinds the eyes of the wise, and twists the words of the just to set them askew.)
Justice, only pursue justice! So you may live, and possess the land the Lord gives you.
You shall not plant any tree beside the Lord your God's altar, nor shall you fabricate
Any type of tree-thing, nor set up a stone pillar—these are things the Lord your God hates.

Deuteronomy 17

"Beasts you slaughter to God may not have any flaw.
Those who serve other gods, you shall stone them with stones.
You need word from two witnesses, this is the law
To put someone to death, lest you break guiltless bones.
When you enter the land that the Lord God gives you,
If you think to yourself, "We should all have a king,"
God shall choose one. But no riches shall he accrue,
He shall copy these rules, and to them he shall cling."

You shall not sacrifice to the Lord your God an ox or sheep if it has a defect,
Any blemish at all; that is abhorrent to the Lord your God, and shows disrespect.

If there is found among you in any of your towns the Lord your God is giving you
Any woman or any man who has done wicked actions in the Lord your God's view,
In transgressing His covenant, going to serve other gods, worshipping them as well,
(Either the sun, or the moon, or any of the host of heaven I did not impel

You to worship), and you are told of it, then hear it. An inquiry shall be begun,
And if you find out it is true, in Israel such abominations have been done,
Then you shall bring that man or that woman, the one who has done the thing that is wicked,
Out to your gates, where you will stone that man or that woman with stones until they are dead.

On the testimony of two witnesses, or three, let the one to die receive death.
But you are not put a man to death on testimony from a single witness.
The hand of the witnesses shall be the first against him, (proof they think his guilt does exist)
To make him die, followed by the hand of all the people, to purge evil from your midst.

If a case should arise that is too difficult to judge, like a bloody homicide,
A dispute over civil judgments, or assaults, any case which you cannot decide
In your town, then get up and go to the place that the Lord your God chooses. Then appear
Before the Levite priests and the judge in office, to consult them. And then you will hear
The sentence of judgment. You shall follow that sentence, in the place the Lord your God chose,
Taking care to do as they instruct you. Precisely according to what they propose,
You shall act. Do not deviate from their sentence, do not sway to the left or the right.
If a man acts presumptuously and does not heed the priest who stands in the Lord's sight,
Or the judge, then that man shall die. This is how you shall burn out evil from Israel.
And all the people shall hear, and fear, and no more act presumptuously or rebel.

When you enter the land the Lord your God gives you, to possess it and dwell on that ground,
If you say, "I will set a king over me, just like the nations that are all around."
Then you may indeed set a king over you, one the Lord will choose from all your brethren.
(For you shall not have a foreign man serve as king over you, who is not of your kin).
But he shall not gain more horses for himself, nor return the people to Egypt's land
To gain more horses. For the Lord told you, "Do not go back ever again, you are banned!"
He shall not gain more wives for himself, lest his heart turn away, nor shall he strive to own
An excessive amount of silver or of gold. But when he sits on his kingdom's throne,
He shall write a copy of this law for himself in a book, before the Levite priests.
And the book shall stay with him, and he shall read it all his life until his breath does cease,
So he may learn to fear the Lord his God, and so he will hold the Lord his God in awe,
By abiding by the words in these instructions, and observing these statutes and laws.
Hence he will not be raised above his brothers, nor deviate from these commands I list,
So both he and his sons may prolong their days over his kingdom in Israel's midst.

Deuteronomy 18

"The Levitical priests, the whole tribe of Levi,
Has no portion with Israel; theirs is apart.
You shall tithe them from slaughters and grain, and thereby
They are paid for attending the Lord from the start.
When you enter the land God is giving to you,
Ignore abominations from those nations there.
They heed sorcerers, and prophets that don't speak true,
So don't follow them, otherwise their fate you'll share."

The Levitical priests, all the tribe of Levi, has no portion of inheritance
With Israel, but shall eat the fire-offerings to the Lord, and his inheritance.
They shall have no land inheritance like their brother tribes, the Lord shall be their portion,
As He promised them. And this shall be the priests' due portion from the people, everyone
Who gives a sacrifice, be it ox or sheep, shall give the priest the cheeks, stomach, and shoulder.
You shall also give him the first fruits of your grain, wine, and oil. (The first fruits, nothing older)
For the Lord your God has chosen him from all your tribes to minister in the Lord's name,
He and his sons forever. Now if a Levite leaves any town in Israel's reign,
where he lives, and comes with his desire to the place the Lord chooses to minister there,
And does so in the name of the Lord his God, like all his fellow Levites. And their share
Shall be equal to the standard portion of food, aside from revenue that they earn
From selling their father's property. When you enter the land the Lord gives you, don't learn
To follow the abominations of those nations. There shall not be found among you
Anyone who has his son or daughter pass through fire, any sorcerer, anyone who
Practices divination, any enchanters, any augurers who use augury,
Any charmers, spellcasters, people who consort with spirits, those who do wizardry,
Or any necromancers. For in the Lord's eyes, all of these are an abomination,
Which is why the Lord drives them out from before you, He finds abhorrent all these vocations.
You shall be wholly perfect before the Lord your God. These nations you will dispossess
Listen to sorcerers and diviners, but not you, the Lord did not give you that mess.

The Lord your God will raise a prophet from your midst, like me, you shall heed him
   with no doubt,
Just as you asked the Lord your God at Horev on the day of Assembly, and cried out,
'let me not hear the Lord my God's voice or see this great fire anymore, else I will die!'
And the Lord said to me, 'they have spoken rightly, and so a prophet I will supply,

Raising one from their brethren, like you. I shall put My words in his mouth and he shall speak,
Saying to them all that I command him. And whoever ignores these words and critiques
All the words that he speaks in My name, those people I shall call to account and require
That they follow my words. But if a prophet speaks and you find out that what has transpired
Is that he has presumed to speak words in My name that I did not command him to say,
Or he speaks in the name of other gods instead, that prophet shall die and pass away.'
Now you might ask yourselves, 'How will we know the Lord did not say what the
     prophet proclaims?'
Well, the answer is this: If the prophet you listen to speaks in the Lord your God's name,
Yet the words he speaks do not come true, then they are not the words the Lord spoke,
     that is clear.
And since that prophet has spoken presumptuously, of him you are to have no fear.

Deuteronomy 19

> "When the Lord your God cuts off the nations whose land
> The Lord God gives to you, set three cities aside
> Where a manslaughterer may flee, safe from the hand
> Of those who would kill him; towns of refuge to hide.
> But if it was on purpose, and not accidental,
> Throw him from the town, let the murderer die.
> Now if there's a false witness who's being judgmental,
> Kill him, for he tried to kill; Eye for an eye."

When the Lord your God cuts off the nations whose land the Lord your God is giving to you,
And you dispossess them and settle in their cities and houses, here's what you must do:
You shall set aside three cities in the land that the Lord your God gives you to possess.
Measure the roads and trisect your land the Lord gives you, so a manslayer in distress
Can flee to those areas. Now an accidental killer who flees there to survive,
One who kills his neighbor without malice aforethought (no past grudge that's been kept alive),
Or a man who goes into the forest with his neighbor to chop wood, and when he chops,
His hand swings the axe, and the head leaves the handle, striking his neighbor so his life stops,
He may flee to one of these cities and survive. Otherwise the avenger of blood
(Seeking to repay the accidental death) will pursue, with emotions in a flood
And in hot anger, overtakes and kills the manslayer, since the way is far to trudge,
Even though the manslayer did not deserve death, as he bore his neighbor no past grudge.

That is why I command you, 'set aside three cities.' And if the Lord makes your land grow,
As He swore to your fathers, and gives you all the land He swore to them he would bestow,
(That is, only if you observe all these commandments that I am telling you today,
To love the Lord your God, and for the rest of your life to walk in the Lord your God's ways),
Then you shall add another three cities to these three, so the blood of the innocent
Shall not be shed within your land, the land the Lord your God gives you as inheritance,
Lest you be guilty of blood. But if a man hates his neighbor, and then he lies in wait,
Then attacks him and mortally wounds him, and flees to these cities, though he killed in hate,
Then the elders of his city shall have him sent from there, giving him into the hand
Of the avenger of blood, so he dies. Your eye shall not pity him; murder was planned.
So you shall purge the innocent blood-guilt from Israel, and things will go well with you.

In your inheritance-portion of the land that the Lord your God gives you to possess,
You shall not move the border-marks of your neighbor, set by generations previous.

A single witness shall not rise up against a man for iniquity, or for sin,
Or for any wrong he has committed. At least two witnesses must speak to begin
A legal matter. If a malicious witness should rise up, accusing any man
Of wrongdoing, then both the accuser and the person who is accused are to stand
Before the Lord's presence, before the priests, and before the judges who are in office.
And the judges shall investigate, and if they find the witness was a false witness
Who falsely accused his brother, you shall do to him what he planned to do to his brother.
This is how you shall purge evil from your midst, those left will hear and fear. All of those others
Will no longer commit any evil deeds in your midst. Your eye shall not take pity,
A life for a life, eye for eye, tooth for tooth, hand for hand, and foot for foot it shall be.

Deuteronomy 20

"When you battle your foes and you see their large force,
Do not fear. Have the priest say, "The Lord is with you."
The officials will say, "We shall have no remorse;
Men with business undone, they may go back and do."
When approaching a town, you shall offer a peace.
If they take it, don't kill them, for they don't oppose.
But if they reject peace, then kill them and don't cease,
Only leave all the trees, for the trees aren't your foes."

When you go out to war against your enemies, and see horses, and chariots too,
And a larger army than yours, you shall not fear them, for the Lord your God is with you,
The one who brought you from Egypt's land. And when you near the battle, the priest
    shall approach
And speak to the people, saying, "Hear O Israel, you draw near to battle your foes
On this day. Do not let your heart be weak, do not fear them, have dread, or in panic flee,
For the Lord your God goes with you to fight your foes for you and will bring you victory.
Then the officers shall speak to the people and say, "What man here has built a new house,
But has not dedicated it yet? Let him not go forth now, but return to his house,
Lest he die in the war and another man dedicate it. And what man has been planting,
Planting a vineyard but has not yet gotten to enjoy the fruit that it will be granting?
Let him go back to his house, lest he die in battle, and some other man eat the fruit.
And what man here has betrothed a woman, but has not married the object of his suit?
Let him go and return to his house, lest he die in battle, and some other take her."
And the officers shall speak more to the people, saying, "What man will let fear occur
And is faint-hearted and afraid? Let him go and return to his house, so he does not
Make the hearts of his brothers weak like his." And when the officials are done with
    these thoughts,
And have finished speaking to the people, the army commanders shall take a head count,
And be appointed at the head of the fighting people. When you draw near to a town,
To battle against it, offer terms of peace. If it responds with peace and lets you in,
All the people of the town shall be servants of labor for you, all people within.
But if they will not make peace with you, and make war against you, then you shall besiege it.
And when the Lord your God gives them into your hand, every male with your sword
    you shall hit,
Striking them down, and taking the women and children and cattle as your spoils of war.
You may enjoy the plunder of your foes the Lord your God has given to you as yours.
You shall do this to all cities far away from you, not cities of these nations here.
But in the towns of peoples the Lord your God is giving you as inheritance share,
You shall not leave alive anything that breathes. Destroy them for the Lord: All the Hittites,
And the Amorites, the Canaanites, the Perizzites, the Hivvites, and the Jebusites,
As the Lord your God commanded you, lest they teach you to do all their practices odd
And abominable that they do with their gods, and you sin against the Lord your God.

When you besiege a town for a long time, and war against it so you can capture it,
You must not destroy its trees by cutting them with an ax. You can eat their fruit a bit,
But do not cut them down. For are trees of the field men who will battle you in a siege?
No, of course they are not. Trees are the life of man, so you may only cut down the trees
That you know produce no food. They may be destroyed, cut down to produce siegeworks and all,
Which will be brought against the town that makes war with you, until it meets with its downfall.

Deuteronomy 21

> "If a man is found slain, and it's not known by whom,
> Then the nearest town's elders will have to atone.
> They shall break a calf's neck, and avoid guilt and doom,
> When they vow that the blood shed was not by their own.
> If war brings you a captive that you wish to wed,
> Have her shave her head, see if she still brings delight.
> When a man has two wives, and one son they've each bred,
> No matter which he likes, the firstborn gets his rights."

If a corpse is found slain in the land the Lord your God gives you, lying out in the field,
And it is not known who slew it, your elders and judges shall work to make it revealed.
They shall go out and measure the distance from the corpse to each town nearby that's a neighbor,
And the elders of the nearest town to the corpse shall take a calf that has done no labor,
And has never pulled a yoke. They shall take the calf, and into a wadi they shall trek,
One that has had no labor done (plowing or sowing), and there they shall break the calf's neck.
Then the priests, sons of Levi, shall come forth (because the Lord chose them to serve at His side,
And give blessings in God's name, and all legal cases will be for their words to decide),
And all elders of that town shall wash their hands over the calf that has had its neck broken,
And then say, "Our hands did not shed this blood, nor did our eyes see it. O Lord, take this token
And forgive Your people Israel, whom You redeemed. Do not leave blood-guilt unresolved
For the innocent blood with Your people Israel. For this blood, let them be absolved,
And so You shall purge the guilt of innocent bloodshed from your midst, and do what is right
In the eyes of the Lord.

[Ki Teitzei]

When you go out to war against your enemies in a fight,
And the Lord your God delivers them into your hands, and numerous captives you take,
And you see among the captives a beautiful woman, of whom you'd like to partake
As a wife, bring her into your house, where she shall shave her head and cut short all her nails,
And discard her captivity clothes. She shall sit, while both of her parents she bewails,
For a month. After that, you shall come into her, be her husband and she as your wife.
Then if you are not pleased with her, set her free. But you may not sell for profit her life,
Do not treat her as a slave, since you had your way with her. Now, if a man has two wives,
One he loves and one he hates, and they both bear him children, and the first one that arrives

Is the son of the one that he hates, when it comes time for inheritance to be done,
He shall not treat as firstborn the son of the loved one before the proper firstborn son.
The son of the one he hates, the true firstborn son, he must recognize as is proper,
Giving him two thirds of the inheritance, since he is the firstborn one of his father,
And it is his strong birthright. When a man has a son rebellious of stubborn will,
Who does not heed the voice of his father or mother, and although they chastise him, still,
He will not obey them, then his father and his mother shall grab him and bring him down
To the elders of his town, the gates of his place. They shall tell the elders of his town,
"Our son here is a stubborn rebel who does not obey us, a drunk and a glutton!"
Then all the men of the town shall stone him to death. This is how evil shall be undone,
And you shall burn out the evil from your midst, and all Israel will hear and fear it.
When a man has committed a sin of such guilt that a penalty of death would fit,
And he is put to death, and you hang him from a wooden stake so he will inspire fright,
Then you must take him down; you shall not leave his carcass to stay on the stake overnight.
On that very same day you shall bury him, (for a hanged body gives your God offense),
So you won't make your soil unclean which the Lord your God gives you as an inheritance.

Deuteronomy 22

"If you see a man's animals wander away,
Then return them to him; don't pretend not to see.
When you take a nest's eggs, let the mother bird stay.
Build all roofs with a guardrail, so no one falls free.
Don't sow fields of two kinds, plow with beasts of two kinds,
Or wear clothes of two kinds. Just use one kind the same.
When a man takes a wife, but then changes his mind,
He shall pay if he lies to give her a bad name."

If you see your brother's ox or sheep go astray, do not hide and pretend to ignore it,
But take action and bring it back to him. If your fellow man loses something, restore it!
And if the man does not live near you, or you do not know him, then you shall bring it home,
Where it shall stay until he seeks it, then you shall return to him his beast that has roamed.
You shall do this with his donkey, with his garments, and with all that your brother may lose.
If you find it, you must bring it back. To ignore it is not an action you may choose.
If you see the donkey or ox of your brother has fallen down by the wayside,
You must help him raise it up. You shall not pretend you do not see his plight, and go hide.

A woman shall not wear the clothes of a man, nor shall a man in woman's clothes be dressed,
Anyone who does is an abomination to the Lord. If you see a bird's nest
In your way, be it in a tree or on the ground, and there are fledgling birds or some eggs,
And the mother bird is sitting on them, you are not to take the mother with her eggs.
Let the mother go free, though the young you may take for yourself, so it goes well for you,
And may live a long life. When you make a new house, construct a parapet for your roof,
So you don't have the guilt of innocent blood spilled on your house if someone falls from it..
You shall not sow your vineyard with two kinds of seed, or the entire yield shall be forfeit
As holy to the Lord. You shall not plow with donkey and ox together. Do not wear
Garments made of wool and linen together. You shall make tassels which you shall prepare
At the four corners of the cloak with which you cover yourself. When a man takes a wife,
And goes into her and then hates her and makes charges that she has led an evil life,
Giving her a bad name, saying, "I took this woman in marriage, but when I came near,
I did not find in her signs of virginity," Then the girl's parents are to appear
And bring her and the signs of her virginity to the town's elders, at the town's gate.
Then the girl's father shall say to the elders, "I gave my daughter to this man, yet hate
Is what he feels for her now, so he made a false charge and said "This girl is no virgin,"
But here is evidence, you shall know of my daughter's virginity by this token!"
He shall spread out the garment before the town's elders, and the elders shall flog the man.
They shall fine him one hundred silver shekels, to give to the father of the woman,
For he gave a bad name to a virgin of Israel, and she shall remain his wife.
From then on, he shall never be able to send her away, they are married for life.
But if the charge proves true, and no signs of the woman's virginity were ever found,
They shall bring the woman to the entrance of her father's house, where the men of her town
Shall stone her to death with stones, because she has disgraced Israel by playing the whore
In her father's house. So you shall burn away evil out of your midst forever more.

If a man is found lying with the wife of another man, they shall both die—The two,
Both the woman and the man with her, so evil will be purged from Israel by you.

When there is a virgin girl betrothed to a man, and another man finds her in town
And lies with her, you shall take them both to the town gate, and stone them until they fall down
And they die. The girl because though she was in town she did not cry for help to assist,
And the man because he humbled his neighbor's wife. So you shall purge evil from your midst.

But if the man should come across the engaged girl in the country, and take her by force,
And lies with her, then just the man shall die, but the girl's life shall be left to run its course.
The girl has no sin worthy of death, this is like when a man attacks and kills his neighbor,
For he found her in the country, so when she cried out, there was nobody to come save her.

When a man finds a virgin girl, but she is not engaged, and by force he lies with her,
When they are discovered, then the man who lay with her shall pay to the woman's father

Fifty silver shekels. And then she shall be his, and eternally serve as his wife.
Since he has violated her, he cannot send her away for the rest of his life.

Deuteronomy 23

> "A man is not to marry his own father's wife.
> Here are membership rules for the Lord's assembly:
> Moabites, Ammonites, cannot enter for life,
> Egyptians, Edomites, in generation three.
> When you camp to make war, you must keep the camp clean.
> Any man or thing unclean, let them go outside.
> What you vow, you must do, so say just what you mean.
> Eat your neighbors grapes only till hunger subsides."

No man shall marry his father's wife, because no man is to expose his father's skirt.
(Since her nakedness is for his father.) Nobody whose testicles are crushed and hurt,
Or whose private member is cut off shall enter the assembly of the Lord, not one.
A bastard shall not enter the Lord's assembly, even to the tenth generation
Of his descendants; none of them shall enter the Lord's assembly. And no Ammonite
Or Moabite shall enter the Lord's assembly, for such is never to be their right,
Even the tenth generation of their descendants from the Lord's assembly are banned,
Because they did not meet you with bread and water on your journey out of Egypt's land,
And hired Bilam son of Beor from Petor, Mesopotamia to place a curse
Upon you. But the Lord your God would not heed Bilam, and instead the Lord did reverse
The curse and turn it into a blessing, for the Lord your God loves you. Don't be concerned
With the peace or prosperity of these people, because all their ill fate has been earned.

You shall not abhor an Edomite, for he is your brother, nor are you to abhor
An Egyptian, for you were a sojourner in his land. All of the children they bore
In the third generation can enter the Lord's assembly. When you go as a troop
Against your enemies, be sure to keep away from all evil things. If in your group
There is a man who has become unclean because of an accident during the night,
He shall go outside the camp, and shall not come back into camp until things are set right.
When the sun begins to set, he shall wash with water, and when the sun has fully set,
He may come back into the camp. You shall have a place outside camp to which you can get,
And you shall have a spike with your weapons, so when you go to relieve yourself outside,
You will dig a hole with it, and cover your excrement, something which you have to hide.

For the Lord your God walks through your camp to protect you and deliver you your enemies,
So it must be holy, lest He turn away from you because he sees indecencies.

You shall not return a slave to his lord who sought you to escape the lord that he flees.
You shall let him live with you, among you, anywhere in your settlement that he please,
You shall not oppress him. No daughter of Israel is to be a cult prostitute,
Nor shall any son of Israel be a dog (a man who follows the same pursuit).
You shall not bring the fee of a harlot or dog into the house of the Lord your God,
Not for any vow. Because they are both an abomination to the Lord your God.

You shall not charge interest on a loan to your brother man, interest in food or silver,
Or in anything that can be charged as interest. Although you can charge the foreigner,
You may not charge your brother any interest, in order that the Lord your God may bless
You in everything that you set your hand to, in the land you will enter and possess.

When you make a vow to the Lord your God, in completing the vow you shall not delay,
For the Lord your God requires it of you, and you will have sinned if you act in this way.
But if you do not vow in the first place, then there will be no guilt of a sin with you,
And so you should be careful that you can do whatever it is that you vowed to do,
For you vowed to the Lord willingly with your own mouth the thing you have promised will be.
When you come into your neighbor's vineyard, to eat all the grapes that you want you are free.
Eat your fill, but you must not put any grapes into your vessel, not one single grape!
(For they are not yours to take, but only to make sure that from hunger you can escape).
When you come into your neighbor's standing grain field, you may pluck what you like
    with your hands,
But you shall not swing a sickle to harvest his grain (since the reason from above stands).

Deuteronomy 24

"When a man takes a wife whom he comes to abhor,
He may write her a document granting divorce.
When a man takes a wife, he should not go to war
Until one year together has first passed its course.
Don't seize millstones for payments, for that's how man lives.
Should a man pledge his coat, give it back, don't be mean.
Don't pluck every last grape, leave a few the vine gives
For the sojourner, widow, and orphan to glean."

When a man takes a wife in marriage and she finds no favor in his eyes in due course,
Because he has found some indecency in her, he shall write her a bill of divorce.
He shall place it in her hand and send her away from his house. Now when she leaves his house,
If she goes and becomes the wife of another man, and he too does not like this spouse,
And he too writes her a bill of divorce to place in her hand and then sends her away,
Or if he dies, then her former husband (who divorced her, and said that she could not stay)
May not take her as his wife again, for she has been defiled at another man's hands.
It would be an abomination to the Lord, so do not bring sin guilt on the land
That the Lord your God gives you as inheritance. Now when any man takes a new wife,
He shall not join the army for war or any purpose for the first year of their life
Together. He shall be free at home for one year, to give joy to the wife he has taken.
You shall not take a millstone or handmill as payment pledge, lest someone's life be forsaken.
(For the millstone and handmill are tools that are needed in order to make daily bread,
And if you seized them as payment, the one you took them from soon would be starving,
      and dead.)
If a man is found stealing one of his brothers, an Israelite seized in his fist,
To enslave or sell him, the kidnapper shall die; so you shall purge evil from your midst.
Be careful in all matters of leprosy, heeding the exact rules given to you
By all of the Levitical priests. As I commanded them, that is what you shall do.
Remember what the Lord your God did to Miriam on your way out of Egypt's land.

When you lend to a neighbor, you shall not enter his home to seize payment. You shall stand
Outside of his house, and the man to whom you loaned shall bring his payment to you, outside.
And if he is a poor man, you shall not sleep in his pledged cloak, but when the sun subsides,
You shall return his cloak to him, so he may sleep in it, and from the cold have defense.
He will bless you, and then you will have righteous merit before the Lord your God's presence.

You shall not oppress a hired servant who is poor and needy by withholding pay,
Whether he be one of your brothers or a stranger who passes through your land that day.
On his payday you shall give him his wage before the sun sets on him, for he is poor
And his heart is set on the wage so he can live, otherwise he will cry to the Lord
Against you, and you will have the guilt of a sin. Fathers shall not be killed for their sons,
Nor shall sons be killed due to their fathers. Each man shall die only for sins he has done.

You shall not pervert the justice due a stranger or an orphan. Don't seize with your hand
The clothing of a widow in payment. Remember, you were a slave in Egypt's land,
And the Lord your God redeemed you from there. Therefore, I command you to do as I've said.
When you reap the harvest of your field, and forget a sheaf there, you are prohibited
From returning to get it. It shall be for the sojourner, the orphan, and widow,
So the Lord your God may bless you in all that you set your hand to. And so when you go
To knock the olives off of your olive trees, boughs you have dealt with are not to be checked,
The remains are for the sojourner, orphan, and widow. And when you go to collect
Grapes from your vineyard, don't pick twice. Leave them for the stranger, orphan, and
      widow's gleaning.
Remember that you were a slave in Egypt's land, so I command you to do these things.

Deuteronomy 25

> "When two men dispute, and one man's guilt is complete,
> Do not strike him too much, lest he end up degraded.
> Don't muzzle a threshing ox so it can't eat.
> If a man dies, his wife should take someone related.
> The woman shall marry her dead husband's brother.
> When measuring weights by the ephah or stone,
> Don't have more weight on one and then less on the other;
> A perfect and fair set of weights you shall own."

If there should be a legal dispute between two men, and they seek the court for judgment,
And the judges decide the verdict, saying who is guilty and who is innocent,
If the guilty man deserves to be beaten, the judge shall have him lie down and be hit,
Beaten in his presence a number of times based on his guilt. Forty is the limit,
Strike him no more than forty times. If you flog him more, he is degraded in your eyes.
(And you should not beat your brother so many times that he becomes something you despise.)

You shall not muzzle an ox while it threshes grain (making it wait to eat 'til it's done).
When brothers dwell together and one of them dies, and the one who has died leaves no son,
The wife of the dead man shall not go outside the family to marry a stranger,
But her husband's brother shall go into her, and do his duty by marrying her.
The first son she bears shall have the dead brother's name, so that his name does not disappear
From Israel. But if when it comes time to marry her, the man does not volunteer,
Then the woman shall go up to the elders at the gate and say, "My brother-in-law
Will not perpetuate his brother's name in Israel, from his duty he withdraws."
Then the elders of his town shall call him and speak to him, and if the man still replies,
"I don't want to take her," Then his brother's wife shall approach him before the elders' eyes,
Pull his sandal off of his foot, spit in his face, and stand to make this declaration,
"To the man who won't build up the house of his brother, these shameful things will all be done!"
And the man's name shall be "The House of the Man with One Sandal" throughout Israel's land.

When two men fight with each other, and the wife of one comes near to rescue her husband
From the hand of the man who is striking him, and grabs that man's genitals with her hand,
You shall cut off her hand, and hold no pity in your eyes. All such behavior is banned.

You shall not have in your pouch two sets of weights, one which is larger and one which is smaller,
Nor shall you in your house have two sets of measures, one that's shorter and one that is taller.
You shall have just and equal weights and measures; in all your dealings be honest and true,
In order that your days may be prolonged in the land the Lord your God is giving you.
For all who do such things, and act dishonestly, are abhorrent to the Lord your God.
Remember what Amalek did to you on the way as out of Egypt's land you trod,
How he surprised you on the way while you were famished and weary, and attacked your rear,
Killing all the stragglers who lagged behind you, showing that of your God he had no fear.
Therefore it shall be that when the Lord your God has given you rest from all of your foes,
And has granted you safety from your enemies, all who surround you whom you oppose
In the land that the Lord your God gives you as inheritance so you can possess it,
You shall blot out the name of Amalek from under heaven; you are not to forget.

Deuteronomy 26

"When you enter the land God is giving to you,
Take the first of your grain, go to the priest, and say,
'I have entered the land God had swore would come true.
My ancestor was an Aramean astray,
Who in Egypt had sojourned, and suffered, until
God brought us to this place, with His strong, mighty hand;
So I bring you these firstfruits, O Lord.' Thus fulfill
All the tithes, and take care that you keep God's command."

[Ki Tavo]

When you enter the land that the Lord God gives you as inheritance you can possess
And then settle in, you shall take some of the firstfruits that off of the ground you harvest
From the land that the Lord your God gives you. You shall put it into a basket and go
To the place where the Lord God will choose to establish His name. And then you are to go
To the priest who's in office at that time, and say to him, "Now I declare on this day
To the Lord your God that I have entered the land which He swore to our fathers He'd lay
In our hands." Then the priest is to take up the basket from your hand, to place on display
At the altar of the Lord your God. Then before the Lord's presence you shall speak, and say,
"My ancestor was an Aramean astray, who went to Egypt, sojourned at length,
He began with few people, but became a nation, one great both in number and strength.
The Egyptians dealt harshly with us and afflicted us with labor of slavery.
We cried out to the Lord who is God of our fathers, the Lord our God heeded our plea.
The Lord saw our affliction, our toil and oppression, and brought us out of Egypt's land
With His awesome power and great terror, with an outstretched arm and with a mighty hand,
And with signs and with wonders. Then He brought us into this place, gave us this land, which flows
With both honey and milk. Therefore now, I have brought the first fruits that this very land grows,
The land that you have given me, O Lord." And then set it down before the Lord your God,
And bow low before the presence of the Lord your God, and then worship the Lord your God;
Then you are to rejoice in all of the good things that the Lord your God has given you,
And has given your household, and given the Levite and sojourner among you, too.

When you finish in paying the tithe of your produce in the tithing year (that's the third),
Give it to the Levite, the sojourner, the orphan, and widow. Once this has occurred,

So that they can eat within your towns and be full, before the Lord your God you shall say,
"I have cleared out the sacred part from my house, and also, I gave some of it away
To the Levite, the sojourner, orphan, and widow, according to Your commandments
You've commanded me. I have not strayed away from or forgotten all Your commandments.
I have not eaten any while mourning, nor cleared any out while I have been unclean,
I have not given any of it to the dead, but have followed Your words, as You've seen.
I have done as the Lord my God gave me commandment. Look down from Your holy abode,
And give blessing to Your people, Israel, and bless the ground which to us you bestowed,
As you swore to our fathers, a land that is flowing with honey and milk." On this day,
The Lord your God commands you to do these statutes, so take care to observe and obey
With all your heart and soul. You've declared on this day that the Lord will be a god for you,
That you'll walk in His ways, His commandments obey, and heed His voice, as you swore to do.
And the Lord, as He promised, declared on this day that you are His people whom He treasures,
Who will follow all He has commanded. He shall set you far above others in measures
Of honor, of praise, and of fame, above all other nations that He has created,
So you will be a people holy to the Lord your God, just as the Lord your God stated.

Deuteronomy 27

> Moses said: "Keep these laws, write them down on the stones
> That you'll use for an altar to God." And then when
> All are gathered, the Levites shall speak in loud tones,
> "Cursed be he who makes idols." All shall say, "Amen."
> "Cursed be he who insults parents, shrinks neighbor's land,
> With his sister or mother or animals lay,
> He who takes bribes for murder, or kills with his hand,
> Or does not follow these laws." "Amen," all shall say.

And now Moses along with all Israel's elders commanded the people and said,
"You shall keep all commandments that I command you on this day. And once your path has led
Over the Jordan River, across to the land that the Lord your God gives you to master,
You shall set up large stones, and then coat them with plaster. And you shall inscribe in
     this plaster
All the words of this law, when you cross over into the land that the Lord God gives you,
A land flowing with honey and milk, as the Lord God of your fathers promised to do.

And when you have crossed over the Jordan, you shall set up stones, these same ones which
    I've noted
About which I command you today, on Mount Ebal. With plaster you shall have them coated.
You shall build there an altar to the Lord your God, one of stone, not by iron tools hit.
But with whole unhewn stones you shall build the Lord's altar, and then you shall offer on it
Some burnt offerings to the Lord your God. You shall slaughter offerings of shalom too,
Then eat them and rejoice before the presence of the Lord your God, as He bid you do.
You shall write on the stones every word of this teaching, and make it abundantly clear.

Moses and the Levitical priests said to Israel, "Silence, Israel, and hear:
On this day you become the people of the Lord your God. Therefore, you are to obey
The voice of the Lord your God, and keep his commandments and laws I command you today."

That day, Moses commanded the people as well, saying, "You shall have these people stand
On Mount Gerizim to bless the people when you have crossed the Jordan into your land:
Shimon, Levi, and Judah, and Issachar, Benjamin, Joseph. These six you shall plan
To have stand on Mount Ebal to curse: Reuben, Gad, Asher, Zebulun, Naphtali, Dan.
And the Levites shall then in a loud voice declare to Israel's men this declaration—

'Cursed shall be the man who makes a graven image, which the Lord has judged abomination,
Something handmade by craftsmen, and set up in secret.' The people shall answer, 'Amen'.
'Cursed be he who dishonors his mother or father.' The people shall all say, 'Amen.'
'Cursed be he who removes the landmark of his neighbor.' The people shall all say, 'Amen.'
'Cursed be he who misleads a blind man on the road.' And the people shall all say, 'Amen.'
'Cursed be he who perverts justice due stranger, orphan, or widow.' They shall say, 'Amen.'
'Cursed be he who lies with father's wife, thus exposing his skirt.' They shall all say 'Amen.'
'Cursed be he who with any beast ever lies down.' And the people shall all say, 'Amen.'
'Cursed be he who lies with sister, daughter of father or mother.' They shall say, 'Amen.'
'Cursed be he who has struck down his neighbor in secret.' The people shall all say, 'Amen.'
'Cursed be he who takes bribes for the murder of innocent life.' They shall all say 'Amen.'
'Cursed be he who does not confirm these laws, and do them.' The people shall all say, 'Amen.'

Deuteronomy 28

"If you heed the Lord's voice, you shall always be blessed.
But if not, you and all of your life will be cursed:
You will find yourself fearful, confused, and distressed,
Such bad things will strike, you can't imagine the worst.
God will plague you with fever, consumption, and blight,
Though you plant many fields, you will never be fed.
You will flee those with fierce face each day and each night,
And you'll spend every moment in horror and dread."

Now if you will obey the great voice of the Lord your God, doing all His commandments
I command you this day, then above all earth's nations, the Lord God shall grant you ascent.
And then all of these blessings shall fall on you and take effect, if you will but obey
The great voice of the Lord your God. Blessed be you in town, and blessed in the field far away.
And blessed shall be your fruit, both the fruit of your womb, and the fruit (or produce) of
    your ground,
And the fruit of your animals, offspring of your cattle and of your flock all around.
Blessed shall be both your basket and kneading-bowl. Blessed be you as you come and you go.
The Lord shall cause your enemies who rise against you to become defeated. And though
They will march out against you by one road, by seven roads they will flee from before you.
The Lord shall ordain blessings for you in your barns, in all things that you set your hand to,
And will bless you in the land the Lord your God gives you. As He swore in earlier days,
The Lord God will establish you as holy people to Him, if you walk in His ways
And do keep the commandments of the Lord your God. Now when all peoples of the earth see
That you bear the Lord's name, they will fear you. He will grant you abounding prosperity,
In the fruit of your womb, in the fruit of your animals, and in the fruit of your ground,
On the land that the Lord swore to give to your fathers. Your prosperity shall abound,
And the Lord shall then open to you His great treasury, the heavens over the land,
And give rain to your soil in its season, and then bless all things to which you set your hand.
You shall lend to nations, but not borrow from one. The Lord makes you the head, not the tail.
You will always be up, never down, at the top you'll succeed, never at bottom fail—
If you heed the commandments of the Lord your God, the same ones I command you this day,
And are careful to do them, and don't turn aside from the words I command you this day
To the right or the left, to follow other gods and serve them. But, if you don't obey
And do not heed the voice of the Lord, His commandments and laws I command you today,

Then you shall be cursed! All these curses shall effect you: Cursed be you in town and in field,
Cursed be your basket, cursed be your kneading-bowl. Cursed shall be your fruit and all
    of your yield,
Cursed be fruit of your womb, cursed be fruit of your soil, cursed be offspring your cattle
    will sprout,
Cursed be lambs from your flock, and cursed be you in your coming in and in your going out.

The Lord shall set confusion, vexation, and curses on you, and all you undertake,
Until you are destroyed and die quickly, because of the great evil of your mistake
In forsaking me. The Lord will make pestilence cling to you, until you are consumed
From the land you enter to possess. The Lord will strike you, by these things you will be doomed:
Consumption, fever with inflammation, extreme scorching heat, dehydration, and blight,
Along with jaundice, these things shall pursue you until you die; such is to be your plight.
Then the earth under your feet shall turn to iron, as heavens overhead turn to brass,
The Lord will make the rain of your land powdered dust, coming down until your life does pass.
The Lord shall cause your enemies to defeat you; though you march against them on one road,
You shall flee them by seven roads. You shall be a horror to all who make their abode
On the earth. Your carcass shall be food for all birds of the air and all beasts on the soil,
With nobody to frighten them off. The Lord will strike you down with the Egyptian boils,
And with hemorrhoids, scabs, and an itching from which you can't be healed; no cure
    shall be found.
The Lord shall strike you with madness, blindness, confusion of heart. And you shall
    grope around
In the bright sun of noon like a blind person feels around in the deep darkness of night,
You will not succeed in your ways, but become robbed and oppressed constantly as your plight,
With no deliverer. You shall betroth a wife, and another man with her shall lie,
You shall build a house, but you shall not dwell in it. You shall plant a vineyard to the sky,
But shall not gather one single grape. And your ox shall be slaughtered before your own eyes,
But you will not eat of it. Your ass will be robbed from you in your sight, but your lost prize
Shall not come back to you. And your sheep will be given to your foes, your most hated ones,
And you shall have no deliverer to help you. Then your daughters and also your sons
Will be given to another people, while your eyes look on with a longing and strain
For the whole of the day, but what your eyes desire, your hand will lack the strength to attain.
Then the fruit of your soil and all your ceaseless toil shall be eaten by a random nation
Who you don't even know. And you will only know oppression and a ceaseless frustration,
Until you have gone mad from all your eyes have seen. Then the Lord with boils shall
    strike you down,
Boils on your knees and thighs, from which you can't be healed, from your foot-soles right up to
    your crown.

And the Lord will drive you, and the king you chose, into a nation that you have not known,
Neither you nor your fathers. And there you shall serve other gods, gods of wood and of stone.

You shall be an example, a horror, a proverb for all nations where the Lord leads you.
You shall carry much seed out to the field, however, you shall gather little to feed you,
For locusts will consume it. You'll plant and till vineyards, but never shall drink of the wine,
Nor get grapes, for the worms will eat them. You will have olive trees through you land by design,
But shall never anoint yourself with the oil, for all your olives shall drop off the tree.
You shall bear sons and daughters, but they won't be yours, for they'll go into captivity.
All your trees and the fruit of your land shall be consumed by locusts, and cause you great sorrow.
And the stranger in your midst shall rise high above you as you fall low, you'll need to borrow,
As he lends to you, but you will not lend to him. He shall be the head, you'll be the tail.
All these curses shall fall on you and overtake you until you're destroyed, since you failed
To obey the Lord your God and keep His commandments and statutes He commanded you.
They shall serve as a sign and a portent, forever, for you and your seed after you.

Because you did not serve the Lord your God with joyfulness and with a gladness of heart
For abundance of all things, you shall serve your enemies, whom the Lord God for His part
Will send out against you, leaving you in thirst, hunger, and nakedness, lacking all things.
He shall put a yoke of iron upon your neck, until your own destruction it brings.
He shall raise against you a nation from afar, from the end of earth and its land,
Which will swoop down on you like an eagle; a nation whose language you don't understand,
A nation that's both fierce-faced and ruthless, without regard for age or mercy for youth,
It will eat all the fruit of your cattle, and fruit of your land, until you are destroyed.
It shall not leave you corn, wine, nor oil, nor offspring of your animals. You'll be devoid,
Until it has destroyed you. It shall besiege you in your towns, until your strong high walls
That you trusted in crumble throughout your land. And even as they continue to fall,
It shall still besiege you in all your towns throughout the land that the Lord your God gave you.
And you shall eat the fruit of your own womb, the flesh of your sons, and of your daughters too,
Which the Lord your God gave you, in the siege and rough straits your enemies have put you in.
The most tender and delicate man among you will have evil's glint shine in his eye,
And not share with his brother, his wife, or remaining children, flesh of those who did die
Because he does not have one thing left in the siege and distress your foe brings to your towns.
The most tender and delicate woman among you, who'd not set her foot's sole on ground
Out of tenderness, her eye shall turn evil against her husband, her daughter, her son,
All of birth which comes out from between her legs, children she bears. For she'll eat them
    when done,
In secret, since she lacks everything, in the siege and distress your foe brings to your towns.

If you don't observe all the words of this Instruction, the laws that are here written down
To revere this most fearful and glorious name, the Lord your God, then He will inflict
On both you and your offspring great plagues that will last long, and make you exceedingly sick.
He will bring every illness of Egypt upon you, the very ones that you had feared,
Which shall cling to you. And every illness and plague which has not in this writing appeared,

The Lord will bring them on you as well, until you are destroyed. Your number shall be few
That remain, though you once were as many as stars in the heaven, no more, because you
Did not obey the voice of the Lord your God. While to do you good was once His delight,
And to multiply you, He shall now delight to destroy you. This is to be your plight,
He shall wipe you out, and you'll be pulled up from whatever land you might try to possess.
The Lord shall scatter you among all peoples, from one end of earth to ends yet unknown.
There you'll serve other gods not known to you or your fathers, gods made of wood and of stone.
And among all these nations you'll find no repose, nor shall you find rest for your foot's sole,
The Lord will give you there a heart that trembles, eyes that are failing, and a sorrowed soul,
And your life will hang in doubt before you. Not sure you'll survive, you will fear day and night,
In the morning you'll say: "God, I wish it were evening!" At night, "God, I wish it were light!",
All because of what your heart will dread, and what your eyes will see. And the Lord will
      bring you
Back to Egypt in ships, by the route which I said that you'd never again get to view,
And there you will all offer yourselves up for sale to your enemies, as a slave crew,
With the men as servants and the women as maids, but not a single man will buy you.

Deuteronomy 29

> Moses said to all Israel, "You have all seen
> What the Lord did in Egypt, so you should take care
> That you follow these words and you know what they mean.
> And the covenant that we now make and declare
> Is not only with you, but those not here as well.
> Let no man turn from God, for His anger will blast.
> Folk will ask, "Why did God strike the land where they dwell?"
> The reply, "They forsook the Lord's covenant past.""

These are the words of the covenant the Lord commanded Moses make with the Children
Of Israel in Moab's land, aside from the one at Horeb that he made with them.

Moses summoned all Israel and said to them, "You yourselves have seen within your view
All the Lord did in the land of Egypt to Pharaoh, to his servants, and his land too,
The great trials your eyes saw, those great signs and wonders, but until this day I decree
That the Lord has not given you a mind to know, ears to hear, or even eyes to see.
I led you through the wilderness for forty years, the clothes on your back did not wear out,
Nor the sandals on your feet. You did not eat bread, or drink wine, so you know without doubt

I am the Lord your God. When you came to this place, Sihon who was the king of Heshbon
And Og, king of Bashan, came against us in battle. We struck them down, now they are gone,
And we took their land, giving it as an inheritance to the Gadites, Reubenites,
And half-tribe of Manasseh. So follow the words of the covenant that I now cite,
So that you may then prosper in everything that you do.

                                                                      [Nitzavim]

                                                            You stand this day, all of you,
Before the Lord your God—The heads of your tribes, and your elders, and your officers too,
All the men of Israel, your little-ones, your wives, the sojourner amidst your camp,
From the woodchopper who hews your wood, to the waterdrawer who keeps all your
    mouths damp—
To cross into the covenant of the Lord your God He makes with you this day, and oaths,
So that He may establish you as a people holy to Him, and be your God, both
As he promised you, and as he swore to your fathers, Jacob, Isaac, and Abraham.
Not with you alone do I make this covenant and oath, but both with those who here stand
Now amongst us today before the Lord our God, and with those who are not here today.
For you know how we settled in Egypt's land, and how we crossed though other nation's ways,
And you saw their abominations, idols of wood, stone, silver, and gold they possessed.
Beware lest there be among you man, woman, family, or tribe whose heart has now transgressed
On this day away from the Lord our God by going to worship the gods of these nations,
Lest there be among you a root bearing wormwood and bad fruit. When one of such persuasion
Hears the words of this oath, he shall think that he is immune, saying, "My safety I'll gain,
Though I follow my own stubborn heart and bring ruin on those parched and those drenched
    by rain,"

The Lord won't pardon him, but will kindle His anger and jealousy against that man,
And then all of the curses shall fall upon him that are mentioned in this book's full span,

And the Lord will blot out his name from under heaven, and single them out for the worse
Among all of the tribes of Israel, according to the covenant and every curse
That is written in this book of law. Generations to come, your children after you,
And the stranger who comes from a far-off land, when all the plagues upon this land they view—
With its sicknesses with which the Lord made it sick, the whole land burnt with brimstone
    and salt,
It cannot be sown, cannot sprout anything, herbage cannot sprout amidst this assault,
Like the overthrow of Sodom and Gomorrah, Admah and Zeboim, which the Lord
Overturned in his flaring wrath and anger—The nations shall ask, in one chord,
"Why did the Lord do this to the land? Who knows, whole, why such flaming wrath has
    been displayed?"
And they will be told, "It is because they abandoned the covenant that they had made

With the Lord God of their fathers when He took them out of the land of Egypt. They went
And served other gods, bowing to them, gods whom they had not known and whom God had
    not sent.
So the Lord's anger flared up against this land, bringing it all curses writ in this tome.
The Lord uprooted them from their land in wrath, fury, and anger, cast them to a new home
In another land, as is this day. Secret things are the Lord's, but revealed things we saw
Belong to us and our children for the ages, to observe all the words of this law.

Deuteronomy 30

> "When these things all occur, and you take them to heart,
> Then the Lord will restore you your fortunes of old.
> God returns to you, even though you did depart,
> If you heed the Lord's voice and do what you are told.
> The commandment I tell you is not far away,
> Over oceans of water, or up in the sky,
> But it's set in your heart, so observe it today!
> For if you do not heed it, then you will soon die."

When these things all befall you, the blessing and also the curse I have set before you,
And you take them to heart among all of the nations where the Lord your God has cast you,
And return to the Lord your God, you and your children, and His voice you heed and obey
Both with all of your heart and with all of your soul, in all things I command you today,
Then the Lord your God will restore your fortunes. Having compassion on you, He will gather
All of you, returning to collect you from all the peoples where by God you were scattered.
Though your outcasts may be at the ends of the earth, the Lord your God will take you
    from there,
Gather you and bring you to the land that your fathers possessed, it will serve as your share.
He will make you more prosperous and numerous than your fathers when they were alive,
Open your (and your seed's) heart, to love God with all your heart and soul, so that you survive.
The Lord your God will place all those curses on your foes, who persecute you and who hate you,
And you shall again heed the Lord's voice, and keep all His commandments that I now relate you.
The Lord your God will grant you prosperity in everything to which you set your hand,
In the fruit of your womb, in the fruit of your animals, and in the fruit of your land.
Then the Lord will return to delighting in you, and your prosperity which he'll cause,
If you will heed the voice of the Lord God again, and keep all His commandments and laws

Writ in this book of law, and return to the Lord your God with all your heart and your soul.
For the commandment I command you this day is not confusing or too far a goal.
It is not in the heavens, to cause you to say, "Who shall go up to heaven for us,
And then bring it to us so we hear and can do it?" (There shall be no cause for this fuss)
Nor does it lie across the sea, so you must say, "Who shall cross for us, across the sea,
And then bring it to us so we hear and can do it?" The word is as close as can be,
In your mouth and your heart, so that you can do it. See, I have set before you today
Life and good, death and evil. For I now command you to love the Lord, walk in His ways,
Keep His commandments, His laws and judgments, so that by the Lord you will be blessed,
So you may stay alive and increase in the land that you are entering to possess.

Now if your heart should turn, and you will not hear, but worship other gods you're
    lured to serve,
I tell you this day that you shall perish, and not long live on the land you don't deserve
That you cross the Jordan to possess. As witness against you I call heaven and earth
On this day, that I have set before you the options of life and death, blessing and curse.

Now choose life, so that you will continue to live, you and your seed, so that you may love
The Lord your God, by heeding His voice, cleaving to Him, for He is your life, and length of
All your days, that you may settle on the same soil that the Lord to your fathers once swore,
Swore to Abraham, Isaac, and Jacob, to give them as a possession evermore.

Deuteronomy 31

> Moses said, "I'm one hundred and twenty. No more
> Can I come and go. God told me: You shall not cross.
> Joshua, you shall bring them to the land God swore
> To their fathers. God's with you, so you'll face no loss."
> Then the Lord said to Moses, "Once you lose life's spark,
> Then this people will sin against Me and do wrong."
> Moses wrote all these laws down, put them in the ark,
> Then said, "Gather, all Israel, now hear this song:"

[Vayelech]

Moses went and was speaking these words to all Israel, then he said to them, "Today,
I am one hundred twenty years old; I can no longer come and go. The Lord did say

To me: 'You shall not cross over this Jordan.' The Lord your God is to cross at your head;
He will wipe out those nations before you, so you dispossess them. As the Lord has said,
Joshua will cross over before you. The Lord will deal with them like Og and Sihon,
(Who were kings of the Amorites), and their land, when he destroyed them until they were gone.
And the Lord will deliver them up to you, so you may do to them as I command,
In accordance with these commandments. Be strong, have courage, don't let your fear of
    them stand,
For the Lord your God is the one who goes with you, He will not fail you or forsake you.
Moses called Joshua, and told him in all Israel's sight: 'Be strong, let courage take you,
For you go with this people into the land that the Lord swore to their fathers to give,
It is you who shall cause them to inherit it. And the Lord, He shall cause you to live,
For He goes before you, He will be with you, and not forsake or fail you in the least.
Have no fear, and do not be dismayed.' Moses wrote down this law, and gave it to the priests,
To the Sons of Levi, who had carried the Ark of the Lord's covenant, and also
To the elders of Israel. Moses instructed them, "When every seventh year goes,
The set time of the Year of Release, and the feast of Sukkot, when all Israel comes
To appear before the Lord your God at the place He will choose, this law you shall read from,
Before all Israel in their ears. Gather the people, men, women, children to hear,
And the stranger within your gates, so they may listen, and learn that the Lord should be feared,
And that they should be careful to follow each word of this law. And their children as well,
Who do not know may hear, learn to fear and revere the Lord your God as long as they dwell
On the soil of the land that you soon shall posses, crossing the Jordan to occupy.

And the Lord said to Moses, "Behold, the time is drawing near for you when you must die.
Now call Joshua and set yourselves in the Tent of Meeting, where I'll give him command."
So both Moses and Joshua went to present themselves, and at the Tent they did stand.

And the Lord appeared in the tent in a cloud column, which stood by the door of the tent.
The Lord said to Moses, "You shall soon lie with your fathers; this people shall make descent
And proceed to go whoring after foreign gods, gods of strangers (since they're in their midst),
In the land they shall enter. They will forsake Me, and break My covenant that exists,
Which I made with them. My anger will flare against them, I shall forsake them on that day,
And hide My face from them. Many ills and evils will befall them. They'll be ready prey.
And they'll say on that day, "Have not these ills befallen us since God is not in our midst?"
But I shall hide My face on that day, on account of the evil they've done, which consists
Of their turning to other gods. Now, therefore, write this song, teach it to all Israel,
Putting it in their mouths, so that it may be witness for me against all Israel.

When I have brought them into the land that I swore to their fathers, a land that does flow
Both with milk and with honey, And they eat until they are filled, and quite fat they will grow,
They shall turn away to other gods and serve them, despise Me and break My covenant.
And it will be, when troubles and ills all befall them, this song will serve to represent

As a witness confronting them, (since from the mouths of their seed it shall not be forgotten),
For before I bring them into the land I swore, I know their plans today (which are rotten).

Therefore Moses wrote down this song that day, and taught it to the children of Israel.
And He charged Joshua son of Nun, and said, "Be strong and let courage in your heart dwell,
For you shall bring the children of Israel into the same land that to them I swore,
And I will be with you." When Moses finished writing the words of this law and this lore
In a book, until they were completed, he commanded the Levites (who bore the ark
Of the Lord's covenant), saying, "Take this book of the law, put it just beside the ark
Of the Lord's covenant, and let it remain there to serve as a witness among you.
For I know you are stubborn and rebellious, while I am today alive to view,
You have already rebelled against the Lord. How much more after the end of my years?
Gather all your officials and tribe elders to me, so I may speak words in their ears
And call heaven and earth to witness against them. For I know that after my demise
You will corrupt yourselves and act wickedly, and from the way I command, turn aside.
You will cause evil to befall you in your latter days, turning from what I command,
Because you have done evil in the Lord's sight, vexing Him with all the deeds of your hand."

And then Moses spoke into the ears of all Israel, to the whole congregation,
All the words of this song, of the following poem, until every last word was done:

Deuteronomy 32

"Hear, O heaven and earth, let my words come like rain.
I proclaim the Lord—Glory to this faithful Rock!
Jacob wandered, God fed him with grapes he could drain,
But then Jeshurun sinned and he left the Lord's flock.
God said, "I will destroy them for sinning, or would,
But their foes would then think they defeated my hand,
So I vindicate My people, bringing them good."
God told Moses, "You'll see, but not enter the land."

[Haazinu]

Now give ear, O ye heavens, and I will speak. Hear, O ye earth, all the words my mouth utters.
Let my teachings drop like rain, my words flow like dew, like the raindrops on young herbs
     that flutter,

Like the showers on grass. For the name of the Lord I proclaim: Give glory to our God!
As The Rock, all His work is perfection, His ways are all just. A corruption-less God,
Always faithful and upright is He. Yet His Children corrupted themselves and persisted,
'til this defect made them not deserve to be His, because their generation was twisted,
And perverse. Is this how you repay the Lord, O people foolish and lacking all sense?
Is He not your creator, your father, who made you and brought you into existence?
Regard days of old, look back and think on the years spanning some generations ago.
Ask your father, and he will then show you, your elders, they will tell you that this is so:

When the Most High gave nations inheritance, and the entire human race he divided,
In relation to Israel's numbers (the sons of God), people's boundaries He provided.
For the Lord's portion is His own people, and Jacob His own allotment to possess.
He found him in a region of desert, an empty wasteland of howling wilderness.
He encircled him, led him about, and instructed him as the apple of his eye.
Like an eagle protecting his nest, stirring up all the little ones, hovering by,
One who spreads out its wings, and then catches them, bearing them on its pinions as it glides.
So the Lord alone did guide him, there was no foreign or alien god at his side.
He made him ride the highlands of all the earth, to eat the field's full yield of crops;
And he suckled him with honey drawn from a boulder, and oil from a flinty rock.
Curds from the herd, and milk from the flock, with the best of the fat lambs and rams he did eat,
Of the herds of Bashan and the goats. Wine from blood of grapes, and finest kidneys of wheat.
But Jeshurun grew fat and kicked - you grew fat and gross, forgetting since you were so gorged -
He forsook the God that made him, scoffing at The Rock by whom his deliverance was forged.
They incensed Him with alien gods, their abominations made his jealous wrath show.
They were sacrificing to demons, who were not-gods, and gods that they never did know,
To new gods who'd come lately, gods your fathers never had feared. You neglected the Rock
That had given you birth, forgot the God who brought you forth onto this earth where you walk.
When the Lord saw, He spurned them, due to the vexation He got from His daughters and sons.
He said: I will hide My face from them, and see how they fare, this perverse generation,
Children faithless who made Me get jealous with not-gods, vexed Me with idols 'gainst My rules.
So I will make them jealous with not-people, vexing them back with a nation of fools.

For a fire has flared in My anger, and burned to the bottom of Sheol, below,
It devours the earth and its yield, sets ablaze the whole base of the hills with its glow.
I will sweep heaping evils upon them, spend all of My arrows against them, and then
Draining famine, devouring and burning plague, bitter pestilence, shall fall on them,
And I will send the teeth of wild beasts out against them, the venom of dust's creepy-crawlers.
On the outside the sword shall deal death, on the inside the terror shall cause all to holler,
Dealing death to both young men and virgins alike, nurselings along with men of grey hair.
I'd have said, "I shall scatter them to nothing, make all remembrance of them disappear
Among men," but for fear of vexation from foes, for the enemy might judge amiss,
And say, "We have prevailed by the strength of our own hand, the Lord had no bearing on this."

For they are a nation void of counsel, a people who have no discernment on hand.
If they only were wise, they would contemplate this, and their future they would understand.
How could one person pursue a thousand, how could only two put ten thousand to flight,
Unless their Rock had sold them, and the Lord had given them over to suffer this plight?
For their rock is not like our Rock, our Lord, as even our enemies admit is so.
After all, from the vine of Sodom their vine comes, in the fields of Gomorrah it grows.
Their grapes are poison grapes, and their clusters are bitter, their wine is the venom of snakes,
The cruel poison of vipers. Is this not laid up in store with Me, all of these mistakes,
Sealed up in My treasuries? Vengeance and payback are Mine! For their foot shall soon falter
And their day of calamity is coming quickly, a swift destiny they can't alter.

For the Lord will soon judge for His people, and then for His servants, repent and relent,
When he sees that their hands have no strength, and none bonded or free have might
    to represent.
He will say, "Where are their gods, the rock where they sought refuge, who ate their sacrificed fat,
And drank their wine libations? Let them rise and help you, let them protect you! Just try that.
See now that I am He, there's no god beside Me. I deal death and bring life. Understand?
I both wound and I heal. There are none on this earth who can deliver out of My hand.

For I lift My hand up to the heavens and say, "As I live forever, it shall be,
When I sharpen My lightning sword, My hand shall take hold of judgment and then you will see
How I take vengeance on all My foes, those who hate Me I will pay back. See what they gain:
I will make My arrows drunk with blood, as My sword devours flesh from the blood of the slain,
From the captives, and from hairy heads of My foes." Give His people acclaim, O you nations,
For He will avenge His servants' blood, and wreck vengeance on his foes, then make expiation
For the land of His people, wipe their tears away." Moses came and spoke this entire song,
Every word in the ears of the people, with Hoshea son of Nun (who came along).
Now when Moses had finished reciting all these words to Israel and had his say,
Then he said to them, "Take to heart all of the words with which I have enjoined you today,
So that you may command all your children to follow each word of this law that I give.
For this is no mere empty word, it is your life; through this word you'll be able to live
And prolong your days on the soil you cross the Jordan to possess, the land where you go."

On that same day the Lord said to Moses, "Ascend the heights of Abarim, Mount Nebo,
In the land of Moab, in the region across facing Jericho, and view the land
Of Canaan that I give to the Children of Israel, as possession for their hand.
You shall die on the mountain that you will ascend, and shall be gathered in to your kin,
Just as Aaron your brother had died on Mount Hor and to his kinfolk was gathered in,
Because you broke faith with Me just as he had done in the Children of Israel's midst
At the waters of Meribah Kadesh, a quarrel that took place in Sin's wilderness

Because you did not properly sanctify Me, your transgression was very severe,
For amidst all the Children of Israel, My holiness you had failed to revere.
So you shall see the land from a distance, the land where the Israelites will all dwell,
But you shall not go there, into the land which I give to the Children of Israel.

Deuteronomy 33

> Before Moses died, he told the Israelites,
> "God came from Sinai. Let Reuben live and not die.
> O Lord, Hear Judah's voice, be his hands in his fights.
> Give your Thummim and Urim to faithful Levi.
> Benjamin is loved in safety, Joseph is blessed,
> Zebulun journeys with joy. In tents, Issachar.
> Gad a lion. A whelp, Dan. Naphtali possessed
> The lake. Asher, like Israel, happy you are."

[V'Zot HaBerachah]

Now this is the blessing that Moses the man of God gave to the Israelites
To bid all of them farewell before his death. He said, "The Lord came from Mount Sinai's heights,
He shone forth from Seir on them, dawned on them from Mount Paran, and approaching
     He came
From Riboth Kodesh, with ten thousands of saints, at His right hand a fiery flame.
He indeed loved the peoples, all His holy ones are in your hand. They sat at your feet,
And they followed your steps, and accepted all of Your commands in the list that's complete,
From when Moses commanded us law as possession for Jacob's entire congregation.
So the Lord became King in Jeshurun, where gathered the heads of all Israel's nation,
All of Israel's tribes. Now let Reuben live on, and not die, though his men number few."
And of Judah he said, "Hear, O Lord, Judah's voice, bring him in to his kin, and may You
Strive for him through his hands, help against all his foes, when with Your strength his
     hands are invested."
Then of Levi he said, "Give your Thummim and Urim to your faithful man, whom you tested
At the grounds of Massa, whom you strove with at Meribah's waters, the same man who said
Of his father and mother, "I see them not." His brothers found no regard in their stead,
His own children he even ignored. For they guarded Your sayings, kept Your covenant.
Let them teach Your law to Jacob, Your law to Israel. They shall offer You incense,

And whole offerings upon Your altar. Bless, O Lord, his substance, and works of his hand,
Crush the loins of his foes that rise up against him, so that against him they cannot stand."
Of Benjamin he said, "Beloved of the Lord, who beside Him securely does rest,
He surrounds and protects him all day, dwells between his shoulders." Of Joseph, he said, "Blessed
By the Lord be his land, with the bounty of heaven's dew, and the deep ocean below,
With the most precious fruits that the sun can provide, with the best crop the moon can bestow,
With abundance from the ancient mountains, and the bounty from the age-old hills, and from
The best gifts of the earth and its fullness, the favor of the bush-Dweller, may it come
On the head of Joseph, on the crown of the one chosen from among his brothers' stocks.
Like a firstling bull, he has a splendor, and he has horns like the horns of a wild ox;
And with them he shall gore all the people, to the very ends of the earth they'll be torn,
Using Ephraim's myriads as one horn, Manasseh's thousands as the other horn."

And of Zebulun he said, "Rejoice, Zebulun, on your journeys. Rejoice, Issachar,
In your tents. They call their peoples to the mountain where their sacrifices offered are
Of success, for they draw from the wealth of the sea, and the hidden treasures of the sand."

Of Gad he said, "Blessed be he who enlarges Gad. Like the king of beasts who rules the land,
He is poised like a lion to tear off the arm, and to tear off the crown of the head.
Then he chose for himself the best part of the land, a part reserved for rulers who led.
He approached with the heads of the people, and did the Lord's judgment along with their help,
Executing all of His commands." And of Dan he then said, "Dan is a lion's whelp
That leaps forth from Bashan." Of Naphtali he said, "O, Naphtali is sated with favor,
And the full blessing of the Lord, taking possession of both Sea and southland to savor."

Of Asher he said, "Most blessed of sons is Asher, of his brothers let him gain most praise,
And dip his foot in oil. Your bolts shall be of iron and bronze, and strength last all your days.

There is none like the God of Jeshurun, who rides through the heavens above to help you,
Through the skies in His majesty. The God eternal is a shelter, ageless and true,
Beneath the everlasting arms. He drove your foes from before you, commanding: Destroy.
So Israel will dwell in security, with Jacob's fountain untroubled. In joy,
His abode is alone in a land of both grain and wine, under heavens dripping dew.
And all this is your happiness, O Israel, you are happy. For who is like you,
People saved by the Lord, He your shield that protects you, your sword that in triumph attacks,
So your foes shall come cringing before you, and you shall tread on their high places and backs.

Deuteronomy 34

> Moses went up Mount Nebo to see all the land.
> God said, "This is the land to your fathers I swore.
> You have seen it, but never shall step on its sand."
> Then died God's servant Moses, laid near Beth Peor.
> Thirty days Israel wept for Moses. And then
> Joshua, son of Nun, led the Israelites.
> But no prophet like Moses rose ever again,
> Whom the Lord had known face to face, with deeds of might.

Moses went from the Plains of Moab to Mount Nebo, upon Pisgah's top he did stand
Facing Jericho. And the Lord let him see all the land, Gilead as far as Dan,
All Naphtali, the land of Ephraim and Manasseh, and Judah's land out as far
As the Western Sea, Negev, and Valley of Jericho's city of palms, to Zoar.
The Lord said to him: "This is the land that I swore to Abraham, Jacob, and Isaac,
'I will give it to your offspring.' I let your eyes see it, but there you shall never walk."

And so Moses, servant of the Lord, died there, in Moab's land, by the word of the Lord.
And He buried him deep in the valley in the land of Moab, nearby Beth-peor,
And no man knows the site of his burial place to this day, where the Lord buried him.
Moses was a full hundred and twenty years old at his death, but his eye was not dim,
Nor his vigor and lifeforce diminished. For Moses, the Children of Israel wept
In the plains of Moab for a full thirty days. And when thirty days' mourning they'd kept,
Then the days of the weeping for Moses were ended. Now Joshua the son of Nun,
He was filled with the spirit of wisdom, for Moses had laid hands on him with this boon,
So the Israelites heeded him, doing as the Lord commanded Moses they do.
And there never again rose a prophet in Israel like Moses, whom the Lord knew
Face-to-face, singled out, in the various portents and signs He sent him to display
In the land of Egypt, to Pharaoh, to all his servants, and his whole country's array,
And in all of the glorious power and awesome might, great strength of hand, and as well,
All the deeds great and terrible Moses had wrought in the sight of all of Israel.

About the Author

Seth Brown was born in Rhode Island and now lives in Massachusetts. From 1997-2000, his rhyming column "Issue of the week" appeared on Sundays in the Providence Journal. In 2001, he was named Poet Laureate of the Williams College Debate Society, and in 2004, became a Contributing Editor to the OEDILF *(Omnificent English Dictionary In Limerick Form)*. He has previously versified everything from the dialogues of Plato to presidential debates. He took 3rd place in the 2008 Western Massachusetts Poetry Slam Competition, and frequently performs poetry and rap around the Berkshires.

Outside of the poetry world, Seth's work has appeared in various places ranging from the Washington Post's Style Invitational to USA Today. He has held humor columns in publications such as JVibe Magazine and the Berkshire Advocate, and currently writes his award-winning column "The Pun Also Rises" for the North Adams Transcript. He is the author of *Think You're The Only One?* (Barnes & Noble, 2004) and *Rhode Island Curiosities* (Globe Pequot Press, 2007).

His website is www.RisingPun.com.